A HISTORY OF KINGSTON, R.I., 1700-1900

Heart of Rural South County

Christian M. McBurney

To Gerard:

Happy History on behalf
of Donna and Alex!

Christian McBurney

Pettaquamscutt Historical Society, Kingston, R.I.

A HISTORY OF KINGSTON, R.I., 1700-1900
Heart of Rural South County

By Christian M. McBurney

Pettaquamscutt Historical Society
Kingston, Rhode Island

©2004

To order more books: go to www.freewebs.com/kingstonrihistory

On front cover: (left) Elisha R. Potter, Jr.; (center) the "Cat Inspector"; (right) Sarah Harris Fayerweather

TABLE OF CONTENTS

- iii -

TABLE OF ILLUSTRATIONS

Forward

Kingston's history in the 18th and 19th centuries is as rich as any village in New England (at least among those not named Lexington or Concord). The key to this rich history is that for almost 150 years, Kingston served as the county seat for South County, for 125 years it served as the town seat for South Kingstown (then including Narragansett), and for 100 years it served as one of the five rotating state capitals of Rhode Island. Thus, it was the location for sessions of the General Assembly, state party conventions and rallies, county and town elections, town meetings, county court trials, jail breaks, and the last hanging in South County. While this book is a general history of Kingston from 1700 to 1900, due to Kingston's role as a government seat, it serves as a mirror of South County's other villages and towns.

A definite theme rises from the retelling of Kingston's past. The theme relates to a world dominated by agriculture that is now lost. Kingston (the name was changed from Little Rest in 1825) grew as a hub of South County's agricultural economy in colonial times. South County developed a unique economy in colonial New England with plantation-type estates that produced dairy and livestock surpluses for trade to nearby Newport merchants, who used the goods to trade with Caribbean and Southern planters. Little Rest grew to service South County farmers, as a place for general stores; artisans such as blacksmiths, silversmiths and tanners; taverns; and churches. When the county and colony seat was removed from Tower Hill to Little Rest in 1752, Little Rest served as South County's political and legal capital.

After the American Revolution, as a result of a decline in agriculture, heavy taxation, and increasing industrialization, South County farmers felt that their interests were under attack. The first manifestation of this separate interest was dramatically demonstrated in Little Rest in March 1790, when a convention of Rhode Island delegates met in the Court House but refused to ratify the U.S. Constitution, making Rhode Island the only one of the original thirteen colonies to refuse to do so. A primary reason for the failure of Rhode Island to ratify the U.S. Constitution was the opposition of South County farmers, who felt that ratification could increase taxes on their lands and reduce their domination of the state government. Ultimately, in Newport two months later, Rhode Island ratified the constitution. But South County's deep concern about its agricultural interests being under attack survived.

In the 19th century, Kingston failed to make the transition to changes brought by the age of industrialization – the rise of wool and cotton factories, railroads and urban immigration. Kingston's talented leaders at the state level – Elisha R. Potter, Sr., his son Elisha R. Potter, Jr., and Wilkins Updike –

fought to suppress what they perceived as threats to their traditional, agricultural and Protestant way of life. They perceived the main threats to be the rise of factories and the increasing numbers of urban Catholic Irish immigrants in Providence and the northern part of the state. This struggle culminated in the failure of the rural interests to agree to reform Rhode Island's antiquated voting and representation laws that prevented urban immigrants in Providence and northern towns from having a proportionate say in state affairs and allowed rural interests to dominate the state government in the first part of the 19th century. This failure led to the Dorr Rebellion, the most traumatic event in the state's history.

As Kingston's efforts to attract manufacturing and railroads to the village failed, and as neighboring towns of Wakefield, Peace Dale and Narragansett Pier prospered in the new industrialized age as the 19th century progressed, Kingston gradually and then dramatically lost its influence in the state, county and town. In the space of several years, Kingston lost its role as a state capitol, then as the town seat, and finally as the county seat. Ultimately, Kingston's decline was halted as a result of the successful effort, led by Bernon Helme of Kingston, to locate next to the village the state's agricultural college. Helme's goal was to rejuvenate agriculture in the state. While the effort to locate a college in Kingston was successful, ironically, the forerunner of the University of Rhode Island grew into much more than an agricultural school and provided the sons and daughters of Rhode Island parents opportunities in many economic fields. It saved Kingston from oblivion as well.

Another theme of the book is the importance, and changing nature over time, of black and white relations in Kingston and South County. In colonial times, the Narragansett country had the highest percentage of black slaves of any rural area in New England. For example, in 1730, more than one in three persons in South Kingstown was a black slave. Some residents of colonial Little Rest held black slaves. After the American Revolution, slaves were gradually freed. The transition from slave to full citizen is part of Kingston's history. The transition was not smooth. This book recounts the effort by the South Kingstown town council to prevent Elisha Gardiner from freeing his slave in 1806. It recounts how the powerful Elisha R. Potter, Sr. used his power to put one of his black servants (who was a former slave) in the Little Rest jail merely because the servant wanted to take Sundays off to preach at local churches. The General Assembly voted to exclude blacks from voting in 1822. But change did occur. George Fayerweather, the son of a slave, moved to Little Rest as a free man to start his own blacksmithing business. As with many South County blacks, he married an Indian woman and had several children. His sons continued the profitable business in Little Rest into the late 19th century. In 1837, white and black Kingston residents formed the Kingston Anti-Slavery Society, which promoted the end of slavery in the South and full rights of citizenship for Rhode Island blacks. After the Civil War, an ex-slave from Virginia moved to Kingston. By the 1880s, most of Rhode Island's discriminatory laws had been banished from the law books, and white and black children attended public schools together in Kingston. Accordingly, this book discusses both the dark side and the bright side of race relations. It is often the case in history books that one topic is discussed to the exclusion of the other.

A third theme is Kingston's role in the liberal reforms that took hold in 19th century America prior to the Civil War. Kingston and South County sometimes fought to prevent the steady march to transform society by advancing the dignity of all persons. The failure of South County's rural interests to permit a liberalization of voting rights by permitting voting without regard to ownership of land has been discussed. In addition, the slow but inexorable liberalization in the treatment of black persons has been discussed. Another area for liberal reform was the movement to ban corporal punishment and the death penalty. In Kingston, criminals were often subject to horrific punishments, including being placed in the pillory, whipped on the "naked back," branded with the letter "R" on both cheeks, and having a piece of each ear "cropped" (cut off). Those convicted in the Little Rest Court House of stealing a substantial amount of goods were sometimes sentenced to die by hanging. Other areas for liberal reform included the movement to prohibit the jailing of debtors; the movement to improve the treatment of the poor; and the movement to promote public schools. While perhaps not a liberal reform, the goal of the temperance movement to reduce alcohol consumption was intended to improve the lives of citizens and society as a whole.

In its history, Kingston has had more than its share of fascinating characters. They include Elisha Gardiner, the "Cat Inspector" who was the head of a club of practical jokers in the early 1800s; Samuel Casey, master colonial silversmith turned counterfeiter; Sarah Harris Fayerweather, African-American heroine and abolitionist; Elisha Reynolds Potter, Sr., the larger-than-life state politician; Jemima Wilkinson, religious prophet and utopian leader; Thomas Mount, the last man hanged in South County; Wilkins Updike, the acerbic politician who was accused of insulting practically every important person in the state; and Elisha R. Potter, Jr., an erudite and sensitive man who was thrust into the role of having to defend Kingston and South County from the forces of modernization.

* * *

When I was fifteen years old, while a resident of Kingston and a student at South Kingstown High School, I wrote and had published *Kingston: A Forgotten History* (1975). Why am I revisiting the same subject? I have several reasons. First, I want to do it "right" this time. In this book, I attempt to make the history come alive by putting in the historical context and including the drama and humor that appear so often in the events that occurred in this village. In addition, my previous book relied heavily on romantic late 19th and early 20th century histories. In this book, I include aspects of real life in Kingston, some of which are not attractive, but which nonetheless are part of a history that should be told and not forgotten. In short, this book is not a rewrite, it is an entirely new (and I hope better) book.

In writing this book, I did considerable research using original resources, and was able to associate with Kingston new sources that had not previously appeared in histories of Kingston, including the story of Elisha Potter and his black servant Cato Pearce; the refusal of the town council to permit Elisha Gardiner to free his slave; Thomas Taylor's general store records; Von Clausen's journal entries relating to George Washington's visit to Little Rest; James B. M. Potter's statement of his hope that the South would win the Civil War and his later letter recounting his recollections of the assassination of President Lincoln; and numerous contemporary broadsides and pamphlets related to Kingston. Furthermore, I was able to have the benefit of several books with Kingston included as its subject that were published after my first book was published: William D. Metz's *Kingston Congregational Church, A History* (2000); Christopher Bickford's *Crime, Punishment and the Washington County Jail, Hard Time in Kingston, Rhode Island* (2002); and the *Journal of Daniel Stedman* (2003). I was also able to include material from my Brown University honors thesis, "South Kingstown Planters: Country Gentry in Colonial New England, 1770-1775." In addition, I happily read widely in modern scholarly books and college theses on Rhode Island history that mention Kingston, including books on race relations and controversies in Rhode Island on the ratification of the United States Constitution and the Dorr Rebellion.

Finally, I am writing this book in honor of my father, Dr. Alexander A. McBurney and my stepmother, Donna McBurney. They have been wonderful stewards of the Elisha R. Potter Homestead property, and I have always enjoyed returning to visit them each year, now with my own family.

I am virtually a stranger in Kingston now. With my perspective of time and distance, how would I like to see Kingston improve? First, I wish that the Rhode Island government would show the political will to build a highway that diverts Newport and beach traffic from passing through the village. Second, Kingston has an unusual number of buildings not owned by private individuals: the Kingston Free Library and Reading Room;

Kingston Congregational Church; Washington County Jail (Pettaquamscutt Historical Society); Helme House and Old School House (South County Art Association); the Tavern Hall Club; and the Fayerweather House (Kingston Improvement Association). This is wonderful, but it does make it difficult sometimes for proper maintenance to be funded. Third, a number of the historic residences have been converted to boarding houses for University of Rhode Island students. The maintenance of these rentals is also an issue at times. Fifth, more houses in Kingston should be on the National Register of Historic Places. Sixth, I fervently wish that the village would change its name back to the charming name of "Little Rest." Read the chapter on the village voting to change its name from Little Rest to Kingston in 1825 and see if you agree!

I would like to extend my gratitude to Dr. William Metz and Dr. Christopher Bickford for commenting on drafts of this book. Furthermore, I would like to thank Taylor McBurney and Kyle McBurney for assisting me on some research. I would also like to thank all of the wonderful archivists and librarians who assisted me at the Pettaquamscutt Historical Society (Dr. Christopher Bickford, Craig Anthony and Katherine Bossy in particular), University of Rhode Island Library (Special Collections) (David Maslyn in particular), Kingston Free Library and Reading Room (Pam Mead in particular), Library of Congress (Ronald Roache), Rhode Island Historical Society, John Hay Library at Brown University, Baker Library at Harvard University, Rhode Island Judicial Archives (Andrew Smith in particular) and South Kingstown Town Hall.

Most of all, I would like to thank my wife, Margaret, and children, Ryan, Kyle and Victoria, for their support and patience as I wrote this book.

Map of Rhode Island, 1806-1854. John Hutchins Cady, *Rhode Island Boundaries, 1636-1936* (State Planning Board, Providence, 1936).

KINGSTON VILLAGE
HISTORIC DISTRICT

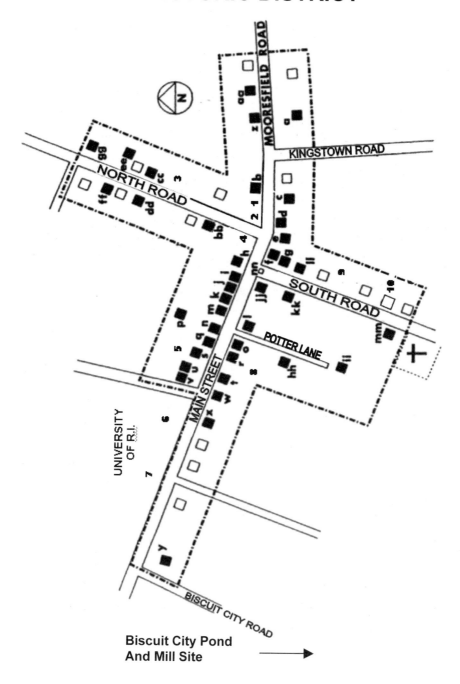

Biscuit City Pond
And Mill Site →

a. **Sherwell (1893)**
- Herbert J. Wells House (1893-1933)

b. **William H. Case House (1826)**
- William H. Case House (~1826-33)
- William French House (~1857)
- Harley Family House (~1860-95)

c. **Mansard House (1875)**
- Site of John P. Case House (~1826)
- Site of Blacksmith Shop (~1860)
- Benj. & Fannie Brown House (1875)

d. **Wilkins Updike House (1819)**
- Site of Joseph Case House (~1710)
- Wilkins Updike House (1819-67)

e. **Kingston Hill Store (1897)**
- Site of Immanuel Case Store (~1771)
- Site of George Fayerweather Blacksmith Shop (~1804-1820)
- Site of John P. Case Store (1822-58)
- Site of Charles Aldrich "Marble Shop" (~1870-76)
- Alonzo Greenman Store (~1897)

f. **John Moore House (1710)**
- John Moore House & Shop (1710-15)
- Abraham Perkins House & Shop (1715-44)
- Nathaniel Perkins & Shop (1744-55)
- Christopher Comstock House (~1826-33)
- Luke Aldrich House (~1857-62)

g. **Wilkins Updike Law Office (~1826)**
- Wilkins Updike Law Office (~1826-60) (moved from Asa Potter House site)
- Elisha C. Clarke Law Office (~1866)

h. **Asa Potter House (1829)**
- Site of Wilkins Updike Law Office (~1826)
- Site of John G. Clarke Shop (~1826)
- Asa Potter House (1829-37)
- James B. M. Potter House (~1848-60)
- Samuel Rodman House (~1860)
- William H. Potter House (1870-82)

i. **Asa Potter Law Office (1831)**
- Site of William Lunt Shop & House (1777-~1830)
- Asa Potter Law Office (~1831)

- Watson & Greenman Store (~1837-60)
- Dr. Thomas A. Hazard Office (~1860-84)

j. **Abel Cottrell House (1818)**
- Site of Abel Cottrell House (1775-1818)
- Abel Cottrell Jr. House & Shop (1775-1833)
- George Champlin House & Shop (~1833-57)
- Rose Sisters House & Hat Shop (~1860-89)

k. **Thomas S. Taylor House (1775/1827)**
- Joseph Perkins House & Shop (1775-89)
- Mary Perkins House (1775-93)
- John Hagadorn House (1812-13)
- Wilkins Updike House (1814-19)
- Thomas S. Taylor House (1825-44)
- W. C. Watson House (~1857-60)
- John G. Perry House (~1869-89)

l. **John Douglass House (1753)**
- John Douglass House & Shop (1753-72)
- George Teft House & Shop (1772-92)
- Lucy & Hannah Champlin House (1844-1906)

m. **Joseph Reynolds Tavern (1774)**
- Caleb Wescott House (1774-83)
- Joseph Reynolds Tavern (1795-1823)
- John N. Reynolds Tavern (1823-36)
- Philip Taylor Tavern (1836-51)
- John N. Taylor Tavern (1852-~90)
- John N. and Philip K. Taylor House (1890-through 1900)

n. **Private School (1759)**
- Private School (1759-1790s)
- Thomas S. Taylor Store (1807-1844)
- Mrs. Taylor Store (~1857)
- Powell Helme Store (~1860-80)
- Bernon & Nath. Helme Store (~1880-through 1900)
- Post Office (20th century)
- South County Art Association (present)

o. **Matthew Waite House (1819)**
- Site of William Caswell House (~1755)
- Site of John Waite House (1769-1817)
- Matthew Waite & Family (1819-84)
- Elisha C. Clarke (~1870)

p. **Taylor Stage Coach Barn (1825)**
- John Nichols Barn (~1824)
- John N. Taylor Barn (~1870)

q. **Helme House (1802/1818)**
- Site of Dan. Weeden House & Shop (~1754)
- Site of John Weeden House & Shop (1775-97)
- John Nichols and Son House & Shop (1792-~1860)
- Law Offices (~1818)
- Landholders Bank Office (1818-1925)
- Town Clerk's Office (~1800-28)
- South County Art Association (present)

r. **Kingston Inn (1755)**
- John Potter Tavern (1755-1771)
- John Peck Rathbun Tavern (~1780)
- Charles Barker Tavern (1796-1820)
- Mary Barker Tavern (1820-27)
- Jesse and John Babcock Tavern (1836-73)
- J. S. Brown Inn (~1875-95)

s. **Peckham Tavern (1820)**
- Timothy Peckham Tavern (1820-21)
- Dr. Daniel Watson House (~1826)
- Robinson & Anthony Store (1831-~55)
- George Robinson Store (~1857)
- Robinson Family House (~1897)

t. **Thomas P. Wells House (1832)**
- Site of First Colony House (1752-75)
- Site of First County Court House (!752-75)
- Site of William W. Pollack House (~1788)
- Site of Levi Totten Office (~1826)
- Thomas P. Wells House & Store (1832-43)
- Rev. J. H. Wells House (1854-70)
- Thomas P. Wells House (1861-84)

- Church Parish House (present)

u. **County Court House (1776)**
- State House (1776-1853)
- County Court House (1776-1894)
- Town Meeting Hall (1776-1877)
- Town Clerk's Office (1828-77)
- Town Council Meeting (1856-77)
- Kingston Free Library & Reading Room (1895-present)

v. **County Records Office (1857)**
- County Records Office (1857-94)

w. **Kingston Congregational Church (1820)**
- Kingston Congregational Church (1820-present)

x. **County Jail (1792/1858/1861)**
- County Jail (1792-1956)
- Pettaquamscutt Historical Society (present)

y. **John Potter House (~1775)**
- John Potter House & Shop (~1775)
- Joseph Stanton House & Tanyard (1783-~1826)

z. **George Fayerweather House (1820)**
- George Fayerweather House & Shop (1820-41)
- Nancy Fayerweather House (1820-65)
- Fayerweather Family (through 1900)
- Fayerweather Craft Guild (present)

aa. **Solomon Fayerweather House (1852)**
- Solomon and Louise Fayerweather House (1852-1901)

bb. **Peckham House (1796)**
- Joshua Clarke House (~1801-17)
- Samuel Helme House (~1817-37)
- Henry Barber (~1857)
- Powell Helme House (~1860)
- Bernon and Nathaniel Helme House (~1880)

cc. **Thomas R. Wells House (1750/1820)**
- Site of House (1750)
- Thomas R. Wells House (1820-35)
- Christopher Comstock House & Boarding House (~1835-55)
- William Hazard (1855-75)

dd. **Henry Eldred House (1833)**
- Henry Eldred House (1833-40)
- Dr. Thomas Hazard House (1847-64)

- Wells Family House (1864-1919)

ee. **Kingston Female Seminary School (1853)**
  - Kingston Female Seminary School (1853-63)

ff. **Luke Aldrich House (1829)**
  - Luke Aldrich House (1829-36)
  - John G. Clarke House (1836-38)
  - Thomas Vernon House & School (~1838)
  - Job W. Watson House (~1853-62)

gg. **S. Perry House (1862)**

hh. **Old Manor House (early 20th century)**

ii. **Elisha Reynolds Potter Homestead (1809)**
  - Elisha R. Potter, Sr. House (1809-35)
  - Elisha R. Potter, Jr. House (1835-82)
  - William H. Potter House (1882-1906)
  - Mary LeMoine Potter House (1906-38)

jj. **Elisha Reynolds House**
  - Elisha Reynolds House & Store (1738-90)
  - Thomas R. Wells Store (1804-22)
  - Dr. John Aldrich House (~1826)
  - Philip Taylor House & Boarding House (~1830)
  - *Rhode Island Advocate* Office (1831-32)
  - Kingston Boot & Shoe Factory (1838-42)
  - Kingston Circulating Library (1852-73)
  - Rose Sisters House & Store (~1855-60)
  - Potter & Vernon School (~1863)
  - J. H. Wells House (~1874)
  - Thomas M. Potter House (~1843; 1876-89)

kk. **Sara Fellows House (1820/1862)**
  - Site of Stephen Green House and Shop (~1813-19)
  - Christopher Gardner House (~1826-33)
  - Sara Fellows House (~1862)

ll. **Elisha R. Gardner House (1803)**
  - Site of Barker House (1770-93)
  - Elisha R. Gardiner House (1793-1823)
  - Kingston Academy Boarding House (~1823)
  - Rev. Oliver Brown House (~1833)

mm. **Robert Helme House (1786)**
  - Robert Helme House (1786-88)
  - Sylvester Robinson House (1800-10)
  - Benjamin Storer House (~1826-33)
  - James B. M. Potter (1882-1900)

nn. **Village Well (1826)**

1. **Former Site of Samuel Casey/James Helme House (1764)**
  - Caleb Gardner House (1747-50)
  - Samuel Casey House & Shop (1750-70)
  - James Helme House & Shop (1777-1823)
  - William Helme Case House (1828-57)
  - Sara and George Fayerweather House (1853-1878)

2. **Former Site of Shops (1793)**
  - Nicholas Pettis Shop (1793-97)
  - Joshua Clarke Shop (~1801-18)
  - John G. Clarke & George C. Clarke Shop (~1820-38)
  - John P. Case Shop (~1826)
  - William H. Case Shop (~1833-57)
  - Dixon and Newell Law Office (1816-37)

3. **Former Site of Kingston Academy School House (1823)**
  - Kingston Academy School House (1823-1844)
  - South Kingstown District School House No. 3 (1844-82)

4. **Former Site of Thomas Potter Tavern (1760)**
  - Elisha Reynolds Building (1740)
  - Thomas Potter Tavern & Store (1760-93)
  - Stephen Green House & Shop (~1810)
  - Samuel Coy House (1820)
  - James B. M. Potter House (~1835)

5. **Former Site of Robert Potter Homestead and Tavern (1731)**
  - Robert Potter and Son Homestead & Tavern (1731-96)

- Timothy Peckham Homestead and Tavern (1796-1820)

6. **Former Site of French Homestead (1792)**
   - Nathaniel Helme House & Shop (~1740)
   - First County Jail (1752-92)
   - Cyrus French (1792-1826)
   - William French (1820-63)
   - Dr. Peleg Johnson (1822-59)
   - French Family (through 1900)

7. **Former Site of House**
   - London Rhodes (~1870)
   - Henry Thomas (~1880)

8. **Former Site of Stores**
   - Palmer & Browning Store & Tavern (~1830)
   - Thomas P. Wells Store (1837-43)
   - B. Palmer & J.H. Wells Store (1862-67)
   - J. S. Brown Shop (~1870)

9. **Former Site of Shops**
   - Elijah Kenyon Shop (~1812-26)
   - Luke Aldrich & Son Shop (~1826-70)

10. **Former Site of Clarke Homestead**
   - William Case Clarke House (~1805-33)
   - George C. Clarke House (~1855)

*** This list is not intended to be comprehensive. It is intended to list residents of buildings, not owners. The "~" mark indicates estimated time-frame. The map shows the original boundaries of the Kingston Village Historic District, which have since been enlarged to reflect current property divisions. Shaded buildings are listed on the National Register of Historic Places.

I. LITTLE REST IN THE COLONIAL ERA:

HUB OF THE NARRAGANSETT COUNTRY,

(1675-1774)

John Potter and Family, with Slave. Potter was one of the wealthiest Narragansett planters in the colonial period and the brother of William Potter, a Narragansett planter who lived north of Little Rest on North Road. John Potter is displaying his high social status, by showing his family in fine clothes, drinking tea with a porcelain set, with a black domestic slave. Oil on panel painting, artist unknown, circa 1765. *Newport Historical Society.*

Little Rest's Beginnings

The first white settlers in Newport and the surrounding area in the mid-17th century looked longingly at the rich lands across Narragansett Bay. Most of them had been farmers in England and they looked to duplicate their farming lives in the New World. The world that they lived in – in the pre-industrial age – was dominated by agriculture. Compared to the relatively expensive, small and crowded farms of the old country, they saw the opportunity to buy large tracts of inexpensive land that could be turned into large farms. Some enterprising men sought to make money on land speculation, by buying cheap land and reselling it to new white settlers.

The problem for the first white settlers in Newport was that the lands they coveted across Narragansett Bay were already inhabited by the Narragansett tribe. The Narragansetts, part of the Algonquin family of Indian nations, subsisted on farming, fishing and hunting. In 1636, when Roger Williams arrived in Rhode Island, there were approximately 7,000 Narragansetts Indians. They dominated southern Rhode Island.

A group of white speculators from Newport and the surrounding area accomplished the goal of acquiring a large amount of cheap, open land by taking advantage of the Narragansett's ignorance of white concepts of property ownership. In 1657, in what is called the Pettaquamscutt Purchase, this group purchased from Narragansett sachems a tract of land about twelve square miles in size for the measly sum of £16. The Pettaquamscutt Purchasers allotted the land among themselves and a few other men.

The area that would later give rise to Kingston village (formerly Little Rest) was one of the focal points of the Pettaquamscutt Purchasers. Large tracts of land were allotted on the northern and southern crests of Kingston Hill. A few adventurous men built houses on their land. In 1668, Jireh Bull acquired 480 acres of land on the east slope of Kingston Hill; there is evidence that a building was constructed on the land shortly thereafter. In 1671, William Knowles purchased 500 acres of land in what would become the heart of the Potter Homestead farm in Kingston; he built a house soon thereafter on this land.

The Indian "problem" was "solved" when the Narragansetts were virtually wiped out as a result of a surprise attack. In December 1675, white Massachusetts and Connecticut settlers were engaged in a fierce war, known as King Philip's War, with many of the Native American tribes in New England. Prior to this time, the Narragansett sachems, led by Canonchet, had largely kept their tribe out of the conflict. But English settlers from Massachusetts and Connecticut became concerned that the powerful tribe was about to join forces with the warring Wampanoag and other New England tribes, led by King Philip. Massachusetts and Connecticut settlers decided to make a preemptive strike against the Narragansett tribe.

The Massachusetts troops camped in Wickford at Cocumscussoc. They had intended to join with the Connecticut forces and seek shelter at Jireh Bull's stone garrison house at Pettaquamscutt (near current-day Middle Bridge), but some Narragansett warriors, fully aware of the intentions of the invading force, had attacked it and burned it to the ground. Fifteen white men, women and children were killed. The Massachusetts and Connecticut forces on December 18, 1675, camped outside on the grounds of the burned structure, exposed to the bitter cold. The next day, with snow on the ground and still in the bitter cold, an army of about 1,000 men tramped towards the well-protected winter camping grounds of the Narragansetts in the Great Swamp, the site of which was about three miles west of Kingston.

During the arduous march to the Great Swamp, legend has it that the Massachusetts and Connecticut forces had a "little rest" on the hill now known as Kingston Hill. This is probably how Kingston obtained its prior name – Little Rest. Whether, in fact, the troops did pass through what would become Little Rest is not known for certain. One historian believes that the troops marched between Thirty-Acre Pond and Larkin's Pond, a route that would have by-passed Little Rest Hill.

The Narragansett tribe, with perhaps 3,500 men, women and children, had set up in the Great Swamp approximately 500 wigwams behind a tall pointed-stick palisaded fort surrounded by felled trees. They were well supplied with enough corn, beans, dried fish, and venison to last the winter. The Massachusetts and Connecticut army, with the invaluable assistance of a captured Indian guide, successfully located the vulnerable point in the Narragansetts' palisaded fort. After a fierce struggle with Narragansett defenders, the Massachusetts and Connecticut troops breached the ramparts of the fort. Somehow, whether as a result of an accident or an intentional act is not clear, some wigwams caught fire. Strong winds caused the blaze to engulf all of the wigwams in fire, destroying the winter camp of the Narragansetts, in what is known as either the Great Swamp Fight or the Great Swamp Massacre. Estimates of Narragansett losses range from 300 to 3,000, many of whom were women and children. In any event, the power of the Narragansett tribe had been broken, as its winter camp and food supplies had been destroyed in the midst of a bitter winter.

The Massachusetts and Connecticut men marched back to Cocumscussoc. Carrying their dead and assisting their wounded, the men continued to suffer in the extreme winter conditions. They also had few food supplies. Inexplicably, they had burned all of the Narragansett's food supplies rather than saving some for themselves. The exhausted, hungry men on the return trip may have had another "little rest" at the top of Little Rest Hill. In the end, the army lost more than 200 killed or wounded, with many of the deaths occurring during the return march.

The Rhode Island settlers paid a heavy price for the invasion by the Massachusetts and Connecticut army. When the army left Cocumscussoc in late January, surviving Narragansett warriors ravaged the entire countryside in southern Rhode Island, destroying crops and cattle, burning houses and barns, and killing any white settlers who did not seek refuge in Newport. Most probably, all of the houses around Little Rest Hill were destroyed, including those owned by William Knowles and Jireh Bull, even though the white settlers apparently had good relations with the Narragansetts. It is said that on the day preceding the attack in the Great Swamp that "the Indians had exchanged neighborly kindnesses with a family by the name of Knowles . . . who resided within a short distance of their encampment . . . ." Knowles's house was about three miles from the site of the Great Swamp encampment, near what would become Little Rest village.

King Philip's War came to an end with the captures and executions of Canonchet, the Narragansett sachem, and King Philip, the latter occurring on August 12, 1676. Settlers who had fled to Newport began to resettle on the western side of Narragansett Bay in what would become known as "the Narragansett country" -- the former lands of the Narragansett tribe. Returning survivors noted that the area had "became a desolate wilderness againe . . . replenished with howling wolves and other wild creatures."

Despite the end of the war, a border dispute between Rhode Island, Massachusetts and Connecticut over the Narragansett country limited migration of farmers to the lands of the Pettaquamscutt Purchase. The Pettaquamscutt Purchasers were backed by Rhode Island, and another group of white speculators was backed by Massachusetts and Connecticut. Once this border dispute was settled in Rhode Island's favor by the British government in 1694, settlers began to stream into Kingstown (incorporated in 1674)[1] to take advantage of the abundant, inexpensive and fertile land.

When the Pettaquamscutt Purchasers divided their lands, they carved out an east-west highway that would become the main street of Little Rest. The east-west highway extended east to Tower Hill and west to Henry's Elbow (near the current Fernwood cemeteries). Deeds indicate that the farms

---

[1] The name of Kingstown itself then referred to most of South County, with the exception of Westerly. The town of Kingstown was renamed Rochester in 1686 when Governor Edmund Andros assumed control of Rhode Island. When Andros was deposed in 1689, the town reassumed its name of Kingstown. It is sometimes reported that Kingston village's first name was Rochester and that its second name was Little Rest, but Kingston's name was never Rochester. The confusion likely was caused by Rhode Island history books written in the early 19th century, in which the term "Kingston" was sometimes erroneously used for "Kingstown."

of Pettaquamscutt Purchasers Mumford, Hull, Sewall, Porter, Wilson, Wilbor and Brenton were laid out north of what is now main street, while the farms of Bull, Knowles, Teft and Helme were laid out south of what is now main street. Importantly, the land of Samuel Wilbor had as its southern boundary what would become main street of the village of Little Rest, while the land of William Knowles had main street as its northern boundary.

The lands of the Pettaquamscutt Purchasers were also bounded east and west by a road that started south of what would become Little Rest, which road crossed main street in the village near the village well, and proceeded north of the village. These roads, called South and North Roads, may have been laid out on an ancient Indian trail.

Some of the original purchasers, and others who acquired tracts through purchase or inheritance, began to settle the land and build houses in the area that would become Little Rest. Samuel Wilson built a house on his land before 1682, and Robert Hazard was living in a house on his land in 1688. Ezekiel Bull deeded land and buildings in 1693. In 1705, Solomon Carpenter built on his farm off of South Road a one and one-half story house, which currently is the oldest surviving house in the area. Original purchaser William Knowles, after King Philip's War, probably rebuilt a house on his land south of what would become main street in Little Rest. Robert Potter, Sr. bought the land of original purchaser Samuel Wilbor in 1684, thereby acquiring most of the lots on the north side of what would become main street. Potter built a house part of the way down Little Rest Hill on its north side shortly thereafter.

To the west of what would become Little Rest, Robert Hannah built his dwelling house. Hannah acquired the 260-acre plot through his marriage to the daughter of Pettaquamscutt Purchaser Samuel Wilson. At his death in 1706, probate records indicate that he owned 154 sheep, 41 cattle, 6 oxen, 3 hogs, and one female black slave with five children.

One of the key tasks of the settlers of early Kingstown was the "laying out" of highways and country roads. The Pettaquamscutt Purchasers in allocating lands among themselves in 1657 had marked the road that would become main street in Little Rest village, and South and North Roads, but in general the original Purchasers did not make much of an effort to make the roads proper roads. In the early 1700s, the Kingstown town council worked to widen, improve and extend roads. For example, in 1703, the town meeting of Kingstown selected twelve men to improve and widen South Road. In 1715, a road was extended from "Henry's Elbow" (at the curve where Old Fernwood cemetery is located on the way to West Kingston) to the west. The work to fell and clear trees on the land for these roads must have been extremely difficult, and may have been performed in part by black slaves. In 1688, Robert Hazard began performing another important task – surveying land boundaries to provide comfort to purchasers that land titles were valid.

The conditions for a village rising on Little Rest Hill were ideal. The farms laid out around Little Rest Hill were bounded by an east-west highway (including what would become main street). What is more, there was a cross-road, North Road (to the north of main street) and South Road (directly opposite of North Road and south of main street). The farmers who lived on their tracts of land far from each other around Little Rest Hill needed a central area in which to obtain services such as blacksmithing and to buy useful articles in a store. In addition, the area of what would become Little Rest was on the crest of a hill, with a marvelous view of the lower lands to the west.

The first houses built on main street were built at or near the "Four Corners," the cross-roads of main street and North and South Roads. The first house on main street in Little Rest was built by John Moore in about 1710. It was a small, gambrel-roofed one-cell structure at the east corner of main street and South Road. This house still stands; the eastern part of the building is the original part. In 1715, Moore sold the house to Abraham Perkins, who was a blacksmith and a storekeeper. Perkins probably expanded the house shortly thereafter. Sometime around this period, Joseph Case constructed a house on main street to the east of Perkins's house, in the area of the current Wilkins Updike house. At his death in 1739, probate records indicate that Case had owned 65 sheep, 16 cattle, 4 horses, 11 hogs, 6 chickens, and four black slaves (two adult females, one elderly male, and one boy).

Robert Potter, Sr., who owned the lots on main street's north side, may have persuaded Elisha Reynolds to move to the Four Corners. Reynold's father and Potter's father both had migrated from Portsmouth, Rhode Island to North Kingstown. Reynolds, born in 1706, was a shopkeeper on the rise. In 1728, he married the daughter of Robert Potter, Susannah. In 1733, Robert Potter, Sr. sold to Elisha Reynolds the lot on the west corner of main street and North Road. Reynolds built a house on this land in about 1736 and opened a small store. Four years later, he sold the land and house to Stephen Mumford, a shopkeeper. Reynolds reacquired the land and house in 1745. In 1738 and 1739, Elisha Reynolds purchased 670 acres of lands in and around Little Rest owned by William Knowles. This was prime land, as it included lots on main street's south side. The land extended approximately from South Road west to what would become Biscuit City Road. This land included a lot on the southwest corner of main street and South Road, on which Reynolds built a large house in 1738. Due to its relatively large size, it was called the "mansion house" in land records. It is the second-oldest surviving building in the village today, and is now known as the Tavern Hall Club.

In 1693, Robert Hannah acquired a key tract of land (about 260 acres), which had as its western border North Road and as its southern border what would become the village's main street. It does not appear that Hannah built a house on this land.[2] The first house was constructed in about 1747 by Caleb Gardner, who would become a wealthy farmer. Thus, by 1747, each of the four lots on the "Four Corners" of the village had houses built on them.

In the early years of Little Rest, Robert Potter, Sr. and Elisha Reynolds may have intended to establish a community of Six Principle Baptists. Early residents, including Elisha Reynolds, Robert Potter and Caleb Gardner, were Baptists. Soon after their arrival they helped to establish a Baptist church, the first one in South Kingstown. It met in the new colony and court house built on Tower Hill in 1729.

The Little Rest Baptists were "Six Principle Baptists." The Six Principle Baptists were distinguished by their insistence on the "laying of hands" as a requirement for membership – the "sixth principle." As a ritual, the "laying of hands" tended to place all members regardless of their economic status on the same spiritual level. In addition, Six Principle Baptists opposed congregation singing (preferring to hear only single voices at one time), and refused to pay the salary of their pastors or have educated pastors (who were deliberately called "elders"). The leveling aspects of the Six Principle Baptists made this sect unpalatable to the religious tastes of many of the increasingly wealthy farmers, but it attracted ordinary rural folk.

While Six Principle Baptists did not have educated, paid ministers, the South Kingstown church's preacher, Daniel Everitt, achieved fame in the area as a preacher beginning in about 1725. A letter from the Baptist church in 1731, written "by the hands of our beloved Brother and Teacher Daniel Everitt," was signed by eleven church members, including four women. Among the signers were three Tefts and Solomon Carpenter, who were farmers down South Road, and three Little Rest men, Elisha Reynolds, Robert Potter, Sr. and his son, Robert Potter, Jr.

While Elisha Reynolds initially may have been attracted to the area that would become Little Rest by a desire to develop a Baptist community, he also must have recognized the opportunity for land speculation around Little Rest. He must have realized that Little Rest was a natural location for a village and that his acquisition of the Knowles tract, which bounded main street on its northern edge, placed him in an excellent position to profit from lot resales in future years. At this time, around 1740, what would become Little Rest was a mere collection of ordinary houses at a muddy cross-roads. As we will see, by 1752, Elisha Reynolds had a clever plan to convert the area into a true village, which would increase the value of his lands and enable him to earn profits from land resales.

---

[2] Robert Hannah is sometimes credited with building a house on this land by 1706, but town records indicate that that was unlikely. This lot is sometimes confused with the lot and house that Hannah owned to the west of the village.

Little Rest: Rising Hub of the Narragansett Country

The rise of Little Rest was intimately related to the rise of a group of commercial farmers called the "Narragansett planters" in South Kingstown and other towns in southern Rhode Island in the 18th century. In 1729, the Narragansett country was formally organized as King's County. It consisted of the current towns of South Kingstown, Narragansett, North Kingstown, Exeter, Hopkinton, Richmond, Charlestown and Westerly.[3]

While rural Rhode Island and the rest of New England was dominated by villages, small farms and a few wealthy men, the Narragansett planters succeeded in developing a plantation-based economy. In part, large and isolated farms were the product of the Pettaquamscutt Purchasers' approach in allotting large land tracts among themselves. Moreover, the boundary dispute with Connecticut and Massachusetts inhibited settlement. Conservative Puritans from those colonies were hesitant to establish villages in the Narragansett country, for fear that Rhode Island would win the border dispute and the settlers would have to live with freedom of religion, which they considered heresy. Thus, settlers from Newport and the surrounding islands were able to acquire vast tracts of cheap land in the Narragansett country. Once they began stock and dairy farming, they benefited from their proximity to Newport. They enjoyed a rising demand for their surplus livestock and dairy produce from nearby Newport merchants, who discovered eager markets for foodstuffs in the English colonial plantation settlements in the Caribbean and the American South.

The fertile soil, high quality grass, open pastures and relatively mild winters near the ocean made the Narragansett country suited for developing a commercial economy based on grazing. By 1730, successful Narragansett planters – notably the Hazard, Robinson, Gardner, Potter, Niles, Watson, Brown, Perry and Babcock families -- owned thousands of acres of land. The average Narragansett planter between 1730 and 1760 held about 400 sheep, 80 cattle and 20 horses. These holdings were far greater than in other Rhode Island towns. South Kingstown (which then included the current town of Narragansett) became the premier cheese-producing town in New England. It was also probably New England's most important horse-raising town, specializing in the famed Narragansett Pacer, a favorite breed of planters in the Caribbean and the southern colonies. Newport merchant records indicate

---

[3] Southern Rhode Island originally consisted of Kingstown and Westerly. Kingstown was divided into North and South Kingstown in 1723. Charlestown was formed from Westerly in 1738. Exeter was formed from North Kingstown in 1743. Richmond was formed from Charlestown in 1747. Hopkinton was formed from Westerly in 1757. Narragansett was formed from South Kingstown in 1901.

that the planters frequently traded "Rhode Island cheese," horses, sheep, and cattle in exchange for rum and luxuries such as silks, clothing, dinnerware, ribbons and chocolates. Newport merchants then shipped the stock and dairy produce to markets in the Caribbean and southern colonies.

The Narragansett planters desired a large, cheap labor force to clear the land, tend to their large herds and cultivate their farms. As did other English plantation-based societies in the early 18th century, they turned to buying black slaves. South Kingstown became the most important slave-holding town in rural New England. Probate and census records indicate that Narragansett planters on the average held between 5 and 20 black slaves.

The Narragansett planters were successful commercial farmers by New England standards. They created a society based on social distinctions in imitation of the English country gentry. But the amounts of land and slaves they owned, and the quality of their houses and household furniture, paled in comparison to those held by Virginia and other southern planters.

A few Narragansett planters had their estates in the immediate vicinity of Little Rest. One of them was Caleb Gardner, who owned two farms in the area, one near current West Kingston and the second one to the east of North Road and to the north of main street, just above the lots fronting on main street. By 1744, Gardner was successful enough in his commercial farming operations that he was in the top 10% of taxpayers in South Kingstown; he maintained this position throughout the colonial period. His wealth is indicated by purchases from an account book of a village store; Gardner purchased luxuries such as silk, velvet and chocolates, items that few other villagers could afford. As did other Narragansett planters, Gardner served in political offices, serving many terms as a member of the South Kingstown town council from the 1740s to the 1770s. In 1774, Gardner was reported in a colony census as having six blacks and three Indian residing at his farms. The black persons were likely slaves and the Indians were likely Narragansetts who were bonded servants. In 1747, Gardner built a house on main street on the northeast lot on the Four Corners.

In 1739, Narragansett planter William Potter inherited from his father, John Potter, one of the wealthiest Narragansett planters in the colonial period, a large farm about one mile north of Little Rest on North Road. In 1750, William Potter married Penelope Hazard, the daughter of wealthy Narragansett planter Thomas Hazard. Potter became a very successful commercial farmer. By 1759, he was one of the top 10% of taxpayers in South Kingstown, and by 1774 he paid the second highest amount of taxes in the town. The census of 1774 indicates that he had eleven black persons residing at his estate, most or all of them likely slaves. His estate, called the "Abbey," was described by a contemporary as containing a large house, an elegant garden "with parterres, borders, shrubbery, summer house, [and] fruit

"S.W. View of the Seat of Hon. Henry Marchant, Esq., in South Kingstown, State of Rhode Island." A typical Narragansett planter farm estate. Ink on paper, unknown artist, circa 1790. *Rhode Island Historical Society, RHi X3 3019.*

orchard," as well as "high and costly fences, outhouses, and cookery establishment." Potter served for many years as town clerk and as chief justice of the county court of common pleas, and served as a member in the General Assembly and on the South Kingstown town council.

Another Narragansett planter who resided just outside Little Rest was Benjamin Peckham, whose farm was a short way up North Road and south of William Potter's land. Peckham paid the fifth highest amount of taxes in South Kingstown in 1759. He then apparently transferred some of his estate to his eldest son, Josephus, as the census of 1774 indicates that he and Josephus each had four black slaves. In describing his property, Peckham wrote that his house had a "Great Room" and that in addition his property included a barn, cheese house, and other buildings, as well as an orchard.

As in the American southern plantation colonies, few notable towns arose in the Narragansett country. The Narragansett planters generally were spread throughout southern Rhode Island on their estates. Still, villages such as Little Rest were needed in order for Narragansett planters (and less successful farmers) to obtain the services of tradesmen. Little Rest began to fill that role. Tradesmen included John Douglass, blacksmith; Elisha Reynolds, storekeeper and small merchant; Samuel Casey, a talented and rising silversmith; and Nathaniel Helme, shoemaker.

Elisha Reynolds, who first purchased land in Little Rest in 1733, became more than a mere shopkeeper. He acquired wealth through land speculation and by acting as a middle-man "factor" between local farmers and Newport and other merchants. Scraps from his account book indicate that he purchased from local farmers cheese, which he resold at a profit to Newport merchants and even Boston merchants. For example, in 1767, he purchased 9,849 pounds of cheese from a local farmer. By the 1750s and through 1774, Reynolds was one of the wealthiest men in South Kingstown, paying enough taxes to put him in the top 10% of South Kingstown taxpayers.

Little Rest's other large landholder was Robert Potter, Jr. In 1746, he inherited from his father most of the land to the north of main street in Little Rest. This included a house that the father had built on the north side of main street in 1731, after moving from his house part-way down Little Rest Hill.

Little Rest was growing, slowly, as a hub to service the Narragansett planters and other farmers in the surrounding area. By the early 1750s, it had several shopkeepers. It had a Baptist meeting. Several farmers also resided in the village. It was probably around this time that Little Rest was substantial enough to earn a name as a village. It was not markedly different from other Narragansett country villages, but that was about to change.[4]

---

[4] The notes to this chapter discuss a book allegedly published in Boston in 1747 that describes Little Rest in 1743 that is probably not authentic.

The Removal of the Court House and Jail
from Tower Hill to Little Rest

The two largest landholders of lots on Little Rest's main street, Elisha Reynolds and Robert Potter, Jr., faced a challenge. How could they attract more families and businesses to Little Rest? If they could do so, their landholdings would dramatically increase in value and they could resell lots on main street at a profit. In 1752, Reynolds, Potter and others villagers saw their opportunity.

When the colony of Rhode Island was divided into counties in 1729, each county was ordered to have its own court house and jail. In King's County (the current Washington County, which is also known as South County), these buildings were constructed at the village on Tower Hill. The colony's General Assembly met periodically at Tower Hill, taking turns with the court houses in Newport, Providence and other county seats. In addition, the county court held its sessions at the court house, and the court house was the location for town meetings and elections. A jail accompanied the court house. As a result of the construction of the court house and jail, Tower Hill grew to be a thriving village.

Fortunately for the influential men of Little Rest, by 1752, the court house at Tower Hill had fallen into disrepair and had other problems. Reynolds, Potter and other enterprising residents of Little Rest saw their chance to relocate the court house and jail to their village. In February 1752, while the General Assembly was sitting at Tower Hill, they persuaded a number of "gentlemen and others" from King's County to petition the General Assembly requesting that a new court house and jail be built in Little Rest. The petition pointed out the many inconveniences of the Tower Hill court house, including that it was miserably built and scarcely fit for use, would be a continual charge to the public funds to keep it fit for minimal use, and was inconveniently located in the southeast corner of King's County. In pointing out the inadequacy of the court house to members of the General Assembly, the petitioners wrote that it "should so endanger your lives as to sit in it this time of year when a hard storm would almost blow it down." The petitioners further pointed out that members of the General Assembly and the court judges suffered from the lack of proper accommodations at Tower Hill, particularly in the winter season.

In supporting Little Rest as the best location in the county for the construction of a new court house, the petitioners argued to the General Assembly that Little Rest was a more central location within King's County than Tower Hill. The petitioners pointed out that Little Rest was now a village with "many Handsome estates & good settlers," was "surrounded with all the conveniences of Life of all sorts," and would soon have "Three good

Taverns well furnished & supplied for ye Entertainment." Importantly, the petitioners noted that Col. Elisha Reynolds would deed land for the court house, Robert Potter would deed land for a jail and yard, and Little Rest residents would fund at their own expense construction of "a Handsome Court House & Gaol."

Tower Hill residents were enraged by the bold petition. They also petitioned the General Assembly, criticizing the "absurdities and misrepresentations made by the Little Rest promoters." In what was probably an exaggeration, the petitioners complained that Little Rest had water "loathsome to the taste," "rocky and miry" roads, and cellars "filled with water." The petitioners stated that it was "absurd" for the Little Rest petitioners to claim that their houses were better and that gentlemen would be better entertained at Little Rest than at Tower Hill. With some justification, the Tower Hill petitioners pointed out that they had built houses at Tower Hill in reliance on the court house and jail being located there, and that removing them would render their property "of Little or no value." The petitioners offered to repair the Tower Hill court house and jail at their own expense.

The General Assembly permitted the King's County towns to vote on the issue. South Kingstown voters preferred Little Rest by a vote of 51 to 21. The voters of Richmond, Westerly and Charlestown, who desired a shorter trip to Little Rest, overwhelmingly supported the change (the vote in Richmond was 54 to 0). With support for the move demonstrated, the General Assembly granted the petition to remove the court house and jail to Little Rest, "Provided Col. Elisha Reynolds, Mr. Wm Potter and Major Latham Clarke give bonds in the sum of $20,000 for the performance of all the conditions mentioned in their petition."

Pursuant to the conditions, on the same day, on September 22, 1752, Elisha Reynolds and Robert Potter, Jr. deeded land in Little Rest for the construction of the court house and jail, respectively. Little Rest villagers paid for the construction of a court house and jail. Thus, Little Rest won the struggle to become the new county seat in King's County.

As storekeepers, tavern keepers and artisans moved to Little Rest after 1752 to take advantage of the location of the court house and jail in the village, Reynolds sold at a profit land for houses on main street's south side and Robert Potter, Jr. sold at a profit land for houses on main street's north side. The removal of the court house and jail spurred a small boom in Little Rest. Between 1752 and 1755, in addition to the construction of the new court house and jail, at least five new houses were built in Little Rest. New tradesmen moved to Little Rest to service Narragansett planters, including a silversmith (Samuel Casey's brother), a blacksmith, a tanner, and a leatherworker. In 1752, Robert Potter, Jr. opened a tavern in his house on main street. Captain John Potter leased a house and opened a tavern in Little

Rest in 1753. He bought land from Elisha Reynolds next to the new court house in 1755 and built a tavern. Immediately, the South Kingstown town council began holding its meetings at the two taverns. In 1759, twelve villagers jointly purchased land from Robert Potter on the north side of main street and built a small school house next to the current Helme House. A school teacher was retained, with the parents of the students paying the school fees.

Construction continued into the 1770s. In 1769, silversmith and locksmith John Waite built a house on main street next to blacksmith John Douglass' house. Joseph Perkins, the silversmith, storekeeper and innkeeper, built a house on main street in 1774, as did carpenter Caleb Wescott and tailor Abel Cottrell. John Potter, turning to the tanning business, built a cottage at the corner of Biscuit City Road and main street in 1775.

Little Rest also became a hub for storekeepers, including Samuel Casey, beginning in the 1750s. Thomas Potter opened a store around 1760. Immanuel Case opened up a store in Little Rest around 1771, probably near the current location of the Kingston Hill Store. From Newport merchants, he stocked his store with "European" goods such as broadcloths; silk; men's beaver and felt hats; men's black breeches; white, green and black satins; women's hats; women's black and colored mittens; white and pompadour gloves; powder, shot and flints; snuff boxes; knives and forks; and "West India" goods such as tea, coffee, rum and molasses. Joseph Perkins kept a small store starting in 1771. In 1777, James Helme, Jr. purchased Samuel Casey's former store, which he operated until around 1816. Records indicate that storekeepers attracted customers from all over King's County. With the artisans, storekeepers and tavern keepers, Little Rest became dominated by families in the middle ranks of the social scale.

Little Rest's gain was Tower Hill's loss. With the loss of the court house and jail, Tower Hill slowly withered away. Many Tower Hill residents moved to Little Rest. After the son of Judge James Helme, James Helme, Jr., moved to Little Rest in 1777, most of his brothers followed him. Wilson Pollack, carpenter, moved from Tower Hill to Little Rest in 1787. Saddlemaker John Nichols moved from Tower Hill to Little Rest around 1790. Tower Hill's quasi-public institutions, the Congregational Church and a small private school with a healthy endowment, would finally move to Little Rest around 1820. Today, no physical trace of 18th century Tower Hill remains.

The removal of the court house and jail to Little Rest not only increased the wealth of village landowners Elisha Reynolds and Robert Potter, Jr., it brought them more respectability. Each man began performing public service at the colony level. Reynolds became a colonel in the militia, and in 1758 he served on the colony's court martial board. Robert Potter, Jr. served

James Helme's Wedding Suit, Silk Vest and Breeches. Helme was married in 1777 in Tower Hill, before he moved to Little Rest later that year. *Pettaquamscutt Historical Society.*

James Helme House and Store, circa 1890. Helme added an addition to the right side, making it his general store from 1777-1816. The building was demolished in 1910. *Pettaquamscutt Historical Society.*

on the colony's exclusive Committee of War from 1757 through 1762, during the height of the French and Indian War. He also served with Elisha Reynolds on the colony's court martial board in 1758. He later served a term each on the town council and as a deputy in the lower house of the General Assembly.

In 1763, four Little Rest Baptists – Elisha Reynolds, his son-in-law Thomas Potter, Jr., Robert Potter and nearby Narragansett planter Caleb Gardner – joined other prominent colony Baptists in a petition to the General Assembly to charter a Baptist-dominated college in the colony. In the next year, the petition succeeded, with Reynolds and Potter becoming two of the incorporators of the first college in the colony, Brown University.

A sign of the Baptist meeting's increase in respectability is that it began to interact with other sects. In 1755, Narragansett planter Jeffrey Watson, a Quaker, reported in his diary that he openly listened to a preacher at a Baptist meeting in Little Rest and afterwards had dinner at Elisha Reynold's house. The Anglican minister in the Narragansett country, Samuel Fayerweather, preached several times at " the Baptist (Anabaptist) Meeting House on Little Rest Hill." Fayerweather made sure that he "Carried on All the Publick Exercises According to the Method practiced in the Church of England."

By 1774, there was a warning sign on the horizon for Little Rest's Six Principle Baptist Church. In 1755, Elisha Reynolds had given half an acre of land for the purpose of building a meeting house for the sect, but no progress had yet been made.

Little Rest also had a number of families that were members of the Congregational Church. A Congregational Church was built in Tower Hill in the early 18th century, but the minister, Dr. Joseph Torrey, refused to move the church to Little Rest after the court house and jail were removed to Little Rest in 1752. Accordingly, Little Rest Congregationalists seeking to attend Sunday services either had to make the long ride by horseback to Tower Hill, or, more commonly, met in the Court House.

The following page has a chart of persons whom the author believes were the Little Rest inhabitants listed in Rhode Island's 1774 census, with each head of household's occupation added. Each household was quite large – on the average about 8 persons per household. The "household" for Royzell (not Roswell) Smith was the county jail. There were about 126 persons in the village. What jumps out most prominently is that black and Indian persons were separately counted and that there were about 18 black and three Indian persons in Little Rest. As explained in a subsequent chapter, black persons were held as slaves in Little Rest.

	White Males	White Females	Black Persons	Indian Persons	Total Persons
Benjamin Barker (shopkeeper)	3	1			4
Abel Cottrel (tailor)	4	2			6
David Douglass (blacksmith)	5	2			7
Jonathan Hassard (tavern keeper)	2	5	2		9
Timothy Peckham (farmer)	4	9	1	2	16
Joseph Perkins (storekeeper, silversmith)	2	1			3
Nathaniel Perkins (blacksmith)	3	6			9
Robert Potter (tavern keeper, farmer)	1	4	5		10
Thomas Potter (tavern keeper, storekeeper)	6	4	3		13
William Potter (tailor)	2	2			4
Elisha Reynolds (merchant, farmer)	3	3	4		10
Henry Reynolds (storekeeper, farmer)	3	5	3		11
Roswell Smith (jailer)	7	2		1	10
George Teft (blacksmith)	3	5			8
John Waite (silversmith)	3	3			6
	51	54	18	3	126

The Court House: The Heart of Little Rest

The most imposing structure on Little Rest's main street was the Court House; it remains the most imposing structure today, housing the Kingston Free Library. Just as the University of Rhode Island is to Kingston today, the Court House was the heart of Little Rest. Without it, Little Rest likely would have never have amounted to anything more than an ordinary village. The Court House was the location for sessions of the General Assembly (colony and state), sessions of the county court for all of King's County (now Washington County or South County), and town meetings for South Kingstown (then including Narragansett).

The Court House Building

Built in 1776, the Court House is the oldest government building in Washington County. It was the second court house constructed in Little Rest. The original court house built in 1752 stood across the street from the current Court House on the site where the Church House stands next to the Kingston Congregational Church. This first court house in Little Rest apparently was built no better than the former court house in Tower Hill -- it was too small (45 by 30 feet) and by 1773 was in bad repair. In October 1773, the General Assembly voted to build a new court house in Little Rest. A committee was appointed to "Consider the Bigness and Form of said House and make a Plan thereof." In June 1774, William Potter, by then a wealthy planter who lived one mile up North Road, was appointed by the General Assembly to oversee the construction of a new court house, on the basis of contracts granted after advertising and the receipt of sealed bids. This time the court house was to be built at public expense.

Potter selected a new site for the new court house, on a lot of land on the opposite side of main street from the first court house. Prior to this time, the lot was "all open and used as a Race Ground" for horses and their riders. Robert Potter, Jr. deeded the lot for the court house. William Potter advanced his own funds for the construction expenses and was later reimbursed by the General Assembly. He selected Caleb Wescott, a skilled carpenter in Little Rest, to begin construction of a new court house in 1775. This time, the building was made to last. The Court House was built from lumber sawed from South Kingstown trees. The frame was made of solid oak, the window frames were made with red cedar and the clapboards were made from white cedar. The builders put in solid 4 by 5 inch studs (today builders use one inch studs). Construction was at first slow. The General Assembly decided not to meet in the old court house in Little Rest in 1775. The General Assembly urged Potter on by voting to have the new court house "glazed, painted, and finished as soon as possible." In October 1776, although not entirely completed, the General Assembly met in the new Court House for the first time.

The General Assembly and county court met on the second floor. The original stairway may be seen in the old Reading Room in the library. Originally, fine Windsor chairs were used to seat members of the General Assembly. In addition, benches were arranged in a semicircular row and had spindle backs with beautiful San Domingo mahogany wood tips. The judge's bench was located at one end of the room and was enclosed by a handsome railing.

An 1857 drawing of the Court House in Kingston shows a plain structure, with a steep gable roof, side chimneys, bell tower and doorway ornamented by a triangular pediment. The Court House resembles a barn, which is perhaps appropriate since Little Rest was the government seat for the state's most important agricultural area, South County. The mansard roof, front stairs and other Victorian ornamentation were added in 1876, one hundred years after the Court House was built.

The Court House at the Colony and State Level

The court houses in Little Rest served as one of the five capitols of the colony of Rhode Island. Rhode Island was the only colony to rotate its capitols among more than two towns. This gave Little Rest the opportunity to gain prominence that other villages in Rhode Island lacked. Sessions of the General Assembly were held in Little Rest once or twice a year – each October and every other February. Accordingly, many of the colony's most prestigious citizens visited Little Rest.

The Court House was also the location for colony and later state elections. Only "freemen" could vote – adult males who (i) owned real estate of at least a minimum value or who paid a minimum amount of rent on real estate, or (ii) were the eldest son of a freeman. In the mid-1700s, about 60 to 75 percent of the adult white males in Rhode Island held sufficient property to vote. However, these percentages were about 20 percent less in South Kingstown, where a substantial disparity existed between the wealthy Narragansett planters and ordinary struggling farmers and tradesmen. In addition, black and Indian males and all women were not entitled to vote in 18th century Rhode Island, and Jews and Catholics were excluded from voting between 1719 and 1783.

Each April, the freemen of King's County held a town meeting in the Court House in Little Rest and voted to elect a governor, a deputy-governor, and ten assistants (at large) to form the upper house of the General Assembly. Two deputies for the lower house from South Kingstown were elected bi-annually at town meetings in April and August prior to the two regular sessions of the General Assembly held in May and October. South

Kingstown was entitled to send two deputies to the lower house (under the Royal Charter granted to Rhode Island in 1663, Newport had six deputies; Providence, Warwick and Portsmouth had four each; and the remaining towns had two each).

In April and August of each year, when approximately 70 Narragansett planters and other white "freemen" who owned sufficient property in South Kingstown converged by horseback on Little Rest for election day, Little Rest bustled with the town's wealthiest men, dressed in fine clothes, riding fine horses and often attended by their black domestic servants. With colony and county offices at stake, the atmosphere in Little Rest must have been tense and planters must have struggled to maintain civility.

Narragansett planters participated in the fierce political struggle that rocked Rhode Island from 1757 to 1770, known as the Ward-Hopkins controversy. The Ward-Hopkins controversy was essentially a factional struggle for government offices, masked by the competition between Newport and Providence merchants. It was not a struggle of country interests versus city interests. Instead, Newport and Providence merchants vied to attract Narragansett planters to their side. Yet tangible issues such as the taxation of towns were at stake. When one faction won, invariably the tax burden of the faction's allied towns was reduced and the tax burden of towns allied with opponents was increased.

Samuel Ward was the leader of the faction supported by most Newport merchants, and South Kingstown was primarily Samuel Ward country. Narragansett planters, led by Jeffrey Watson and Judge James Helme of Tower Hill, joined with Newport merchants to support Ward. But Stephen Hopkins of Providence (later a signer of the Declaration of Independence) also had solid support in the town, led by the Hazards. In part, the factions were divided along religious lines. Narragansett planters who were Congregationalists and Anglicans tended to support Ward (a Congregationalist), and planters who were Quakers tended to support Hopkins (a Quaker). When one side won the election, it gained key county offices, with its members filling positions as judges, court clerk, sheriff, and justices of the peace.

In 1761, Jeffrey Watson described some typical tough electioneering in Little Rest for seats as town delegates to the lower house of the General Assembly. On August 25, 1761, Watson wrote in his diary, "I was at Little Rest where we met to agree upon our Deputies. 26 of us their met and set up William Potter and Hezekiah Babcock" as the candidates for the Ward faction for the two seats from South Kingstown for deputies to the General Assembly. The result of this Ward faction's pre-election meeting paid off, as the next day, Watson wrote, "I was at a Town Meeting. Potter and Babcock was chose

Deputies by 30 majority after a great deal of fending and probing. Hard words and a Great Strife but ended well." Ward won the governorship and his supporters took over colony and county offices previously held by Hopkins' supporters. For example, James Helme was selected as chief justice of the county court of common pleas. He replaced Stephen Hazard, a Hopkins supporter who had previously held the judgeship. Hazard regained the post in 1763 and 1764.

Sometimes, the parties engaged in highly questionable electioneering practices. During the 1767 election, a note from ardent Hopkins supporters in Providence refers to money from them to be used "in order for payg off all those who may be agreed with by our Friends" in the southern part of the colony. Another note during the same election from a committee in Providence to Beriah Brown of North Kingstown mentions sending $100 to be used by Brown for obtaining "both Deputies and a considerable majority in Proxies in favor of Mr. Hopkins." The electioneering worked as Hopkins garnered his majority, and Beriah Brown was appointed as county sheriff.

Despite the occasional fierce elections, whichever side won the election, a Narragansett planter typically would assume the contested colony, county or town office. Middling tradesmen and farmers typically were not elected to these offices. They generally deferred to their "betters" and supported as their "natural" leaders townsmen from the class of Narragansett planter families. This situation continued until the American Revolution, when Rhode Island elites turned to the struggle over the ideas of independence from England, liberty and equality. An unintended consequence of the American Revolution was that ordinary Americans would participate more in wielding positions of power. In addition, it was not until after the American Revolution that farmers in Little Rest and other parts of South County began to view themselves as having a separate country interest that needed defending from commercial, urban interests.

During the American Revolutionary War, many sessions of the General Assembly were held in the Court House in Little Rest. With the British occupying Newport for much of the war and controlling most of Narragansett Bay, General Assembly sessions generally rotated between Providence, East Greenwich and Little Rest. The most significant legislation passed in Little Rest was the bill that prohibited Rhode Islanders from engaging in the slave trade, making Rhode Island in 1787 the first state to outlaw that trade. In 1781, the General Assembly meeting in Little Rest passed a bill renaming King's County after George Washington.

The Court House was almost the location for a major historical event, when the Rhode Island convention for the ratification of the United States Constitution met in Little Rest in March of 1790. This story is told in a chapter at the end of Part II.

Even after Rhode Island ratified the Constitution in 1790, the Court House continued to serve as one of Rhode Island's five state houses for sessions of the General Assembly until 1853. Indeed, the building was often called the "State House." The General Assembly usually sat in the State House in the last week of October, at first annually and later every two years. The General Assembly typically paid Little Rest villagers for providing firewood in winter sessions, for providing candles for evening sessions, and for serving as waiters.

The Court House and the County Court

The Court House in Little Rest was the meeting place for the county court for all of King's County (now Washington County or South County). There were three levels of courts in the county.

The lowest tribunal in Rhode Island's county-based structure was the local court of the justice of the peace. Cases could be heard at any time by a local justice of the peace and were often held in people's houses or in taverns. The bulk of the cases were for debts owed, many to Little Rest shopkeepers.

The next level up was the inferior court of common pleas. It sat in Little Rest twice a year, typically in February and August. The bulk of the cases involved creditors attempting to collect debts owed to them. Many cases were brought by Little Rest shopkeepers. The ease of enforcing debts against customers was a factor motivating shopkeepers to locate in Little Rest. In periods of economic distress when cash was in short supply, the number of cases filed by Little Rest shopkeepers rose dramatically. For example, in the February 1762 court of common pleas session, Little Rest shopkeepers brought the following cases: Thomas Potter, Jr., shopkeeper/merchant, 26 cases; Samuel Casey, ten cases (eight in his capacity as silversmith and two in his capacity as shopkeeper); Elisha Reynolds, shopkeeper/merchant, seven cases; Robert Potter, innholder, three cases; John Potter, innholder, one case, and John Douglass, blacksmith, one case. The customers who owed the debts came from all of the towns of King's County, indicating that Little Rest served the entire county.

Cases filed in the court of common pleas sometimes involved Narragansett planters from around the county. They sometimes sued other planters. For example, Jeffrey Watson, in his diary, mentions in 1759 his attending "Court at Little Rest to hear a case tried between John Potter and George Hazard which went in Hazard's favor." Sometimes planters were sued by Newport merchants to whom they owed money. Cases filed in the court of common pleas sometimes involved parties outside of King's County. For example, it was not uncommon for Newport and Providence merchants to be sued for nonpayment of debts in the court of common pleas by wealthier merchants from Boston, New York City and even London.

The second county court that regularly sat in the Little Rest Court House was the superior court. This court heard all appeals from the court of common pleas and was the trial court for all criminal cases, including capital cases. It sat in Little Rest twice a year, typically in April and October. Juries, consisting of white male voters, were selected to hear the criminal cases.

Official county positions were selected by the colony governor; they were not elected by the towns. There were justices of the peace who could both charge persons and sit as a court on minor matters. There were the county sheriff and a deputy sheriff who could charge persons with civil and criminal violations. For each county court, there were judges, a county court clerk and a court sergeant-at-arms. And there was a jailer to watch over the incarcerated criminals and debtors in Little Rest. Many of these positions, particularly the positions of jailers and clerks, were filled by Little Rest men. William Potter, who lived one mile north of Little Rest, and later Little Rest silversmith John Waite, served many terms as judges on the court of common pleas. Nathaniel Helme served as clerk of the superior court from 1785 to 1790. His uncle with the same name served as jailer from 1753 to 1761.

The Court House at the Town Level

On the first Tuesday of June of each year, South Kingstown freemen assembled at the Court House in Little Rest to hold a town meeting to elect town officers for a year term. The town offices included a town clerk, six town council members, a town sergeant, a town tax collector, a town treasurer, and an overseer of the poor.

The town clerk was the key town government official, as he prepared the official documents of the town. His duty was to write down every document that became part of the official town record: land transfers, public indentures, orders removing poor persons, tax lists, voting lists, probate records, and town meeting and town council minutes. Men in and around Little Rest typically served as the town clerk, no doubt in part because of the need to be close to the town's records that were stored in or near the Court House. There was also little turnover in the office. William Potter, the Narragansett planter who lived one mile north of Little Rest on North Road, served as town clerk from 1753 to 1779. Little Rest villager James Helme, Jr. followed him, serving as town clerk from 1779 to 1812. The job of town clerk required long hours bent over town books and diverted time away from other occupations (Potter was a farmer and Helme was a storekeeper). It did not pay well either. For example, Helme in 1785 received six shillings for drawing up 37 citations. This represented several days of labor and Helme was paid a laborer's wage for the work.

The town council was the most important governing body at the town level. It met about four to ten times a year in colonial times. It often met in one of

Little Rest's taverns. Its duties covered a wide range of administrative and judicial functions, many based on old English traditions, including the following:

- Probating wills and recording estate inventories for residents who had died.
- Giving directions in emergencies, such as outbreaks of smallpox or threat of invasion during wartime.
- Authorizing the construction of new roads and bridges, and supervising maintenance of roads and bridges.
- Granting liquor licenses, resolving complaints against tavern keepers, and disciplining habitual drunkards.
- Reimbursing people who had provided goods and services for the town's poor.
- Providing care for town's poor and sick who were incapable of caring for themselves.
- Appointing guardians for orphaned children and for aged and ill adults.
- Setting up "indenture" contracts, for poor children and for irresponsible or indebted adults to work off their debts, with local farmers.
- Granting departure certificates for inhabitants who wished to move to another town.
- Warning out transient people who moved to the town and became a risk of requiring support by the town.

In colonial times, prestigious Narragansett planters often served on the town council. Council members included Narragansett planters William Potter, who resided about one mile north of Little Rest, and Caleb Gardner, who resided in Little Rest on North Road.

The town sergeant dealt with offenders against town rules and town standards of conduct. He brought offenders – such as drunkards, transients, and women who bore illegitimate children – before the town council to discuss their conduct. If the council imposed a fine and the offender could not pay, the town sergeant could put the offender to work at a short-term contract, perhaps maintaining roads. The town sergeant also publicized the holding of special town meetings, often by posting notices on local taverns.

The overseer of the poor was responsible for identifying poor or sick persons who needed support of the town and for providing them with the food, clothing and cash that they needed. He also arranged for children and adults able to work to be "bound out" under indenture contracts as servants to town farmers.

The tax collector had the duty of collecting colony and town taxes. He usually went from house to house collecting taxes. The tax collector typically received a percentage of the taxes as a fee. It was not a pleasant job. The tax collector was pressured by the town treasurer to collect town taxes and by the county sheriff if it was a colony tax. The tax collector then had to squeeze taxes out of the town's residents.

The treasurer received the taxes from the tax collector, paid out funds as directed by the town council, and kept orderly books. The treasurer used the Little Rest jail to store the town's cash.

The Court House served as the location for town meetings. In addition to the town meetings in Little Rest to elect colony and town officials three times per year, South Kingstown freemen typically held town meetings at Little Rest several times a year to discuss pressing issues of the day. The town meeting provided a forum for all freemen – those white males who had enough property to vote. Some of the matters dealt with by the town meeting affected the town: selecting town officers, identifying qualifying residents as freemen entitled to vote, levying town taxes, and creating new roads. Other matters affected the colony or the state, including the casting of votes for governor and members of the General Assembly. When important matters in the colony (or state) were at issue, the town meeting sometimes instructed their town's General Assembly members on how to vote. In one town meeting vote held in the Court House in 1783, the preamble read, "it is the undoubted Right of the Freemen to instruct their Deputies at all times & highly expedient upon great & Momentous Questions. . . ." For example, the town meeting voted to instruct the town's delegates to use their utmost endeavors to prevent the calling of a convention for Rhode Island to ratify the U.S. Constitution. Thus, the town meeting allowed freemen the opportunity to participate in deciding the key political issues of the day.

The first business of most meetings was the election of a town moderator, who by law ran the town meeting. The moderator typically was an established authority figure in the town, someone who could command the respect of all freemen, in order to make it easier to control quarrelling townsmen. William Potter served as moderator for many years. During the American Revolution, the village's most important patriot officer, Colonel Thomas Potter, served as moderator of many town meetings.

The King's County Jail

As promised to the General Assembly, in 1752, Robert Potter, Jr. deeded land to the colony for the construction of a new King's County jail in Little Rest. The original jail was located on the north side of main street, on the west edge of the village, west of the second Court House. The first jail was a small, two-story wood building that housed the jailer and his family on the first floor and the prisoners on the second floor. The General Assembly committee designated to insure that the Little Rest men met their obligations to build a proper court house and jail at their own expense pointed out some faults in the construction of the jail. In October 1753, two of the men still under bond to complete the project, Elisha Reynolds and William Potter, agreed at their own expense to "instantly line the northernmost jail-room below with two inch plank & the other jail rooms be made as strong as they can be made with the plank that is already provided."

The job of jailer of the King's County jail in Little Rest was difficult. The jailer could earn fees from prisoners, the creditors of jailed debtors, and the colony for keeping poor prisoners in the jail and feeding them. Nathaniel Helme, the jailer from 1753 to 1761, however, blamed the colony for his inability to earn fees from prisoners. The colony released prisoners incarcerated for indebtedness on condition that they enlist in military forces raised by Rhode Island to help the colonies and British fight the French in the French and Indian War. Even though Helme had paid for their "Victuals and Drink," the prisoners who were released never repaid him. Thus, Helme explained, this circumstance resulted in his inability to pay his own debts. In a petition to the General Assembly submitted in 1762, Helme requested permission to hold a lottery to sell his "good Dwelling House, a large Barn, and a Shoemaker's Shop" next to the jail. Permission was granted, but the lottery was not successful, as Helme remained in debt.

The King's County jail was not strong enough to prevent a determined prisoner from escaping. Henry Reynolds in 1754, William Wilson in 1763, Nathan Butler in 1765, and Thomas Smith in 1768 all escaped from the Little Rest jail. In 1773 and 1774, three more men escaped.

The jail was, of course, designed to imprison individuals convicted in the courts of a crime. The usual crime was theft. South Kingstown also had an extraordinary number of criminals who were caught committing the crime of counterfeiting. This phenomenon was perhaps attributable to the large number of silversmiths in South Kingstown, who had the technical skills to make dies for printing fake money, and to the scramble for wealth in the Narragansett country. In 1753, for example, the town justices ordered Henry Reynolds of Exeter to be apprehended, questioned and committed to the jail in Little Rest on suspicion of counterfeiting money. An attempt was made to free the prisoner, and a special guard was provided to prevent future occurrences. Despite this, on March 15, 1754, Reynolds, in the company of another man who had been held for failure to pay his debt, broke out of jail and fled. The town sheriff offered a reward of £150 for the capture of Reynolds, who was described as being about 27 years old, with a thick sandy beard and a downcast look. He was wearing a blue double-breasted coat with brass buttons, an old camblet coat under it, and leather breaches. John Waite, town justice and later Little Rest silversmith, pursued Reynolds on horseback for seven days and finally caught him. Reynolds and an accomplice were found guilty of counterfeiting and sentenced to stand an hour in the pillory at Little Rest, to be cropped in the ears and branded, and to pay double damages. As described later in this Part I, in 1770 there would be an even more dramatic counterfeiting episode and jail break in Little Rest by one of its most prominent residents, silversmith Samuel Casey. In 1784, three more men were convicted of counterfeiting; they also broke out of the Little Rest jail.

One of the most common reasons for an individual to be incarcerated in the jail was for non-payment of debts. Debtors were not treated as harshly as criminals, and they were sometimes permitted to continue their trade, but they were forced to remain in the jail until their debts were paid off. Not even the jailers who were hired to keep the jail were immune from being imprisoned for nonpayment of debts. In 1764, Nathaniel Helme, the jailer of the Little Rest jail for eight years, was committed to the jail for two years for failure to pay his debts. To debtors, the Little Rest jail did not have satisfactory accommodations. In a petition to the General Assembly, Helme protested that the limits of the "yard," the area in which debtors were allowed freedom of movement, had been reduced to the point that he could not work at his trade (shoemaking). His petition for a more extensive jail yard was signed by twenty Little Rest villagers and others.

In 1785, Matthew Robinson, at the time elderly but in his prime one of the most influential attorneys in the state, was confined to the jail for debt. He protested to the General Assembly that conditions were so bad that only criminals and not debtors deserved to be locked up in the jail. The General Assembly, taking pity on Robinson's sorry plight, allowed the sheriff to find a house in the village for Robinson to occupy that would be designated his "jail." With this precedent set, another debtor in 1786 successfully petitioned the General Assembly to be lodged in a house in Little Rest. In the next year, the General Assembly extended the practice to a convicted criminal (a sheep thief), and allowed the criminal to be boarded at a villager's house for five days. By 1790, the General Assembly sought to limit this practice and ordered the county sheriff to remove the jail keeper if he continued to permit prisoners charged with crimes "to go at large."

By the 1780s, the jail was in such poor condition that guards were hired to watch over prisoners at night. In 1786, two men were hired to stand guard over James Rogers for seven nights, and on four occasions in 1790 as many as thirteen men were hired to help prevent jail breaks. In 1791, serious criminals were housed in the Newport jail.

In 1789, the General Assembly appointed attorney Rowse Helme and others to consider a new site in Little Rest for the county jail. In 1790, a committee informed the General Assembly that it had contracted with Col. Thomas Potter (son-in-law of Elisha Reynolds) to purchase a lot on the south side of main street opposite the old jail. It submitted a plan for a "convenient" jail. The plan called for a two-story, central hall building with four rooms on the first floor and five cells (three small and two larger) on the second. The jail was to measure 40 by 32 feet. The General Assembly authorized the construction of the wood jail house, which was completed in 1792.

Christopher Bickford, in his *Crime, Punishment and the Washington County Jail, Hard Time in Kingston, Rhode Island,* states that the "1792 Washington County jail had a kitchen and, most probably, a jailer's office on the first floor, leaving two rooms on the first floor and two rooms upstairs for the use of the jailer's family. The physical arrangement, which placed criminals and the jailer's family in close proximity, was less than satisfactory."

While the primary task of a jail in colonial times was to prevent the escape of criminals and debtors, the approach of the criminal system was more focused on corporal punishment than incarceration. The point was not to lock a criminal away for an extended stay, but to humiliate the criminal and shame him in the eyes of the community, in the hope that he would reform himself. It was also cheaper to whip the back or crop the ears of a criminal than to incarcerate him for a long period. Accordingly, Little Rest was the scene for the infliction of horrible punishments. In 1770, a man convicted of counterfeiting was sentenced to stand in the pillory in Little Rest and to be whipped thirty-nine lashes. In 1787, a man convicted of stealing a horse was sentenced to pay a stiff fine, and if he could not pay the fine, he was to "be whipped on his naked back in thirty nine stripes at the tail of a cart or dung cart at three of the most public places on Little Rest Hill."

It appears that a frequent location for inflicting punishments was in the front yard of the Court House. For example, in 1784, five men convicted of counterfeiting were each sentenced to stand "in the Pillory in the front of the State House" for one hour. In 1788, a man convicted of stealing a horse was sentenced to pay a stiff fine, and if he could not pay the fine, he was to "be whipped on his naked back twenty stripes in front of the Court House on Little Rest Hill." At a South Kingstown town meeting held in the Court House in September 1788, it was voted that Colonel Thomas Potter purchase "a pair of Stocks & Whipping Post" for use in Little Rest.

"Three Good Taverns"

When Little Rest villagers petitioned the General Assembly to remove the court house to their village in 1752, they promised that "three good taverns" would be available to house and entertain the legislators. While two taverns sprang up in Little Rest almost immediately, it was not until 1770 that a third tavern appeared.

In a time when horses were the primary mode of transportation, it was important for legislators and their retinues to have sufficient taverns to host them. Legislators who traveled on horseback from as far away as Providence, Newport, Bristol, Smithfield and Little Compton were forced to spend several days or even a few weeks in the village. When the General Assembly was in session, the Little Rest tavern keepers hosted the most important men from all over the colony. During General Assembly sessions, the Little Rest taverns were so crowded that their guests sometimes had to sleep "head-to-toe" in their beds.

There were other special days that would transform Little Rest into a bustling community and increase the business of its tavern keepers. Sessions of the county court frequently led attorneys and their clients from throughout King's County to spend time in village taverns. Colony and town election days, and other town meeting days, attracted men from all over the large town and county, sometimes requiring them to stay overnight in a tavern. In addition, the town council often met in one of the taverns in Little Rest. Invariably, the South Kingstown town council's last act each meeting was to authorize funds for its own "victuals and drink."

From the era of the French and Indian Wars on, Little Rest was also a location for county militias to hold musters. For example, in accordance with an act of the General Assembly in 1757, at a time when Rhode Island was attempting to raise troops to join in the fight against the French in Canada, Little Rest was selected as the "rendezvous" for all officers and men of the militia raised in King's County. Guns were fired at Little Rest in celebration of the American victory over the British at Yorktown in 1781. In 1793, Thomas Hazard noted in his journal that "the Melisha all Turned out this day at Little Rest." After the musters, large crowds would fill the local taverns "with jolly company, drumming, fifing, wrestling and joking."

In order to maintain an inn for overnight guests, a tavern keeper had to buy provisions for man and horse, provide bedding, maintain fires, purchase candles, and maintain tables, chairs, beds and other furniture and fixtures. Little Rest tavern keepers bought some supplies from village stores, but they bought most of their supplies (especially rum) from Newport merchants.

In addition to hosting travelers and visitors, taverngoing by local men was a central feature of village life. Taverns facilitated the exchange of information and community. They were important gathering places and informal clubs for village men, who could share a friendly drink, swap stories, gather news, make business deals or discuss politics. Taverns were exclusive in that town officials permitted only white men to frequent them.

At the time of the vote to remove the court house to Little Rest in 1752, Little Rest did not have a tavern. Robert Potter, Sr. sold alcohol from his house in Little Rest in 1723, but this enterprise was short-lived. Once the General Assembly made the decision to move the court house and jail to Little Rest, son Robert Potter, Jr. converted his house, located in the area of the current Court House, set off just north of main street, into a tavern. Robert Potter, Jr. was issued a liquor license by the town council in July 1752. In the next year, the town council began holding some of its meetings at Potter's tavern. This tavern had stable ownership, as it was operated by the Potter family until 1796.

A second tavern, currently known as the Kingston Inn, was built in Little Rest in 1755. In March 1753, John Potter (also known as John Potter the 3rd) leased a house in Little Rest, obtained a liquor license from the town council, and opened a tavern. The town council met at his tavern for the first of many times in September 1753. In 1755, John Potter bought land from Elisha Reynolds and erected a building designed to serve as a tavern. The town council met at his tavern in 1755, granting him a license to keep the tavern, provided he first paid £14 to the town treasurer, which "he done in ye face of this Town Council." As did many villagers at the time, Potter had more than one occupation. He was also a tanner and he may have started the tanning operations that continued for many years at the corner of main street and Biscuit City Road. Potter was also an officer of the King's County militia, rising to the rank of colonel in 1763 and 1764.

Potter served as tavern keeper until his death in 1771. A tavern keeper's death often resulted in difficulties finding a new, regular tavern keeper. After Potter's death, various members of his extended family operated the tavern sporadically. In July 1780, John Peck Rathbun, a local naval hero of the American Revolution, purchased the tavern. But before he operated the tavern, the ship he was commanding was captured by the British off the coast of England in 1782 and he died shortly thereafter in prison. In 1782, Rathbun's heirs leased the tavern to Ray Sands, and after him to his son Robert Sands, who operated the tavern for more than ten years. In 1911, during a restoration of the Kingston Inn, a lifting wall was discovered, which was hooked to the ceiling and could be dropped on Sundays to comply with the local liquor laws. In addition, colorful stencil patterns from the 18th century were found on one of the room's inside walls.

A third tavern was operated by Thomas Potter, Jr. In 1760, Elisha Reynolds, the village's wealthiest man, conveyed to his son-in-law Thomas Potter, a large house on the west corner of main street and North Road. Jeffrey Watson, in his diary, reported that in June 1760, "I was at Colonel Reynold's. He raised his house in corner of his land, a Very Large Building. Abundance of people." This was apparently the building Reynolds conveyed to Potter.

At first, from his new home in Little Rest, following his father-in-law's footsteps, Thomas Potter conducted a storekeeping and merchant business. The following is a letter, dated October 10, 1770, from Thomas Potter of Little Rest to Aaron Lopez, the wealthiest Newport merchant in the 1770s (and a member of Newport's Jewish community):

> Sir,
>
> We are out of Salt and want some more over as soon as possible. I have taken in uperds of 30 Casks of Seed. the Forty Bushels Salt that came over last did not last 4 howers. if the Bote cant come to Newport on Monday I desire you would git some frait Bote that belongs somewhare up the River to bring over a 100 or 150 Busheles untill franklins Bote [Franklin's Ferry at South Ferry] can come over. pray let the Salt be as large as possible. I have likewise sent the Hors [horse] I spoke with you about by the barrer [bearer of the letter], which I think there ant [is not] a better Shippin Hors in the Government [Colony] you, Sir will have no Commisions or Charge on this Hors; the prime Cost is all which I did not mean to be out the way in, and am, Sir, your Humble Servant,
>
> Thomas Potter, Jr.
>
> N.B. I dare venter to expect 100 Casks of Seed at least, if can be suplied with Salt of equil quallity with the other.

The letter is revealing in several ways. First, it shows that Potter acted as a middle-man merchant between Newport merchants and local residents. He traded a horse to Lopez (who regularly shipped horses to the English colonies in the Caribbean and the southern American colonies) in exchange for salt, which Potter resold to local residents. Aaron Lopez's records also indicate that Potter ordered from him various goods such as paper, "long pipes," felt hats, and dinnerware. Second, of course, is that the letter's spelling and grammar are atrocious. Even Lopez must have had difficulty discerning the letter's meaning; letters to Lopez by other men often demonstrate impeccable spelling and grammar.

In July 1770, Potter turned his home into a tavern, calling it the "Sign of the Dove" and obtaining his first liquor license from the town council. Thomas Potter served several terms in the lower house of the General Assembly, before becoming a lieutenant-colonel in the militia in the Revolutionary War. As explained in Part II, Colonel Potter hosted General George Washington and his staff at his tavern in 1781 and hosted patriot committees in 1779. The town council met many times at his tavern. Colonel Potter was the father of Elisha Reynolds Potter, Sr., who would become Little Rest's most influential resident. Potter maintained a tavern until his death in 1793. But Thomas Potter was not a success as a tavern keeper or merchant. In 1767, his father-in-law, Elisha Reynolds, had to loan him some money. In 1769, Potter he became insolvent. When he died in 1793, Potter's estate was insolvent.

Each year any person desiring to sell alcohol in South Kingstown had to obtain a license from the town council. The most successful taverns were charged the highest fee and the least successful taverns were charged low or no fees, an early form of progressive taxation. As the operators of the three taverns described above typically paid the highest fee, it can be concluded that the Little Rest taverns were the most successful in the town. Other persons in Little Rest also obtained liquor licenses. For example, storeowners frequently obtained liquor licenses, which could support their business of selling alcohol by the bottle as opposed to the glass. James and Samuel Helme opened a dry goods store in Little Rest in about 1777. Ten years later, they obtained a license to sell "Strong Spirits" in as small a portion as "one pint." Joseph Perkins operated a store on the north side of main street in the village, and he obtained his first liquor license in 1782 (although his store records indicate that he was selling rum as early as 1771). The town council also permitted individuals to sell alcohol by the glass out of their homes. It was a way in which middling persons could start as tavern keepers, and was also a way for poor persons to make some money so that the town council would not have to support them. William Pollack, who owned a house where the Church House is now located, was granted liquor licenses beginning in 1782. He typically paid less than half of the license fee paid by the village's established tavern keepers. A poor licensee would have his fee waived.

The town council supervised tavern keepers, including resolving complaints against tavern keepers for keeping disorderly taverns. These problems did not arise in Little Rest; a complaint was lodged against a tavern keeper in South Kingstown outside of Little Rest in 1753 for "Keeping a Disorderly house allowing people to play Cards and Entertaining Indeons Negroes &c." The town council also notified tavern keepers of drunkards who were dissipating their money and were not to be served any alcohol.

Samuel Casey and the Other Silversmiths of Little Rest

In addition to serving as a government seat and as a place for taverns, Little Rest was a hub where surrounding Narragansett planters and ordinary farmers could have tradesmen perform services for them. In colonial times, the following tradesmen were present in Little Rest: silversmith, blacksmith, leatherworker, tanner, shoemaker, wheelwright, clock and watchmaker, storekeeper, carpenter, tailor and locksmith.

The silversmith was the most impressive craftsmen in colonial times. Little Rest supported, at different times, six silversmiths, including Samuel Casey, one of the finest silversmiths in all of the thirteen colonies. Little Rest village was able to support these highly-skilled craftsmen because it had become the main village in the Narragansett country, which was dominated by wealthy Narragansett planters. These planters had the extra savings and the social pretensions to desire to own fine silverware.[5] Moreover, the silversmiths could rely on wealthy men from throughout the colony, county and town visiting Little Rest on days when the General Assembly or the county court was in session, or on town meeting days. It should also be noted that all of the silversmiths supplemented their incomes with other work.

In the colonial period, before banks and reliable paper money, silverware was important. Coins could easily be stolen out of poor safes and stolen coins could not be identified. But wealthy planters could have their savings converted to silver and made into items that had the unique engraved markings of the silversmith and the customer. In addition, wealthy planters could acquire beautifully made silver teapots, trays, tankards and dinnerware to display their wealth. In the 18th century, the teapot was at the center of a social ritual of taking tea, with the host sharing food, drink and conversation with other planter families.

A list of silver made by Little Rest silversmiths that is held by museums is set forth in Appendix A to this book.

Samuel Casey

Of all the silversmiths in Little Rest, Samuel Casey was the most skilled. Casey was the undisputed master silversmith in King's County and

---

[5] A valuation of Rhode Island towns adopted by the General Assembly in 1780 indicated that South Kingstown had 2,614 ounces of silver plate, second in the state only to Providence (4,075 ounces). Newport would have had the most silver, but its silver was not valued because at the time it was occupied by British soldiers in the Revolutionary War. South Kingstown's 2,614 ounces was substantially greater than that reported for other South County towns: North Kingstown (1,363); Westerly (879); Exeter (488); Charlestown (324); Hopkinton (293); and Richmond (170).

one of the finest in the colonies. An expert in the area of collectible colonial silverware recently stated that Casey was second only to Paul Revere in the skill that he brought to the silversmith craft. His tankards and teapots demonstrate gracefulness, fine design, and expert handling of the silver metal.

Samuel Casey was probably born in Newport in 1724. He may have served as an apprentice to silversmith Jacob Hurd in Boston before setting up shop as a silversmith in Exeter, Rhode Island. Casey was admitted as a freeman of Exeter in 1745. In 1750, he moved to Little Rest and spent his most productive years there. In 1750, he purchased Caleb Gardner's house on the north side of the main street in Little Rest to the west of North Road.[6] Next to his house, Casey built a forge to perform his work. Here, Samuel Casey worked as a silversmith. From 1753 to 1762, he partnered with his brother Gideon, who was a part-time goldsmith. In 1753, Casey married Martha Martin. Feeling the need to supplement his income, Casey also operated a dry goods store in the village. His silversmith and storekeeping businesses thrived. Court records indicate that he had customers from all of the towns in King's County and Newport. But disaster struck on a September night in 1764. Samuel Casey's house burned down as a result of a fire that started in his forge. Casey rebuilt the house and carried on with his silversmith and storekeeping businesses, but financial pressures apparently caused Casey to engage in illegal counterfeiting, which is described in the next chapter. He might have avoided his financial troubles and pressures to turn to counterfeiting if he had plied his silversmith trade in Newport.

The Smithsonian Institution in Washington, D.C. holds a fine example of one of Samuel Casey's teapots. The teapot was made by Casey for Abigail Robinson, the daughter of a wealthy Narragansett planter. The teapot dates to 1752, the year Abigail married John Wanton, the son of the governor of Rhode Island. It was passed down in her family until 1979. Ezra Stiles, then president of Yale College and earlier a Congregationalist minister in Newport, in 1755 received a tankard made by Samuel Casey. It is now in the possession of the Yale University Art Gallery.

---

[6] In his *The Silversmiths of Little Rest* (Kingston, R.I., 1928), William Davis Miller states that Casey's house was at Curtis Corner Road about two miles south of Little Rest village. This statement has been relied upon by later historians, but it is not accurate. South Kingstown land records indicate that Casey purchased Caleb Gardner's house on main street in Little Rest village, which house Gardner built around 1747 on the southern border of his land in Little Rest. By being located in Little Rest, Casey's potential customers had easier access to him, as they visited Little Rest's Court House, taverns and shops. Samuel sold a ½ interest in this property to his brother Gideon in 1753.

Gideon Casey

Samuel Casey's brother, Gideon Casey, partnered with Samuel in Little Rest, in both the silversmith and storekeeping businesses, from about 1753 to 1762. In 1753, Gideon purchased a ½ interest in his brother's property. Gideon worked in gold and pewter, as well as silver. In the diary of the Reverend James MacSparran, the Anglican minister of St. Paul's church then located a few miles north of Little Rest, MacSparran writes in 1751 that "Gideon Casey bro't my Gold Buttons for mending [for which] I gave him 30 shillings." In 1762, Gideon sold his ½ interest in the property back to Samuel and returned to his hometown of Exeter. He later worked in Warwick and Providence. Gideon was a "shady" character, as is explained in the next chapter on counterfeiting.

John Waite

John Waite was born in Wickford in 1742. In 1769, "John Waite . . . silversmith, of South Kingstown" purchased land from Elisha Reynolds, tore down the house that was on it, and built a new house to the right of Potter Lane. Waite's shop was in the basement of his house, and he worked there until his death in 1817.

Waite was not the master silversmith that Casey was, but he had some fine skills. Waite was selected by the General Assembly to make the print plates for the Rhode Island paper money issue of September 1776. This was the first Rhode Island issue of paper money to use the term "dollars" and was the first time the term "State of Rhode Island and Providence Plantations" was used (replacing the former term, "Colony of Rhode Island").

In an excerpt from Waite's account book that reflects his work from 1785 to 1800 for a successful local farmer, Waite made silver knee buckles, a silver thimble, and a pair of gold earrings, and mended tea tongs, a punch strainer and shoe buckles. Waite also worked as a locksmith, mending broken locks.

During the American Revolution, Waite became captain of the Kingston Reds, a local independent military company. He served as a justice of the peace from 1796 until his death in 1817. Although never receiving a formal legal education, Waite served several terms as judge on the Washington County inferior court of common pleas from 1796 until 1803.

Joseph Perkins

Joseph Perkins was born, probably in Little Rest, in 1749. He was the grandson of former Rhode Island governor and Newport merchant William Brenton. In 1771, Perkins opened a shop in Little Rest, from which he sold a variety of dry goods and alcohol. He also sold silver that he made: spoons, plates, a thimble, and a pepper castor. He benefited from being close to village artisans, as he made silver buckles for shoes made by shoemaker John Weeden and silver buttons for clothes made by tailor Abel Cottrell. Perkins sold a set of silver spoons to Experience Gardner, the daughter of wealthy Narragansett planter Caleb Gardner who resided near Little Rest. Correspondence from 1789 indicates that Hannah Potter, the daughter of William Potter, took some of Perkins' silverware with her to sell on consignment when her family moved to upstate New York in following the religious prophet Jemima Wilkinson, with Perkins giving her a 7% commission. In April 1774, calling himself a goldsmith, Perkins purchased a small plot of land on the north side of main street from Robert Potter. The house that Perkins then built now forms the ell of the Thomas Taylor house.

During the Revolutionary War, in 1775, Perkins was chosen by the town meeting to go to New York to purchase one hundred firearms, and he joined the Kingston Reds as a private. Later he was promoted to ensign. On June 16, 1776, Joseph Perkins married Mary Gardner, daughter of Little Rest Narragansett planter Caleb Gardner, in a service performed by the Congregationalist minister in Tower Hill, Dr. Joseph Torrey.

While Joseph Perkins started out as a silversmith (often called a "goldsmith" in court records, which was equivalent to a silversmith), he later spent more time as a shopkeeper, innkeeper and merchant. In 1782, he obtained a license to sell liquor by the glass. On several occasions, he hosted meetings of the town council, including serving dinners to the members. He also served as a middle-man merchant, buying local farm produce such as cheese and corn and reselling it to Newport merchants, who in turn supplied him with goods for his store. He may have also had a money lending business. In the 1780s, the county justices court often met at his house to address cases that Perkins brought against persons who owed him money, either "by book" (the store) or "by note" (the merchant business). Perkins became one of the village's wealthiest men. At his death at the young age of 40 in 1789, he owned several farms and a number of promissory notes payable to him, including one for £363 due from the state of Rhode Island. He also was wealthy enough to have three young apprentices, each of whom received $100 in his will, and one adult assistant, Adam Helme, who received $500.

Nathaniel Helme

Little Rest might have produced a second master silversmith had Nathaniel Helme not died in 1789 at the early age of 29. Helme's few surviving works are beautifully made, including a pepper castor sold to Experience Gardner, daughter of Narragansett planter Caleb Gardner who resided near Little Rest.

Helme, born in 1761, was the youngest son of Judge James Helme of Tower Hill. It is probable that Nathaniel followed his brothers to Little Rest. James Jr. moved to Little Rest to set up a general store in 1777 and became town clerk in 1779. Brothers Samuel, Robert and Adam also resided in Little Rest in the 1780s. Nathaniel Helme served from 1785 to 1789 as justice of the peace and as clerk of the county superior court. These were other indications that he probably lived in Little Rest.

In his 1777 will, James Helme, Sr., the father, directed his eldest son Powell "to procure some Proper place for his Brother Nathaniel and put him out to some proper Tradesman or merchant to learn how to get a living in the World." Powell probably arranged for 16 year-old Nathaniel to serve as an apprentice to Little Rest silversmith John Waite. Helme worked as a silversmith from 1782 until his death in 1789. Among the numerous tools that were listed in Helme's estate (which was handled in part by John Waite) included a goldsmith forge anvil, bellows and bench, and ten goldsmith hammers. His estate also included a silver watch, a silver tankard, gold fillings, and 40 pewter buttons.

Jeremiah Niles Sands

A goldsmith who has not previously been tied to Little Rest is Jeremiah Niles Sands. In addition to working as a goldsmith, Sands worked in another impressive craft, clock and watchmaking. In 1791, he entered into a 99-year lease of land on the north side of main street on which he was to build a "goldsmith shop." Sands worked in Little Rest for about three years, but apparently his business was not successful. In January 1795, Sands advertised in the *Newport Mercury* that he had "removed from Little Rest to Wickford where he carries on clock, watchmaking and goldsmiths' business in all their branches . . . cash for old gold and silver." Sands then moved to Newport, but met with no success there either. In January 1798, he published a notice in the *Newport Mercury* that he was an insolvent Newport goldsmith. By 1801, Sands had moved to Boston to practice his craft. In 1809, two Little Rest men filed suits in the Court House against Jeremiah Sands "of Portland, Maine" for debts incurred in 1797, but they never recovered anything from him. The author is not aware of any gold or silver pieces that have been attributed to Sands.

Samuel Casey Silver Teapot, circa 1760. Casey made this teapot at his forge and shop in Little Rest. *Redwood Library and Athenaeum (currently on display at the Newport History Museum).*

Die Used for Counterfeiting by Samuel Casey, 1770, and Coin. The die was found in the garret of the James Helme house before it was demolished in 1910. The coin was recently minted from a mold that was made using the die. *Pettaquamscutt Historical Society.*

Samuel Casey: Master Silversmith and Smalltime Counterfeiter

Samuel Casey was a brilliant silversmith. His craftsmanship of silver tankards and teapots made him known throughout the Narragansett country and beyond. But Casey turned to counterfeiting coins, which proved to be his downfall and ended in a dramatic jailbreak in Little Rest.

Counterfeiting money in colonial Rhode Island, including in South Kingstown, was a surprisingly common crime. This phenomenon was in part attributable to the large number of silversmiths in Rhode Island, and in particular in South Kingstown. Silversmiths had the technical skills to make dies for printing fake money. Indeed, silversmiths were hired by the colony to make devices for making official coins and printing official paper money. The frequency of counterfeiting may also reflect the uninhibited scramble for wealth in Rhode Island.

Samuel and Gideon Casey seemed to have become involved in counterfeiting at an early time in their careers as silversmiths. In 1752, when in Philadelphia, Gideon was thrown into jail for passing counterfeit money, found guilty at a trial, and fined £50. In 1754, Samuel and Gideon became persons of interest in an investigation of a counterfeiting ring in Rhode Island, but only three other men from West Greenwich and Exeter were tried and convicted in the Little Rest Court House. In 1768, authorities suspected that Gideon was the head of a gang of counterfeiters who operated around the Connecticut and Rhode Island border. After escaping Rhode Island, Gideon was caught on a schooner in New York City with counterfeiting dies and money. He was acquitted after a trial in New York "for want of sufficient evidence."

Samuel Casey may have considered counterfeiting in earnest as a result of a personal disaster that occurred in 1764. His house, which was located on main street in Little Rest across from the current Kingston Hill Store, burned down, caused by a fire in his forge. The *Boston News-Letter* reported the following item:

> Last Tuesday morning the House of Samuel Casey, Esq., at South Kingstown, Rhode Island, was reduced to Ashes. A large Variety of Furniture, a considerable Quantity of European goods, with Drugs, Medicines, etc. makes Mr. Casey's Loss, as we are informed, amount to more than Two Thousand Pounds Sterling. The most of his Books, and a small Part of his Furniture, were the principal of what was saved. This Misfortune, we hear, was occasioned by a large Fire being kept the Day preceding in his Goldsmith's Forge, which was so intense as to set Fire to a Poll at the back part of the Chimney.

The considerable sum that Casey lost demonstrates his success as a silversmith and storekeeper. In an age lacking fire insurance, much of the savings that Casey had worked for all these years disappeared in flames.

After the fire, Samuel Casey rebuilt a house and forge at the same site. Casey borrowed money to rebuild, using his remaining household goods and silversmith tools as collateral. Samuel continued to conduct his silversmith and storekeeping businesses at his house, without Gideon.

From Casey's later testimony, Casey began associating with counterfeiters at this house in 1764, the year his house burned down. As early as February 1768, Massachusetts authorities were informed of Casey's connections with a notorious Boston counterfeiter. Casey's silversmith business apparently was not sufficient to repay his heavy debts and he turned to counterfeiting to supplement his income. Casey's financial problems broke out in the open in March 1770, when he submitted a petition of insolvency to the General Assembly, signed by 27 of his creditors, including many prominent Newport merchants. In April 1770, the *Newport Mercury* published a notice that Samuel Casey was insolvent.

Regardless of the motive, Samuel Casey fell for the temptation of illicit money. His house in Little Rest became the headquarters for his gang of silversmith counterfeiters. Most of the counterfeiting of the bogus money took place in the attic of Casey's house. Samuel Wilson of Tower Hill, and William Reynolds of Richmond, also counterfeited some money. Among the people who were present during the illegal activities were Noah Colton, William Reynolds, Samuel Wilson, and Gideon Casey. All of these men were silversmiths. The men had great screws and melted metal, which they used to turn out coined money. Sometimes their customers would bring them blanks of mixed metal to be stamped.

Apparently, a number of townsmen passed the money. Elisha Reynolds (of Exeter, not the Little Rest merchant and founder), and Immanuel Case, a storekeeper in Little Rest, were a few of the townsmen who were caught passing Casey's coins. Casey was proud of his work and boasted to his nephew that his dollars would "pass through the world."

One of the gravest dangers for any gang of counterfeiters was the threat of having a member betray the gang's counterfeiting activities. To address this risk, Samuel Casey required everyone in his gang to take a solemn oath not to reveal "the secrets of any other man, woman or child without the consent of company or companions and to swear 'If I am not true to you and do not keep all your council and your secrets I pray God to shut me out of Heaven and make all my Prayers to become sin.'"

With the flood of counterfeit money, it was only a matter of time before the local authorities caught up with Samuel Casey. In July 1770, a local man, Thomas Clarke, was caught passing counterfeit coins. He confessed that the bad money was made "by the ole man upon the Hill," meaning Casey on Little Rest Hill.

Casey was tipped off about the interest of the authorities. Casey ordered his nephew to take his counterfeiting tools and dies and throw them "into a sunken Swamp on Caleb Gardner's Ground, where they cannot be found." (Gardner, who lived immediately north of Casey, also owned a farm to the west near the Chipuxet River.) Casey also wrote a note of warning (with poor spelling) to his accomplice Samuel Wilson.

Casey was not quick enough. An immediate search was made in Casey's home where a press for counterfeiting was found. In addition, Casey's desperate note of warning addressed to Wilson was found. Under questioning, Casey admitted that two squares in the note were meant to indicate dies for counterfeiting. Numerous suspected counterfeiters were taken into custody. But only Samuel Casey, William Reynolds, Thomas Clarke, Samuel Wilson and Elisha Reynolds (of Exeter) were indicted at the October 1770 session of the superior court held at the Court House in Little Rest. These men were put in the King's County Jail in Little Rest.

Prior to the trial, Casey made a full confession of his counterfeiting activities to the court sitting at Newport. He stated that he had made about 300 Spanish milled dollars and about 40 Portuguese coins. Nevertheless, he denied that he had passed any of the coins, but had merely given them to others, who had placed them into circulation.

In the October 1770 session of the superior court held at the Court House in Little Rest, Casey and the other four indicted men were placed on trial. They were represented by prominent attorneys Matthew Robinson of Newport and South Kingstown, and James Varnum of East Greenwich. The "Counsel for the King" also were prominent attorneys: James Honeyman and Henry Marchant of Newport. Presumably, the jury included many friends and acquaintances of Casey's. The trial was presided over by a five-judge panel.

During the trial, Casey pleaded "not guilty" and the jury agreed, bringing in a verdict of "not guilty," apparently on the ground that his confessions made in Newport were not admissible evidence. The five-judge panel was not satisfied with the verdict and ordered the jury to go out another time and reconsider the verdict. This time the jury found Casey guilty on the condition that Casey's confession was admissible. The court determined that the evidence was admissible and that therefore Casey was guilty.

Counterfeiting was treated as a serious crime in colonial times, as it not only cheated the individuals who found themselves with worthless money, it undermined confidence in a pillar of the colony's economy, its money supply. The *Connecticut Courant* decried that "a more horrid and extensive combination to defraud the public, has never been heard of in New England." The judges sentenced Casey to be hanged "until he be dead" between the hours of nine in the morning and two in the afternoon on a day in the near future.

Casey's accomplices, Samuel Wilson, William Reynolds, Elisha Reynolds, and Thomas Clark, were also found guilty. Wilson's trial lasted ten hours, but the jury convicted him in ten minutes. The *Providence Gazette,* on October 20, 1770, reported the following shocking news:

> At the Superior Court held for King's County, on Thursday last, Samuel Casey, of South Kingstown, received Sentence of Death, for making and passing counterfeit Money. Samuel Wilson, of the same Town, was sentenced to stand in the Pillory, be branded on both Cheeks, have both Ears cropped, and pay a Fine of Six Hundred Pounds Lawful Money. William Reynolds, of Richmond, was sentenced to stand in the Pillory, have both ears cropped, and pay a Fine of Three Hundred Pounds Lawful Money. Thomas Clark, of the same Town, was sentenced to stand in the Pillory, be branded on both Cheeks, have both ears cropped, and pay a Fine of One Hundred Pounds Lawful Money. Elisha Reynolds was sentenced to stand in the Pillory, and to be whipped Thirty-nine Lashes; all for the like Crimes.

The punishments were originally to be inflicted at the pillory in Little Rest. But perhaps to accommodate the expected large crowds, the punishments instead were meted out at Tower Hill. The story of Samuel Casey and his accomplices was soon so widely known that it was reported that on October 26, 1770, more than 3,000 people gathered on Tower Hill to witness the tortures inflicted upon Wilson, Clark, and William Reynolds. The crowd's morbid fascination was satisfied as each convicted man was branded on both cheeks with a hot iron with the letter "R" on it (for "rogue") and had his ears cropped (a piece of each ear was cut off).

Elisha Reynolds of Exeter was not reported to have been punished at Tower Hill. His punishment of standing in the pillory for one hour and being whipped with "thirty nine lashes on his naked back" may have been carried out in Little Rest.[7]

---

[7] In *Counterfeiting in Colonial America,* at page 234, Kenneth Scott writes that "Elisha Reynolds does not seem to have been tried, and it may be suspected that he was received as king's evidence." Other authors repeat this claim. However, superior court records are clear that Reynolds was tried and convicted. In addition, two newspapers, the *Providence Gazette* and the *Connecticut Courant,* both reported that Reynolds had been convicted and sentenced to stand in the pillory for one hour and to be whipped. The confusion with Reynolds may be that this man was mistakenly confused with Elisha Reynolds of Little Rest, whom authors may have sought to protect from criticism due to his role as a key founder of Little Rest.

Samuel Casey was scheduled to hang after the punishments were meted out to his four accomplices. His hanging may have been delayed in order for the General Assembly to consider his petition for reducing his penalty. Casey, however, had many friends in Little Rest and King's County, as was evidenced by the reluctance of the jury to convict him. These men felt that Casey's sentence of death by hanging was too harsh. At a time when criminal punishments were often overly harsh in light of the crime committed, citizens sometimes took justice into their own hands in order to apply leniency. Friends of Casey's, from around the county and village, gathered at Thomas Potter's tavern in Little Rest on the night of November 3, 1770 and made plans to free him. That night, "a considerable Number of People riotously assembled" in Little Rest and headed for the jail where Casey was being kept. With "Iron-bars and Pick-axes," the men broke open the outer door of "his Majesty's Gaol" and set Casey free. The other four convicted counterfeiters were also freed. With a death sentence hanging over his head, Samuel Casey was then furnished with a horse and he rode as fast as possible towards Connecticut. He never returned to Little Rest.

Immediately after the dramatic jailbreak, the General Assembly offered a reward of £50 for any information leading to the arrest of anyone involved. Although numerous arrests were made, at the April 1771 session of the superior court in Little Rest, only three men were punished with stiff fines. At the same session, a fifth man, William Carlisle of Exeter, was convicted of passing counterfeit money. He was sentenced to stand an hour in the Little Rest pillory, be branded with the letter "R" on both cheeks, and have both ears cropped.

Samuel Casey left Rhode Island and, according to his petition for amnesty drawn up by his wife in 1779, "wandered in exile nine years forlorn and forsaken and destitute of every means of support . . . separated from his wife and offspring." The General Assembly, voted to pardon the silversmith, but Samuel never took advantage of it. It may have been that he could not possibly have done so. A Canadian descendant of Samuel's reported that he was loyal to King George III in the American Revolutionary War and was killed as a Tory. This report is somewhat supported by evidence that Samuel Casey's son fought as a Tory and after the war fled to Canada.

Casey's house, which became known as the old Helme House as it housed James Helme's store and family, was torn down in 1910. Prior to the demolition, a search of the attic turned up a pressing die, which was determined to have been used for counterfeiting by Samuel Casey.

Slavery in Colonial Little Rest

A few families in colonial Little Rest held black men, women and children as slaves. As was discussed earlier in this Part I, Little Rest arose to become the hub of the Narragansett country. The Narragansett country – primarily the current South Kingstown, Narragansett, and parts of North Kingstown, Charlestown and Exeter – was unique in 18th century rural New England. While the rest of Rhode Island and New England was dominated by small farms surrounding villages, the Narragansett country was dominated by plantation-style estates. The Narragansett planters maintained large stock and dairy farms, which were worked by black slaves. Black slaves were first used to clear forests and meadows for cultivation and pasture. Then they were needed to watch over the increasing holdings of sheep, cattle and horses, and to cultivate the fields and harvest the crops. Some black slaves were used to perform domestic work in planter houses and to run errands in Little Rest or Newport, while a few were trained in skilled crafts such as blacksmithing.

Narragansett planters generally owned between five and twenty slaves. While the black population of Rhode Island in the 18th century ranged from 6 to 10 percent (the highest in New England), in South Kingstown (then including Narragansett) the black population ranged from 16 to 25 percent. As the hub of the Narragansett country, in this environment during colonial times when slavery was an accepted practice, it is not surprising that some Little Rest families acquired slaves.

Black slaves appear in town records dealing with land transactions in what would become Little Rest in the early 1700s. Robert Hannah, who had his house just west of what would become Little Rest, owned at his death in 1706 154 sheep, 41 cattle, 6 oxen, 3 hogs and one black female slave with five children. His son's estate, in 1736, showed four black slaves.

The earliest reference to slavery in Little Rest is in the land evidence records relating to Abraham Perkins, a blacksmith and storekeeper whose house was in the southeast corner of the Four Corners. In 1718, Perkins was recorded as having a "right to a Negro girl named Rose." Joseph Case, who built a house to the east of Perkins' house, died in 1739; the inventory of his estate indicates that he held the following black slaves: two adult females named Opera and Dinah, an elderly male named Roger, and a young boy. He also had rights to the services of an Indian girl until she turned age 18.

In the 1774 Rhode Island census, the following Little Rest villagers were recorded as having blacks in their households, who most likely were slaves: Elisha Reynolds, one of the village's founders (four blacks); Henry Reynolds, Elisha's son (three blacks); Robert Potter, Jr., the tavern keeper and farmer (five blacks); Thomas Potter, the tavern keeper and merchant (three blacks); Jonathan Hassard, who took over the Kingston Inn from John Potter in 1772 (two blacks); and farmer Timothy Peckham (one black). The Reynolds' slaves were probably used as field hands on the extensive farms held by the Reynolds family, and as domestic help in Little Rest itself. Elisha Reynolds' records indicate that in 1761 he purchased "a negro woman named Binor about forty or fifty years of age," who may have been used for domestic service. Slaves held by Thomas Potter, Jonathan Hassard and Robert Potter were probably used to help operate their taverns, with the tasks of caring for the horses of customers, acting as waiters, washing dishes, cleaning rooms, and running errands.

Little Rest was surrounded by farms on which black slaves worked the fields and served in planter households. For example, Narragansett planter Caleb Gardner had a farm to the east of North Road and a second farm to the west of Little Rest across the Chipuxet River. In 1774, Gardner was recorded as having six blacks and three Indians residing at his farms. Most of the black persons were likely slaves and the Indians were likely local Narragansetts who were indentured or temporary servants (by law they could not be enslaved in the colony). In 1774, William Potter had eleven black slaves at his estate about one mile north of Little Rest off North Road. Just a short way up North Road from Little Rest, Benjamin Peckham and his son Josephus each owned four black slaves. It was probably quite common to see black slaves in Little Rest, sent on errands to purchase articles from a village store or to have a blacksmith or other artisan fix an article for a planter.

Slaves in Little Rest likely generally resided in the main houses of their white owners. Caleb Gardner's slaves who worked on his farm to the west of Little Rest probably lived in a barn located on the farm. The farms of William Potter and Benjamin Peckham, in addition to their main houses, had several out buildings, some of which may have been used as slave quarters.[8]

Slavery was not the only condition of servitude in Little Rest. Free white, black and Indian persons could be "bound out" to white masters, meaning that they were required to work for their master for a number of years before they would be released from service. Frequently, the binding out was approved by the town council as a way to prevent the servant from becoming a burden on taxpayers by having to receive poor relief from the town. Sometimes the arrangements were voluntarily entered into, with the servant seeking regular food and shelter. Timothy Peckham, a farmer who

---

[8] Robert Fitts, in his *Inventing New England's Slave Paradise*, found in South Kingstown probate records that black slaves slept in the following locations: Stone House; Old House Chamber; Master's Chamber; On Farm; In Storage Area; Cellar; Barn; West Lower Room; Lower Bedroom; Garret; Kitchen Chamber; On Farm; West Chamber; On Farm; Kitchen & Storage Area; Kitchen; North Chamber; East Chamber; Separate Quarters; Kitchen.

resided in Little Rest, had two Native American servants, both probably members of the Narragansett tribe. The working conditions of indentured servants were similar to those of slaves. In 1775, Peckham advertised a reward in the *Newport Mercury* for the return of a runaway Indian servant named Joseph Hazard. The advertisement informed the readers that Hazard, as may have been the case with many Narragansetts, "commonly ties his hair behind."

In the first part of the 18th century, the South Kingstown town meeting passed a number of ordinances designed to reduce the risk of a slave rebellion. In 1724, the town meeting enacted an ordinance prohibiting a slave from visiting the house of a free black in the town. In 1726, the town meeting passed an ordinance prohibiting black slaves and free persons, as well as Indians, from gathering for their annual festival "in the third week of June."[9] The ordinance apparently was not heeded, as in 1737 a second ordinance was enacted. In 1724, the town meeting also forbade all blacks (even free persons) from keeping cattle, hogs and other farm animals. The punishment for violation of each ordinance was a public whipping at the discretion of the town justice. However, none of the ordinances was effective for long.

From early in the colonial period, it appears that local blacks and Narragansett Indians inter-married and had children together. This is indicated by the references in South Kingstown legal records to "mustees," who are children of mixed black and Indian parents. The ineffective town ordinances outlawing Indians and blacks from attending the June festivals are also an indication of the mixing of the two races. While Indians could not be enslaved, it appears that their children with a black parent could be enslaved.

As in other slave-holding societies, the existence of slaves raised vexing legal questions at the local court. In court, could a slave be sued or testify? If a slave was like a wagon – an inanimate piece of property – the answer could be no. If the court recognized that slaves were human beings, the answer could be yes. In 1765, in the county court of common pleas in Little Rest, Narragansett planter George Hazard sued Ben, a slave belonging to Narragansett planter Jonathan Hazard, for trespass. At trial, Hazard argued that the case against Ben should be dismissed, because as a slave, he was incapable of paying damages or owning any property. Hazard also argued that "being a Slave," Ben could not make a legal appearance in court. Hazard also argued that the plaintiff's deposition of Cuff, a black slave belonging to a Newport master, should not be admitted as evidence before a jury because Cuff was "a Heathen & Slave" and was "infamous." The court rejected all of these arguments and allowed the case to continue, finding in favor of the plaintiff and ordering Hazard to pay the damages and court costs.

---

[9] The "Negro Election" festival is described in more detail in a chapter in Part III, entitled "Elisha R. Potter, Sr. and Continuing Badges of Slavery in Little Rest."

An early historian of black slavery in the Narragansett country, Elisha R. Potter, Jr. of Little Rest, reported that the conditions of slavery in the Narragansett country were relatively mild compared to the harsher conditions in the colonial South. In an 1840 speech, Potter stated: "It is believed that while slavery existed in Rhode Island, the slaves were always treated with humanity, and that they were generally rather a burden than a source of profit to their owners." Potter repeated this position in an 1851 address, in which he stated that "public opinion would not sanction over-work or ill treatment" of slaves in the Narragansett country. These statements may generally be accurate, but they miss the primary point. The main point of slavery was to take away the liberty of an individual by force and to force the individual to perform labor for his or her master free of charge.

At its core, slavery was a relationship based on terror. White masters used terror to keep black slaves from rebelling, running away or disobeying. Despite the tradition of mild treatment of slaves in the Narragansett country, there are reported examples of harsh punishments being meted out on them. Consider the following examples.

- In 1707, a black slave killed the wife of his white master in Kingstown. Realizing what punishment would be inflicted on him, the slave committed suicide. Nevertheless, the General Assembly, wanting to strike fear in the local slave population, ordered that the dead man's "head, legs, and arms be cut from his body, and hung up in some public place, near the town, to public view and his body to be burnt to ashes, that it may, if it please God, be something of a terror to others from perpetrating of the like barbarity for the future."[10]
- A South Kingstown male runaway slave who was captured reportedly was tied to a stake in a swamp, left overnight, and died of exposure to mosquitoes.
- Another runaway male slave apparently as punishment had the big toe of each foot cut off.
- The Reverend James MacSparran in his diary of the 1750s reports that on several occasions he whipped his male and female slaves for "disobedience." On the occasion of a particularly harsh beating, a male slave ran away. The slave was caught and returned with "Pothooks put about his Neck."

---

[10] This report is quoted in Irving Barlett's *From Slave to Citizen* (1954), pages 15-16. Bartlett states that the incident occurred in Kingston, but he is incorrect. It occurred in Kingstown. At this time, in the colonial period, Little Rest was not even named Kingston. The original quote is in Bartlett, John R. (ed.), *Records of the Colony of Rhode Island,* vol. 4, page 27.

- Cato Pearce, a black slave whose story is told later in this book, ran away from his North Kingstown farm but was later caught and whipped by his master.
- A woman in 1770 was accused by her Quaker sect of "encouraging the unmerciful whipping or beating of her negro man slave, he being stripped naked and hanged by the hands in his masters house."
- In 1773, a North Kingstown slaveowner, after his male slave failed to obey his order to perform some work, struck the slave's head with a pair of iron tongs, causing a severe wound.

By the early 1770s, there were indications that the moral environment in South Kingstown regarding slavery and the treatment of slaves was beginning to change. Quakers, led by South Kingstown's Thomas Hazard, were the first to question the morality of slavery. In May 1760, the influential Quaker elder John Woolman visited Newport and spoke out against slavery and the slave trade. "The great number of slaves in these parts and the continuance of a Trade . . . made deep impressions on me," he wrote. In the early 1760s, the South Kingstown Quaker monthly meeting began disciplining members who purchased slaves. In one case, a member, Joseph

South Kingstown, June 15.
RUN AWAY from the Subscriber, on Thursday the 4th Instant, a Negro Man named Cæsar, about 5 Feet 9 Inches high; had on when he went away, a cloth-coloured Serge Coat, a striped Jacket, and striped Trowsers, also a Pair of Silver Shoe Buckles. Said Fellow is very black, and well proportioned every Way, hath a Scar on one of his Cheeks, is a Blacksmith by Trade, but has principally followed Anchor-making. Whoever apprehends said Fellow, and secures him in any of his Majesty's Goals, or brings him to me, shall have Eight Dollars Reward, and reasonable Charges paid. EBER SWEET.

Run-away Slave Advertisement, June 15-25, 1767, *Newport Mercury*. The South Kingstown run-away was well positioned for freedom, as he had been trained as a blacksmith and anchor maker. *Library of Congress.*

Rathbun, resisted and purchased a black girl in 1765. The monthly meeting threatened Rathbun with expulsion on several occasions if he did not free the girl. Rathbun reacted in 1771 by selling the girl to another slaveowner outside the colony, a violation of Quaker rules. The monthly meeting responded by expelling Rathbun. In 1771, the monthly meeting took the next step and threatened to expel members who kept slaves. In June 1773, South Kingstown Quakers appointed to "Visit Slave Keepers" proudly reported that "they don't find there is any held as Slaves by Friends." Little Rest, however, did not have Quakers, so this reform movement did not free any of its its slaves.

There were other indications that a more liberal and compassionate attitude in dealing with slaves was taking hold in South Kingstown by the 1770s. In 1771, Jeffrey Watson, a prominent Narragansett planter, and several other men apparently agreed upon a sordid scheme to sell into slavery members of the Wamsley family. It was not clear whether Mary Wamsley and her daughter were slaves or whether they had become free; there was conflicting evidence on the point. Watson took control of the bankrupt estate of James Gardner and claimed that Mary Wamsley and her daughter Susannah had been Gardner's slaves. Mary had lived in the Gardner household for many years and Susannah was working as a bonded servant for another white family. Watson arranged for the sale of Susannah for only £10 to an accomplice, Colonel Samuel Rose. Rose then sold Susannah to a man in Connecticut, who was to resell her for a much higher price. Mary Wamsley found out that Jeffrey Watson was searching for her and her daughter to "enslave them." Mary found shelter in the home of a sympathetic white benefactor, Samuel Rodman, for several months. Mary remained in "great ... apprehension of Danger." Eventually Watson found Mary and had her sent to Connecticut. Mary then brought suit against Watson for false imprisonment in 1772 in Newport. After hearing the evidence, including the allegation that Watson, Col. Rose and the Connecticut man were to divide the proceeds of the intended sale among them, the jury ruled that "we find that Mary Wamsley and Susannah Wamsley are free." This verdict demonstrates that townsmen were growing less tolerant of the extremes of slavery and more sympathetic to the legal rights of free blacks.

The North Kingstown slaveowner who in 1773 struck his slave in the head with iron tongs was charged for the assault. While the grand jury in the Little Rest Court House chose not to bring the case to trial, the fact that a charge for striking a slave was filed at all by authorities showed that there was a concern about limits to the punishments inflicted by slaveowners.

Two incidents showed that South Kingstown men began making a distinction between slavery in South Kingstown and the more brutal form of slavery in the South. In 1773, the county superior court, meeting in the Little Rest Court House, ordered a North Carolina slaveowner to return Sarah, a woman of mixed black and Indian parents, to South Kingstown. The North Carolina man, John Walker, had purchased Sarah under the apparent belief that Sarah was a slave. When it was later revealed that Sarah was free and not a slave, Walker, fearing that he might lose Sarah, shipped her out on the next boat to North Carolina. The court, however, ordered that Walker be committed to the custody of the King's County sheriff until Sarah was returned to South Kingstown. In addition, in 1779, a North Carolina slaveowner passing through South Kingstown purchased a female slave, Abigail, and her three young children. When it became clear at a stop in nearby Charlestown that the North Carolina man wanted to bring Abigail down south with him, Abigail understandably panicked. She took her children and ran away, and local white Charlestown men warned the North Carolinian not to follow them. The North Carolinian in October 1779 petitioned the General Assembly sitting in Little Rest for relief, but was refused; instead, the General Assembly passed a law prohibiting the sale of slaves outside the state without their consent. This incident showed that local sentiment in South County abhorred the extremes of slavery in the South (but not to the extent to free their own slaves).

With the rhetoric of the American Revolution at a high pitch by 1774, Rhode Islanders became uncomfortable by the incongruity of white Americans demanding liberty from English "slavery," while in practice white Americans denied liberty to black Americans in their own homes. In June 1774, the General Assembly passed an act "prohibiting the importation of Negroes into this Colony." The preamble reflected the tension between revolutionary rhetoric and reality, as it acknowledged that "those who are desirous of enjoying all the advantages of liberty themselves, should be willing to extend personal liberty to others." Unfortunately, there were several exemptions that weakened the act, but it was a start on the road towards emancipation for Little Rest slaves and other Rhode Island slaves. The new sentiment went only so far. When a proposal to abolish slavery in Rhode Island was floated in 1775, the South Kingstown town meeting voted to oppose it. The proposal did not advance in the General Assembly.

The preamble to the 1779 act prohibiting the sale of slaves outside the state expressed hope that slavery would soon be abolished. But while Rhode Island remained at war with Great Britain, it chose not to act on the matter.

With the coming American Revolution, life in Little Rest, as in the rest of Rhode Island, would dramatically change. Not only would white Americans gain their freedom from Britain, black Americans also would benefit from the realization by whites that holding blacks in slavery was inconsistent with the liberty that they were seeking from Great Britain. The Revolutionary War did not bring immediate change, but it laid the groundwork for the change that eventually came.

II. LITTLE REST IN THE REVOLUTIONARY ERA,

(1775-1791)

State House and Washington County Court House at Little Rest. The General
Assembly often met here during the Revolutionary War. Scene of the Rhode Island
constitutional convention that met in March 1790. Detail of map of South Kingstown
by Henry Walling, 1857. *Rhode Island Historical Society,* RHi X3 853.

Little Rest and the Coming American Revolution

Resistance Against British Authority

Rhode Island, with its long tradition of self-government, decentralized government and evasion of British trading laws, naturally resisted Britain's attempts to tighten its control over the American colonies in the 1760s and 1770s. With other towns in Rhode Island, Little Rest became caught up in the swirl of events that culminated with the Battle of Lexington and Concord in April 1775, Rhode Island renouncing its allegiance to King George III in May 1776, and delegates from all of the American colonies signing the Declaration of Independence in July 1776.

While the focus of the resistance in Rhode Island occurred in the commercial seaports of Newport and Providence, the rural South County towns, including South Kingstown, supported the patriot side. In December 1773, South Kingstown freemen gathered in a town meeting, as usual held at the Little Rest Court House, concerning the duty placed on tea "to draw up Resolutions for this Town to enter into respecting the East India Company's importing Tea into America whilst subject to a Duty." A committee of leading citizens, including Narragansett planters William Potter and Benjamin Peckham who both lived on North Road just north of Little Rest, was formed to draft these resolutions, which appeared in the next issue of the *Newport Mercury* newspaper. The strongest section in the resolutions charged the King with establishing "taxes and monopolies upon all the necessaries of life in America." The town pledged neither to buy nor sell tea that was subject to the hated tax. The resolutions ended with a declaration of support for the centers of patriot activity: "We revere the sister colonies Boston, Virginia, and Philadelphia, for their virtuous and noble stand in defense of the common liberties of America and stand with hearts full of gratitude, thank the towns of Newport and Westerly for their resolutions in the present alarming situation of the colonies."

Following the Boston Tea Party, British authorities closed the port of Boston. In order to assist Boston, in August 1774, the South Kingstown town meeting donated money and 135 sheep to Boston. In October 1774, the town meeting also organized a committee of correspondence, along with other New England towns sympathetic to the patriot cause. The committee probably met in Little Rest's taverns. Pursuant to resolutions passed by the Continental Congress, the committee ordered the town to receive no British imports after December 1, 1774.

The Problem of Loyalists

There were divisions in the colony of Rhode Island, including in South Kingstown. Many influential townsmen supported the Crown. The colony's government and the South Kingstown town council were, however, dominated by patriots. They had to face the issue of how to deal with loyalists (later called Tories).

In 1773, the General Assembly threw George Rome of North Kingstown into the King's County jail at Little Rest. Rome was an English agent of London creditors whose job it was to collect on the debts of Newport merchants and Narragansett planters. If this was not bad enough to make him unpopular, he was also a well-known loyalist. His fatal mistake was writing a letter to his friend, Dr. Moffat of Newport, in which he severely criticized Rhode Island's judicial system for failing to allow him to collect properly on debts owed to him. Rome made the audacious (at least to Rhode Islanders' ears) suggestion that the British Crown ought to assume the power to appoint judges, rather than the freemen of Rhode Island. Moffat forwarded the letter to the British ministry in London. In London, however, Benjamin Franklin somehow got hold of the letter and through back channels it was printed in New England newspapers. The whole colony rose up in a rage against Rome. He was sued in twelve separate actions for defamation, each for £290, just below the minimum value that would allow him to appeal to England. The General Assembly, meeting in Little Rest in October 1773, issued a warrant for the sheriff to bring Rome before the deputies. Rome was brought before the lower house and read the charges against him. When Rome was asked if he wrote the contents described in the letter, Rome demonstrated his knowledge of English common law. He responded, "I cannot be legally called to the bar of this house to accuse myself." Because the General Assembly did not possess the original letter, Rome's assertion of the right against self-incrimination would appear to have won the day. But these were unusual times! The General Assembly found Rome to be in contempt of the lower house, issued a warrant for his arrest, and committed him to His Majesty's jail in Little Rest where he stayed until the session ended. In October 1775, the General Assembly voted to void all deeds of real estate made by Rome, and in June 1776 it ordered all of his real estate to be confiscated.[11]

As early as 1774, the Reverend Samuel Fayerweather, rector of the

---

[11] In 1776, Rome escaped another jailing for his loyalist leanings by rowing out to the British ship *Rose* from his sumptuous estate in North Kingstown and sailing back to Britain. The grounds of his former estate, including Rome Point from where Rome rowed to safety, is a new state park.

Episcopal Church (which was then located about two miles north of Little Rest and is now St. Paul's in Wickford) received objections from his Narragansett planter congregation on the ground that he read the prayers for the king and royal family. Fayerweather could not, he said, omit them without violating his church vows and so the church was temporarily closed. (In August 1778, the Reverend Fayerweather applied to the South Kingstown town council to take the oath of allegiance to the patriot cause. The town council accepted the Reverend Fayerweather's application, but stated that "this Counsel expects that for the future he prays for the Congress and the United States.")

Judge William Potter, the chief justice of the court of common pleas, and co-author of the previous resolutions supporting the patriot cause in 1774, also found himself in trouble. A week after the Battle of Lexington and Concord, on April 22, 1775, the General Assembly authorized raising a 1,500 man "army of observation" with Nathaniel Greene as its commander. But when the army started its march to Boston, Governor Wanton of Rhode Island ordered the soldiers to return. Judge Potter openly supported the Governor's decision. Rhode Island patriots raised such an uproar that Potter was forced to write a letter of apology to the General Assembly. Potter explained that he had thought that perhaps a settlement could still be reached that would save Rhode Island commerce, "particularly the town of Newport." Potter admitted his indiscretion and gave the following powerful oath:

> No man hath been more deeply impressed with the calamities to which America is reduced by a corrupt administration, than myself. No man exerted himself more, in private and public life, to relieve ourselves from our oppressions, and no man hath held himself more readily to sacrifice his life and fortune in the arduous struggles now making throughout America, for the preservation of our just rights and liberties, and in these sentiments I am determined to live and die.

The General Assembly forgave Potter, and at the same session, re-elected him chief justice, a post which he served until 1778.

The South Kingstown town meeting feared that some Narragansett planters sympathized with the Crown. In June 1775, a decree against "Enimies of American Liberty" was enacted by the town meeting. The decree promised that any person in the town who aided the British would be subjected to an economic and social boycott by the townspeople of South Kingstown and held "in ye utmost Contempt." In July 1775, Benjamin Shearman was brought before the town meeting and denounced as an enemy of the patriot cause. Shearman's fellow townsmen were ordered to cease "all intercourse, trade and dealings" with him.

On May 4, 1776, Rhode Island became the first colony to renounce allegiance to King George III. It declared that it assumed full sovereignty under the existing Rhode Island constitution and laws, and that all British officials were stripped of authority. Ten weeks later, on July 18th, 1776, the General Assembly ratified the Declaration of Independence. But it would take war against the mightiest power in the world at that time, Britain, for the American colonies to truly gain their independence.

Mustering for War in Little Rest

Throughout the colonial period, Little Rest was the primary location in King's County for military musters. This role continued as the Revolutionary War moved to its military phase.

At the outbreak of the Revolutionary War in April 1775, the active military force of Rhode Island consisted of several independent companies. None were from King's County, until November 1775, when a number of Little Rest and other South Kingstown men petitioned the General Assembly to organize as an independent unit the Kingston Reds.[12] The Kingston Reds' main duty was to patrol the southern Rhode Island coastline.

The Kingston Reds likely mustered in Little Rest. The uniform of the Reds -- a red coat with black facings -- was a near approximation of the uniforms of British regular troops. The parade of soldiers in their red uniforms must have caused much excitement in the village. In addition, at least ten of the 43 men listed in a May 1776 roll resided in Little Rest: John Waite, silversmith; Joseph Perkins, silversmith and storekeeper; David Douglass, blacksmith; Thomas Potter, tavern keeper; Henry Reynolds, son of Elisha Reynolds; Caleb Wescott, carpenter; George Teft, blacksmith; John Weeden, leather worker; and William and John Clarke, farmers. Villager John Waite eventually became captain of the Reds and headed the Reds for most of the war. In May 1776, Thomas Potter was second-in-command.

In October 1775, the town meeting took several actions to prepare the town for war against the British. Little Rest blacksmith George Teft was hired to make 100 guns, with each gun barrell to be three-feet eight inches long and each bayonet to be eighteen inches long. Little Rest blacksmith Nathaniel Perkins was hired to make 100 gun locks for the guns. In the meantime, Little Rest silversmith Joseph Perkins was ordered to ride to New York to purchase 100 guns on the best terms he could obtain. Benjamin

---

[12] The name of the unit is, from the act of incorporation and most subsequent military lists, the "Kingston" Reds. The name of Kingston for the village would not be adopted for another fifty years. The name "Kingston" Reds in fact probably was based on a misspelling of the word "South Kingstown," which was often misspelled as "South Kingston" in legal records.

Peckham was authorized to purchase 100 bayonet belts.

During the war years, the demand for skilled labor for the manufacture of war material was so great that the General Assembly sometimes exempted men thus employed from serving in the military forces. In 1777, George Teft and Jeremiah Sheffield, members of the Kingston Reds, were excused from duty, as they were employed in the "making and stocking guns." Two other men were also released from service on the ground that they were engaged in the making of cartridge paper for muskets.

Little Rest's highest ranking patriot officers were brothers Thomas Potter, the tavern keeper, and William Potter, a tailor (he was not the Judge William Potter who lived up North Road). When two King's County militia regiments were established in November 1776, Thomas Potter was chosen as major. In August 1777, he was appointed as one of the recruiting officers for South Kingstown. In May 1778, he was appointed lieutenant colonel of the 2nd Regiment of King's County militia and served in that position through 1780. His brother, William Potter, joined as an ensign in Rhode Island's 1,500-man "army of observation" that joined in the siege on Boston in May 1775. In 1776, William was appointed a lieutenant in the 11th Continental Regiment. From January 1777 to April 1779, he served as captain of a company in Col. Israel Angell's 2nd Rhode Island Continental Regiment. Captain Potter led his 50-man company, which included a fifer and a drummer, in the battles of White Plains, Germantown and Red Bank. At Red Bank, in New Jersey, he reportedly "mounted the ramparts in spite of warnings and kept up a galling fire on the enemy."

Common soldiers at first showed Narragansett planters deference by making them leaders of the King's County regiments. But as the war went on, perhaps inspired by the egalitarian rhetoric of the patriots and by the need to place the best military leaders in charge regardless of background, men from more ordinary backgrounds were selected as officers. Narragansett planter John Gardiner was the first captain of the Kingston Reds, but he later gave way to John Waite, a mere tradesman (a silversmith).

The preparations of the soldiers from Little Rest and elsewhere in the Narragansett country were for good reason. A flotilla of British ships, including the *Rose* captained by James Wallace, patrolled the waters of Narragansett Bay, interrupting commercial shipping and grabbing livestock and farm produce from coastal areas. South Kingstown freemen, having been notified by "several expresses sent to different parts of this town," gathered at the Little Rest Court House on January 4, 1776 "on account of an alarm last night" and proceeded to arrange for the townspeople to be armed and for a watch to be set up on the shoreline. On January 13, 1776, a British raiding party landed on Point Judith and seized a number of sheep and cattle. The excitement was heightened when it was determined that several local Tories had aided the "land pirates," as they were called.

The British Occupy Newport

By November 1776, the British commander in America, General William Howe, with a force of approximately 34,000 soldiers and sailors, had soundly defeated Washington's army and had captured New York City. With the objective of mounting an invasion of New England in the spring, Howe sent a strong detachment to seize Newport, Rhode Island. On December 8, 1776, General Henry Clinton and 6,000 British and Hessian troops, supported by more than 40 British ships, easily captured Newport.

The British occupied Newport for almost three years. This occupation had a significant impact on Little Rest. First, Little Rest became more crowded and had more of a bustling air. A number of prominent Newport patriots, their families and their black slaves fled to the safety of Little Rest, where they stayed with friends or in one of the taverns. The Rhode Island military census of 1777 lists eleven white men and five black male slaves who formerly had resided in Newport and who were staying temporarily in Little Rest. Little Rest also continued to host musters of local militias. In 1778, the state reimbursed tavern keeper Robert Potter for serving dinner to 33 Massachusetts soldiers, who were guarding the coastline. In 1779, the state reimbursed tavern keeper Thomas Potter for hosting a state committee on removing Tories and another state committee on illegal trading with the British. In his diary, Colonel Israel Angell, commanding a regiment of continental troops stationed at Boston Neck, wrote that in October 1779, he was invited to dine with Governor Bradford, General James Varnum, Colonel Thomas Potter, "and a number of Gentlemen of the Superior Court" then in session at Little Rest. They probably met at Potter's tavern.

In addition, due to the occupation of Newport and the threat of raids to the coastline, the General Assembly met frequently in Little Rest during the war years – three times in 1777, twice in 1779, and three times in 1781. Laws adopted by the General Assembly in Little Rest included the confiscation of Tory property, punishment for treason, and provisions for the raising and equipping of troops. To make the Court House more accessible, the General Assembly in 1779 ordered that a set of stone steps be built on the east entrance of the "State House."

An important impact of the British occupation of Newport was to shift the state's tax burden to South County towns. With Newport, Portsmouth, Jamestown, Middletown and Block Island either occupied by the British or under constant danger of attack, and with the British fleet largely shutting off trade by Providence and Bristol merchants, the General Assembly had to rely heavily on South Kingstown and other South County towns to raise taxes to support the war effort. South Kingstown was then the wealthiest rural town in the state, and during the war would become the state's heaviest taxed town. The South Kingstown town meeting continually protested the heavy taxation, but to no avail. As the war dragged on and the burden on the rural South County towns increased, the discontent would eventually boil over, as will be seen in upcoming chapters.

In February 1777, dropping plans to invade the New England mainland, General Clinton withdrew half of his troops from Newport. With the American victory at Saratoga in October 1777, only Newport and New York remained in British hands. In August of 1778, American and French forces made a concerted effort to recapture Newport. General John Sullivan gathered militia from Rhode Island and other parts of New England. He was joined by units of the Continental Army under General Marquis de Lafayette and Rhode Island's own General Nathaniel Greene. The Americans were to receive additional help from a squadron of French ships with a contingent of 2,000 French troops led by Admiral Comte d'Estaing. When d'Estaing's ships sailed successfully past the Newport harbor batteries, the chances of capturing Newport and perhaps ending the war were encouraging. But when a squadron of British ships arrived off of Newport, d'Estaing felt he had to avoid being bottled up in Narragansett Bay. He had his French ships sail out of the harbor to give battle, but a violent wind storm damaged the fleets of both countries. The French admiral sailed to Boston to have his ships repaired, leaving Newport open for British reinforcement and the Americans with less support. Sullivan's 8,000 men, many of whom were inexperienced militia, could not dislodge the 6,000 British and Hessian professional troops in Newport. As Sullivan pulled back his forces, the British attacked. The Americans did succeed in repelling the British, but they suffered heavier casualties.

One of the American regiments that fought in the Battle of Newport was the 1st Rhode Island regiment, which included the first all-black battalion of the war. Desperate for troops, the General Assembly in early 1778 enacted a law providing that any slave volunteering for the new battalion would be "absolutely FREE, as though he had never been encumbered with any kind of servitude or slavery," with the same wages and bounties as regular soldiers, and with the master being reimbursed by the state. Six General Assemblymen from South County fired off an ineffective petition, claiming among a litany of protests that the idea would "produce an opinion in the world that the state had purchased a band of slaves to be employed in the defense of our rights and liberties of our country." On March 19, 1778, a white captain held a recruitment assembly in South Kingstown (perhaps in Little Rest, a frequent locale for musters), and was pleased that a "large number of Negroes collected together apparently desirous of Enlisting." One white Narragansett planter also attended and attempted, without success, to discourage enlistment, predicting that the black soldiers who were "taken prisoners would

not be exchanged, but were to be sent to the West Indies & sold as slaves."
From a partial list of 73 black men who joined the regiment, most of them
came from South County and at least 23 of them hailed from South
Kingstown. It is does not appear that any from this list came from Little Rest.
However, muster rolls of the 1st Rhode Island Regiment indicate that former
slaves Sampson Reynolds and Mingo Reynolds served as privates. These
men could have been from Little Rest, as former slaves of Elisha Reynolds or
his son Henry.[13] The battalion successfully fought a key delaying action
against Hessian troops in the Battle of Newport, performed well in the
remainder of the war, and was present at the British surrender in Yorktown,
Virginia in 1783. In a brutal action late in the war, their white commander,
Colonel Greene was killed in close range fighting with British soldiers using
bayonets, but only after the black soldiers guarding him fought heroically
before being killed. A French officer, the Marquis de Chastellux, in his
journal entry for January 1781, wrote of meeting the 1st Rhode Island at a
ferry crossing. He noted that "The majority of the enlisted men are Negroes
or mulattoes; but they are strong, robust men, and those I saw made a very
good appearance." The bravery of the black soldiers was later cited as one of
the reasons to abolish slavery and extend voting and other rights to blacks in
Rhode Island. Still, the breakthrough in race relations was incomplete. The
General Assembly ended the enlistment of slaves on June 10, 1778; and it
never included black males as subject to the state's military draft, despite the
pressing need for troops.

      Captain William Potter, of Little Rest, led a company of soldiers in
Col. Israel Angell's 2nd Rhode Island Continental Regiment, General James
Varnum's brigade, in the Battle of Newport. It is not clear if the Kingston

---

[13] On March 10, 1794, at a meeting of the South Kingstown town council, it was
voted that "Administration be granted to Elisha Gardner on the Estate of Sampson
Reynolds a Continental Solder Dec'd [deceased]." The author believes that
Sampson Reynolds was likely a former black slave of Elisha Reynolds (or of his
son, Henry) who served in the 1st Regiment for the following reasons: (i) slaves
were typically given the last names of their masters and Elisha Reynolds (and his
son, Henry) were the only Reynolds reported as having blacks living in their
households in the 1774 census of South Kingstown; (ii) Elisha Reynolds and his
son also had black slaves living in their households according to the 1790 census
and Elisha Reynolds' 1791 will; (iii) the service of Gardner, and two other Little
Rest men, to administer Sampson's estate suggests that Sampson was from Little
Rest, as often administrators of estates were selected who resided near the
deceased. Regiment records indicate that Sampson Reynolds enlisted in June 1778
and remained with the regiment until his death in August 1781. Records indicate
that Mingo Reynolds, who also could have been a former slave owned by Elisha or
Henry Reynolds, enlisted in July 1778 and was taken prisoner in Newport.

Reds fought in the Battle of Newport. A member of the Rose family, in the early 1800s, recollected that James Rose, a private in the Reds, served under General Sullivan at the Battle of Newport. It may have been that the unit served in a reserve capacity during the battle.[14]

Little Rest villagers were constantly concerned that the British army would at any time invade the mainland or raid the coast. Their worries were realized in the spring of 1779, as a result of the shortage of supplies to support the British and Hessian troops in Newport. Jeffrey Watson, in his diary, reported on May 8, 1779, that British "Land Pirates" captured John Gardiner and "his 9 workmen" and grabbed livestock as well. On May 21, 1779, a British raiding party of 150 men from a fleet of nine ships landed in South Kingstown, burned one house, plundered two others, and made prisoners of fifteen townsmen, including some slaves. In a skirmish with patriot forces, the British party was driven off, with the patriot forces capturing one British sloop and five sailors. That same day, another foraging party landed in Point Judith and carried off eight prisoners and more livestock. They were again driven off by patriot troops. The next morning, the British landed at another exposed part of the town's coastline and burned two houses. At about the same time, a band of Tories raided Point Judith and carried off more livestock. "Nailer Tom" Hazard made the following entries in his diary on June 6th and 8th: "Regulars landed and took Samuel Congden" and "The Regulars burnt two houses last night." Another entry on June 12th reported "an alarm in the night." Jeffrey Watson reported that on June 25, 1779, Land Pirates took about 700 sheep and some cattle from his relative, Job Watson. Watson later reported that Land Pirates landed again off Point Judith and "caryed away from John Gardiner between two and three hundred wait of cheese and some of his wife's wearing close" and took from Job Watson "two negro men and four white men that was at work for him." One can imagine the fear that South Kingstown residents faced in these difficult months. Ironically, for the black slaves who were "carried away" by the "Land Pirates," it usually meant freedom.

---

[14] The woman who provides an eyewitness account of General Washington's visit to Little Rest (see page 62) reports that Captain William Potter, brother to Colonel Thomas Potter, was killed in General Sullivan's expedition at Newport. But records indicate that Captain William Potter resigned his commission in April 1779, earned a revolutionary war pension, and died in 1822. Captain William Potter was a different man from the Narragansett planter William Potter who became a disciple of Jemima Wilkinson.

General Washington has a "Little Rest"

In October 1779, the British began to focus their efforts on the American South and evacuated Newport, to the great relief of all Rhode Island inhabitants. On June 10, 1780, Newport was occupied a second time, but this time it was by the allies of the patriot cause, the French. Count Rochambeau, with 6,000 troops and a fleet of 46 ships, waited in Newport for the right opportunity to help General George Washington and his troops. The British blockaded the mouth of Narragansett Bay most of the time, allowing the French few chances to help the Americans and further inhibiting trade by Newport and Providence merchants.

In March 1781, General Washington and members of his staff, including Alexander Hamilton and Tench Tilghman, traveled from their headquarters in New Windsor, New York to Newport, Rhode Island for the purpose of consulting with the French allies about how the French troops could best assist the American war efforts. While traveling to Newport, General Washington and his staff stayed at Thomas Potter's tavern in Little Rest.

Fortunately for posterity, Baron Ludwig Von Closen, the French aide of Count Rochambeau who was selected to ride to New Windsor, New York and make advance plans for Washington's visit, kept a marvelous journal. On February 25, 1781, Von Closen wrote that he was "delighted at the prospect of at last seeing General Washington, whom I had heard described so many times as the most interesting man on the Continent." The next day, Von Closen started his trip to New Windsor, passing through Little Rest and Westerly, and Norwich and Lebanon, Connecticut. At Lebanon, Von Closen met the Duc de Lauzun, who was stationed there with his French troops. The next day, making good time, Von Closen reached New Windsor and met General Washington. Upon meeting Washington, Von Closen said he "was not at all disappointed in my expectation." On March 2d, General Washington, aides Alexander Hamilton and Tench Tilghman, and Von Closen started their journey to Newport. On March 4th, Von Closen rode ahead of Washington's group in order to alert residents of Hartford and the French troops stationed in Lebanon of Washington's expected arrival.

On March 5th, retracing his ride back through western Rhode Island on his way to Newport to alert Count Rochambeau of General Washington's expected arrival, Von Closen halted at Little Rest. He then "ordered the night's lodging at Little Rest, where we had 8 hussars [French cavalry] stationed for communications. I cautioned the cavalry corporal that they would have to guard him [Washington] carefully during the night, as there were many Tories in the neighborhood." Von Closen then continued on to Newport, where his announcement that Washington would visit the next day "created a general sensation throughout the army and among all the residents of Newport and the surrounding area."

Meanwhile, General Washington's trusted aide, Colonel Tench Tilghman, kept a detailed record of the expenses incurred on this trip. Tilghman recorded expenses for shoeing horses and taking ferries across rivers. Washington passed through Norwich, Connecticut and from North Stonington, Connecticut, struck across country. Due to the lack of roads from the border of Connecticut east to Little Rest, Tilghman hired three guides to lead the way. Finally, Tilghman wrote the following entry: "Little Rest potters $2796." A summary prepared later by Tilghman provides "Potter's at Little Rest $2796." These references establish that General Washington spent the night at Colonel Thomas Potter's tavern in Little Rest on March 5, 1781. The substantial expenditure indicates that a large party spent the night at the tavern, had their meals, and had their horses attended to and fed. It is likely that there was not sufficient room at Potter's tavern to host the entire party and that the cost includes board at other taverns and houses in the village. The total cost would have included the eight French cavalry troopers who spent the previous night at the tavern waiting for General Washington. Fortunately, no "Tories in the neighborhood" disturbed General Washington's rest that evening.

Colonel Potter's daughter and youngest child, Elizabeth, as an adult, told villagers of General Washington visiting Little Rest, stopping at her father's tavern, and holding her as a child on his knee. Elizabeth (Potter) Randolph gave the following account as an adult, probably some time in the 1830s or 1840s:

> General Washington came to my father's house, Col. Thomas Potter. He took me on his knee. Gen. Hamilton [Alexander Hamilton, Washington's aide-de-camp] was with him, a fine looking man. About a dozen others [were also there] from Hartford. William Lee, Gen. Washington's black servant was with him. Washington was dressed in [a] faded uniform patched at the elbows and all the American officers [were] badly clothed . . . . French officers, Count Rochambeau, Duke Larein and others splendidly dressed. They learned English readily and carried grammar and dictionary [books] with them. . . . Washington passed up and down the street [presumably, main street in Little Rest] with head uncovered [with no hat or wig]. He was shaved by the village barber, Major Lunt!

One must be careful about taking 19th century recollections at face value. Often, they contain valuable kernels of truth, but may be embellished with

Vanderbergs	483
Morehouses	1034
Getting out the Horse Bell &c Wat	215
Litchfield	687
Shoing Horses	34
Farmington	1048½
Ferry at Hartford	84
Bolton	540
Shoing Horses	45
Tracy Norwich	214
Lothrops do	720
Ferry do	143
For a Guide	150
Preston	1072
do	32
Lewis Kenniens	1900
a Guide	100
do	74
Little Rest potters	2796
Narraganset Ferry	280
Connamicut do	280
Carried over	11947⅞

Excerpt from Tench Tilghman Expense Account Book. The reference to "Little Rest potters $2796" is proof that General Washington visited Little Rest in 1781 and stayed at Potter's Tavern. *Library of Congress, Manuscript Division.*

time. Elizabeth's recollections of Hamilton and General Washington's black servant, as well as the recollection of French troops staying at her father's tavern that night, are accurate, but she did not meet Count Rochambeau or Duke de Lauzin that day. Count Rochambeau was in Newport waiting for General Washington to visit the next day, and Duke de Lauzin was absent from Lebanon, Connecticut when General Washington visited the previous day and reviewed the Duke's troops. The Major Lunt mentioned in the above recollection was William Lunt, who was born in 1745 in Newburyport, Massachusetts and moved to Little Rest just prior to the war. Major Lunt served as a soldier and barber in the Rhode Island militia, until he was accidentally wounded by a defective gun that misfired. In his later years, he gained the unofficial title of "major" and received a pension beginning in 1794. Until his death in 1840, he enjoyed informing his Little Rest customers that they were being shaved by the same blade that was applied to General Washington's face.

Early the next morning, on March 6, 1781, General Washington and his staff saddled their horses in Little Rest and rode towards Tower Hill and South Ferry in order to catch the ferry to Jamestown. But first, General Washington and his staff may have stopped at the Rose family's house, which still stands a short way down the road in Mooresfield. Elizabeth (Potter) Randolph also reported that she was told the following by Mary Rose, a contemporary of Elizabeth's who lived in Mooresfield.

Washington with a number of officers both French and American passed through Kingston on their way to Newport in 1781. They spent the night in this village. Washington with some of his party stayed at a Potter house which stood somewhere on the lot now occupied by Mr. William Potter. Not having room for them all there, some of the French officers were entertained at what is now known as the Aldri[ch] house next to the Post Office.[15] The party left the next morning and dined at the house of Mr. John Rose of Mooresfield. The family are still in possession of the decanter and wine glass which Washington used at that time. This Rose homestead stood on the farm now owned by Watsons in Mooresfield. Washington's object in coming here was to see Mr.

---

[15] It is not clear what house is referred to. At the time Elizabeth Randolph related her recollections, general stores typically served as post offices. It may have been Luke Aldrich's house, which was built in 1829 and was located just up North Road. The William Potter referenced was one of the sons of Elisha Potter, Sr., who at the time lived in the former Asa Potter house, to the west of the corner lot formerly occupied by Col. Thomas Potter's tavern.

John Rose and tell him of the capture and death of his son Philip on the prison ship Jersey. Philip Rose not only held office of aid to Washington but was a friend as well and Washington took this way of seeing the family, to give them these sad particulars.

While General Washington may have stopped at the Rose house for breakfast, the author has been unable to confirm the role of Philip Rose. The author has not found any reference to a Philip Rose or any other Rose from Rhode Island serving on Washington's staff or being killed as a solider. There was a Philip Rose who served in a Rhode Island artillery company in 1776. It is conceivable that this was the same Philip Rose referred to in Mary Rose's recollection and that he was killed as a soldier.

General Washington and his staff continued on their way to South Ferry. They rode by the house of Jeffrey Watson, who lived near South Ferry, about one mile south of Saunderstown. On that day, Watson recorded in his journal, "General Washington Rode by our House with about Twenty Soldiers for a guard about ten o'clock." Colonel Tilghman shows expenses for the South Ferry and the Jamestown Ferry. A French soldier stationed on a French ship in Narragansett Bay wrote in his diary, "This day General Washington, who was expected, arrived about two o'clock. He first went [from the ferry at Jamestown, by the admiral's barge] to the *Duc de Bourgogne* [the flagship], where all the generals were." Von Closen wrote, "All the fleet was decked with flags and saluted him with 13 canon shots.

After a council of war that lasted two hours, General Washington was "taken ashore to the great wharf [in Newport], from which the troops lined the road to M. de Rochambeau's house. The ground batteries saluted him with a dozen canon shots, and the troops rendered him the honors of a marshal of France." South Kingstown diarist "Nailer Tom" Hazard wrote on March 6th, "Generril Washington went to Newport this day. The town was elluminated." The illumination was from candles in house windows of Newport residents to welcome Washington's arrival. Because the seaport was in financial difficulties, the Newport town council purchased the candles for Newport residents to use. When one British sympathizer failed to place candles in his window, outraged patriots began throwing objects to break his windows until he finally joined the rest of his fellow Newport residents by placing lit candles in his windows. General Washington stayed for several days in Newport, dancing with Newport's beautiful Peggy Champlin at an evening ball. General Washington then traveled to Providence and later returned to his headquarters in New Windsor, New York, passing through western Rhode Island in the northern part of the state.

While staying at Potter's tavern in Little Rest, General Washington apparently disclosed to Colonel Potter his need for support from local militia troops. On March 6, 1781, the same day that General Washington and his staff departed Colonel Potter's tavern in Little Rest, the South Kingstown town council met at Colonel Potter's tavern. While the town council was in part basking in the recent glory brought by General Washington's visit, it also had important business to attend to, probably spurred on by Washington himself. The members voted to insure that soldiers who lacked weapons would be so equipped and for cartridge boxes and guns that were stored at a local farm to be obtained for use. Perhaps the town council was stirred to action by Colonel Potter informing it of General Washington's desire for support from local troops. General Washington's goal on his trip to Newport was to persuade Count Rochambeau to have the French fleet leave Newport and engage in actions against the British fleet. During his meeting with Count Rochambeau in Newport, Washington assured Rochambeau that if the French fleet sailed south, the militia of the surrounding countryside could supplement his remaining forces at Newport. The General Assembly was asked to supply 500 soldiers for this purpose at its meeting in Little Rest later in March 1781. In May, the General Assembly responded by ordering one-half the men belonging to the state's independent companies, including the Kingston Reds, and the King's County militia regiments, to be stationed outside Newport on or before June 5, 1781. Lieutenant Colonel Thomas Potter was second-in-command of the militia. The troops camped about four miles outside Newport, remaining there until late August 1781.

"Our Best Blood and Treasure"

Von Closen's concern about keeping a close watch on General Washington during his stay in Little Rest due to "Tories in the neighborhood" was prudent, but was exaggerated. The Rhode Island General Assembly and South Kingstown town council kept a close eye on Tories and continued to punish persons who expressed any support for the British Crown. In January 1781, for example, the General Assembly determined that prominent local lawyer Matthew Robinson had "publickly manifested principles inimical and dangerous to the liberties of the United States of America," and ordered that Robinson "be taken into custody by the sheriff of King's County, and committed to the jail in said county." Robinson's friends (including patriot officers John Waite and John Peck Rathbun) and a letter from a local "Practitioner Physick" on the 72-year old Robinson's poor health, later persuaded the General Assembly to release the lawyer from jail.

In June 1781, Count Rochambeau and his troops left Newport and marched across Connecticut to join the Continental Army threatening the British in New York City. But General Washington changed his plans and joined forces with the French fleet under Comte de Grasse in an effort to trap General Cornwallis in Yorktown, Virginia. Nailer Tom Hazard recorded the results of the allied effort that won the war against the British in a diary entry in October 1781: "Fired guns at Little Rest for the taking of Cornwallis and his army in Virginia." It must have been an exciting day to be in Little Rest.

In October 1781, meeting in Little Rest, the General Assembly voted to change the name of King's County to Washington County, in "perpetual and grateful remembrance" of Washington's "distinguished services and heroic actions." Despite the goal of the "rising republic" to "obliterate" all traces of British royalty, the names of North and South Kingstown went unchanged.

Little Rest villagers were no doubt saddened to learn of the death of John Peck Rathbun. Rathbun was born in Exeter in 1746 and lived in South Kingstown with his wife, Mary. In 1776, he served in the Continental Navy as a first lieutenant under John Paul Jones on the Rhode Island sloop *Providence*. A recent biography of Jones calls Rathbun the most able second-in-command to serve under Jones. Promoted to captain of the sloop, Rathbun and his small crew successfully raided the British outpost in New Providence, Bermuda in January 1778. While captain of a larger vessel, his flotilla of three ships captured eleven British merchant vessels off Newfoundland, Canada, with a value of nearly $1 million. In 1780, Rathbun must have returned to South Kingstown for a brief visit, as he purchased the tavern in Little Rest formerly owned by John Potter, perhaps with his share of the profits from the spoils of the British ships. Later in 1780, Rathbun and his crew went ashore and helped to defend Charleston, South Carolina from a British invasion, until the city fell in May 1781. Taken prisoner, Rathbun was later paroled. Rather than quietly operate his tavern in Little Rest, Rathbun continued to seek action, although no Continental Navy ships were then available for command. He took command of a privateer and set sail for England. Unfortunately, Rathbun and his crew were captured by a larger British vessel after a 24-hour chase. They were imprisoned in the notorious Kinsale Prison in Cork, Ireland, where seventeen crew members died. Rathbun himself died at the notorious Mill Prison in Plymouth, England on June 20, 1782, at the young age of 36.[16]

The town became concerned that Tories would return, some of whom had their property confiscated. In April 1783, at a town meeting in the Court House moderated by Col. Thomas Potter, the town's deputies in the General Assembly were instructed to guard against "Enemies" and "traitors" from introducing "themselves again as Citizens of this State wishing to partake of the Liberties and privileges purchased at the Expense of our best Blood and treasure." But no further actions were taken against Tories. Col. Thomas Potter and some of his militia patrolling the shoreline were awarded cattle, sheep and oxen that they seized on South Kingstown's beaches. The court of common pleas approved the seizures, ruling that the farm stock was intended to have been surreptitiously traded to British forces.

Perhaps the most lasting impact on South Kingstown and other South County towns from the Revolutionary War years was the outlay of "treasure" – the burden of heavy taxation. Prior to the outbreak of the war, South Kingstown typically paid the second highest amount of taxes in the colony. Newport was the wealthiest town in the colony and therefore paid the most taxes; but South Kingstown usually paid more taxes than the colony's rising port, Providence. During the early years of the war, with Newport suffering from British occupation and British ships blockading Narragansett Bay, the state looked to South Kingstown and other rural South County towns to bear the brunt of taxation. In June 1779, South Kingstown deputies protested the amount of taxes apportioned to the town. The town typically was late paying its taxes and satisfying its quota of beef and grain. Frequently, the town meeting requested its deputies to petition the General Assembly "for relief in the burdensome taxes ordered." The General Assembly typically extended the deadline for South County towns to meet their quotas.

Anger in the southern towns boiled over in 1782. In that year, a new tax assessment apportioning taxes among the towns was put into effect,

---

[16] In 1969, the U.S. Navy named a frigate in Rathbun's honor, but misspelled his name as "Rathbourne." In the will that Rathbun signed in the town records, his name is clearly spelled "Rathbun."

showing South Kingstown as the heaviest taxed town in the state. The value of South Kingstown's property was set at £292,300, compared to Providence in a distant second at £217,000. Not only had South Kingstown's share of the tax burden increased, the amount of the tax burden had also increased. According to one historian, in 1782, South Kingstown paid a crippling per capita tax of $2.05, in contrast to an average of $.26 for the period of 1778 to 1789. In January 1782, in a petition to the General Assembly requesting further time to collect a tax, the citizens of South Kingstown cited an unfair tax estimate, the scarcity of cash and the damage caused by British raids as their reasons for not paying in full their share of the tax. South Kingstown and other South County taxpayers were in an uproar. Their agricultural economy, with its dependence on trade by Newport merchants, had been severely disrupted. The bulk of their wealth was in illiquid land and cash was scarce. Yet they were being required to pay heavy taxes in cash.

In April 1782, as a result of a request made by the Charlestown town meeting, a convention of representatives from South County towns was held at the Court House in Little Rest. The delegates to the convention agreed that their towns had been "aggrieved and burthened with heavy Impositions and Assessments." They blamed the new estimate for the circumstance in which many other areas of the state did not contribute as much as they did and yet those regions had "thrice & twice the number of Voices in assessing the same." The delegates adopted a resolution urging the holding of a state constitutional convention in order to rectify the situation. The movement, however, never got off the ground. A similar effort in Little Rest to call for a state convention in 1784 failed.

If a town failed to pay its share of state taxes, the state would bring a lawsuit against the town treasurer and obtain a court order to put him in jail until the tax was paid. In October 1782, the General Assembly became annoyed at South Kingstown's town meeting for relieving some taxpayers of their tax burdens. It authorized villager Col. Thomas Potter, representing the state, to bring a suit against the town treasurer, George Babcock, for the town's failure to pay its taxes. Babcock was alternately placed in jail for the town's failure to pay back taxes and released by the General Assembly on the promise of payment three times in 1782 and 1783. When this occurred, the town typically paid Babcock a fee for each day he spent in jail. In addition, town expenses increased as the town council had to pay more for poor relief for returning soldiers and widows and orphans of killed soldiers. All other South County towns experienced similar problems. South Kingstown and other South County rural voters' deep concern over heavy taxation led to the emergence of a country party that promoted rural interests in South County. This was to have dramatic consequences later in Rhode Island's history.

The Indentured Servitude of Alice Franklin

There were a variety of ways for the South Kingstown town council to deal with poor orphans and illegitimate children from poor parents who could not financially support their children. Indentured servitude was the most common way. The town council "bound out" the child to another family in the town, usually one that wanted help working a farm. Indentured servitude could happen to white, black or Indian children. In addition, the town council often required parents of illegitimate children to pay costs of raising illegitimate children.

In 1773, a poor unmarried black woman in South Kingstown, Hannah Franklin, gave birth to a girl, Alice Franklin. Hannah had already been bound out to a white family until she was able to pay for the money the town council had previously spent on her and her previous children on poor relief. When baby Alice was eighteen months old, the town council ordered Alice to be "Bound Out" to Little Rest Narragansett planter Caleb Gardner. The town council ordered the town treasurer to provide a new suit of clothes for Alice. Why would Gardner agree to this transaction? Once Alice became older, she would be required to work as a servant for Gardner without wages (except for room and board) until she attained age eighteen years when she would be freed. Because Alice was an infant and could not perform services for Gardner for some years, the town council agreed to pay Gardner £6 as an incentive to undertake the indenture. As a condition to the arrangement, the town was no longer obligated to pay for Alice's board, clothing or other expenses.

The indenture did not work out as planned by Gardner. When Alice Franklin was fourteen years old and still Gardner's indentured servant, she gave birth to a son named Cato. In 1787, the town council authorized Gardner to "find a place & put out to board" baby Cato at the town's expense. The bearing of the child at such a young age apparently caused Alice health problems, as she was described as in a "delirious" state at Gardner's house.

In late 1787, Caleb Gardner attempted to solve his problem of an unproductive servant by dropping off Alice at the house of the town's overseer of the poor, Rowse Potter. Gardner explained his action by claiming that Alice had reached the age of eighteen and was now free. In December 1787, Gardner was called to appear before the town council, which was meeting at Robert Potter's tavern in Little Rest. At the meeting, Gardner claimed that Alice, who "is delirious and unable to Support herself," had reached eighteen years of age and therefore was no longer his responsibility to support. However, the town council reviewed its own records and determined that Alice was only fourteen years old. The council then voted to have the town sergeant pick up Alice from Rowse Potter's and "Convey her to Mr.

Caleb Gardner and there deliver her."

Caleb Gardner apparently refused to receive and care for Alice. In January 1788, the town council voted to hire attorney Rowse Helme to bring a lawsuit against Gardner "for the Support of his apprentice Alice Franklin and Her Infant Child." This must have been difficult for the town council to do, as Gardner in previous years had served many terms as a town council member.

Two years later, Alice Franklin must have recovered her health to some extent, as she was living independently and not as a bound servant. In February 1790, the town council decided that seventeen-year old Alice was now "well able to support" her son, Cato. The town council warned that if she refused to support Cato, the council would bind out Alice again as an indentured servant to repay the town its expenses of caring for Cato.

The story of Alice Franklin reveals the manner in which the town leaders controlled poor children. The town council, town sergeant and town overseer of the poor all worked together with the primary goal of reducing the town's costs. They did not have as their primary role the welfare of the children. The story also reveals the difficult circumstances that poor young women with children found themselves in during the 18th century.

Men who were identified as the fathers of "bastard" children were forced in law suits brought by the town to pay for child support. A poor man could also be a victim of this system. For example, in 1811, a man was put in jail on a charge of "bastardy" and the town council ordered him to be "bound out" to a family until he paid for the town's costs of his illegitimate child.

Jemima Wilkinson: Prophet of God and Utopian Leader

Little Rest had in its midst one of the first female religious prophets and utopian leaders in early America. Her name was Jemima Wilkinson. She lived in a time when religion was vitally important to ordinary persons and when many religious sects sought the attention of religious enthusiasts in rural areas.

Wilkinson was born into a Quaker family in Cumberland, Rhode Island, in 1752. She grew up on her father's marginal farm in Cumberland. When Wilkinson was eighteen, she became caught up in the last wave of a religious revival, known as the Great Awakening, when the English evangelical preacher, George Whitefield, visited Rhode Island in 1770. Wilkinson began attending evangelical "New Light" meetings outside the Quaker meeting, which resulted in her expulsion from the Quaker meeting.

In 1776, Wilkinson fell ill with typhoid fever for several days and apparently became unconscious for a short time. When she awoke, Wilkinson declared that she had actually passed through the gates of heaven and had been raised from the dead. She announced that she had a new spirit within her, the "Publick Universal Friend." From that day on, for the next forty-three years, Wilkinson preached to "a dying and sinful world." Wherever she went in southern New England, she attracted large crowds of people, eager to hear her spiritual message, or perhaps curious to see a woman who was a powerful speaker and who claimed to have been raised from the dead. In time, she began to attract a devoted following of men and women, some of whom were financially well off.

Wilkinson's doctrines were similar to those of the Quakers, dwelling on the divinity of all people. Like her contemporary, Ann Lee of the Shaker movement, she advocated celibacy. Wilkinson also advocated pacifism, which was not popular during the war years. She predicted the second-coming of Christ. Disturbingly, a few followers believed that she was the female incarnation of God.

Wilkinson spoke in front of crowds in and near Little Rest that included local elites, not just those on the lower end of the social scale. On November 15, 1778, Daniel Updike, from a prominent North Kingstown planter family, "went to the Hill to hear Miss Wilkinson preach who I liked very well." Two days later, Updike went to the "Hill" again to hear her preach and described the crowd as a "gallery." The "Hill" could have been Little Rest Hill or Tower Hill. "Nailer Tom" Hazard traveled to hear Wilkinson speak in or near Little Rest on March 2, 1779.

In 1778, Wilkinson's persuasive powers led to one of her most important converts, Judge William Potter, one of the most influential men in southern Rhode Island at the time. Potter, a Narragansett planter, inherited a large landed estate from his father, John Potter, who was one of the wealthiest Narragansett planters in the colonial period. William Potter's house and large farm were located about one mile north of Little Rest off North Road. Potter had a distinguished political career, serving several terms in the General Assembly, and several terms as chief justice of the King's County court of common pleas. He also served for many years as a member of the South Kingstown town council and as town clerk. In 1750, Potter married Penelope Hazard, daughter of prominent Narragansett planter Thomas Hazard, in a service presided over by the Anglican minister, the Reverend James MacSparran. But in 1778, both William and Penelope, and several of their children, left the traditional Anglican church and became converts to Jemima Wilkinson.

Ezra Stiles, Newport's accomplished Congregationalist minister, wrote in his diary, "When I was at Narragansett Sept. 24, 1779 I heard much about Jemima who calls herself the *Publick Universal Friend*." Stiles reported that Henry Marchant's wife lodged with William Potter that day and spoke to Potter's daughter, Alice. Stiles wrote that when praying, Alice "addresses the public Friend whom she says is omnipresent, & calls her *Messiah* & herself her *Prophet* – she says Jemima is the *son of God*." Stiles explained the Potter family's unorthodox interest in Wilkinson as a response to a son who had become insane at age 17. (Stiles later reported that Wilkinson herself did not claim that she was the son of god.)

In 1779, William Potter lost both his position as town clerk and his judgeship on the county court of common pleas. Potter's loss of offices probably was the result of a reaction by townsmen against what they perceived to be his unorthodox religious leanings.

Wilkinson's influence on the Potters was felt in many ways. The 1774 census indicated that William Potter had eleven blacks residing at his property, most of whom were likely slaves. Wilkinson opposed slavery and distinctions of color. After joining Wilkinson, Potter began to free his slaves. In certificates of manumission dated March 27, 1780, he gave freedom to two of his slaves, Mingo and Cesaer, with two members of the Universal Friend's society serving as witnesses.

Judge Potter built a large addition of fourteen rooms to his house, which was called by locals "the Abbey." This served as Wilkinson's headquarters of operation for several years. The 1790 Rhode Island census indicates that 14 white persons and 13 free black persons (who probably worked as paid farm workers and domestic servants) resided on Potter's estate. Many of the black persons probably lived in outbuildings away from the "the Abbey." The white persons probably included Wilkinson and a few of her supporters, as well as Judge Potter, his wife Penelope, and some of their elderly children. When traveling, Judge Potter usually rode with

Jemima Wilkinson, Prophet and Utopian Leader (1752-1819). Canvas painting, John L. D. Mathies, 1816. *Yates County Genealogical & Historical Society, Penn Yan, New York.*

Jemima, who rode a horse equipped with white leather straps and a blue velvet saddle, wore white or black flowing robes and a wide brimmed hat, and was accompanied by ten or so of her followers riding two-by-two behind her.

Jemima Wilkinson created controversy in Little Rest and the other towns in which she traveled in southern New England, and similar stories were told in these various towns. In 1780, she reportedly tried to raise from the dead the recently deceased twenty-two year old daughter of Judge Potter. Wilkinson reportedly blamed her failure on the lack of faith of the crowd. On another occasion, Wilkinson claimed that she could duplicate Christ's feat of walking on water. On the appointed day, with many spectators, she proceeded to Biscuit City Pond (some stories say it was Larkin's Pond or other local ponds), where she said she would perform the promised miracle. Upon reaching the water's edge, she abandoned the attempt, explaining to the crowd that its lack of faith was the reason she had failed.

In another instance, at the North Ferry in South Kingstown near Saunderstown, Wilkinson reportedly tried to bring a recently deceased disciple back to life. She said that he would rise from the dead on the third day. On the appointed day, she had the body brought out into the yard in order to show everyone the miracle. Some patriot soldiers were in the crowd, and their captain, who wanted proof that the man was dead, requested permission to drive his sword through the body. After this request was made, the "corpse" sprang to life and ran into the house, dragging the sheet that had been laid on him in his coffin behind him.

One story about Wilkinson that circulated in South Kingstown was almost certainly a fabrication. It is repeated here to demonstrate the concern and jealousy that townspeople had about a woman who had assumed a position of such power. One day, Jemima Wilkinson was visiting Judge Potter, who was feeling poorly and in need of spiritual comfort. The Judge's wife, who had been away when Jemima arrived at the house, came home unexpectedly and found Wilkinson in her husband's bedchamber, in rather close proximity to the ailing jurist. Wilkinson said that it was all right for God's lambs to love one another, because her religion believed in love. Mrs. Potter cut her off abruptly. "Minister to your lambs all you want," the angry woman was supposed to have said, "but in the future, please leave my old ram alone!" This story was told even though Wilkinson advocated celibacy and had attracted a following of women, as well as men. Indeed, Penelope Potter, the Judge's wife, was even more devoted to Wilkinson than Judge Potter himself.

The story goes that Jemima Wilkinson was forced out of Rhode Island and moved to upstate New York. She was obviously a source of controversy, a woman in a world dominated by men, yet having men under her sway. In addition, many interpreted her claim of death and resurrection as a blasphemous attempt to duplicate the feat of Jesus Christ. Furthermore, Wilkinson's advocacy of a curious brand of celibacy was blamed for breaking up marriages. However, it may simply have been the case that in moving to upstate New York, Wilkinson was seeking to attain her dream of establishing a utopian colony of her own followers. In 1786, Wilkinson sent a member to explore upstate New York. In 1788, twenty-five members of her church (including Stephen Card who lived just west of Little Rest) founded a new town in upstate New York in the wilderness region of Genesee County. In 1790, Wilkinson, Judge Potter and her other remaining followers departed Little Rest and moved to the new town in New York state, which at the time had 260 residents.

Wilkinson wanted to develop a community far from persons outside her sect. She did not want any distinctions of wealth and foresaw a community whose residents owned land in common. But land speculators became interested in the town. In response, Wilkinson moved her sect even further west, founding New Jerusalem.

The utopian community developed friction caused in part by Judge Potter's greed for land. Potter's disagreements with Wilkinson led him to resign from the sect. Before he resigned, he secured papers from many of the town's settlers releasing all their lands to him, possibly because he had helped fund the original purchases of the land. Potter then sued Wilkinson in court for blasphemy, but lost when the judge noted that Potter must have been blasphemous as well since he had been a devoted follower. Potter sued Wilkinson again, this time for ejectment from the land. At trial Wilkinson won by producing a document with signatures from all of her followers that established that control of the lands stayed with Wilkinson. Judge Potter left the courtroom in disgrace with a large bill of court costs to pay. Still, Judge Potter reportedly acquired about 16,000 acres of land in the Genesee country.

Potter's house in New Jerusalem became the center of the town's anti-Wilkinson feelings. Eventually Potter returned to his farm north of Little Rest, leaving his wife Penelope behind. But he found that townspeople still resented his behavior. Running short of money, he returned to New Jerusalem. Before he died in 1814, Potter and Wilkinson reportedly reconciled their differences. Wilkinson passed away in 1819 at age 68. Elisha R. Potter, Sr. acquired the Abbey and its surrounding farm from William Potter's son, but he did not preserve the mansion, elegant gardens, fruit orchard and high fences, which quickly fell into ruins.

The Execution of Thomas Mount

Capital punishment was not unknown in Little Rest and the rest of South County in colonial times. In 1751, a stranger to South Kingstown, Thomas Carter, robbed and killed a Virginia merchant, William Jackson. Carter was convicted of the crime and was hung before a large crowd at Tower Hill (then the county seat of government). Carter's body was then placed in a gibbet and left to rot, as a means of terrorizing others from committing a like crime. In 1770, Little Rest silversmith Samuel Casey was convicted of counterfeiting and sentenced to hang until dead, but he escaped the gallows when villagers dramatically freed him from the Little Rest jail.

In 1771, a North Kingstown black slave, Caesar Hazard, killed a white laborer by striking him in the head with a hedge stake. Hazard reportedly fled the scene after the violent encounter. Hazard was caught by authorities, incarcerated at the Little Rest jail, charged with attempted murder, and put on trial at the Little Rest Court House. The October trial "took up the greatest Part of the day," but it took the jury only fifteen minutes to return with a guilty verdict. The judges sentenced Hazard to "be hanged by the neck until he be Dead Dead" on November 15, 1771. A gallows was built in Little Rest, a hangman was hired, and six townsmen were hired to view the public execution. Hazard escaped from the jail, was caught again, and ultimately was hung in Little Rest. The case would not be remarkable if it was a death sentence in response to a true murder. Given that Hazard was a slave, we do not know if he was acting in self-defense, perhaps in response to a threatened lashing. The court record does not indicate the grounds of his defense.

Thomas Mount was also hanged in Little Rest. What makes this event extraordinary was the crime that led to his death sentence: burglary. The crime of burglary does not seem particularly egregious in the modern world, and even then many questioned whether it was a hanging offense. While burglary was a hanging offense under Rhode Island statutes, it was rarely applied by the courts. Rhode Island's list of capital crimes included arson, rape, robbery, burglary, as well as murder. Mount's death caused Rhode Islanders to question this harsh punishment in the case of petty crimes.

The 27-year old Mount was caught stealing from a store in Hopkinton, Rhode Island, and was tied to earlier thefts in Newport. He was sent to the Newport jail, probably because at the time the Washington County jail in Little Rest was in poor condition and was easy to break out of, and Mount was a known jail breaker. While confined in jail, and after his conviction at trial and death sentence, Mount decided to write his "confession." He admitted to numerous acts of theft. Perhaps Mount wrote the remarkable document in the hope that his honest account and repentance would win sympathetic support and perhaps a reprieve from the death sentence by the state governor. Or perhaps Mount simply felt a need to unburden himself before he met his fate.

According to Thomas Mount, he was born in 1764 in New Jersey, the son of unmarried parents. He began a life of crime when he moved to New York by playing truant and "upon Sundays especially was fond of doing mischief such as robbing orchards and spreading my wicked example among all the boys I could get acquainted with." In the Revolutionary War, seeking enlistment bounties, he joined the Continental Army, later deserted to join the British ranks, and then returned to patriot ranks. Tiring of the army, Mount left for the sea where he led a life of securing advance pay and "jumping" ships. For the next twelve years, back on land, he engaged in thefts, robberies, and house and jail breakings throughout the colonies. For one act of theft, he was given 100 lashes and 25 more for "giving the court saucy answers." He then came to Newport where he engaged in further thefts, until he came to Hopkinton, where he was caught stealing. Here is Mount's own account from his "confession."

> Next night Stanton, Williams, and I set off to break into Joseph Potter's store; I broke open a mill and took a crowbar out of it, and we all three went in, I first, and they following, I being most forward in this business. I lighted a candle and handed down the goods, about several hundred dollars worth, and some money, two or three dollars, and carried them to Stanton's house, where we divided them into three parts and cast lots. Williams and I took our shares, after giving Stanton out of my share 8 or 9 pounds worth of goods for a mare, and hiding the goods under two corn stalks and under a barn about five miles from Stanton's house, we set off for Voluntown, there were apprehended and brought back to Hopkinton, where Stanton, I and my wife were tried for breaking open the mill; Stanton's wife and Williams were admitted as State's evidence. Accordingly I was sentenced to receive 20 lashes and my wife 10 (although she was innocent). I paid the fine by giving up part of my clothes, then committed to Newport gaol, tried for breaking Potter's shop, found guilty, and received the sentence of death.
> —And the Lord have mercy upon me.

The trial of the accused was held in Newport in 1791. One of his attorneys was Elisha Reynolds Potter, Sr., the prominent citizen of Little Rest. Potter apparently assisted Mount on humanitarian grounds. Potter's efforts were to no avail, as the jury convicted him. The death penalty was rarely imposed by Rhode Island judges for the crime of burglary. An unfortunate man had been convicted of burglary and hanged in Newport in 1764, but he had been the last. Shockingly, the three-judge panel sentenced Mount to "be hanged by the Neck till he be dead." They were likely influenced by the high value of goods stolen – "several hundred dollars worth" of goods, according to Mount. Such a theft may have resulted in the bankruptcy of the storeowner, Joseph Potter. Mount's accomplice, Joseph Stanton, also received a death sentence.

Both Mount and Stanton filed petitions for pardons with the General Assembly. Stanton's petition was granted, but Mount's was not. Perhaps the General Assembly felt that Mount was beyond redemption and applied an early and harsh form of the "three strikes and you are out" rule. In the trial, Mount also failed to show remorse, which did not help his cause.

Mount was ordered back to the Newport jail, where he tried two jail breaks. One attempt failed due to Mount's "unaccountable absence of mind." Mount reacted, "I have broke every Prison in which I hitherto have been confined – but defeated twice – in this I see the Hand of God."

Four days before his execution, Washington County deputy sheriff Robert Sands transported Mount and his wife Catherine to the Little Rest jail (Sands, from Little Rest, also helped to capture Mount). Sheriff Beriah Brown and jailer William Wilson Pollack took no chances. They hired about a dozen men to guard against a last-minute escape by Mount. Elisha Potter, to his credit, spent Mount's last night with Mount to hearten his spirits.

Many people thought that execution was too harsh a penalty for burglary. This feeling seems quite evident from the following account in the *United States Chronicle*, a Providence newspaper, dated June 16, 1791.

> Passing over many Things relative to his Behavior while in prison at Little Rest, and during the Interval of his leaving the Prison, and going to the Place of Execution, suffice it to be remarked, that firm to the last, his Mind averted from Sublimary Things and steadfastly fixed on God and ascending up to Heaven in Holy Extacy of Prayer he declared his "willingness to be offered up a Sacrifice to divine & human Justice—he forgave all men in Hopes of finding Forgiveness with God"—and after he was turned off—he was distinctly heard to breath his last in prayer— "Lord have mercy on me—Lord"—here he was suffocated.

> Multitudes mourned and bewailed him—No triumph over his melancholy end disgraced the feelings of humanity—for the space of a quarter of an hour nothing was to be heard but prayers mixed with sighs and groans. Every face displayed the signs of being affected with the solemnities of his death and most tender sympathies of woe trickled down almost every cheek.

The place of execution reportedly was about one-quarter mile below the Court House down Little Rest Hill. (This was probably the same location where Caesar Hazard was hanged in 1771.) Reportedly, Mount was buried close by and his grave was visible as late as 1869, but his gravesite now is unknown.

Here is a poignant poem written by Thomas Mount in his "confession":

> Thomas Mount it is my name
> And to my shame cannot deny;
> In New Jersey I was born,
> And on Little Rest now must die.

Mount's execution apparently caused some judges and the General Assembly (which could and did grant pardons) to be more reluctant to impose the death penalty in cases of burglary and other property crimes. From 1798 to 1831, there were no executions by the state of Rhode Island, although there were many instances of criminals convicted of burglary. This leniency shown by judges and the General Assembly came too late for Thomas Mount.

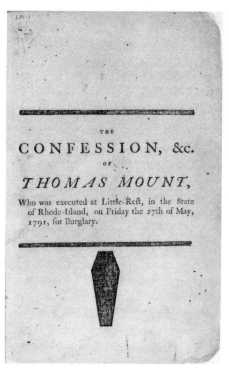

Cover of "The Confession of Thomas Mount." Pamphlet, unknown artist, 1791. *Rhode Island Historical Society, RHi X3 7655.*

Little Rest in the Census of 1790: Slavery, Freedom and Family

Set forth below is a list of Little Rest residents in 1790:

	White Males	White Females	Free Blacks	Black Slaves	Total
Charles Barker	5	3	1		9
Hannah Champlin		2		1	3
William Case Clark	4	3			7
Abe Cottrell	5	4			9
David Douglass	6	1			7
Elisha Gardner	1	3			4
Sarah Gardner		2			2
James Helme	5	3	2		10
William Lunt	3	3			6
John Nichols	6				6
George Peckham	6	3			9
Timothy Peckham	3	2	1		6
William W. Pollack	7	2	1		10
Elisha Potter	3	2	1		6
Thomas Potter	2	4	3		9
William Potter	3	3			6
Col. Robert Potter & Dr. Shearman	6	4		5	15
Elisha Reynolds	1			4	5
Henry Reynolds	3	2		1	6
Robert G. Sands	2	2		1	5
George Teft	3	6			9
John L. Totten	2	1			3
John Waite	2	5			7
John Weeden	4	4			8
Joseph Stanton	2	4	2		8
West Cross (Negro)			4		4
John Larkin	1	4			5
TOTALS	85	72	15	12	183

The above list is made possible primarily by the federal census of 1790, which is in the order of the houses of where the census takers found them. The Little Rest residents as recorded in the 1790 Rhode Island census are set forth above in alphabetical order by last name, except for the last three entries.

What jumps out at the reader first from viewing the 1790 census is that in Little Rest there continued to be some black persons held as slaves. The ideas underlying the American Revolution ultimately would lead many Narragansett planters to free their slaves, but the transformation was not immediate. Once the Revolutionary War ended, the General Assembly finally turned its attention to important deferred non-military matters. Led by Moses Brown from Providence, an emancipation bill was proposed in 1784. Still, in a show of self-interest, the South Kingstown town meeting in February 1784 voted to oppose enactment of any emancipation law by the General Assembly. Nonetheless, an emancipation bill did pass in 1784 providing that any black person born after March 1, 1784 was to be considered a free person. This meant that black persons born before 1784 continued to be slaves.

In South Kingstown, 1790 census takers reported 180 slaves and 468 non-white free persons. From the 1774 and 1790 censuses, the number of slaves in Little Rest decreased only by six, from 18 to 12. This indicates that Little Rest inhabitants were somewhat slow to free their slaves. But the new moral environment did lead some slaveholders to free their slaves when they did not have to in the case of slaves born before 1784.

In the 1790 census, the following Little Rest white persons were recorded as holding slaves: Elisha Reynolds (4); Colonel Robert Potter (5); Henry Reynolds (1); Robert Sands (1); and Hannah Champlin (1). Hannah Champlin, described as a widow in the census, probably used her slave as a domestic servant. Robert Sands operated a tavern (the current Kingston Inn), using his slave to help run the business. Elisha Reynolds was the only white person in his household, which included two female and two male black slaves. Of the five Little Rest slaveholders in 1774: Elisha Reynolds continued to hold four slaves; Henry Reynolds went from three slaves to one in 1790; Robert Potter continued to hold five slaves; Thomas Potter, who held three slaves in 1774, had three free black servants in 1790; Timothy Peckham, who likely had one black slave in 1774, had one free black servant in 1790.

In addition to black slaves, the 1790 census indicates that there were 15 free black persons in Little Rest. There was one independent household of four free black persons headed by a free black man, West Cross. The 1790 census takers had a tendency to go in order of houses. Joseph Stanton, who was listed immediately before Cross's name in the census, lived in the former John Potter cottage just before Biscuit City Road. Land purchase records indicate that in 1783, Joseph Stanton and John Cross purchased the tannery business. They operated the tannery business, but John Cross apparently departed from the area shortly thereafter. It is likely that West Cross was a slave owned by John Cross and that he remained in Little Rest, perhaps was given his freedom, and was employed by Stanton in the tannery business. West Cross was thus able to reside in his own house with his family nearby to the tannery. In addition to Cross, eleven other free blacks lived with white families, as paid servants. Joseph Stanton employed two other free blacks in his tannery business who resided in his house. Charles Barker, Thomas Potter and Timothy Peckham were tavern keepers who probably used their black servants (five in the aggregate) to help operate their tavern businesses.

It must have distressed the village's free black persons to know that about half their number continued to be held as slaves in the village. Free blacks and black slaves did not live in the same household. Slaveholders probably felt that that would result in discipline problems with slaves.

There were two Indians in the household of Timothy Peckham and one incarcerated in the jail. The Indians likely were from the Narragansett tribe. Peckham's servants probably were bound out to him, required to work off debts until they were repaid. By law, Indians could not be enslaved.

The 1790 census indicates that the population of the village increased by about one-third, increasing from about 126 in 1774 to 183 in 1790. The village was in a growth phase. The number of persons in each household was 6.53, compared to 8.4 in 1774. The number of whites per household (not including Cross's) was 6.63 in 1790, compared to 6.93 in 1774. Most of the white male heads of households were or would become freemen, able to vote in town and state elections. Seven of them voted against ratification of the U.S. Constitution in Rhode Island's vote in 1788.

A few individual listings stand out. John Nichols had six white males living in his household, with five listed as under 16 years old. Nichols was a saddlemaker who also operated a boarding house, including for out-of-town students attending the village's one-room school. A total of 15 persons lived in Colonel Robert Potter's and Dr. Shearman's household. Potter operated a tavern and farmed land as well. William Wilson Pollack kept the jail.

Outside Little Rest, but close by up North Road, several white men had blacks residing in their households. Narragansett planter William Potter maintained a household of 27 persons – 14 whites and 13 blacks. The whites included Potter's family, but also likely included Jemima Wilkinson and some of her followers. Wilkinson, Potter and other followers departed for upstate New York later in 1790, as described in an earlier chapter. The 13 black persons were all free, compared to 1774 when they were likely mostly slaves. As discussed previously, the Jemima Wilkinson influenced Potter to free his slaves. In addition, Narragansett planter Caleb Gardner had a household of 18 persons – 7 whites, 7 black slaves, and 4 non-white servants (either free black or Indian servants). The laborers may have included persons residing at Gardner's farm bordering Little Rest, as well as persons residing at Gardner's farm to the west of Little Rest. Furthermore, a short way up North Road from Little Rest, farmers Benjamin Peckham and Josephus Peckham (Benjamin's son) each had four slaves.

The Rise of the Country Party and the Failure of
Rhode Island to Ratify the U.S. Constitution in Little Rest in 1790

Why was Rhode Island the last of the original thirteen states to ratify the United States Constitution? By July 26, 1788, Rhode Island was one of two states that had failed to ratify the Constitution. On November 21, 1789, Rhode Island became the last holdout. A Rhode Island convention did not even meet until March 1790, when it met in Little Rest. Supporters did not have, however, sufficient votes to ratify the Constitution at this convention in Little Rest. The reason for the failure relates to the emergence of a country party in the agricultural towns in Rhode Island, led by towns in South County. The farmers in South County suffered financially during the American Revolution, and after the war they suffered under the weight of heavy taxation to repay war debts.   Farmers feared direct taxation of their lands and otherwise felt threatened. They did not see any advantage to joining the union of states. This would not be the first time that rural interests in South County would influence important events in Rhode Island. This time, however, it had national implications.

Rhode Island always had an individualistic streak during the colonial era. It was founded by Roger Williams on the then radical notion of religious tolerance. Its government was never closely controlled by Britain and was not formed under a royal charter. Its merchants developed a tradition of evading British trade laws, becoming renowned for smuggling. For these reasons, Rhode Island was a leader in the revolutionary movement against Britain, as demonstrated by the burning of the British revenue schooner, *Gaspee,* in 1772. Rhode Island was the first colony to declare independence from the Crown, two months before the Continental Congress did so in July 1776.

An indication that Rhode Island would continue its independent streak occurred in 1781. When the Continental Congress sought to improve the credit of the new nation by amending the Articles of Confederation to permit collection of a five percent import duty, Rhode Island alone of all the thirteen states refused ratification. Rhode Island merchants feared that such a tax would unfairly burden the state, which was heavily dependent on foreign trade.   In addition, Rhode Island farmers feared that if the national government was given the power to tax, it would ultimately tax their farmland. Due to Rhode Island's holdout, the effort to strengthen the national government failed. A legislator in the Continental Congress declared, "the cursed state ought to be erased out of the Confederation, and I was going to say out of the earth, if any worse place could be found for them." Even Thomas Paine, the radical pamphleteer, spent part of the winter of 1782 in Providence attempting in vain to convince the public of the common sense in giving Congress the taxing power.

During the Revolutionary War, many state legislatures were dominated by radical democrats. After the war, in a reaction to the perceived chaos engendered by excesses of democracy, these states turned to more traditional, conservative elitist leaders. Such men tended to support a stronger national government. Rhode Island, however, did not experience such a reaction. Instead, its government beginning in 1786 became dominated by the Country party, led by the brilliant Jonathan J. Hazard of Charlestown. Hazard was a "natural orator" who was "ingenious in debate" and was a politician who had no match in the state. He used his skills to blame merchants for the distressing times of 1784 to 1786.

The rise of the Country party in Rhode Island was the first time that farmers saw themselves as having a separate interest that needed defending and the first time that agricultural interests banded together as a political force. The rise of power of the Country party in part was due to the decline of the strength of merchants in Rhode Island. Newport in particular had been devastated during the war. In addition, the interests of Rhode Island merchants and farmers on the national impost issue began to diverge. Although Rhode Island merchants had initially opposed the effort by the national government to obtain a taxing power, between 1783 and 1786, merchants began to see that a national tax would be preferable to multiple tax schemes by the many states.

A key factor leading to the emergence of the Country party as a party promoting rural interests was the disruption and decline of farming in South County during and after the American Revolution. Prior to the American Revolution, the Narragansett planters had built a successful commercial farming economy, with their large estates producing surplus dairy products, horses and other products for trade to Newport merchants, who shipped them to eager markets in the West Indies and the American South. But by 1775, the Narragansett planters were already experiencing a decline, in large part due to the division of their estates among younger sons. The Revolutionary War hastened the downfall of the Narragansett planters, due to the burden of heavy taxation, the decline of Newport as a commercial center, and, significantly, the loss of British markets in the West Indies during the war for what surplus goods they had. The decline in agriculture also affected all farmers, not just Narragansett planters.

South County farmers expressed their frustration through the state's tax policies. During the American Revolution, with Newport devastated and Providence merchants bottled up by British naval forces for much of the war, South County towns bore the brunt of taxation. As the wealthiest agricultural town, with fine soil and proximity to seaports, South Kingstown became the heaviest taxed town in the state in 1782. Yet it had great difficulty meeting its obligations and frequently appealed for relief from the General Assembly.

Most of South Kingstown's wealth was tied up in land, which could not easily be converted to cash to pay taxes. In 1780, for example, 86 percent of South Kingstown's estimated taxable value was in land. In 1782 and 1784, South County towns held two conventions in the Little Rest Court House with the goal of changing the state's system of taxation and representation, but the efforts failed.

After the Revolutionary War, Rhode Island, with other states, had assumed a portion of the national debt incurred to finance American war efforts. Rhode Island's share was more than £120,000. Rhode Island also had incurred its own state debts. South County farmers became alarmed as they saw a decline in their incomes and at the same time an increase in their obligation to pay their share of interest on the state's debt. In fact, South Kingstown, embarrassingly, often could not meet its tax obligations, with the result that the state incarcerated the town's treasurer in the Little Rest jail. In Rhode Island, the taxes were actually assessed and collected by the towns, and when a town was delinquent the state treasurer would bring suit against the town treasurer and send him to jail. To be a town treasurer in Rhode Island in the period following the Revolution was a hazardous occupation. Before anyone would accept the position, it was customary for the town to agree on a fee which the town treasurer would receive for each day he might have to spend in jail. Records show that the South Kingstown town treasurer was jailed in the Little Rest jail as early as 1774 and as late as 1787. George Babcock served as the town treasurer for much of this period and therefore spent a considerable amount of time in jail. He was jailed four times between 1785 and 1787. In 1788, Babcock submitted a bill to the town meeting for the astounding amount of £512 for "lying in Jail in the years 1785 & 1786 . . . ." Other towns in South County had similar difficulties. South County farmers also were concerned that the increasing debt load could result in increasing taxation of their lands. While a farmer may have owned a good amount of land, it was difficult to convert the land into cash to pay taxes. To make matters worse, the debt was largely held by a few wealthy Providence merchants. In effect, through the government as an intermediary that imposed taxes, ordinary farmers had to pay principal and interest to a few wealthy merchants who were making a healthy return on their investments.

In this heated environment, farmers in Rhode Island, and in particular in South County, began to view their rural economy and lifestyle as a separate interest from the commercial, urban interests of Newport and Providence. They became attracted by the ideas of Jonathan Hazard, the scion of a prominent Charlestown family and tax collector of the town, who promoted a plan among South County farmers to issue paper money that would ease the payment of the state debt and debts owed by farmers. Rhode Island farmers created the Country party. In the Spring elections of 1786, led by Jonathan

Hazard, the Country party swept into power. The election transformed the Rhode Island government from the merchant dominated government that it had been during the colonial era to one dominated by rural interests.

Once in power, Jonathan Hazard pushed through the General Assembly his bold plan authorizing the issuance of new paper money. The paper money was backed by mortgages on the land of farmers. The paper money could be borrowed only by those who owned real property worth twice the sum of the loan. The loan was to remain outstanding for fourteen years, bearing interest at a rate of four percent. The paper money was to be distributed to the towns in proportion to the tax each town owed.

Little Rest's Colonel Thomas Potter, a Country party supporter, vowed that the value of the paper money would be "equal to gold." This vow was not met. The value of the paper money was not worth its face on the open market, declining to a value of about eight cents on the dollar. Creditors would sometimes hide in their basements or even leave the state in order to avoid being paid. The General Assembly then adopted a rule that debts could be repaid by leaving payment with the county court or a justice of the peace. George Washington called Rhode Island's policies at that time "scandalous," and James Madison condemned it for political "wickedness and folly." While controversial with creditors and New England merchants, the paper money in fact enabled Rhode Island to pay off its entire war debt by 1789 and enabled farmers to pay their debts to creditors and pay their state taxes. The paper money issue worked well for Rhode Island farmers, and played a role in insuring that they did not follow the lead of the Massachusetts farmers in the Shays' Rebellion in 1786.

The paper money plan was popular in South Kingstown. The South Kingstown town meeting (as usual, held at the Court House) in July 1786 "without a dissention" instructed its delegates to oppose the plan, perhaps as a result of lobbying by Newport merchants, whom South Kingstown farmers traditionally followed. But after seeing the support for the paper money plan in the other South County towns, those instructions were reversed. By September 1786, South Kingstown became a firm advocate of the paper money system and the Country party. Rowse Helme, a well-respected attorney who often appeared in Little Rest, opposed the paper money plan in the General Assembly. Despite his prominence and his holding several statewide offices in the Revolutionary War, the voters of South Kingstown punished Helme by refusing to re-elect him to the General Assembly.

The national movement to create a stronger central government resulted in the drafting of the United States Constitution, which Congress sent to the states for ratification on September 28, 1787. Every state but Rhode Island elected a ratifying convention in 1787 and 1788. By July 1788, eleven states had ratified the Constitution, with only Rhode Island and North

Carolina as the holdouts. Between November 1787 and October 1789, the General Assembly expressly rejected calling a convention seven times.

Rhode Island did submit the Constitution to its town meetings in the only popular vote held on whether to ratify the Constitution in any of the original thirteen states. In a vote boycotted by most Federalist supporters of the Constitution, who complained of the irregular procedure, the voters rejected it 2,711 to 239. Had the vote included the Federalists, Rhode Island voters probably still would have rejected the Constitution by a wide margin. In Little Rest at the Court House, on March 4, 1788, South Kingstown freemen held a town meeting, with Col. Thomas Potter serving as moderator, to vote on the adoption of the U.S. Constitution. The debate must have been one-sided. Out of the 124 town voters, only one supported the adoption of the constitution. The lone supporter was Joseph Perkins, the Little Rest merchant, shopkeeper, silversmith and landowner. Perhaps Perkins was influenced in his outlook by his close contacts with the suppliers for his store -- Newport merchants, who tended to support adoption of the U.S. Constitution and who thought that ratification would help their commercial businesses. Perkins was also the wealthiest villager and held a note payable to him by the state of Rhode Island in the amount of £363. Those villagers voting against adoption were Elisha Potter (apprentice attorney), Timothy Peckham (tavern keeper and landowner), Henry Reynolds (farmer), John Weeden (leatherworker) and John Larkin (mill owner).

Pressure on Rhode Island to ratify the Constitution increased as North Carolina ratified it on November 21, 1789. But Rhode Islanders resisted the pressure. Rural voters were quite satisfied with local control of the state government and the paper money policy. This meant that the threat of heavy taxation of the lands could be contained. In 1788, a Rhode Island farmer reported that with light taxes and the use of taxes to pay down the greatest part of the state debt, conditions in the state for farmers had never been better. Rhode Islanders were also concerned about domination by the larger states, and were perfectly content acting independently. They had a tradition of being close to their elected leaders, with annual elections of state legislators and officers, which tradition would be undermined by the U.S. Constitution. In addition, the state's influential Quaker community was concerned about the recognition of slavery in the Constitution itself. The Constitution implicitly assented to slavery through three clauses – the 3/5ths representation clause, the fugitive slave clause, and the 20-year ban on the slave trade (with no ban on slavery itself).

The pressure on Rhode Island continued to build. Advocates of the Constitution warned that the United States would invade Rhode Island and partition it between Massachusetts and Connecticut. Rhode Islanders were embarrassed that George Washington had avoided Rhode Island during his fall tour of New England in 1789 to celebrate ratification by the other New England states. Even Jonathan Hazard and Governor John Collins had secretly agreed that the time for ratification had come, as the paper money scheme had achieved the goal of turning around the state's finances. Still, the South Kingstown town meeting on October 12, 1789 instructed its deputies (including Hazard) to oppose the calling of a convention, "there being but one vote for a Convention" (i.e., the popular vote held in 1788).

Ominously, Congress voted to enact a tax on all Rhode Island goods exported to other states that were not of Rhode Island "growth or manufacture." Governor Collins managed to persuade Congress to suspend the tax "until the first day of April next, and no longer." Hazard and his friends had to do something. Hazard, Collins and others steered through the General Assembly a resolution calling for a ratifying convention to meet in Little Rest on March 1, 1790. The bill was introduced by Henry Marchant, a prominent Newport Federalist who would later move to an estate in South Kingstown. Even this action barely succeeded, as Governor Collins courageously incurred the wrath of Country party voters by breaking a tied vote in order to pass the resolution. Rural voters never forgave Collins for his perceived treachery, which effectively ended Collins' career in politics.

Just prior to the convention in Little Rest, Vice President John Adams confided to Federalist merchants in Providence that he was "really much affected at the obstinate infatuation of so great a part of the People of Rhode Island." He admonished, "If the Convention should reject the Constitution or adjourn without adopting it, Congress will probably find it necessary to treat them as they are, Foreigners . . . ."

Little Rest wanted to be a good host for the convention. At a town meeting at the Court House in February, Robert Potter was instructed to "have the lower part of the Court House cleared out and proper seats erected for the Inception of the Convention which is to meet here the first of March next . . . ." Village blacksmith David Douglas agreed to serve as a waiter and courier for delegates.[17]

In this heated atmosphere, about 70 Rhode Island delegates traveled by horseback to Little Rest in early March 1790 for the state convention to vote to ratify the Constitution. Henry Marchant, the Newport Federalist leader, two weeks before the session convened wrote a letter expressing his

---

[17] In Theodore Foster's *Minutes of the Convention,* at p. 61, it is reported that a committee to draft amendments to the Constitution "sent Word by Mr. Douglass the Waiter that they will report in 15 minutes." Douglass, a village blacksmith, frequently served as a waiter and handyman at sessions of the General Assembly. He also tended the fire in the fireplace and lit candles for evening sessions. For his work at the convention, Douglass was paid £27.

doubts that the delegates were ready to vote in favor of ratification. "The Antis are about ten majority. I have hopes however they will not totally reject the Constitution but I think they may adjourn it over our Gen[eral] Election," which was to be held in April.

If the convention had voted at the session in Little Rest, it likely would have soundly rejected the Constitution. Little Rest would have been known for making a different sort of history. Instead, Hazard and other Country party leaders, convinced that ratification was necessary, steered the convention to proposing amendments, then to adjournment in order to let the voters in the towns express their views in the upcoming general election.

At three o'clock in the afternoon on Monday, March 1, 1790, the 70 delegates began their deliberations on the U.S. Constitution in the Little Rest Court House. The anti-federalists showed their strength by electing one of their own, Daniel Updike of North Kingstown, to keep the official minutes of the convention. His record, however, is incomplete. Theodore Foster, a delegate from Providence who supported the Constitution, kept a more detailed account of the proceedings. The major points of discussion during the six-day convention were the allocation of representatives, direct taxation, the slave trade, the method of adopting future amendments, the ratification of the congressionally proposed Bill of Rights, and the power of the convention to adopt the Constitution. The convention adopted a "declaration of rights" and advanced eighteen other amendments. Hazard and his allies wanted to adjourn the convention and have these amendments sent to the voters of the towns for consideration. They did not want to vote in favor of or against ratification of the Constitution until they were returned to power in the upcoming April elections. Thus, Hazard and his allies agreed to attempt to adjourn the convention until late April or early May.

On Saturday, March 6th, Henry Marchant rose in the Little Rest Court House and moved for the delegates to ratify the U.S. Constitution. An anti-federalist delegate instead moved to adjourn the convention. After a spirited debate, the convention voted 41-28 to adjourn the convention. It was later voted for the convention to meet in Newport on May 24th. The vote margin was probably a fair indication at the convention of the relative strength of the supporters for and against the Constitution.

The Country party held a meeting at the Little Rest Court House and selected its slate of candidates for the April elections, minus Governor Collins. The April elections again showed the solid support of the Country party. Nevertheless, pressure mounted on Rhode Island to ratify the Constitution. Despite the pressure, in a town meeting in Little Rest in May, South Kingstown continued to oppose ratification. But on May 28, 1790, at the meeting of the convention in Newport, the convention ratified the Constitution by the bare majority of 34-32. President George Washington made a special visit to Newport and Providence in August 1790 to celebrate Rhode Island's entry into the union. He arrived by ship in Newport harbor on August 17, 1790, traveled to Providence through Bristol, and left the state by ship, thus avoiding having one last "little rest" in Little Rest.

While Little Rest did not obtain the honor of hosting Rhode Island's ratification, it did acquire another honor. At the March convention in Little Rest, the delegates adopted the Bill of Rights, which was close to ratification by the number of states needed to add them as amendments to the U. S. Constitution. The delegates also adopted an additional twenty-one proposed amendments, some of which had been adopted by other states, but a few of which were unique to Rhode Island. During the convention's proceedings in Little Rest, the slave trade provision and other slavery references in the Constitution provoked considerable opposition among antislavery delegates. Some delegates even questioned whether they could personally bring themselves to vote for the U. S. Constitution due to this problem. Other delegates, while expressing unhappiness with the slavery references in the Constitution, realized that the Constitution was a compromise and that the southern states would never enter the union if the slavery references were entirely eliminated from the Constitution. A majority of delegates, however, proposed and adopted an amendment exhorting Congress to ban the slave trade immediately. Rhode Island was the only state to suggest such an amendment to the federal Constitution during the ratification struggle.

The power of the agricultural interests in South County to prevent Rhode Island from adopting the U.S. Constitution in March 1790 in Little Rest was wielded for all of the nation to see. In future years, Little Rest would continue to play a key role in the defense of South County's agricultural interests at the state level.

III. LITTLE REST IN THE EARLY REPUBLIC:

THE GOLDEN AGE,

(1792-1825)

Coastline Scene at South Ferry, Narragansett (formerly part of South Kingstown). The Potter family owned a one-half interest in the ferry and interests in sloops that operated from here. South Ferry was the location where local farmers often sent their surplus for export and where Little Rest general store owners received imports of supplies and goods. James B. M. Potter built the church in the background that still stands today. Lithograph, J. P. Newell, undated, 1860. *Rhode Island Historical Society,* RHi X3 4898.

A Picture of Little Rest in the Early 1800s

Economic Decline in South County and
Golden Age in Little Rest

Little Rest in the early 19th century (its name was changed to Kingston in 1825) enjoyed its golden age. In colonial times, Little Rest had been the hub of the Narragansett country. It was an important village in the county, but the Narragansett country had been dominated by a class of wealthy planters. These planters lived on their estates spread throughout South County, and frequently owned from 5 to 20 black slaves. They relied on Little Rest craftsmen – silversmiths, blacksmiths, leather workers, and carpenters – to perform services for them. They came to Little Rest's Court House and taverns for General Assembly sessions, county court sessions, and town meetings, returning afterwards to their comfortable estates.

By the end of the Revolutionary War, the glory days of the Narragansett planters had passed. Several causes led to their decline. The primary cause was that their estates had been divided so often through inheritance that they no longer had large holdings and could no longer generate large farm surpluses for trade. While the Narragansett planters in colonial times were successful commercial farmers by New England standards, their landholdings were never huge, especially compared to the landholdings of wealthy southern planters. Thus, the division of estates had a significant impact. Narragansett planters also did not, as was done in the colonial South, practice primogeniture, a system of inheritance by which the eldest son inherited the bulk of the land and slaves, with the younger sons left to fend for themselves. Instead, Narragansett planter parents often treated their sons equally in dividing their estates. While this was a more humane practice, it meant that it was difficult to maintain a large estate beyond a few generations. Furthermore, unlike the southern planters who had the lands of the deep South, Kentucky and the West at their doorstep, Narragansett planters did not have cheap, uninhabited land in a close hinterland that could be used to set up younger sons. During the constitutional convention in Little Rest, the disparity of wealth between southern planters compared to Rhode Island farmers was highlighted. One delegate stated that 20 southern planters had more property than 300 Rhode Island farmers. Henry Marchant conceded that a southern planter could "ride in a Coach with 4 or 5 attendants" and "[d]rinks wine [and] lives extravagantly." No Narragansett planter could afford that.

Elisha R. Potter, Jr., in a summary of the history of slavery in South County, thought that slavery itself contributed to the decline of the Narragansett planters, as it made them lazy and less ambitious. Furthermore, the Revolutionary War hastened the downfall of the Narragansett planters, due to the burden of heavy taxation, the decline of Newport as a commercial center, and the loss of British markets in the Caribbean as an outlet for what surplus farm goods they had. Narragansett planters also exported so many Narragansett pacers that the breed became extinct in Rhode Island.

By 1800, South Kingstown (then including Narragansett) was suffering from an economic depression. It was no longer the premier dairy and horse raising town in New England. The decline of the town is reflected in its post-war population decline. In 1790, South Kingstown's population was 4,131. But by 1800, the population had declined to 3,438. The population, stunningly, would not reach pre-war levels until the 1850s. Many farmers migrated to upstate Rhode Island for new manufacturing jobs, or left for upstate New York for cheap land. An observer of those times wrote,

> I can well remember the time when, if a farmer had only one farm, and four or five sons, and as many daughters, all but one, as they married off, were obliged to move into the western country. It was all we could do, to give them a little money, and send them into the wilderness. This was like sending them to the grave. Very often parents and children never met again.

By 1800, the Narragansett country was like the rest of New England, dominated by villages and small farmers struggling to produce a surplus. Despite this period of decline in the agrarian economy, Little Rest retained its economic, political and legal importance in South County. It grew to support more tradesmen, more taverns and more stores to service farmers. It continued to host sessions of the General Assembly (until 1853), sessions of the Washington County court, and town council meetings and town meetings. Its role as a government seat is addressed in more detail in the next chapter.

The year 1800 was still prior to the time that industrialization changed South County. By the 1820s, the wool mills built and operated by the Hazard and other families from Peace Dale and Wakefield had become an important force in employing workers. Eventually, the location of South Kingstown's political and social influence would shift to those towns, as well as to the Narragansett Pier. Little Rest would not successfully adapt to these economic changes. But Little Rest did have its golden age from about 1800 to 1840.

Tavern Life

Taverns continued to be the center of Little Rest's social life. Not only did they host tired travelers, legislators while the General Assembly was in session, lawyers while the court was in session, and town council meetings, taverns also served as the common meeting areas for local villagers.

There were three important taverns in the early 1800s in Little Rest. Charles Barker operated "Barker's Tavern" (the current Kingston Inn) from 1797 until his death in 1819. His wife, Mary Barker, then operated the tavern until 1827. The job of tavern keeper was one of the few jobs that was acceptable for women to pursue, particularly if the woman inherited the tavern. Jesse Babcock operated this tavern from 1834 to about 1855.

When Charles Barker died in 1819, the town made a room-by-room inventory of his personal property, which provides the opportunity to learn about the furnishings of a country tavern at this time.

- Near the front door, Barker had his most prized possession, a mahogany desk, in which he kept his customer account books.
- There were three parlors in which customers could eat meals, drink alcohol or drink tea and coffee. One parlor had "8 slatback chairs" and one square table. A second parlor had two large maple tables, 8 Windsor chairs, 5 banister-back chairs, one armchair, and one rocking chair. A third parlor must have been the main meeting room, as it held 6 "green chairs and one black one," 6 "leather bottom chairs," 8 "fiddle back" chairs, and 6 maple and pine tables. Other possessions in the parlors included a "Backgammon Board with contents," five spitting boxes, 13 wine glasses and six tumblers, tea canisters, coffee mill, candlesticks, lanterns, and shovel and tongs for the fireplace.
- The kitchen had an assortment of iron kettles, pots and griddles; one "large grid iron for broiling pig;" one bread toaster; one potato boiler; one copper tea kettle; coffee pots; and plates and dinnerware to serve about 25 persons, including 10 silver spoons and 6 pewter platters and 8 pewter plates.
- There were twelve bedrooms. Each one had a bed, two pillows with pillowcases, sheets, a quilt (and sometimes another blanket), a bed stand, and little else. There were seven "night mugs."

Accordingly, the rooms were sparsely furnished. The bedrooms had no chairs, wall hangings or curtains. The tables in the parlors had no tablecloths. The parlors also had no wall hangings, except for one small coat of arms. The white parlor walls, however, did have pleasant colored stenciling and curtains.

Thomas Taylor's account books for his general store in Little Rest provide a glimpse of the type of entertainment provided in the Barker tavern. One account book kept between 1824 and 1829 was used solely for his transactions with Mary Barker. Most of Mary Barker's debits were for alcohol (rum, brandy, wine and gin, with lesser amounts of ale and beer). Other debits were for foodstuffs such as coffee, tea, eggs, butter, cheese, corn, goose and cigars, and supplies such as knives, forks, tumblers, playing cards, plaid flannel, bed cord, brooms, bellows, and candles. When the account book is turned over, it lists Barker's credits. Compared to transactions with storekeepers in Little Rest's earlier years, most of the payments were made in cash. Barker also received credits for calf skin, fish, veal, fowl, and hogs, which she obtained from local farmers, and for board for carpenters and other laborers who probably were hired to build Taylor's new house on main street.

In 1796, Robert Potter sold the tavern that had been operated by his family since 1752 to Timothy Peckham, Jr. In 1820, Peckham built a new tavern on the lot to the east of the Court House. This tavern had a roomy drawing room and bar for tavern patrons.

The Joseph Reynolds tavern was built by "house carpenter" Caleb Wescott in 1775, but it was not used as a tavern until later. Joseph Reynolds operated the tavern from about 1796 to 1821. Joseph's son, John, operated the tavern from about 1822 to 1837, when it was taken over by Philip Taylor. The tavern has a huge stone chimney that is almost fourteen square feet at the base. A flight of stone steps is built into one side of it that used to lead from the cellar to the ground floor. The cellar has an enormous fireplace with a heavy oak lintel and each floor has three more fireplaces. Upstairs there was once a large hall with a vaulted ceiling, where "tables were set for meals during sessions of legislature and court, town-meeting days, or other great occasions, and turkey suppers, dances and other entertainments were given there." Joseph Reynolds' day book from 1796 to 1801 demonstrates that his business increased when the county court was in session. During "Court Week," more alcohol and dinners were served, more horses were kept and fed, and more visitors were lodged. After the town meeting in the Court House in April 1800, Elisha R. Potter, Sr. and four other men treated their supporters to 170 gills of rum and 104 gills of brandy. The day book also indicates that Reynolds' bar was popular with local villagers and townsmen.

A Village of Shopkeepers

In addition to taverns, Little Rest grew as a hub for local farmers riding to the village to buy goods from local stores and to obtain services from blacksmiths and other artisans. James Helme opened a store in 1777 and operated it until 1816. In addition, Little Rest attracted two general stores in the early 1800s, one operated by Thomas Taylor and the other by Thomas R. Wells. They provided customers with a wide assortment of manufactured goods, foodstuffs and alcohol. There were always two or three blacksmiths in the village, including one of the members of the Fayerweather family for most of the 1800s. Other artisans included Luke Aldrich, cabinetmaker; Daniel Stedman, Jr., shoemaker; Stephen Greene, gingerbread baker; Joseph Stanton, tanner; Eldred family, stone masons; Abel Cottrell, tailor; William Lunt, wigmaker and barber; and Washington Greenman, wheelwright. Cyrus

French and his son William manufactured hats from their home across the street from the jail for many years. John Nichols and his son operated for many years one of the main saddlemaking shops in the county. In 1855, Orpha Rose supported herself (she was not married) by learning how to make fashionable women's hats in Boston and operating a millinery shop out of the Tavern Hall Club. As one of the few women's hat shops in the county, ladies came from far distances to shop at her store. Importantly, in 1818, a bank was established in Little Rest. Banks provided farmers with hard cash, which they could use to obtain the latest relatively inexpensive manufactured goods from general stores and handmade goods from the artisans.

"Nailer Tom" Hazard, the Wakefield farmer and blacksmith who kept a journal, often traveled to Little Rest to run errands at the village's stores and taverns, sometimes four times per week. He frequently purchased goods at the stores of James Helme, Thomas Taylor and Thomas R. Wells. He often purchased small quantities of gin, rum and other alcohol at those stores, and from the village taverns. He purchased gingerbread from village baker Stephen Greene. He purchased new saddles from John Nichols. He had his hair cut by William Lunt. After the bank was established in the village in 1818, Nailer Tom sometimes rode to Little Rest to draw out cash or to repay his loans. Nailer Tom attended several Quaker meetings at the Court House. He spent many nights lodging at the Joseph Reynolds tavern, Barker tavern and Peckham tavern. Furthermore, Nailer Tom had many friends in Little Rest, and he enjoyed nothing more than having tea with Elisha Potter, John Nichols, Joseph Reynolds, Dr. Thomas Hazard, and other villagers. For example, on January 21, 1807, Nailer Tom "went to Little Rest. Drank tea at Elisha R. Potters. My mare got away from me and returned home on foot."

A new government office became available in the village in 1807: postmaster of the U.S. mail. The first postmasters were all storekeepers: James Helme (1807-09), Thomas R. Wells (1809-20), Thomas S. Taylor (1820-1837), and Thomas P. Wells (1837-1843). The mail was brought by horseback to the village; villagers then picked up the mail at the store, paying a small fee, and dropped off any mail for delivery outside of the village. In the 1830s, a stagecoach line was established between Kingston and Providence for the delivery of the mail. The local stagecoach to and from Providence was driven by men from Little Rest. Passengers could pay $1.25 to hitch a ride to Providence, a trip which took most of the day.

The first long-term, trained physicians appeared in Little Rest with the arrival of Dr. John Aldrich in the early 1800s. Dr. Peleg Johnson (1791-1859) replaced him, moving to Little Rest in 1821. After he retired, Dr. Thomas A. Hazard (1813-86) took over the practice, residing and working in Kingston for many years. Dr. Johnson received training from Yale University and Dr. Hazard received training from the University of Pennsylvania (three courses). All of the doctors made their rounds on horseback, serving a wide area, carrying medicines in their saddlebags. Dr. Johnson kept a diary indicating that in one typical week in 1855 he rode about 75 miles visiting patients. Day books of visits made and medicines sold survive that were kept by Dr. Johnson (from 1827 to 1851) and by Dr. Hazard (from 1839 to 1882). William Gould, a seafarer from Wakefield, reported in his diary calling for Dr. Thomas Hazard of Kingston to visit his Wakefield home many times at $1 per visit for members of his family and himself in the 1850s. But Dr. Hazard was unable to save Gould from dying at early age from illness. The first dentist (J.W. Babcock) held appointments in Kingston in 1863.

Leisure, Voluntary Associations and Reform Activities

Little Rest (Kingston after 1825) became a center for local entertainment. Townspeople sought to enjoy life more to escape the drudgery of work. Traveling circuses with "wild animals" stopped at Little Rest at least as early as the 1820s. Daniel Stedman in his journal reported that the circus performed in Kingston in July 1835, August 1838 and October 1838. In his account book, seafarer William Gould of Wakefield recorded that he spent "50 cts for horse ride to Kingston" on May 29, 1850, where "there was a circus on Kingston Hill." Stedman also recorded that a cattle show was held in Kingston in September 1846. In 1870, an estimated 4,000 persons, the largest crowd to gather in one place in South Kingstown, viewed a circus in Kingston, consisting mostly of riding horses, somersaulting, and tight-rope walking. In addition, July 4th celebrations were held at the Court House. At one July 4th celebration in 1858, the *South County Journal* reported that "The State House, at Kingston, took fire on Monday, from firecrackers thrown from the cupola, but was soon extinguished."

Women also sought entertainment suitable to their tastes. In 1858, an advertisement appeared in the *South County Journal* informing interested readers that on August 3rd at 4 p.m., "The Ladies of Kingston will hold a Tea Party, at the Court House . . . ." In later years, the first floor of the Court House was used for other social occasions, including dances and painting classes. In 1848, the first women's club was formed in Kingston.

In the early 1800s, there was still no meeting house for the Congregational Church built in the village. That would change by 1820, when an impressive meeting house was built at the crest of Little Rest hill opposite the Court House. In addition to tending to the spiritual needs of villagers, the church would be instrumental in creating a Sunday school, a circulating library, a music society and a temperance society. The Six Principle Baptist meeting that had been an important part of Little Rest's early years fell into decline after the Revolution, as it did in the rest of the state.

Kingston became the home of numerous voluntary associations in the mid-1800s, where villagers and others could join together to improve their lives. These voluntary associations did the work of governments. Invariably, they each had constitutions, like a government. William French was said to have formed the first agricultural society in South County, with meetings to discuss the latest scientific farming techniques held in the Court House. Religious fervor spawned by a second religious revival swept the country and spawned a host of reform movements, including in Kingston a temperance society founded in 1829 and an antislavery society founded in 1837.

By the 1820s, as villagers became more educated, they sought more sophisticated entertainments. Tavern-going, an exclusively male preserve, was not enough for them. In 1825, villagers established the Little Rest (later Kingston) Musical Society, a singing club. The preamble to the club's constitution stated the members' lofty goals: "Daily appreciating the importance of cultivating those mental powers with which Providence has blessed us whereby we may be enabled to sing praises to the Giver of all our mercies in a becoming manner, and realizing the necessity of united effort that we may improve in this sublime and delightful employment," the society was formed. The original "gentlemen" who became members numbered 38, while the "Ladies" numbered 32. All the prominent families in the village were represented. As usual with clubs at this time, men served in the officer positions. What was different here was that the women's names were written in a column next to the column of the men's names. In most club minutes, the men's names were placed before the women's names. The club also provided an opportunity for the young men and women of the village to socialize together. The society met weekly, either on a weekday afternoon or a Sunday afternoon. The Kingston Musical Society continued for about five years.

In 1824, a group of villagers met at the Court House to discuss establishing a library. At the meeting, forty-nine men founded a "social Library to be kept at Little Rest." The Reverend Oliver Brown, minister at the Congregational Church, was elected president of the library society and was its first librarian. With subscriptions from the founders and fees and donations, Reverend Brown collected about 150 volumes. The collection would continue to grow over the years, and would serve as the foundation for the current Kingston Free Library and Reading Room.

Hatter and attorney Cyrus French created and tended fine gardens in his leisure time. At his death in 1826, he owned several books on gardening.

A record of the mail received by villagers kept by postmaster Wells from 1837 to 1841 indicates that villagers received a wide assortment of newspapers. Some of the newspapers had a political point of view (*Republican Herald, Liberator, Emancipator*), some had a religious point of view (*Christian Witness, Missionary Herald, Christian Secretary, and New York Evangelist*), and some had a rural point of view (*New England Farmer*).

Doctors Peleg Johnson and Thomas Potter subscribed to the *Medical Examiner* and businessmen Asa Potter, Thomas P. Wells and Isaac P. Hazard (of Peace Dale) subscribed to the *Journal of Commerce.* Elisha R. Potter, Jr. subscribed to eleven different newspapers, Thomas P. Wells nine, and Wilkins Updike four. Newspapers arrived from Washington, D.C., New York, Boston, Philadelphia, Providence and many other cities in the United States. Newspapers and faster transportation helped connect Kingston villagers to the larger world.

The Rise of the Common Man

Little Rest was dominated by ordinary men and women who were down-to-earth, egalitarian, New England Yankee types. There were no pretensions of striving to be like English gentry, as was the case with colonial Narragansett planters. The village's most important resident and one of the most important politicians in the state, Elisha R. Potter, Sr., was a frequent visitor to the Joseph Reynolds tavern, where he "could be seen sitting on the stoop nearly every pleasant afternoon." Unlike Narragansett planters in colonial times, who sought to separate themselves from the middling ranks, Potter sought and enjoyed their company.

A typical resident was William Lunt, the village barber, wigmaker and Revolutionary War veteran. "Major" Lunt enjoyed informing customers that they were being shaved by the same razor that had been applied to the face of General George Washington himself. Lunt's modest house stood on main street, at the site now occupied by the Asa Potter law office. Lunt displayed a barber's pole in front of his shop. He also put his pigpen "before his door and resting on the side-walk." He was noted for having the finest pig in the village, come fair time in the fall. Major Lunt tended a beacon light and an alarm gun in Little Rest during the War of 1812. To obtain his Revolutionary War pension, Lunt had to go to Providence each month, usually riding in the mail wagon. "Old Bill Nichols" of Little Rest carried the mail thirty miles to Providence in a one-horse wagon that took all day. Passengers were charged $1.25 but had to walk up all hills. One day Major Lunt decided to save the cost of the fare and walk the whole way. In an "old brown coat all buttoned down before," Lunt started on his long walk. Fortunately for Lunt, as he approached Wickford on the Post Road, he was hitched a few rides to Providence and actually arrived before the mail coach.

There were other ordinary folks who were characters as well. There was Cyrus French, who made beaver hats in his house across from the Little Rest jail. He enjoyed sauntering over to the Joseph Reynolds tavern during evenings, sitting by the fire, and telling droll stories to local villagers. There was Abel Cottrell, tailor, farmer and sergeant-at-arms in the county court, whom the boys in town enjoyed listening to opening the court: "Hear ye!

Hear ye! Hear ye!" There was Stephen "Baker" Green, who had his shop on South Road and who gained local fame not for his prowess in the court room or in politics, but for baking gingerbread. There was Prince Robinson, an elderly black man who used to stand at the entrance of the court room, selling apples, cider, candies, and Baker Greene's gingerbread. And, as we shall see, there was also Elisha Gardner, deputy sheriff and a skilled practical joker.

For African Americans, Indians and women, equal rights would be realized only in the future. Census records indicate that only one black person was held as a slave in Little Rest in 1800. With 18 black slaves in 1774, and 12 black slaves in 1790, Little Rest white families must have felt moral pressure to free their slaves. The manumission bill of 1784 did not require slaveholders to free their slaves who were born prior to that date, but most slaveholders did so nonetheless. Some were freed upon the death of the white slaveowner. In an upcoming chapter, we shall see that at least one Little Rest villager was prevented from freeing his slave by the South Kingstown town council. By the early 1800s, free blacks began to integrate into the local economy. In 1804, Little Rest attracted the Fayerweathers, a black family of blacksmiths, who performed services for villagers and local farmers for the next 80 years. In addition, whites and free blacks worked side-by-side as temporary hired hands on local farms.

With all this activity, more houses were built in the village. Between 1802 and 1831, 13 dwelling houses and other buildings were constructed in the village, including two fine Federal style residences on main street. In 1825, a hand pump was placed in the village well. The Pease and Niles Gazetteer, published in 1819, described "Little Rest Hill" as a small but pleasant village occupying a prospective and interesting site near the center of town, with about 25 dwellings, the court house, and a bank.

Little Rest's Ties to the Sea

While Little Rest was not a seaport, it did have connections to the sea, due to South Kingstown's proximity to the ocean. Thus, its leading men could engage in mercantile activities. South Kingstown had small ports, at South Ferry and Narragansett Pier. Elisha Reynolds Potter, Sr. of Little Rest acquired a one-half interest at South Ferry, the key ferry to Jamestown and Newport. This ferry had always been important to South Kingstown farmers, as it carried livestock and farm produce to Newport for shipment overseas. In 1824, Potter owned a half interest in a sloop of 25 tons built at Narragansett Pier called the *South Kingstown,* which was a freight sloop (the "fastest in Narragansett Bay") that ran a regular route between South Ferry and Providence, as well as South Ferry and Jamestown. In 1828, records of the port of Providence indicate that on one voyage from Providence to South Ferry, the *South Kingstown* carried 30 bales of wool for Peace Dale manufacturer Rowland Hazard and eleven chests of tea for Anthony Robinson, an owner of a general store in Kingston.

In 1830, Potter and Thomas Taylor, the successful village general storekeeper, paid for a sloop of 100 tons to be built at Narragansett Pier, named the *Kingston*. On the sloop's first journey, she departed South Ferry with a load mostly of South County potatoes and cheese and unloaded them at Philadelphia. The *Kingston* then was loaded with quicksilver and dry goods valued at $30,000, which she carried to Texas. In 1831, Taylor advertised in the village's newspaper, the *Rhode Island Advocate*, that the *Kingston* had just returned from a voyage laden with molasses and that townspeople could purchase the molasses at South Ferry or Newport at favorable prices. Records also indicate that Thomas Taylor invested in the sloop *Wickford* in 1830.

James B. M. Potter, a son of Elisha Potter, Sr., inherited the South Ferry property and interest in the sloop *South Kingstown*. Potter incurred considerable expenses maintaining the *South Kingstown,* including replacing sails and masts. But the sloop met a not infrequent fate. It was wrecked in 1846 off Point Judith. James B. M. Potter had the sloop *Usquepaug* built as South Ferry's new local freight sloop. Potter also erected a church at South Ferry which still stands as a visible marker on Narragansett Bay.

Stone Marker on South Road, Two Miles South of Little Rest. It reads "To Little Rest 2M 1814." The marker is a symbol of Little Rest's prior importance as a market village for outlying South County farmers and a government seat. *Pettaquamscutt Historical Society.*

Little Rest as State, County and Town Seat

The Court House (or State House as it was also known) continued to be the center of the village's success. Until 1853, the General Assembly met on the second floor of the Court House every other year. Those state representatives elected at their town meetings in April sat for the May session in Newport and its June adjourned session in East Greenwich, while those chosen in August sat for the October meeting of the Assembly conducted alternately in Providence and Little Rest, with adjourned sessions held in January in Bristol. The United States Constitution created a new set of elected national officials. U.S. senators from Rhode Island were chosen by the vote of the Grand Committee of the General Assembly (the house and the senate sitting jointly), while U.S. congressmen were elected on an at-large basis by the freemen in August of the odd-numbered years.

County court sessions at the Court House, typically held twice a year each by the court of common pleas and by the supreme court, continued to be important events in the village. Judges, attorneys, parties to lawsuits, members of the jury and witnesses traveled from around the county and the state to Little Rest and often stayed overnight. Important trials became a source of entertainment, attracting visitors from around the county.

In sessions of the court of common pleas, most of the cases continued to be creditors forcing debtors to pay amounts owed to them. Sometimes Little Rest villagers could sit in on trials between fellow villagers, such as in 1809 when general storekeeper James Helme sued tavern keeper Charles Barker for amounts owed, and in 1818 when general storekeeper Thomas Taylor sued attorney Levi Totten for an unpaid debt. Tavern keeper Timothy Peckham sued hatter and attorney Cyrus French for trespass, claiming that six inches of a beam from French's house was on Peckham's land. The case dragged on for years, ending only when the beam rotted. Villagers must have been shocked in 1817 when the litigious Peckham had the audacity to sue Elisha R. Potter, Sr., the village's most important resident, as a result of a land deal gone bad. Potter responded by bringing several cases against Peckham. In addition, villagers could sit it on cases that dealt with disputes involving parties from around Washington County. One significant case involved owners of a mill on the Pawcatuck River, who were accused by a Hopkinton official of failing to create a passage in the mill dam that would permit fish to swim upstream. Furthermore, villagers could sit in on cases that dealt with parties outside the county, such as the time in 1817 when Cuban merchant Juan Julian Martin Guerrero sued eight Providence and other merchants.

Court viewers typically preferred to sit in on county supreme court trials, which included criminal trials. For example, in 1805, Mary Joe, a Narragansett Indian residing in South Kingstown, was placed on trial, accused of secretly giving birth to a live baby, so that the authorities would not be able to determine if the baby was born alive or dead. The baby was found dead by authorities. At trial, the jury found her guilty, and she was fined $200 and sent to prison for four months. Many of the criminal trials involved cash and property. Forging bank notes became a popular past-time among those who would have likely counterfeited money in colonial times. For example, in 1813, James Short was found guilty of forging a bank note, and was sentenced to have a "piece of each of his ears cut off" while standing in the Little Rest pillory for an hour. Villagers could also sit in on divorce proceedings, which started appearing in the Court House in 1792 and became common in the early 1800s. Typically, a wife would bring a proceeding for divorce, charging the husband with physical abuse or adultery. For the first time, abused women had a legal and socially acceptable way to escape a failed marriage.

During county court sessions on the second floor of the Court House, Little Rest attracted the best lawyers in the state, from Providence, Newport, Westerly and East Greenwich. The village also attracted more lawyers as residents, reflecting the increasing importance of lawyers in American life and the increasing litigiousness of American society. Talented lawyers and politicians, including Elisha Reynolds Potter, Sr., resided in the village. In addition, country lawyers such as Levi Totten, Joseph Aplin and William Newell moved to the village. Significantly, Wilkins Updike, whose family had lived at the Smith's Castle estate near Wickford for 120 years, moved to Little Rest to practice law in 1819 and soon had the largest stable of clients. None of these lawyers received formal training in a law school operated by a university. The first trained attorney from Kingston was Asa Potter, Jr., who attended the law school at Litchfield, Connecticut, and in 1827 was admitted to the Rhode Island bar. In the late 1790s, several attorneys banded together to form a bar association for Washington County, with four of the six members hailing from Little Rest (including Elisha Potter and Levi Totten).

With the permission of the county sheriff, who supervised the use of the Court House on behalf of the State, the Court House was used for other business. The first floor of the Court House continued to be used for town meetings and elections. The freemen of the town actively debated pressing issues of the day and expressed their views through voting.

The Court House was put to a new use in 1831, when state members of the Whig Party met at Kingston to elect delegates to meet in Baltimore at the first national party convention. Other party meetings supporting presidential candidates were held at the Court House, including for Henry Clay, Abraham Lincoln and Ulysses Grant. In addition, the Court House was used for non-governmental gatherings. Until 1820, it was used by Congregational Church members to hold Sunday services. The town's Quakers also occasionally used the Court House for meetings in the early

1800s, and a few members of the Episcopal Church held services at the Court House from 1838 to 1840. In 1829, it was used as the location for the annual meeting of the town's temperance society. During a session of the court of common pleas in Kingston in 1840, when important men from throughout South County were in Kingston, a speaker from Boston gave a lecture on currency and the U. S. Treasury.

The South Kingstown town council continued to meet usually in one of Little Rest's taverns. In 1858, town council meetings began to be held in the Court House. These meetings brought economic benefits to Little Rest. Consider the town's payment of expenses in fulfilling its role as caretaker of the town's poor. The town council typically paid a Little Rest doctor fees for caring for the town's poor; paid Little Rest shopkeepers for small items of food and clothing for the town's poor; and paid Luke Aldrich, cabinetmaker, for building coffins for poor persons whose estates could not afford them.

In 1828, the South Kingstown town clerk's office was built in the Court House. The town clerk typically was a Little Rest resident who served for an extraordinarily long time. The following Little Rest villagers served as town clerks in the 19th century: James Helme, Jr. (1779-1812); Thomas R. Wells (1827-53); Powell Helme (1853 to 1858); and John Perry (1858-87).

Occasionally, government authorities acted to protect the dignity of the Court House. In 1790, to prevent townsmen from racing their horses through the village and disrupting General Assembly sessions, the General Assembly passed a law to prevent "excessive riding" (defined as faster than a common traveling pace) within 80 rods of the Court House. For many years, it was not uncommon to see stray hogs, cattle and other farm animals grazing in front of the Court House. In 1855, at the urging of Wilkins Updike, the General Assembly voted to install the ornamental iron fence, which still surrounds the Court House grounds. In June 1861, the town council passed an ordinance against keeping a "Station House" for public use within one-half mile of the Kingston Court House. A station house may have been a stagecoach stop. Perhaps the dignity of the court was affected by the odor or noise caused by horses at a stagecoach stop near the Court House. This ordinance does not seem to have affected the horse stables kept by villager John Taylor for his stagecoach operations. In April 1862, at a well-attended town meeting in the Court House, enterprising vendors placed kegs of beer "all around the court-yard fence, and towards evening their contents produced a serious effect on the conduct of the many outside." At the next town meeting, the sale of alcohol in Kingston on town meeting days was prohibited.

The Washington County jail in Little Rest continued to be an important part of the local legal system. The official criminal and civil legal system included a town sheriff, deputy sheriff, justices of the peace, judges, a court clerk, a sergeant-at-arms, the jury, lawyers and a jailer, selected at the state level. Many of the official positions were held by Little Rest men. For example, Samuel Helme served as clerk of the Washington County court of common pleas from 1802 to 1833. James Helme, Jr. served as clerk of the superior court from 1801 to 1812. William C. Clarke served as judge on the court of common pleas from 1805 to 1817. County sheriffs were assisted by town justices who could charge persons with crimes; there were always two or three justices from Little Rest. Daniel Stedman, the Wakefield diarist, was a town justice for many years; he reported in his journal in March 1826 that William Congden was charged with assaulting his wife. Stedman reported further, "We had a Court at [Congden's] house and from their to Kingston village, & their past sentence upon him and he was put in Jaol that night."

A typical local farmer who frequented Little Rest was "Nailer Tom" Hazard, who kept a journal from the late 1770s to the early 1840s. Many of his trips related to the government institutions in the village. Nailer Tom often attended sessions of the General Assembly when they were held at the Court House, sometimes for three days in a row. One time he was asked to testify on the subject of local fisheries. Nailer Tom attended many town meetings at the Court House. For example, on April 29, 1811, Hazard writes, "I went to Little Rest to Town Meeting. Dined at Elisha R. Potter's. He got a 180 majority." Nailer Tom also came to Little Rest to attend numerous sessions of the county court. He was, at different times, a party to lawsuits, a witness in lawsuits, a member of juries in both civil and criminal cases, and a spectator at many trials. Interestingly, Nailer Tom served as an arbitrator to resolve three disputes held in Little Rest taverns. Rather than hire attorneys, adhere to formal courtroom procedures, and rely on a judge, the parties sought to have local respected townsmen decide the dispute in an informal setting. Nailer Tom also visited the jail at Little Rest, once to give a bond for his son "to have the leberty of the Jail bounds" (son Tom was incarcerated for debt). Nailer Tom rode to Little Rest for other official business, including administering the estates of deceased persons before the town council, paying his town taxes, and inquiring about poor relief for his wayward son.

In addition to being the county government seat, Little Rest continued to be a key location for military musters. Captain Elijah Kenyon, a cabinetmaker who lived and worked at the southeast corner of Main Street and South Road, was the "commander of an independent chartered military company of the town, whose duty it was to muster for discipline and parade three or four times a year." Kenyon served as captain of the Washington Light Infantry from 1818 to 1822. Other military units in Washington County likely held musters in Little Rest or went to its taverns after a muster elsewhere, including the Kingston Reds (until 1808) and the Washington Cavalry. Little Rest hatter William French served as the last captain of the

Kingston Reds. The Washington cavalry, a troop of Washington County horsemen, was active from 1792 until 1841. Little Rest villagers Robert Potter, Adam Helme, Jeremiah N. Sands, and Robert Sands joined in the petition to establish the Washington Cavalry in 1792. John Hagadorn, an attorney who resided in Little Rest and died young in 1813, was appointed as a first lieutenant of the Washington Cavalry in 1807. Daniel Stedman, in his journal, noted that military reviews were held in Kingston in September 1835 and September 1839. In September 1842, the Rhode Island governor reviewed Washington County militia at Kingston. On July 4, 1843, soldiers of the Washington Grenadiers and Narragansett Guards listened to a patriotic speech at the Court House and afterwards retired to a dinner supplied by a local tavern keeper.

Trooper on Horse, Washington Cavalry. Several Little Rest villagers served in this unit, including First Lieutenant John Hagadorn. The uniform is red, the lining is tan, and the breeches are brown. Small watercolor on paper, circa 1800, unknown artist. This painting for many years was in the possession of Kingston's French family. *Pettaquamscutt Historical Society.*

Elisha R. Potter, Sr.: A Natural Born Great Man

In the history of Little Rest (and later Kingston), the most influential resident on a statewide basis was Elisha Reynolds Potter, Sr. In an age when the federal government was relatively weak and state politics were more important than today, Potter's success in state politics made him one of the most influential men in the state for many years, especially in South County. He saw himself as the defender of South County's agricultural interests, and in that role he succeeded. He also used his influence and wealth to improve his village of Little Rest. But being powerful and a benefactor does not, of course, mean that Potter was a "good" man in all respects. He had a mixed record when it came to supporting policies that would have liberalized Rhode Island society – extending the right to vote to men who typically were landless urban immigrants, reducing barbaric penalties meted out to criminals, eliminating the jailing of debtors, and dealing with freed black slaves.

Potter's Early Life

Elisha R. Potter, Sr. was born in Little Rest in 1764. He was a descendant of Nathaniel Potter who came to Rhode Island in 1638. Elisha's father, Thomas Potter, was a village tavern keeper and a lieutenant-colonel of a Washington County militia regiment in the Revolutionary War. Thomas Potter hosted General Washington at his tavern in 1781. He was respected in the village, serving several terms in the General Assembly and often being selected as moderator of the town meetings. Elisha Potter himself, in about 1780 when he was age 16, joined Colonel John Topham's militia regiment, but he saw no active service. Elisha Potter's mother was Susannah Reynolds, the daughter of Elisha Reynolds, the wealthy landowner who played such a vital role in Little Rest's early days.

There probably was some tension between Thomas Potter and Elisha Reynolds, as Thomas Potter became insolvent a number of times. Elisha Potter spent much of his youth with Reynolds, perhaps due in part to his father's financial difficulties. During his youth, Potter worked as a blacksmith and farmer on Reynold's farms. Reynolds must have recognized talent early in Elisha Potter. We saw that Thomas Potter could write, but that his spelling and grammar were very poor. It was probably Elisha Reynolds who made sure that his grandson received a good education. Elisha attended school at Plainfield Academy in Connecticut. Potter then served as a teacher for young students at the local private schools in Little Rest and Tower Hill from 1785 to 1787. He did not attend Brown University or any other college. He studied law under the respected local lawyer Mathew Robinson. Years later, Potter bragged that his legal training consisted mainly of reading only Blackstone's *Commentaries*.

Potter was admitted to the bar in 1789 and he practiced law successfully from the 1790s to the early 1800s, often appearing at the Court House in Little Rest. He even has a catchy legal quote attributed to him: "Human nature constitutes a part of the evidence in every case." In 1790, Potter also started a small storekeeping business, which he kept for a few years. He probably leased Immanuel Case's former village store near the current Kingston Hill Store, which his grandfather Elisha Reynolds had purchased. Potter sold gin, rum, sugar, tea and cloth to local villagers such as Caleb Gardner, Elisha Reynolds, Elisha Gardner, Robert Potter and Elisha Potter's black servant, Cesar Potter.

In 1790, Elisha Potter had the good fortune of marrying Mary Perkins, daughter of Narragansett planter Caleb Gardner, who could afford to purchase items from Potter such as silk, velvet and chocolates, and the widow of Joseph Perkins, the Little Rest storekeeper, innkeeper and silversmith. Mary was described as "a beautiful woman, tall and queenly in appearance, with a charming disposition and a high order of intellect." She brought to the marriage a substantial estate inherited from Joseph, including five farms and several substantial note payables. In 1791, Elisha Reynolds died, and through his will Elisha Potter inherited more property – the land and house on which Potter operated his store, and his parents' land and house. The property from his wife and grandfather gave Elisha Potter a firm financial footing and social standing in the community. Typical of the times, Potter had had several occupations: farmer, blacksmith, teacher, storekeeper and lawyer. As a lawyer and substantial landholder, he could now enter politics.

Potter Establishes his Political Credentials

Potter's true forte lay in politics. "Shepherd Tom" Hazard, writing in 1882, stated that Elisha Potter "was, while in his prime, the autocrat, not only of Little Rest, but of the town and county in which he resided, and for many years, the most influential man in the state, being a natural born great man." Another contemporary observed, "Perhaps no political man in this State ever acquired or maintained . . . a more commanding influence." A Rhode Island historian who knew Elisha Potter described him as an "old-fashioned Rhode Island politician, democrat-aristocrat" who "knew men and things."

In 1786, at the age of 22, Potter received 10 acres of land from his grandfather Elisha Reynolds so that he could qualify as a freeman of the town. In 1788, at a town meeting, he voted against adoption of the U.S. Constitution. At the age of 29, in 1793, Potter was elected as a representative to the lower house of the General Assembly. There he quickly established his reputation by acting as the prime mover in obtaining a reapportionment of the state tax burden away from South Kingstown and other South County towns.

Elisha Reynolds Potter, Sr. (1764-1835). Kingston's most influential person in its history. Painting on canvas, unknown artist, circa 1815. *Pettaquamscutt Historical Society.*

Ever since 1782, South Kingstown had suffered the most under the burden of heavy taxation. With reapportionment, that honor shifted to the state's growing and prosperous metropolis, Providence. In 1795, the General Assembly committee led by Potter placed a value for the entire state at $15.5 million, with Providence's share at $2.95 million and all of South County's share at $2.78 million. South Kingstown's share of the state's taxes, which for many years exceeded Providence's share, was now only one-fourth of Providence's share. Despite the fierce protest of Providence politicians, Potter managed to have the valuation put in effect. This "Herculean" triumph against Providence and the northern towns gave Potter "zealous support of the minority towns, South Kingstown in particular, through [his] life." It thrust him into the role of defender of South County's agricultural interests. Potter gave this role his highest priority. Potter was elected to the state house of representatives from 1793 through 1796, serving as speaker in 1795 and 1796.

Potter as National Congressmen

Potter first entered the national stage when he was elected to the U.S. Congress as a member of the Federalist Party in 1796. He resigned his seat in 1797 and returned to the Rhode Island General Assembly for several years. He returned to his seat in Congress from 1809 to 1815, during the years leading up to and including the War of 1812 against the British. As a result of the Napoleonic Wars, with England's and France's decrees and Jefferson's embargo, Rhode Island's trade with the Caribbean was all but closed. Elisha Potter, while in Congress, vigorously sought to open those markets and to oppose the march to the War of 1812, as did many Federalists in New England. A South Carolina congressman considered him to be the ablest debater on the subject. A letter, dated December 5, 1812, from Elisha Potter to John Hagadorn of Little Rest, expresses his anti-war feelings:

> There is not the least prospect of peace as long as the present rulers are in power. They are now determined to oppress the people with taxes, to draft and Impress the people of the Country to fight Great Britain until she will give up the right to search our merchant vessels to impress their subjects to fight France. I am willing to protect these imported patriots as long as they will remain with-in our territorial jurisdiction, but if they will go to sea and deprive our own sailors of employ, if the English should take the whole of them I would not raise my hand to reclaim them, much more to involve this country, in a ruinous war when it is not in our power to obtain what we are contending for, and it would not be worth anything if we could.

While Potter opposed the War of 1812 (Potter called it on the floor of the House, "Mr. Madison's War"), he also opposed the Hartford Convention where many New England Federalists flirted with leaving the Union.

Although always fighting for the cause in which he believed, as a member of the Federalist Party in the early 1800s, Potter often found himself in the minority. Potter told of one situation:

> I remember a time when we found ourselves in a minority of eleven, and some timid soul had called a sort of meeting, to see if it was worth while to continue the opposition. Some were disposed to be dispirited and I was asked to say a few words to brace them up. Well, it came upon me to say only this: "Friends, just remember that we are as many as the Apostles were after Judas deserted them. Think what *they* did and fight it out." That did the business. We did fight it out and fell fighting for the good cause.

As a member of Congress from Rhode Island, Elisha Potter felt it his obligation to promote commercial interests. In addition, as a Federalist, he forged a successful alliance between Providence and South Kingstown voters. But to the extent Potter defended commercial and manufacturing interests, it was usually in the context of helping farmers – to reduce the costs of manufactured equipment to farmers and to assist merchants carrying farm products on their ships. In Congress, Potter was always against direct taxes, which he felt would place an unfair burden on Rhode Island farmers, who already paid tax on their land. He was against President Jefferson's policy of avoiding war with Britain by ceasing trade with Britain, because he thought such an action would hurt farmers as well as merchants. In Congress, he stated that the embargo raised the price of a farmer's purchases of manufactured goods by 20% to 50%, while at the same time it reduced the price for the farmer's surplus products. Potter also occasionally worked to protect Rhode Island's emerging manufacturing businesses. But inwardly he believed that the ideal life was that of a farmer, which he thought was far better than "being shut up in a manufacturing establishment spinning cotton or making pins and needles." Repeating that quote as evidence, a Providence newspaper in 1810 stated that Potter was "notoriously inimical to the American Manufactures," but that was an exaggeration.

Potter's Character

Potter was a man of enormous size and commanding presence. One description states that he stood more than six feet four inches tall and weighed about 300 pounds. It is said that he paid for two seats when he traveled by coach. In addition, Potter had great charisma. "Wherever he went he was a conspicuous figure, by reason of his gigantic stature, vigorous personality, and keen wit." The influential Federalist leader from Massachusetts, Josiah Quincy, observed that Potter "was one of the men who carry about them a surplus of vital energy." Quincy, Potter and other congressmen, apart from their families in Washington, D.C., often met for dinner together at their boarding house. Quincy recalled of Potter, "I well remember how the faces about Miss Hyer's dining table were wont to be lighted up when he entered the room. Mr. Potter seemed to carry about him a certain homespun certificate of authority, which made it natural for lesser men to accept his conclusions." Potter was not a cultivated speaker or smooth writer, but he was a forceful speaker. He was also a natural politician. One observer noted that his great influence in the state "was the result mainly of his powers and qualities as a man: of his rare natural endowments – his intuitive perceptions of character – his large acquaintance with motives, principles, and passions which belong to human nature and determine the conduct of men."

While Potter could be blustering and boisterous, he had a humble side as well. A man who knew Potter recalled the following exchange after Potter's side was beaten in a town vote.

> Coming down the steps of the old court house – mortified and moody – an inquirer asked about some measure in prospect. "I don't know," said the baffled leader, "I used to have influence enough in South Kingstown to hang any two men in the town. Now I can hardly keep from being hung myself."

On another occasion, an observer wrote that Elisha Potter used to have heated arguments with James Helme and his brothers, who were rival "red-hot Republicans" (James Helme actually served as a state elector in 1804, casting the state's official vote for president for Republican Thomas Jefferson). But when one of the brothers died unexpectedly, Potter permitted the Helme family to use his carriage, attended the funeral and was described as being very much affected. At the national level, while other Federalist Party members, bitter about the War of 1812, avoided their party rivals, Potter "mingled freely with them" and "won them to an easy and generous confidence . . . ."

Potter's Political Influence at the State Level

Potter had his greatest influence in state politics. He served again in the Rhode Island house of representatives from 1798 to 1808, and as speaker in 1802 and from 1806-08. Returning from his seat in Congress, he was elected to the state house of representatives for most years from 1816 to 1835. Potter enjoyed nothing more than on election day in Little Rest, when he would stand near the Court House receiving the homage of his townsmen.

While Potter was all-powerful in South County, he had difficulty winning elections for major offices in statewide elections, probably because of his strong identification with the rural interests in South County. In 1822, seeking to put a cap on his political career, Potter ran for the United States Senate. In those years, the "Grand Committee" of the General Assembly (both houses) selected United States senators by secret ballot. Potter lost by one vote, 30-29, apparently as a result of a double-cross by one of the state senators. In 1827, it was anticipated that Potter would make another run at being selected to the U.S. Senate. The *Manufacturers and Farmers Journal* denounced Potter as an enemy of Providence. A bitter campaign of accusation and recrimination followed. Potter lost his campaign in 1828.

For most of his life, Potter was a loyal member of the Federalist Party, which in the early years of the Republic dominated Rhode Island politics. After the War of 1812, however, the Federalist Party suffered a swift decline. In an age of robust egalitarianism and democracy, the elitist Federalists were seen as an anachronism. Potter ran for governor in 1818 as a Federalist, but he had little chance to win because of the weakness of his party. In their newspapers, Federalists even avoided using the term "Federalist" in speaking of themselves. The Republican Party swept the state elections that year. In 1823, he ran for the United State senate as a Federalist, which contributed to his defeat by a single vote in the Rhode Island legislature. Potter was defeated again as a Federalist in 1828. As the Federalist Party met its demise, Potter had to join another party.

With the Republican Party and later the Whig Party dominated by Providence men with commercial backgrounds whom Potter had battled with over the years in a struggle of city versus country, Potter turned to the new rival party, the Democratic Party, with Andrew Jackson as its national leader. Jacksonian Democrats celebrated the common man, supported agrarian policies, and cast a suspicious eye on large central banks, all of which appealed to Potter. But the party also supported landless, urban workers, which did not appeal to Potter. Potter's switch caused a commotion in Rhode Island, leading even Kingston villager Wilkins Updike to write to a friend, "They came over to Jackson just for what they could get and you see they are governed by no principles . . . ." But given the political realities of the day, Potter cannot be blamed for the switch. In short time, Potter was considered the head of the Jacksonian Democrats in Rhode Island. In 1832, the Democratic Party selected Potter as a delegate to the Democratic convention held in Baltimore, Maryland.

One focus of the national Democratic Party was opposition to powerful central banks. Potter appreciated that local banks (such as his Landholders Bank in Kingston) made cash available to local farmers with produce to sell and that banks paid taxes, which reduced the taxes of farmers. But Potter was justly concerned that a large, central bank that was not under national government control could wield too much power if it issued too much money in one period and at another time restricted the flow of money, resulting in an economic panic and hurting farmers.

The early 1830s were a tumultuous time in Rhode Island politics, with voters having as a choice of political parties Jacksonian Democrats, Whigs, Jeffersonian Republicans (who were on the decline) and Anti-Masons. Potter renewed his campaign for the U.S. Senate in anticipation of the 1833 election. A newspaper that had been moved from Wickford to Kingston in 1831-32, the *Rhode Island Advocate*, printed numerous editorials and advertisements for Democratic candidates. A Republican newspaper accurately stated that the paper was "printed in the garret of one of [Potter's] houses" (it was printed in the current Tavern Hall Club, which Potter then owned). Potter lost the vote in the Grand Committee in the General Assembly to the incumbent. The *Providence Journal* wrote that "Mr. Potter was not personally unpopular, but his Jacksonianism would sink a man ten times more popular than he ever was." However, the election result was challenged on the ground that members of the General Assembly who had been elected as far back as 1831 were not competent to vote for a U.S. Senator to be seated in 1833. After a new election of assemblymen in 1833, with Jacksonian Democrats finally taking control of the General Assembly, Elisha Potter offered a resolution, declaring the previous election null and void. This resolution passed, and a new Grand Committee elected Potter. The incumbent U.S. Senator refused to vacate his seat. One more time, Potter traveled to Washington, D.C., this time to make his case to Congress that he was entitled to the seat. But the U.S. Senate, divided along Whig and Democratic party lines, confirmed that Potter's opponent had been duly elected.

At age 70, in 1835, Potter tried one last time to be elected to the U.S. Senate. An opposition pamphlet, noting his advanced age, conceded that "the vigor of his mind is not diminished by age . . . . He is now, in mental powers, natural and acquired, very much what he was 40 years ago." After an excruciating 20 ballots, the Grand Committee could not arrive at a majority for any candidate, so no U.S. Senator was selected. Potter died later in September 1835, having failed in his quest to be elected to the U.S. Senate.

Potter was accused of questionable electioneering tactics. In 1829, an anti-Potter pamphlet was published in Kingston, entitled *What a Ploughman Said*. The author charged that Potter controlled the votes of all those freemen who had borrowed money from him or from his bank (the Landholders Bank), or who leased farmland from him. Under another arrangement, Potter reportedly leased life interests in small corners of his land to "poor men" who built houses on the land and thereby became "freemen" entitled to vote. The author claimed that all of these men were "bound by the most solemns" to vote for Potter. The pamphleteer also charged that Potter once publicly supported one candidate but ordered his "made" voters to vote against the candidate. Given that the pamphleteer was a political opponent of Potter's, these charges must viewed in that context. It was true, however, that many local men owed Potter money (at least 60 according to an 1816 list), that he hired farmers to work his farms (seven in 1816), and that he controlled the Landholders Bank. Accordingly, many townsmen must have felt pressure to vote according to his wishes. In an age before the secret ballot, influential men such as Potter had means to punish those who were beholden to him but who did not vote his way.

Potter and His Community

While Potter was busy with national and state political concerns, he always had time to devote to his village of Little Rest (Kingston in 1825). He played the key role in organizing the Landholders Bank that was established in Little Rest in 1818, and he served as its president. He donated the most money to the fund for the construction of the Kingston Congregational Church in 1820, despite the fact that he never joined the church as a member. He also donated land for the church's cemetery, Old Fernwood. Furthermore, he was active in the Presbyterian Society, the secular arm of the village Congregational Church that saw to the church's welfare. In addition, Potter played a key role in moving the Tower Hill private school to Little Rest and in establishing the Kingston Academy, the village's fine private school. He served as president and as a trustee of Kingston Academy. In 1826, Potter led a village committee in changing the name of the village from Little Rest to Kingston (see the last chapter in this Part III).

Elisha Potter, Sr. purchased from his cousin Henry Reynolds in 1792 the former home of Elisha Reynolds at the "four corners" and all the farmland behind it (about 650 acres). In 1809, Potter built a three-story house on the land, down a lane off of Main Street across from the old school house. The property, which he called the Homestead, is in fine condition today, with two outbuildings, a large barn, and the remnants of a formal garden. Potter's Homestead farm extended west all the way to Biscuit City Road.

Potter became a wealthy man. In 1816, much of his property was set forth in a list as part of a court case. The list sets forth the following holdings, with an aggregate value of $110,690: eight farms, each with an average value of about $8,000, including farms at Boston Neck, Point Judith, and current West Kingston, and William Potter's former farms up North Road and in western New York; four more lots of land, two of them with houses; stock in the Landholders Bank and "Factory Stock;" notes from 60 different persons indebted to Potter; and (apparently at the Homestead house) three carriages, a pair of bay horses, five other horses; two oxen; 200 sheep; and two cows. In an 1810 circular letter to friends to promote Potter's candidacy to Congress, it was stated that he would represent the agricultural interests, as he was "one of the largest landholders in the State."

After 1816, Potter dabbled in mercantile activities, acquiring a one-half interest in the South Ferry in Narragansett and acquiring partial interests in several sloops built at Narragansett Pier. Potter apparently did sacrifice his principles once by investing in "factory stock."

Potter continued to serve as a lawyer and even made an oral argument in the United States Supreme Court – although the argument was in a case in which he was a party. The case arose out of Potter's purchase for $15,000 of a farm to the west of Little Rest from Ezekiel Gardiner. Gardiner had inherited the land from his father, who in his will stated that the possessor of the land had to "pay all my just debts out of said estate." After Potter purchased the land, Ezekiel Gardiner claimed that Potter was responsible for the estate's debts in the amount of $7,593. In the lawsuit that followed, Potter lost in the Rhode Island state courts, but he was able to have an appeal heard by the United States Supreme Court. Chief Justice John Marshall, writing for a unanimous court in favor of Potter, ruled that "Potter had a right to purchase [the land] free of all such charges and encumbrances."

Potter's first marriage to Mary Perkins ended with Mary's early death in 1809. The couple had no children. A little over a year later, Elisha married Mary Mawney, a niece of Mary Perkins and a descendant from a Huguenot family that had settled in East Greenwich in 1686. Elisha and Mary had five children, four boys and one girl, Mary Elizabeth. Potter's greatest contributions to Little Rest may have been his children. The lives of Elisha Reynolds Potter, Jr., Colonel James B. M. Potter, Dr. Thomas Potter and William Potter fill many pages of this book.

After his last attempt to be elected to the U.S. Senate, Potter told a friend, "My race is run and I shall fall with the next fall of leaves." The day Potter returned from a trip to the west, he discovered that his beloved wife Mary had died and was being buried that same day. A few days later, on September 26, 1835, Elisha Reynolds Potter, Sr.'s full life ended. He was buried in the Potter family cemetery near the Homestead in a large vault.[18]

---

[18] It is sometimes incorrectly reported that Elisha R. Potter, Sr.'s gravesite has been lost. In 1882, at the death of his son, Elisha R. Potter, Jr., a newspaper article stated that Elisha Jr. was laid to rest in "the old family vault back of the house," beside the remains of his father, mother and step-mother. The article stated that "the old vault had not been opened for forty-five years." A recent visit inside the vault by Craig Anthony of the Pettaquamscutt Historical Society confirmed that a marker for the Elisha R. Potter, Sr. still exists.

The Little Rest Village Club of Practical Jokers

In 1806, Charles Comstock of Newport and South Kingstown wrote and had published a most extraordinary book, titled *A History of South Kingstown.* The book had the subtitle *"With a Particular Description of the Hornet's Nest Company, and the Cats Let Out of the Bag."* The author focuses on a club of practical jokers who caused him much grief that was located in the village of Little Rest (he calls it the "Hornet's Nest"), which is now called Kingston. The book is extraordinary because it focuses on the humor of ordinary villagers and the emergence of a popular, entrepreneurial culture in Rhode Island in the early 1800s.

The author does not claim to have discovered Comstock's book. It was actually republished in 1934, with a forward by Washington County historian William Davis Miller. But the author does believe that the book's significance and usefulness as a tool to study the popular culture of the period has been underestimated. There are two likely reasons why the book has been overlooked. First, it is difficult to read. It is written in dense language. Its flow is also frequently interrupted with tangential discussions, many of them of an obscure religious nature. In addition, many of the spaces for names have been left blank in the first part of the book. However, Comstock uses names later in the book, making it is possible to discern who was referenced earlier in the book. This chapter will attempt to make the stories more accessible by paraphrasing and re-ordering them.

A second reason why Comstock's book has been overlooked is that its central story, the "Cat Inspector" story, was retold by a renowned storyteller in the late 19th century. In *The Jonny-Cake Papers,* Thomas R. "Shepherd Tom" Hazard re-told the story in exaggerated form, making it the central story of his book. This has resulted in Comstock's original "Cat Inspector" story being overshadowed, even though in many ways it is the more interesting of the two versions.

Background of Comstock's Book

Comstock's book is a satirical diatribe against certain "cunning" and "unscrupulous" townspeople in South Kingstown. Comstock apparently was motivated to write the book out of anger after he had moved in 1802 from Newport to a farm in South Kingstown, claiming that he was then cheated in a number of business dealings with South Kingstown men. Comstock was also angry because he became a target of one of the Little Rest club's best practical jokes.

Comstock's tone is one of outrage, but clearly, he has a strong sense of humor himself. After he was the target of an elaborate practical joke, Comstock returned to Little Rest to make fun of the episode. He also placed after his name on the title page of the book initials that would indicate that he was a member of the Royal Society of London, a suggestion that can only be a joke.

Comstock's chief antagonist was farmer, merchant and deputy sheriff Elisha Reynolds Gardner. Gardner was well suited for his position as deputy sheriff, as he was "notorious for wit, shrewdness and unpolished intelligence" and was "a large and muscular man." In addition to serving as deputy sheriff, Gardner was a justice of the peace, who could serve court writs and incarcerate in the jail individuals suspected of committing crimes. Gardner also owned farms and engaged in lending money to local persons. In 1803, he built a two-story house at the corner of South Road and main street in Little Rest. He was the grandson of Elisha Reynolds, who played such a vital role in early Little Rest, and the nephew of Caleb Gardner, the Narragansett planter whose farm was located east of North Road just above the village.

In the early 1800s, Little Rest was in its golden age. While physically it only amounted to a collection of about thirty houses and public buildings (many of which survive today), Little Rest had an importance beyond its size. For one, it was the government seat for Washington County. The Court House building on main street at the edge of Little Rest hill served as one of the five rotating state capitals of Rhode Island; it was the location for Washington County's court of common pleas and supreme court, both of which met twice a year; and it was the location for South Kingstown's town meeting. The nearby jail housed criminals and debtors. In addition, Little Rest served as the hub for agricultural Washington County. General stores in Little Rest, in exchange for receiving farm produce, sold foodstuffs, alcohol, useful household items and farm supplies to farmers. Blacksmiths, sadlers (saddle-makers), hatters, tanners, locksmiths and other craftsmen serviced outlying farmers. At least three substantial village taverns serviced locals and visitors. This was a time when agriculture still dominated Washington County, just before the period when wool and cotton mills in Peace Dale, Usquepaug, South Ferry, Davisville and other communities would come to transform rural Washington County.

Elisha Gardner and His Practical Jokes

Comstock professes outrage that practical jokers in Little Rest would "glory" in their jokes rather than be embarrassed by them. Comstock begins his book by describing some of the practical jokes committed by the Little Rest club of practical jokers. "There is a little village in this town, where the court-house stands, called Little Rest. Some people call it Restless Hill. I think it resembles a hornet's nest; for the people are some like hornets." Comstock gives the following examples of "hornet's nest cunning."

The leader of the hornet's nest practical jokers, Elisha Gardner, the deputy sheriff of South Kingstown, was known for dealing in a special way with men who had become drunk in Little Rest. When Gardner would come across a man who was sleeping in a public place in the village in an intoxicated stupor, Gardner would grab a jug of water, pick up one of the man's arms, and pour water into the long-sleeves of the man's shirt. The reaction of the intoxicated man with water floating in his long-sleeves was a source of great mirth for the Little Rest practical jokers.

Comstock was told about an evening in which "an old man got intoxicated at the hornet's nest, and [Elisha Gardner] poured one quart of water in his sleeve." Gardner then pretended that he was not the man who had poured the water and that he would help the man to find the "rogue" who had perpetrated the deed. As Gardner led the angry drunken man to the door to find the "rogue," one of Gardner's Little Rest accomplices blew out the only candle that was providing light and another Little Rest accomplice "threw a pail of water in the old man's face."

In another incident, Comstock witnessed Elisha Gardner "and a number of others making sport of an old man that was somewhat intoxicated." The unsuspecting elderly man, an out-of-towner, informed the group that he had a promissory note that required William Nichols to pay him money. The elderly man did not know Nichols personally and had purchased the note from someone else. The Little Rest men "told the old man that they did not believe he had got such a note" and claimed that it must have been forged. Deputy sheriff Elisha Gardner then sent for Nichols, and when a young man came, Gardner called him William Nichols. Gardner asked the young man if "the old man had a note against him" and the young man "said he had not." The old man disputed the charge, and the younger man "said he would indict him for forgery if he [the old man] did not give up the note, and pay him two dollars." Deputy Sheriff Elisha Gardner advised the old man to comply or he would suffer being "cropt and branded." Gardner and others continued to apply pressure on the older man, who must have been very concerned about his well-being. Of course, the young man was not William Nichols and Gardner had no intention of charging the older man. It was all a practical joke. Comstock complained that the Little Rest practical jokers "abused the old man shamefully with their lies and their hornet's nest cunning."

On another occasion, Elisha Gardner and John Nichols, the sadler, persuaded a male member of the Little Rest club of jokers to dress up as a woman and accuse Joseph Stanton of being the father of "her" child. (Stanton, a tanner, lived with his family in a cottage at the corner of main street and Biscuit City Road.) The female imposter insisted on child support payments from Stanton. Deputy Sheriff Gardner carried the jest to the point where he was about to commit Stanton to jail for failing to give a bond for child support. At that point, the Little Rest practical jokers disclosed the joke to Stanton. Comstock wrote reprovingly, "I think that was too much for a man that has a justices commission."

Comstock also describes "April fools" jokes that Elisha Gardner played on "some of his fellow hornets." Gardner "goes the first day of April to Asa Fellows, who was his brother in law, and told him that Miss Potter (probably the first wife of Elisha Potter, the village's wealthy and powerful politician) wanted to see him; others he told that somebody else wanted to see them." The people he informed naturally spent time in the day seeking out the named party. In these days of travel by horseback or walking, that could take substantial time and effort. Of course, Gardner was making all of this up, making "April fools of them."

Asa Fellows played his own April fools practical joke the next year. Fellows went to the court house and obtained a writ against one Pemberton Belcher, and went to Elisha Gardner, who was still a deputy sheriff, and asked that he serve it on Mr. Belcher. Gardner responded that he had another appointment, but Fellows insisted that Gardner serve the writ. "Fellows told him that he could not get any other officer, and told him further that the man lived out of the state, and that he was afraid he should lose the debt . . . ." Fellows then informed Gardner that Pemberton Belcher likely could be found "at a house about 3 miles from the Hill, which he named." Gardner then agreed to ride his horse the three miles and serve the writ. But when he arrived at the house named by Fellows and asked for Pemberton Belcher, the residents of the house told Gardner that "they did not know such a man; and told him there was a man by the name of Joseph Belcher, that lived about two miles off." Gardner rode there as well, but "could not find a man by the name of Pemberton Belcher." Comstock concluded, "I don't suppose there was such a man to be found." In the meantime, back in Little Rest, Fellows explained to fellow villagers the practical joke he had pulled on Gardner. When Gardner returned, "the people called him April fool." Even Gardner's wife yelled out "April fool" to him! Gardner "was very angry; and swore that he would prosecute Fellows for serving him such a low dirty trick." But Gardner later calmed down and realized that one April fools joke deserved the other.

Comstock also mentions some lewd practical jokes that some of the Little Rest practical jokers played on certain Native American Narragansett women, one of which is too lewd for the author to repeat. The women were poor, in a degraded condition and vulnerable to exploitation. "They term squaw hunting, hunting black rats; and when they say that they have ketched a black rat, their meaning is that they have had to do with a squaw. There is one . . . the hatter, who has frequently told me that he had been a hunting black rats; and that he had ketched black rats; sometimes very large ones; and he did not appear ashamed of it." One of the Little Rest practical jokers told Comstock that while attending the "negro elections" festival, "the old way of inspecting black rats and cheating them, was to grind a copper smooth and pass it to a black rat in the dark for an English shilling, for a chance of inspecting the black rat and boast of it afterwards, and appear to be proud of it for they are not ashamed of cheating any one they can."

Comment. From Comstock's descriptions, it is obvious that Little Rest villagers enjoyed practical jokes. In an age before television, radio, and movies, and located far away from urban centers that at the time had at least some recreational distractions, practical jokes in Little Rest served as a form of entertainment. While much of the humor of this period was based on the country rube being out of place in the city, or the city dweller being out of place in the country, the jokes here focus on country people fooling each other. In rural South Kingstown, where things moved slowly, people had time to plan the jokes and talk and laugh about them later in taverns, shops and houses afterwards. Practical jokes can also be cruel to the jokes' victims. Some villagers, as well as Comstock, may have felt that Gardner at times went too far in the exercise of his deputy sheriff position.

It is noteworthy that Gardner felt that excessive drinking was a problem in Little Rest. There were plenty of outlets for alcohol. At this time, there were at least two general stores in Little Rest that sold rum, gin and other alcohol by the bottle. There were also at least three substantial taverns that sold liquor by the glass. Elisha Gardner himself, after spending one night ill attended by two friends, woke up the next morning feeling better. He promptly ambled over to a general store to buy rum for his two sleep-deprived friends. Eventually, the concern over the problem of excessive drinking, coupled with a powerful evangelical movement, resulted in an organized temperance movement beginning in Rhode Island in the late 1820s. In 1829, Little Rest would have its own temperance society and annual July 4th temperance speeches.

Humor is sometimes made at the expense of a different racial or ethnic group, and here we have humor at the expense of the Narragansett Indian tribe. The Narragansetts had been at the time of the arrival of Roger Williams the most powerful tribe in southern New England, but by the time of Comstock's book had had their way of life destroyed and much of their lands fraudulently acquired by white men. Comstock apparently felt it was acceptable to include these stories of sexual promiscuity so long as they involved Native American women. It was not socially acceptable at the time in "proper" society to have told such stories involving white women. Interestingly, by stating that a "hatter" procured the services of Indian prostitutes, Comstock practically names the man, as there was only one hat-making operation in Little Rest at the time. The master hatters were Cyrus French and his son William French, who operated a hat-making business in their house across the street from the jail. The Frenches were both married.

Despite the fact that Washington County, and South Kingstown in particular, had the highest proportion of black slaves in colonial rural New England, Comstock did not include African-Americans in his story, other than to mention the well-known "negro election" festival. At this annual festival, Washington County black men and women gathered to elect a mock governor, and to enjoy dancing, games and other activities. Comstock's description is useful in that it reminds us that at this time, African-Americans and Native Americans frequently mixed in each other's company, resulting in descendants today of mixed heritage. This mixing occurred in the early colonial period as well. When the town meeting attempted (unsuccessfully) to outlaw the festival in 1726 and again in 1737, it mentioned that the festival was attended by "Indians and Negro servants and others."

Many of the African-Americans in Washington County had been recently freed as a result of the 1784 gradual emancipation legislation and the new moral environment after the end of the American Revolution in 1783 and the state's adoption of the U.S. Constitution in 1790. Some African-Americans remained, however, in bondage. In 1796, Elisha Gardner himself inherited a slave woman, named Patience, from his grandfather who had been a substantial slaveholder in colonial times, with his farm just north of Little Rest. Stunningly, when Gardner brought Patience before the South Kingstown town council in 1806, the town council rejected Gardner's request to approve of Patience's manumission. The town council was concerned that Patience and other freed slaves would become town charges once freed. Gardner sued the town council to free Patience, with the county supreme court ruling in his (and Patience's) favor in 1808.

The elderly man who was accused of forgery and threatened with cropping and branding was right to be concerned about his welfare. At this time, judges often had discretion to crop a criminal's ears or brand the skin of a criminal with a hot poker iron. The crime of forgery was dealt with harshly. In one Little Rest case, a convicted forger had his ears cropped and his face branded while held in a pillory in front of the Court House, after which the man was returned to jail with blood running from his ears. More typically, the choice of corporal punishment was whipping "on the Naked Back," which was inflicted on several men and women each year at the county jail in Little Rest in the early 1800s.

The charge against Joseph Stanton for fathering an illegitimate child was also no laughing matter. In order to avoid illegitimate children from being supported by town funds, the town frequently tracked down the fathers of illegitimate children and forced them to secure a bond and pay for child support. If the accused man could not afford it, he could be placed in jail. As late as 1811, a man was put in jail on a charge of "bastardy" and the town council ordered him to be "bound out" to a family to perform services until he paid the town's costs of his illegitimate child.

'Lisha Gardner, Cat Inspector

The story of "'Lisha Gardner, Cat Inspector," was made famous by the renowned Washington County storyteller, "Shepherd Tom" Hazard in his *Jonny-Cake Papers*. Hazard told the story, based on Charles Comstock's *A History of South Kingstown*, in exaggerated form. The version set forth below closely follows Comstock's original version.

One evening, Charles Comstock was resting in a comfortable chair in the Joseph Reynolds tavern, at the time the premier tavern in Little Rest. With Comstock in the room was a man Comstock did not know. Elisha Gardner walked into the room. The man Comstock did not know shook hands with Elisha Gardner as if they were old acquaintances. Elisha Gardner, turning to Comstock, said, "Mr. Comstock, this is Colonel Cook of New London." Elisha Gardner was aware that Comstock had a side business of purchasing local farm products and shipping them to Nantucket Island (which at the time was experiencing an economic boom from the whaling industry). Gardner knew that Comstock wanted to purchase butter to ship to Nantucket. Gardner asked Colonel Cook what the price of butter was in New London. Cook responded that the price was eleven cents per pound. Gardner then asked if Cook could sell Comstock a quantity of butter. Cook responded that he could sell Gardner 3,000 to 4,000 pounds of butter upon a few days notice, as Cook said that he kept a large stock in New London. Comstock (always eager to make a business deal, but always short of hard cash) told Cook that he would want to purchase the butter on credit. Gardner then interjected that Comstock "was an honest man, and there was no doubt but that he would pay him honestly." Comstock then stated that he would first buy 1,000 pounds of butter on credit, and after being paid upon reselling the butter in Nantucket, he would pay Cook and then buy the remaining 2,000 pounds of butter. Colonel Cook and Comstock agreed to the deal.

After agreeing to the butter deal, Colonel Cook asked Comstock where he could purchase some mules. Cook wanted to ship the mules and sell them to planters in the Caribbean islands. Comstock responded that Connecticut was the best place to buy mules, as few mules were raised for sale in Rhode Island. Colonel Cook informed Comstock that there were no mules to be purchased in Connecticut, as the surplus mules had already been purchased and shipped away by others. Elisha Gardner then asked Colonel Cook what price he would pay for mules in Rhode Island. Cook responded that if the mules were "likely ones," he would pay $60 per head for them. "Then [Gardner] tucked my elbow, and asked me to go aside with him; and when we were aside together he told me that Sylvester Hazard had two mules, that were very likely ones, and he wanted to sell them." Gardner suggested that Comstock could buy them on "long credit." This conversation "embarrassed" Comstock, because deputy sheriff Gardner held two writs that would be served on Comstock if Comstock did not pay two outstanding debts in ten days. (So Gardner knew that Comstock was short of cash and could buy only on credit.) Gardner pressured Comstock, saying that Colonel Cook was anxious to purchase Hazard's two mules, and that Cook had "two bags of money" to purchase mules. Gardner said that he was confident that Cook would pay $70 per head for the mules, so that it was an opportunity for Comstock to make some money. Gardner added that he knew that Sylvester Hazard was at a house in Little Rest, and that Comstock should see Hazard and talk with him about selling the mules to Comstock. Comstock agreed and made the short walk to where Hazard was visiting and "asked if Sylvester Hazard was there." The response was that he had gone home. Comstock stayed to banter a few minutes, when "a number of young men that lived in" Little Rest entered the house and also asked for Hazard. One of the young men said that he had to see Hazard that night or very early the next morning. Gardner, hearing this, then warned Comstock that Comstock should see Hazard that night or very early the next morning before the young man did, so as to purchase the mules before the young man did.

Gardner and Comstock then returned to Joseph Reynolds tavern. Gardner asked Colonel Cook if he would pay $70 per head for the mules. Cook said that he would pay only $60 per head for them, "if they were ever so likely."

Gardner then asked Colonel Cook if Cook wanted to purchase some "Jacks" (cats). Cook said that he did not. Gardner then explained that all the cats had died in two islands in the Caribbean, and that Cook could ship cats to the islands as well as mules, as the cats "would fetch a great price." Cook then changed his mind and said that he would ship cats with his mules. Gardner then agreed with Cook that Gardner would sell Cook 200 cats at 75 cents apiece. Gardner and Cook signed an agreement. Gardner then asked Comstock, George Douglass (a village blacksmith) and one other villager to join him in a partnership to purchase the cats. Gardner put the partnership agreement down in writing, with the condition that if 20 cats could be obtained that night, Cook would purchase 200 cats at 75 cents apiece.

Comstock told Gardner that "it was too late to get any cats that night." Gardner responded that Comstock and Douglass should walk to the house of William French (a hatter in the village) for French "had got six or seven cats." Comstock responded that French would be in bed sleeping. Gardner suggested that Comstock could "call" at French's window and French would "get up." Gardner then said that he would go to collect five or six cats at his own house. Gardner said he would meet with Comstock and

Douglass "at the coffee-house"[19] in half an hour.

Comstock and Douglass walked over to French's house in the pitch dark. Douglass called up to William French at his bedroom window, waking French up. Douglass told French that he wanted to purchase some cats and asked how many cats French had. French said he had seven cats. Comstock did not have cash to purchase the cats, so he attempted to arrange for a barter trade. Comstock said that he would trade French's cats for pigs that Comstock would bring to the village in the next week. French said that he would trade three pounds of pig for one pound of cat. Comstock responded that he thought that a pound of pork meat was worth as much as a pound of cat meat, and that he would not pay that price. Gardner then arrived and argued that Comstock should agree to the terms, as Colonel Cook was thinking of getting out of the agreement to purchase the cats. Time was of the essence. Comstock angrily shooed Gardner away, but he ultimately agreed to French's terms, to trade three pounds of pig for one pound of cat. French found only two of his cats.

The "Cat Company" brought the cats to the Joseph Reynolds tavern, where Colonel Cook was staying. Cook said that the cats "were likely ones" and handed Gardner $1.50 for them. The tavern keeper, who was roused from his sleep, said that his daughter had two cats that she could sell to Cook. The daughter brought them and Cook paid for these as well. The daughter then "went up chamber" and found a cat with six kittens. Cook said that he would pay for four kittens the same as one cat. The Cat Company agreed. Cook then paid the money to Gardner, "for we were all partners together." Comstock then informed Cook that he had five more cats from William French to sell to Cook and Cook said that he would take them. Gardner added that he had been to another local villager's house whose owner had eight cats that he would trade for pigs as well. Gardner added further that other villagers were willing to trade their cats for pigs, including Elisha Potter with seven cats and tavern keeper Charles Barker with five cats. The orders for the cats were written down and Comstock signed the orders.

---

[19] It is not known what Little Rest tavern was associated with the name "coffee-house." Coffee houses had appeared as an alternative to taverns in large cities such as Boston, New York and Philadelphia. It was not likely that an establishment in Little Rest would have been solely devoted to coffee. It is possible that one of the village's taverns was called the "coffee house," but that the tavern served more alcohol than coffee. A study of Massachusetts taverns in the 18th century concluded that "coffee houses" were often misnamed, as they sold more alcohol than coffee. The 1819 inventory of Charles Barker's tavern indicates that he sold coffee and tea. It was probable that one of the village's taverns had a room that was devoted to coffee in the mornings, which room was called the "coffee house."

When the order forms were completed, Gardner exclaimed that the "he had received all the money for all the cats, and for all the orders that Mr. Comstock has turned in, and he had received twenty dollars for Mr. Comstock." Cook responded that he had agreed with William Lunt (the Little Rest barber and wig maker) for Lunt to carry up to 200 cats in a wagon to New London. Cook said that he had also purchased a cow, whose milk could be used to attract cats. Cook added that he wanted 20 cats delivered to Peter Boss's house the next day by 10 o'clock in the morning, and said that if Comstock would deliver them to Boss's house, he would pay Comstock an extra $1. (Boss's house, which was also a small tavern, was located north of the village on North Road.)

The "Cat Company" members agreed that Comstock would wake up George Douglass (a blacksmith) early the next morning. Comstock and the rest of the "Cat Company" must have then caught a little sleep. Early the next morning, Comstock roused Douglass and Gardner out of bed. They went their separate ways in search of cats. Comstock and Douglass rode their horses to Sylvester Hazard's house to purchase his two mules. Hazard, however, would not sell the mules. Douglass then said to Comstock that he knew where they could buy some cats. They bought two cats for six cents a piece from one villager and one other cat from another villager. Comstock then walked with a man to his house about 150 rods from the village and purchased two more cats. In the meantime, Little Rest villagers brought cats they were willing to sell to Joseph Reynolds tavern where they "shut them up in a closet, about sixteen in all." The time was nearing when Comstock had to deliver 20 cats to Colonel Cook at Peter Boss's house.

It was at this point that Sylvester Hazard approached Comstock and informed Comstock that the whole Cat Company business was a joke! James Helme, a respected villager, confirmed with Comstock that the entire affair was a joke. He explained that "Colonel" Cook was in fact Cook, a village hatter who was an apprentice to William French in the hat making trade and that Elisha Gardner had arranged for Cook the apprentice hatter to play the role of Colonel Cook of New London.

Comstock claimed to be unfazed. He told Hazard and Helme that "I had got the cats and that I intended to deliver them according to my agreement, and that I intended that Cook should pay for them or I intended to sue him." Comstock then stuffed about 14 cats in a sack, put the sack on his horse, and rode to Peter Boss's house to wait for Cook. Cook was late, so Comstock asked Boss if Comstock could leave the cats in one of Boss's rooms for Cook to pick up later. Boss responded that he would not give up a room for that purpose. He suggested that Comstock deliver the cats to Cook to establish that Comstock had fulfilled his part of the bargain, so that Comstock "would stand clear to bring an action against Cook." Comstock, again carrying his cats in a bag across his horse, was riding back to Little Rest when he met with Elisha Gardner near Adam Gould's house. Gardner then said that Comstock "had better take the cats off the mare" so that Gardner could "inspect them, and see if they were merchantable." Comstock took the bag of cats off of his horse. Gardner then "took them out of the bag one by one, and inspected them." In inspecting them, Gardner "did not brand them under the tail, for he had no branding iron." Instead, Gardner viewed each cat's eyes and "I believe inspected them faithfully, and I don't think that they can get a better cat inspector in the whole state." Gardner, from then on known as the "Cat Inspector," said that he found two cats that were blind, and that there were only 12 merchantable cats. Gardner ended the meeting with Comstock by stating that he had provided Colonel Cook with 40 cats, that Colonel Cook had not yet paid for the cats, and that Gardner intended to sue Cook.

It was reported later by Little Rest villagers that Adam Gould earlier had predicted that the "New Lights" (the name for church goers who preferred a more evangelical religious experience) would turn into cats. The cats inspected by Gardner escaped into Gould's house. Gould, excited by the deluge, exclaimed that they were "new-lights turned into cats according to his prediction." Gould then began preaching to the cats. Villagers later said that the cats turned into hogs, so that Gould wound up owning 14 hogs.

A few days later, Comstock returned to Little Rest. In a village tavern, Sylvester Hazard (the man who had earlier refused to sell Comstock his two mules) walked up to Comstock and began "meowing" and scratching Comstock on the shoulder. Elisha Gardner, the Cat Inspector, was also in the room. Comstock seized Hazard by his collar and yelled to the "Cat Inspector" that he wanted "this cat inspected." Gardner inspected the cat and pronounced Hazard to be a "mofferadite" cat.[20] Comstock then went over to Cook and informed him that he had had Hazard inspected. Cook agreed to buy Hazard at half price, adding that he wanted a pair of "mofferadite" cats and that he was looking for another cat that was "suitable to span him." Comstock ended, "whether Cook has got him spanned or not, I do not know."

Comstock never did sue Cook to force him to buy the cats. Comstock found out that Cook was so poor that he had to rent out a room in the Little Rest jail, and that he was an apprentice to French in the "hatter's trade." Suing Cook "was like the old saying, 'sue a beggar and catch a louse.'"

Comstock apparently had had enough of Little Rest and South Kingstown. He announced that he was moving to Newport to operate a tavern. Comstock accused Gardner of attempting to gain more official

---

[20] The author does not understand the reference to "mofferadite."

positions. Comstock wrote, sarcastically, "This Elisha R. Gardner is very fond of office, for he has been laying a plan, in order to get another office, and I think he is likely to obtain it, if he gets his branding iron and comes over to Newport and brands the cats when he is requested to, for cats will not sell in the town of Newport unless they are inspected and branded with the letters, E.R.G. under their tails, as cat inspector . . . ." Comstock also wrote, sarcastically, that Gardner "told me that he expected to be a great man like General Washington, and expected that his effigee would be set up at the corners of the streets like Washington . . . ." Elisha Gardner then advised Comstock that in order to attract customers, Comstock should "set up a sign of a cat" on his tavern sign, and that the sign should include "a likeness of the cat inspector also." This Comstock did.

Comment. The "Cat Inspector" story reveals the emergence of an entrepreneurial culture among ordinary persons. We see Charles Comstock and other villagers scrambling to enter into small commercial transactions. Comstock was willing to go to considerable efforts to purchase and gather individual cats in order to resell them at a small profit. He did not have cash reserves or the ability to borrow money, so he arranged for bartering transactions, in which he would fulfill his side of the trade at a later date. The practice of capitalism was in full swing, but on a very small scale.

The "Cat Inspector" story also reveals the importance of taverns as a place to enter into business deals and for local villagers to meet and swap stories. Taverns were, however, a place where only white males congregated.

The "Cat Inspector" story has the ring of a folk tale to it, particularly when the cats reportedly turn into hogs. The author leaves to others possible interpretations of the story in this regard.

Credit Transactions in Little Rest – Comstock's Go Sour

Charles Comstock wrote his *History of South Kingstown* in part to expose what he considered the shady business practices of certain South Kingstown businessmen. Comstock moved from Newport to South Kingstown in 1802 and purchased the large house and farm formerly owned by John Potter, a wealthy Narragansett planter in colonial times. Comstock immediately ran into trouble with some townspeople. "I made the mistake of marking a flock of sheep, and through a mistake marked some that was not mine . . . ." Some townspeople then "reported that I was a thief, and gave me an infamous character." When Comstock then purchased another farm in the town on credit, some townspeople must have been concerned about Comstock's ability to pay for two farms. The rumor was spread that Comstock could not pay for the farms, "which was a notorious falsehood." One of Comstock's neighbors "came riding into the field half drunk and said here is a man who has purchased a farm and, cannot pay for it."

The Cat Inspector.

The "Cat Inspector." Probably a portrait of Elisha R. Gardner, deputy sheriff and practical joker. Cover of pamphlet, Charles Comstock's *A History of South Kingstown,* 1806. *John Hay Library, Brown University.*

Comstock carried on a side business purchasing goods on credit and transporting them by vessel from South Kingstown to Nantucket. While on his trips, Comstock was unable to make payments on his debts to local townsfolk. During one of his trips to Nantucket, "they reported that I had run away. When I returned home, I found seven copies of writs, and one pair of my oxen was carried off." Comstock, understandably, was livid. Comstock had further difficult business dealings. He describes how, in his view, he was cheated out land in complex credit and mortgage dealings by an "unscrupulous" South Kingstown man.

Not surprisingly, Comstock had a difficult time in business matters in Little Rest as well. He had business difficulties with John Nichols, the sadler, who had his house and shop in the current Helme House. Nichols was a member of the Society of Friends, also known as Quakers, who were known for their plain dress and honesty. "There is one John Nichols who is a saddlemaker, that lives at the hornets nest, and wears a plain coat, and he has been in company so much with this cat inspector, that he has learnt to make use of the false tongue." Comstock stated that he entertained "a very good opinion of real Friends, but this John Nichols appears to me, to be a disgrace to the society."

The problem started when Comstock sold Nichols some skins for making saddles, pursuant to an agreement in which Nichols agreed to pay Comstock the money in ten days. Despite numerous efforts by Comstock to collect on the debt and further promises from Nichols, Nichols did not pay. After about six months, Nichols sued Comstock in court to stop the collection efforts! Nichols then promised that he would stop the lawsuit and pay the debt. Another man, to whom Comstock owed money on another matter, purchased some saddles from Nichols on credit by giving Nichols Comstock's note. This last transaction apparently resulted in offsetting and satisfying Nichol's prior debt to Comstock.

Comstock later purchased some saddles from Nichols on credit for $30 and Nichols agreed to take a demand note and wait until Comstock could come up with the money to pay the note. Comstock was able to repay $10 of the debt faster than the parties had anticipated. Nonetheless, without asking Comstock to pay the remaining $20, Nichols sued Comstock for the remaining $20. Comstock confronted Nichols and "asked how he came to treat me in such a shameful manner . . . I asked him whether I had not paid him faster than I talked of paying him, and he said I had paid him sooner than I told him I would pay him." Nichols apparently promised that he would pay Comstock's court costs from the lawsuit, but Nichols "would not pay one cent of it, and his word is not worth one cent in my opinion, unless he is bound in writing."

Comment. In the early 1800s in Rhode Island, few banks loaned money to ordinary people. Little Rest would not have a bank until 1818. It was difficult for ordinary craftsmen, farmers and small merchants to obtain paper money. In colonial times, Rhode Island could and did issue its own paper money, but under the new United States Constitution, only the national government could issue paper money. In order to buy or sell products and services, ordinary people in rural communities often had to buy or sell on credit and engage in barter transactions. In this type of economy, the reputation of a man for honesty and fair dealing was crucial. If people did not believe a man was reputable, he could not buy on credit, and he would have little chance to "get ahead." Comstock was well aware of this circumstance.

The county court of common pleas and local justices courts at this time were primarily devoted to forcing debtors to repay creditors. In each bi-annual session of the county court of common pleas, dozens of cases were brought by merchants, general storekeepers and other shopkeepers to force debtors to repay amounts due "by book" or "by note." John Nichols, described in court records as a "sadler," filed many cases against his customers in the 1790s and early 1800s. Charles Comstock, described in court records as a "trader," also sued a South Kingstown man for nonpayment of a note in 1805.

Elisha R. Gardner Suffers the Last Laugh

"Shepherd Tom" Hazard, in his *The Jonny-Cake Papers,* tells of several more practical jokes played by Elisha Gardner. They celebrate the common man and the rural lifestyle. In one, Little Rest villager (and Irish immigrant) Benjamin Storer is informed that the governor of Rhode Island, Arthur Fenner, who at the time was staying in Little Rest with Elisha Potter, the most powerful politician in Washington County, wanted to view Storer's prize-winning hog, which was kept in a pen in Storer's front yard. Governor Fenner and Elisha Potter amble over to Storer's house. When they arrive, they break into laughter, as Storer's hog is entirely clean-shaven. They learn later that Gardner, upon hearing about the planned visit, paid barber William Lunt to shave the hog.

Ironically, it was Charles Comstock's nemesis in the field of practical jokes, Elisha Gardner, who suffered a severe financial reverse. Gardner reportedly co-signed on a note on behalf of a friend, but the friend defaulted on the note, forcing Gardner to auction his property to pay the note. In about 1823, Gardner and his large family, with a large wagon and two horses remaining, left Little Rest for upstate New York to start a new life. One feels that the loss was Little Rest's.

The Town Council Prevents Elisha Gardner from
Freeing his Slave

With the ideology of equality and natural rights permeating American culture after the Revolutionary War, the system of slavery that had been quietly introduced in the American colonies in colonial times now appeared as an embarrassment. The northern states, starting with Pennsylvania in 1780 and ending with New Jersey in 1804, gradually cleansed themselves of slavery.

Rhode Island did not enact a bill for the immediate abolition of black slaves. Instead, it enacted a gradual emancipation bill. In 1784, the General Assembly enacted a law providing that any black person born after the law was enacted was to be considered a free person. This was far more complicated than a simple immediate abolition. For one, the state and town councils had to determine what to do with children who were born free to mothers who continued as slaves.

The preamble to the 1784 act was written in the ideological language of the day – "Whereas, all men are entitled to life, liberty, and the pursuit of happiness, and the holding mankind in a state of slavery, as private property, which has gradually obtained by unrestrained custom and the permission of the laws, is repugnant to this principle, and subversive of the happiness of mankind, the great end of all civil government. . . ." The body of the act stipulated that "no person or persons, whether negroes, mulattoes, or others, who shall be born within the limits of this state, on or after the first day of March, A.D., 1784, shall be deemed or considered as servants for life, or slaves," and that "all servitude for life, or slavery of children, to be born as aforesaid in consequence of the condition of their mothers, be, and the same is hereby taken away, extinguished, and forever abolished." Noting that "humanity requires" that "children declared free as aforesaid" remain with their mothers "a convenient time" following their birth, the act required town councils to reimburse "those who claim the services" of their mothers for the costs of supporting the children during that time. In addition, the town councils were required to reimburse slaveowners for the educational, moral and religious instruction of such children, according to the "earnest desire of this Assembly." This was a relatively enlightened approach to insure that the children of slaves received a decent upbringing, including some education and religious instruction. Furthermore, the act authorized the town councils to bind out the children as apprentices between the ages of one year and 21 years if males and one year and 18 years if females to achieve these ends. Finally, the act released slaveowners freeing slaves between the ages of 21 (for a male) or 18 (for a female) and 40 from further obligation to financially support the freed slaves, on condition that the town council determine that the freed slave was healthy.

The relatively enlightened approach did not last long. An amendment to the emancipation act was passed in October 1785 that undermined the freedom granted to children in the 1784 act. In the 1784 act, the town councils reimbursed slaveowners for the maintenance of the free-born children This spread the cost among all taxpayers. But the 1785 amendment repealed this public support provision and required "that every negro or mulatto child born after the first day of March, A.D. 1784, be supported and maintained by the owner of the mother of such child, to the age of twenty-one years, provided the owner of the mother shall during that time hold her as a slave." It was likely the case that slaveowners would have little incentive to provide a decent life for the children of their slaves without assistance from the towns. Only the manumission of the mother would discharge the owner from responsibility for the child's support. Moreover, the Assembly's "earnest desire" to educate the children of slaves had evaporated. Finally, the amendment reduced the upper age limit from 40 to 30 years for slaves who might be manumitted without further financial responsibility on the part of the owners.

As we have seen in prior chapters, even after the gradual emancipation act passed in 1784, Little Rest white families continued to hold some black persons as slaves. In the 1790 census, the following Little Rest heads of households were recorded as holding black slaves: Elisha Reynolds (4); Colonel Robert Potter (5); Henry Reynolds (1); Robert Sands (1); and Hannah Champlin (1). The total number of slaves went from 18 in 1774 to 12 in 1790.

By 1800, only one person held a slave in Little Rest. In South Kingstown as a whole, in 1800, census takers counted 375 free blacks and only 44 slaves. It appears that after 1790, the social and moral environment had changed and that holding black slaves was no longer seen as acceptable. This transformation may have been influenced by Rhode Island's adoption of the U.S. Constitution in 1790. Even though legally, slaveholders holding slaves born prior to 1784 did not have to manumit them, they chose not to hold onto them. Most slaves who were born before 1784 were simply freed by their masters. The one reported slave in Little Rest was held by none other than Elisha R. Potter, Sr. He was not reported as holding any slaves before 1800 or after 1800. Elisha Potter's slave was named John Potter, who was born after 1784 to a slave mother. It is not clear how Elisha Potter acquired ownership of John, but he probably inherited him.

Some Little Rest villagers, along with their townsmen, obtained certificates from the town manumitting their black slaves. Others in their wills manumitted black persons who continued to be held as slaves and were not born prior to 1784.

Wills often dealt with the many complex situations that arose. Joseph Perkins, the merchant and silversmith, in his 1789 will, addressed the circumstance of a black slave who had liberated himself by running away. Perkins ordered that "if my Negro Man called Phillip should return" that he be treated as a free man. Perkins generously willed a house and a lot of land to a freed black man who worked for him, Javin Niles.

Elisha Reynolds dealt with five black slaves in his 1791 will. One of the circumstances was complicated, as the slave was a mother who had given birth to a child after 1784. Reynolds freed his slave, Lydia, and gave Lydia the remaining time of her slave daughter Genny, until Genny turned 18, when Genny too would be free. Reynolds also freed his male slave, Tom. He further stipulated that if Lydia and Tom could not support themselves, that income from his estate should be used to support them. Elisha Potter recorded for several years in his expense book charges against Reynolds' estate for boarding Tom and for purchasing leather shoes for Tom. By contrast, Reynolds did not free his other two slaves, female Jesse and male Cesaer. Instead, he gave them to his daughter Elizabeth Potter for her life; after her death Jesse was to be owned by Thomas Potter and Cesaer by Elisha R. Potter. It may have been that Reynolds did not free them because he felt that Jesse and Cesaer could not support themselves, perhaps because they were elderly. Because Thomas Potter died in 1793, Elisha Potter may have inherited Jesse, and she may have been the mother of John Potter. Jesse and Caesar apparently were free persons by 1800. Cesaer purchased goods from Elisha's store in 1791.

In his will in 1790, Narragansett planter Benjamin Peckham, who lived a short way up North Road from Little Rest, transferred ownership of his male slave Philo to his son Josephus. However, Benjamin ordered that in seven years, in 1797, when Philo turned age 33, Philo was to be freed and given "ten silver Spanish milled Dollars." Benjamin Peckham did not manumit another young male slave, named Quom. Quom was born blind and never regained sight. Benjamin wanted his family members to take care of Quom, requesting that Quom "be treated kindly."

The manumission provisions of the gradual emancipation statute were a source of persistent conflict over the support of ex-slaves between town councils and slaveowners. The 1784 act permitted slaveowners to be released from further financial responsibility for a freed slave, if the male slave was freed between the ages of 21 and 30, and if the female slave was freed between the ages of 18 and 30. As a condition to such manumissions, the town councils had to declare that the slave in question was healthy; the town councils wanted to insure that a slave when freed could enter the free work force and support himself or herself without support from town coffers. When South Kingstown slaveowners sought to employ the provision giving them the right to manumit slaves without further financial responsibility for their welfare, resistance of the town council grew. At first, after 1784, the South Kingstown town council regularly found that a black man or woman met the requirements of the emancipation statute. But the town council became increasingly concerned that freed slaves would not be able to support themselves and would thus have to be supported by it, at taxpayer expense.

The concern about emancipating slaves was first expressed by the town council in 1793. Josephus Peckham, who lived a short way up North Road from Little Rest, brought before the town council Philo Peckham, the "Negro Man Slave" that he had inherited in 1790 from his father and requested that Philo be emancipated. Recall that in his father's will, Philo was required to be freed in 1797. Josephus was willing to free Philo prior to that time. Four members of the council agreed that Philo fell within the provisions of the law to be freed, but for the first time, one of the council members dissented. This single dissent eventually grew into a majority. The South Kingstown town council, facing a large number of blacks still held in bondage in the town, stubbornly refused to authorize manumissions of individual black persons who clearly were entitled to be freed under the statute. In 1804, the town council refused to manumit a slave on the ground that "the Town ought not to be put in jeopardy of any expense whatever."

Another rejected manumission led to a lawsuit brought by Elisha Gardner, the Little Rest deputy-sheriff who achieved fame as the master-mind behind the "Cat Inspector" practical joke set forth in the prior chapter. Gardner was the co-executor and a beneficiary of the estate of his uncle, Caleb Gardner, who died in 1796. Caleb Gardner had been a Narragansett planter who had two farms near Little Rest, one of which was located immediately to the north of main street in Little Rest and to the east of North Road. Caleb Gardner was also a long-time slaveholder. He was reported to have six black persons residing on his lands in 1774 (all of whom likely were slaves) and seven black slaves residing on his lands in 1790. The increase was apparently attributable to the birth of Patience after 1784 from a black woman who was a slave owned by Caleb Gardner. Patience was part of Caleb Gardner's estate when he died in 1796. Once Patience reached the age of 18, Elisha Gardner applied to the South Kingstown town council to declare that Patience was healthy and could be set free. On August 11, 1806, at a meeting of the town council in the Joseph Reynolds tavern, Gardner presented Patience and requested "that this Council would manumit said Patience," as her circumstances fell within the 1784 gradual emancipation legislation. However, the town council rejected the request. Gardner filed suit in the Little Rest Court House, but the probate court ruled against Gardner. Finally, in October 1808, the county supreme court reversed the probate court, finding that Patience clearly fell within the terms of the emancipation act and ruling that "Patience be manumitted and forever hereafter liberated and emancipated."

This shameful situation, in which a local government body prevented the freedom of a black slave in clear contradiction to a statute, not to mention morality, must be attributed to several factors. The first factor was the failure of the General Assembly to provide means for the freed black slaves to support themselves. Freed slaves were not given any money or property by the state, and were often forced into servant relationships with their former masters. The second factor was the unsatisfactory system of Rhode Island towns handling poor relief. Since colonial times, town councils had the duty of caring for inhabitants who could not support themselves. The money was given out grudgingly in individual cases. This was not a system that was designed to handle a circumstance such as the freedom of a large number of slaves who previously had not been permitted to educate or support themselves. Under pressure from rebellious taxpayers, and relying on an outmoded welfare system, the South Kingstown town council itself rebelled. Not until later in the 19th century would welfare relief take the form of isolating the poor in "town farms" or in asylums, where they could be supported relatively cheaply. The third factor was that the town council made a value judgment that the freedom of a black slave was worth less than adding to the burden of the town's taxpayers.

In August 1810, Elisha Potter brought his slave John Potter before the town council and the town council agreed to issue John a certificate demonstrating his freedom. Presumably, John Potter had just turned 21 years of age and qualified for emancipation under the 1784 statute. John Potter was Little Rest's last slave.

Elisha R. Potter, Sr. and
Continuing Badges of Slavery in Little Rest

Little is known of the daily life of black people in South Kingstown in the late 18th and early 19th centuries, after many of them had gained their freedom, due to the paucity of surviving written records. This chapter describes one tradition that caught the eye of whites who in the late 19th century reminisced about life in Little Rest – the "Negro Election" festival. This chapter also describes a surviving contemporary description by a black servant in Little Rest who was jailed for desiring to leave his work in the fields in order to attend a religious meeting. Taken together, they suggest that while slavery no longer existed in Little Rest in the early 1800s, badges of slavery did continue to exist.

The "Negro Election" Festival

The "Negro Election" festival was a long-standing tradition in the black and Indian community in the colonial Narragansett country and in other parts of New England as well. Typically, in colonial times in the Narragansett country, black slaves and servants, as well as Indians, met at a location on the third Saturday in June. The object of the gathering was to elect a colony (and later state) "governor." The position was largely an honorary one, but the governor was known to discipline fellow slaves for certain transgressions. Weeks of " 'lectioneering and parmenteerin' " preceded the event. Masters became involved as well, by contributing cash and fine clothes to the candidates. The masters did not want to be embarrassed by having their slaves appear in poor clothing. On the day of the election, many of the blacks rode to the designated election spot on their masters' horses, decked out in fine clothes. The vote was then taken, after which the winner of the campaign was proclaimed, the defeated candidate was selected as chief marshal, and the rest of the afternoon was spent eating a picnic, dancing and playing athletic games.

The tradition of "Negro Elections" continued into the early 19th century in South Kingstown. In 1874, Jonathan Helme, a grandson of James Helme, Jr., wrote a newspaper article in the *Providence Journal* recollecting a "Negro Election" day that occurred in part in Little Rest. In this particular year, perhaps around 1810, a servant of Elisha Reynolds Potter, Sr., John Potter, was elected governor. As explained in the prior chapter, John Potter was Elisha Potter's slave until Elisha Potter had the town council free him in August 1810. If the year was 1810 or before, John Potter's election may have been intended to highlight his continuing slave status and spur Elisha Potter to free John Potter. If the year was after 1810, John Potter's election may have been intended to celebrate his new-found freedom. In any event, John Potter was to be installed as governor in Apponaug. Helme writes,

> On the occasion of his installation, Mr. Potter told his servant
> John to take the best horse in his stable, as he had a number,
> among them a fine span of large bays, for his journey to
> Apponaug, about twenty miles. He selected one of the span, a
> noble large horse and with the assistance of Mr. John T. Nichols,
> his horse was beautifully caparisoned. Early on the morning of
> the day, the governor elect, mounted on his splendid steed,
> dressed in fine style, viz: blue coat, short waist, swallow tail,
> with a profusion of guilt buttons, red sash, black pants, put inside
> of a pair of boots, with white tops, and a handsome pair of silver
> mounted spurs, together with a white hat, a large black plume
> with a red top, completed his regimentals. There were quite a
> number of our citizens assembled to see the governor-elect start
> [from Little Rest] for the capitol.

John Potter rode on to Apponaug, and on the way was met by "a band of
music consisting of three drums and two fifes," which struck up "Hail to the
Chief." Both sides of the road were lined with spectators, "the ladies waving
their handkerchiefs and the gentlemen their hats, while the governor with hat
in hand bowed to the populace, his head nearly touching his horse's head. On
his entrance to the village, the band played 'Washington's March.'"[21] About
this time Elisha Reynolds Potter, Sr. was asked to be a candidate for governor
of the state. He reportedly declined, stating that one governor in a family was
sufficient.

"Negro Election" day was a continuing badge of slavery days. It had
its origins in black and Indian slave festivals early in colonial times. In June
1724, the South Kingstown town meeting passed an ordinance banning blacks
and Indians from leaving work and gathering for a festival in the third week
of June. This ordinance apparently was not effective, as the town meeting reenacted the ordinance in June 1737. The early reference to this black June
festival suggests that it had African roots. The June festival grew into a long-
standing tradition in the black community. Blacks and Indians inter-mixed at
these festivals (as is also indicated in Charles Comstock's book). Black
slaves wanted to have a festival of blacks-and-Indians only, but they had a

---

[21] For the benefit of historians, the entire description by Helme is set forth in
Appendix C. In describing "Negro Elections" in South County, historians have
relied exclusively on the description set forth in Wilkins Updike's *History of the
Episcopal Church in Narragansett* (Merrymount Press 1847), pages 177-79. The
John T. Nichols referenced in the description was the Little Rest saddlemaker
whose shop was next to the old school house.

problem with what white authorities would make of black slaves gathering together. Accordingly, they probably determined that the safest course was to appear to be harmless by imitating their white masters and holding an election day for blacks only. On the other hand, one must not be too harsh in evaluating the festival. Each year the festival was looked forward to by blacks as an opportunity to escape the drudgery of farm work, to socialize among themselves, and to celebrate and have a joyful time. In addition, some historians also argue that the festival both reinforced white control over the slaves and empowered the slaves by institutionalizing a self-governing structure.

With the end of slavery in Rhode Island, the festival continued in South Kingstown for some years. But as black people were able to move to cities and congregate and socialize among themselves freely in cities, the festival had less relevance. Eventually, it was probably viewed as a continuing badge of slavery among freed blacks themselves and the tradition faded away in the early 19th century. "Shepherd Tom" Hazard, writing in 1879, recalls that the last Negro Election was held in South Kingstown some time after 1812. Hazard recalled that in the last election Aaron Potter, a servant in Elisha R. Potter's house, was elected governor at a ceremony held in the Potter woods on Rose Hill. In the recently published journal of Daniel Stedman, who was an ordinary white farmer who lived between Little Rest and Wakefield, Stedman reports a "Negro Lection at Willard Hazard's" (near Wakefield) occurring on June 16, 1827. This is the last report of a Negro election being held in Rhode Island.

There is another story told by a white man reminiscing in the late 19th century, "Shepherd Tom" Hazard, with Elisha Reynolds Potter, Sr. and free black people in Little Rest as the subjects. Hazard wrote that not only did town blacks hold annual elections for governor, they also established a debating society in Little Rest. The first subject debated by the new society was "Who makes thunder?" After three hours of debate, a written resolution was adopted as follows:

> *Resolved*, Maganimously by this here meeting, that while God ormighty make the litenin, it takes Massa 'lisha Potter to make thunder.
> Captain Guy Watson, Esq.
> Moderator, Chairman and President of this here Bating Siety, held in the Siety's room, on Little Rest Hill,
> This here 4th day of July, one thousand eight hundred
> And fifteen, and in the year of our Lord, Hannan Dominy,
> 1815.

Obviously, one must be careful about what one draws from Helme's and Hazard's reminiscences. If the stories had been told about black slaves in the South held by a powerful southern slaveowner in the early 19th century, one would conclude that they were products of a racist society. One can still arrive at the same conclusion with respect to South Kingstown in the late 19th century. In particular, one wonders whether Shepherd Tom Hazard made up the written resolution or whether he really did review an original resolution drafted by Guy Watson (who was well known in the town as a black man who had gained his freedom by joining the Rhode Island black battalion in the Revolutionary War and fighting with distinction). The use of a "negro" dialect by Hazard was in popular use at the time of the writing of his book; it was intended to be humorous, at the expense of blacks, but probably did not actually represent black speech patterns at the time.

Stories by Helme, Hazard and Wilkins Updike in his *History of the Episcopal Church in Narragansett* tend to paint a picture of black society in South Kingstown that was happy, harmonious and romantic. This is not to denigrate the election day festival, as it was an important social event in the lives of black people from colonial times up to the early 19th century. But the use of the event by whites in the late 19th century to paint a picture of harmonious race relations in colonial times and the early 19th century must be viewed with great skepticism.

Cato Pearce, Freed Black Slave in Little Rest

Another badge of slavery was reflected in an extraordinary pamphlet, *A Brief Memoir of the Life and Religious Experience of Cato Pearce a Man of Color*. Cato Pearce was a freed black slave from North Kingstown who at one point was hired as a field hand by Elisha Reynolds Potter, Sr. Pearce tells the story of a time when Potter had Pearce incarcerated in the Little Rest jail for three days because Potter did not want Pearce to leave his farm to preach at Sunday services. The pamphlet was published in Pawtucket by abolitionists in 1842, seven year's after Potter's death, which may explain in part why it has been ignored by most historians.

Cato Pearce, according to his account, was born a slave in North Kingstown in about 1790 (probably around 1788). His mother ran away from their master, leaving behind young Cato and two other siblings. Pearce himself ran away from his master when he was 18, and hired himself out on a ship at sea. But the ship later returned to Wickford, where Pearce's master saw Pearce, captured him, and whipped him. Pearce's master apparently could have freed Pearce after he turned age 18, but he did not do so. Pearce ran away for good two years later.

In what must have been about 1807, Pearce agreed to be hired by Elisha R. Potter, Sr. at the Potter Homestead in Little Rest. At first, Pearce found Elisha Potter and his wife, Mary Potter (the former Mary Perkins), to be "very clever people" and Pearce "had a pretty good time with them." But trouble started when Pearce developed an urge to attend Sunday church services.

At first, Mary Potter encouraged Pearce's interest in religion. Pearce learned of a planned Sunday church service being held three miles away and he informed "Mrs. Potter" of his desire to attend the service. Mary Potter responded, "Well, Cato, you can do all your chores up and go 'arly, if you please." This Pearce did. He was well received at the meeting and was asked to say some words, which he did. Pearce then asked the congregation, which apparently was primarily white, to permit him to preach at the next meeting. The congregation agreed. Pearce went back to the Potter Homestead overjoyed. He "told Mrs. Potter I had got meetin' 'pointed to preach,'" to which she responded that she was pleased that he was engaged in religion.

Pearce prepared diligently for his preaching engagement. He "went into the woods to study what I should say, and sound it out there; and swing my hands." Pearce's preaching engagement was a resounding success. Another meeting was arranged for him to preach. With his farm wages, Pearce purchased clothing to improve his appearance while preaching, including white gloves, white stockings and a breast pin. Mary Potter offered to sew ruffles on to Pearce's white shirt. When the day for preaching arrived, Elisha Potter drove Pearce in a wagon to the town where the church meeting was taking place. In his new clothes, Pearce "thought every body would know I was a minister, and never hardly any body felt as big as I did." At the house designated for the meeting, "hundreds of folks" (again, mostly whites) crowded in and around the house, waiting in anticipation for the preacher to arrive. Pearce managed to squeeze into the house and introduce himself to the waiting host, even though some of the whites on the outside of the house who did not know Pearce was the preacher told him to get lost. The meeting was another success. But perhaps overwhelmed by his success, Pearce decided not to preach for the next year. One day, Mary Potter sent Pearce on an errand to her father's house in East Greenwich. When Pearce arrived, there was a church service in progress (of course, Mary Potter knew this). A chair was offered to Pearce and he was invited to say a few words, which he did, again to good effect.

With this assistance from Mary Potter, Pearce renewed his interest in religion. He was baptized as a member of the Baptist church in South Kingstown, led by Elder Cole. In the winter, Pearce left Potter's employment and preached "both nights and Sundays" at a Baptist church just over the

Connecticut border.[22] In the spring of about 1808, Pearce "had to hire out to work by the month" and he again agreed to be hired by Elisha R. Potter, Sr.

Four weeks later, Pearce asked Potter if he could attend a Baptist meeting the next Sunday at which Pearce had been asked to preach. Potter agreed, but only if Pearce hired another man to do Pearce's chores in case Pearce did not return in time by the next day. Pearce hired a replacement and went off to attend the meeting. He was asked to spend the night at the church elder's house, a common practice in the case of guest preachers.

Early the next morning, Pearce traveled back to the Potter Homestead, arriving before Elisha Potter had finished his breakfast. Pearce did his expected chores, but he did not know that Potter was angry at him and that Potter had refused to allow on his land the man Pearce had hired as his replacement. Pearce described what happened next.

> When Mr. Potter had done his breakfast he come out with his horse-whip in his hand. Says he, "Why wa'nt you here last night to do the chores." I told him I hired some body. He said he wouldn't have him on his place. He said he hired me. He said he didn't understand why I went away to preach. Says he, "I wo'n't have no nigger preachers – I'll horse-whip you;" and he swore. Says I, "Don't strike me, Mr. Potter . . . ." Well he said they had a good minister there, and they wouldn't have no nigger preachers, and said he would put me where he could find me. So he went and got the officer – the jailer – and put me into jail.

Pearce was incarcerated in the jail for "two nights and parts of two days . . . ." Fortunately for Pearce, the county court was in session at the Court House in Little Rest, which meant that attorneys who resided outside Little Rest (and were therefore not under Elisha Potter's influence) were visiting the village.

> Sheriff Allen and a number of the great men came in to visit them that was in prison, and asked me what I was put in for. I told 'em for preachin' – but yet I couldn't help weepin'. [One of the visitors] said, "You won't stay here but a few minutes – he had done parfectly wrong – we will have you out in a few minutes." Then they gave me some money and went out and told Elisha Potter they would give so long to take me out [or] they was goin' to prosecute him if he didn't. About half an hour after that, I could see Elisha Potter through the grate, comin' up the back side and in the back way, and [he] got the jailer to talk with me while

---

[22] Pearce's story is also a good example of how the religious movement in the early 19th century known as the Second Great Awakening attracted African-Americans into the evangelical Protestant fold.

he stood down to the bottom of the stairs. And the jailer took me in another room and told me that Mr. Potter said I might go every Saturday night and stay till Monday mornin' and have meetins where I was a mind to. I told the jailer I had nothin to do with Elisha Potter. "If he had put me in here, amen – if I have got to stay here and die, amen to it: I have nothin to do with him. I never have stole nor cheated nor done any thing wrong to him. . . . I said I hadn't nothin' 'gainst Elisha Potter: I loved him as well as ever. At that Elisha Potter come up stairs and said I had better go to work – he liked me well, and I might go to meetin' when I was a mind to. I told him I didn't calculate to work for him any more. Then he told me to go and git my things, and I come out.

When Pearce was released from jail and stepped out into the street, he was immediately "surrounded by many friends and brethren." Pearce said he "went singin' through the streets, and felt to give God the glory that I wa'nt put in for anything but preachin'."

Comment

It is interesting to contrast Pearce's story, a contemporary tale told by a black man, with this chapter's first two stories, which were reminiscences told by white men. First, there is the threat of violence in the Pearce story, but in the Helme and Hazard stories, there is a theme of harmony. Second, in the Pearce story, Elisha Potter uses a derogatory term for black people and swears; there is no such language used in Helme's and Hazard's romanticized stories. Instead, Potter is viewed as a generous man who helps his servant appear in a splendid outfit and ride a finely equipped horse, and as a man who gains the favorable attention of local blacks. Third, in Hazard's written resolution, the term "Massa" is used to address Elisha Potter. The term "Massa" brings to mind the manner in which a slave might address his master. By contrast, in Pearce's recollection, Pearce addresses Elisha as "Mr. Potter" and does not degrade himself by using the term "Massa."

It is also interesting to note that Potter did not strike Pearce, as he threatened to, but instead Potter "got the officer – the jailer – and put [Pearce] in jail." One wonders what crime Pearce committed to merit being thrown in jail. Was Elisha Potter so powerful that he could use his influence with the local jailer to have a free man thrown in jail for merely failing to abide by Potter's wishes? Potter was not even a justice of the peace or other official in the criminal system. Or was Pearce's incarceration another badge of slavery, in which local government institutions were used to keep free blacks in their places? There were no formal local laws to suppress blacks, as there were enacted in the South Kingstown town records in colonial times; but the informal threat of jail could serve a similar purpose.

It is clear from the stories set forth above that while black persons in Little Rest were free, there were still some badges of slavery remaining in social relations between blacks and whites. In addition, even though blacks were free, many of them continued to work the fields of wealthy white landowners, in conditions that were not too different from those of their forefathers. Pearce hired himself out as a temporary field hand. In the journal of Daniel Stedman, Stedman reports working side-by-side with various black field workers who were hired on a temporary basis by a wealthy white farmer, Jeremiah Niles Potter, including "Gov. John Potter," the black man who won the Negro Election described above. [23] "Nailer Tom" Hazard also hired Potter and other black men and women for temporary farm work.

On occasion, white planters exhibited shockingly bad behavior towards their black laborers. While the General Assembly passed a law prohibiting the sale of slaves outside the state, some planters sold free black persons who were bound by contract to perform labor for a fixed term of years to slaveowners in southern states. Once the term ended, it was not likely that the black persons would be freed. In about 1789, the Rhode Island Society for the Abolition of the Slave Trade caused a criminal action to be brought against Benjamin Peckham, possibly the same planter who lived just north of Little Rest on North Road. The Abolition Society consisted primarily of Quakers who were opposed to slavery, including Moses Brown of Providence and Thomas Hazard of South Kingstown. In the Abolition Society's minutes, it states that a prosecution was commenced against Peckham for selling a free black boy who was bound to him as a servant for a fixed term of years to a South Carolina slaveowner who intended to keep the boy as a permanent slave. But Peckham vociferously denied "that he sold him for a longer time than he was bound to him as an apprentice." Because the Abolition Society could not prove that Peckham sold the boy as a slave, it dismissed the prosecution.

Given this environment in South Kingstown and other parts of South County, it is not surprising that many local black people chose to migrate to Providence and elsewhere. In particular, urban areas gave blacks the opportunity to form communities away from domineering farm overseers. Emigration is indicated by the population of blacks in South Kingstown, which rather than show an increase in the natural growth rate, actually decreased from 648 in 1790 to 390 in 1810. The decrease continued, with only 249 blacks living in South Kingstown by 1850. South County overall experienced a similar decline, from 1,711 blacks in 1790 to 877 in 1810 and

[23] Pearce continued to preach in southern Rhode Island. Stedman records in his journal on October 12, 1827 that "a black man by the [name] of Cato Pearce in Evening had a meeting at Wakefield to Mr. Ray Allen's."

530 in 1850. By contrast, Providence's black population swelled from 475 in 1790 to 871 in 1810 and to 1,499 in 1850.

Still, times had changed from slavery days. Early in Pearce's story, we see Mary Potter encouraging and assisting Pearce's interest in religion. In addition, Pearce preaches before primarily white audiences, and his skill surprises and is appreciated by whites. Furthermore, once prominent whites learned of Potter jailing Pearce, they became so upset that they threatened to prosecute Potter unless Potter released Pearce from jail. Potter did so, and in an act of repentance, invited Pearce to work for him, even allowing Pearce the weekend off to attend Sunday services. But in a demonstration of independence and dignity, Pearce rejected the offer, wanting "nothin to do with Elisha Potter."

One small reflection of the change in race relations was that black persons for the first time beginning in 1795 filed cases in the county court of common pleas in the Little Rest Court House. When a white employer refused to pay the agreed upon amount for temporary labor, free black men and women needed a mechanism to force the employer to meet his obligations. In the August 1795 term of the court of common pleas, Quash Peckham, probably a former slave of Benjamin Peckham of North Road, and his wife Lydia, the former slave of Elisha Reynolds of Little Rest, filed a suit against a white Hopkinton man for failure to pay fees owed. Quash and Lydia were not represented by attorneys, and when the defendant's attorney filed a response, they withdrew their case and were charged with paying court costs of $6.41. But in the next two years, two free black laborers successfully sued their white employers and were awarded by the court amounts owed to them ($90 and $55, respectively, plus court costs). Local whites likely approved of these cases, in part because if the recently-freed black workers were not able to recover in court fees owed to them, they might become town charges and a burden on town taxpayers.

George Fayerweather: A Free Man of Color

An indication that race relations were changing in Little Rest was evidenced by the appearance of George Fayerweather in the village in about 1804. He was a man who successfully experienced the transition from slavery to freedom.

George Fayerweather's father (George I) was a black slave of the Anglican minister of St. Paul's Episcopal Church, Samuel Fayerweather. Samuel Fayerweather served as pastor of St. Paul's from 1760 to 1781. Reverend Fayerweather was relatively enlightened for the day, as he promoted religion among the black slaves. Church records show that in 1767 Reverend Fayerweather "christened his servant man George before a large congregation." Reverend Fayerweather may have taught George to read, as George's sons would be literate. As was the usual custom of the day, George Fayerweather took the last name of his master. In 1774, George had a son, who was also named George (George II). The identity of George II's mother is unknown, as detailed church records were not kept after 1773. Upon Reverend Fayerweather's death in 1781, he was not so liberal that he freed his slave George I in his will. Instead, Reverend Fayerweather willed "his Negro Man called George" to his "friend Matthew Robinson." Robinson was an accomplished attorney and a slaveholder residing at Hopewell Lodge, an estate located near current West Kingston. Interestingly, Samuel Fayerweather and Matthew Robinson both were charged by the town council with having loyalist sympathies during the American Revolution. George I's daughter and another son were willed to Reverend Fayerweather's two sisters residing in Cambridge, Massachusetts.

At some point, George I and his son George II became free men but how and when is not clear. There is evidence that they were freed prior to 1795. The 1790 census indicates that Matthew Robinson had eight free blacks living on his estate. In addition, in January 1792, "Nailer Tom" Hazard records in his journal that George I ate dinner at Nailer Tom's house, which suggests that George I was free, as he had the liberty to travel to Nailer Tom's house. Later in 1792, Nailer Tom purchased some grain from George I, which suggests that he was free to run his own business. On the other hand, Matthew Robinson's 1795 will refers to unnamed slaves, which suggests that Robinson did have slaves. In any event, there is no further record of George I. Ironically, George I's family would have more of an impact in South Kingstown than would the white Samuel Fayerweather's family.

George II married Nancy Rodman, whose father was a Narragansett sachem. George II learned the trade of a blacksmith. He first appears in village records in 1800, when Joseph Reynolds hired him to perform some blacksmith services for tavern customers. George II moved to Little Rest, where he commenced his blacksmith trade, in about 1804. (Elisha Potter's account book indicates that George II began purchasing food and supplies from Potter in 1804). George II rented part of James Helme, Jr.'s house across from the Kingston Hill Store, and his first blacksmith shop was on the site of the Kingston Hill Store. In 1819, George II purchased land from James Helme, Jr., and his blacksmith shop was moved to the north side of Mooresfield Road on the edge of the village. The foundation of the blacksmith shop can still be seen today. George II also built a house on his land in front of his blacksmith shop and facing Mooresfield Road in 1820. The Cape Code-style cottage house is one of the few surviving houses in Rhode Island known to have been inhabited by a middle-class black family in early 19th century Rhode Island. George II and his part-Indian wife had 12 children – three daughters who died young, and eight boys and one daughter who survived childhood and were raised in the house.

"Nailer Tom" Hazard, who was also a blacksmith, in his journal mentions George II several times between 1815 to 1836. In 1821, for example, he reported that "George Fairweather Workt here this day making Plow Irons." The next day, he wrote that "George Fairwether logd here last Night and Supt."

George II maintained a day book that still exists. In it, he wrote down every job that he handled between the years 1809 and 1821. He performed work for more than one hundred persons, both Little Rest villagers and townsmen. He also performed work for several years on the cotton mill located at Biscuit City Pond. Typical blacksmithing chores included shoeing horses, sharpening pitch forks and other farm tools, mending sleighs, and mending wagons. The day book demonstrates good organization typical of efficient shopkeepers of the times, good spelling and good handwriting. The account book shows that his customers paid him in cash, but some were slow to pay. In a letter to Elisha Potter, Jr. in 1836, George II complained that he was short of cash due to the failure of his customers to pay on a timely basis. He only sued once in the county court to collect an unpaid debt.

Post office records kept by postmaster Thomas R. Wells from 1837 to 1841 indicate that George II subscribed to the following newspapers: *The Liberator,* the newspaper edited by radical abolitionist William Lloyd Garrison; *The Coloured American,* a newspaper edited by black Philadelphians; and the *Courier Journal,* a Providence daily newspaper. George II was the first black person listed as a member of the Kingston Anti-Slavery Society that was formed on June 20, 1837. In addition, his wife, Nancy, and two of his children signed on as members. Clearly, George II and his family were concerned about important issues of the day, including the freedom of southern slaves. George II died in October 1841 at the age of 67, and was buried in Little Rest's main cemetery, Old Fernwood.

One of George II's sons, Solomon, carried on the blacksmith trade for many years in the village. He married Louise Weeden of Mooresfield. Solomon built a new house to the east of the blacksmith shop on Mooresfield

Solomon Fayerweather (1820-1901), circa 1890. Standing in front of the Kingston Congregational Church, where he was a member and sextant for many years. His father was born a slave and his mother was part Narragansett Indian. *Pettaquamscutt Historical Society.*

Solomon Fayerweather in His Blacksmith Shop, circa 1890. The shop was a gathering place for villagers to swap news and stories. *Pettaquamscutt Historical Society.*

Road in 1852. He, Louise and his brother Daniel became members of the Kingston Congregational Church. He owned his own pew in the church and voted with other church members on important matters. Solomon was well known in the community for his long-time service as sextant of the church, which involved in part ringing the church bell that was heard daily in the village. Solomon's mother, Nancy, and sister, Isabella, became members of the church in 1836.

Another son, George III, moved to New London, Connecticut and started a blacksmithing business. When he had difficulty with creditors, he sought and received loans from Elisha R. Potter, Jr. After about fifteen years, in 1855, George III returned to Kingston and entered into a partnership with his brother Solomon in the blacksmithing business. From an 1868 account book of the blacksmith shop of George and Solomon Fayerweather, it is apparent that they ran a profitable business. A surviving example of the Fayerweathers' work is the iron bars for the windows in the Washington County jail in Kingston. The Fayerweathers won the contract for making and installing the iron bars when the jail was rebuilt in 1858. A man who resided in Kingston village his entire life described Solomon's shop as a center of village life and as "the constant resort of all whose tools were broken, or whose horse lacked a shoe; and under his skillful treatment many a farming machine led a useful existence long after most mechanics would have condemned it as worn out." Members of the Fayerweather family operated the blacksmith shop in Kingston until 1886. It was an important place in the village for villagers to exchange news and gossip. While the Fayerweathers' shop was successful, and tax records indicate that they were middle class, they never became wealthy; there were usually one or two other blacksmiths in the village as competition.

George III brought with him on his return to Kingston a remarkable woman, abolitionist Sarah Harris Fayerweather, whose story is told in Part IV of this book. Sarah Harris Fayerweather purchased in 1853 one half of the old Helme house, which stood next to the Fayerweather lot. From well-written letters by George III to Sarah, we know that George III traveled to Newport and Providence to purchase manufactured items such as nails, which he resold to villagers. On these trips, he sometimes met up with Sarah while she was visiting friends in Providence.

Glimpses of the Fayerweather home life can be gleaned from a few surviving letters written by Sarah Harris Fayerweather. In 1855 Isabella, the youngest daughter, was attending school in New Bedford. On March 2nd, she had reached her sixteenth birthday. Mother Harris wrote her a letter in which she revealed how she felt upon turning sixteen. Harris urged her daughter to "study all you can to keep up with the sisters and cousins." She wrote that she was making up a package of "Knickknacks" to send her by friends who were going to New Bedford the next day, and apologized for not including "a nice dress or something valuable for a present," explaining that her father (George III) was owed money on several accounts he hoped soon to collect. Apparently they were not usually financially strapped, as Harris added that, "I have bought the pianna that I brought from Providence, so that you can have it when you come home again . . . The girls play very well." Harris concluded with this domestic scene: "Libby [Sarah's daughter, age 19] sits here beside me a mending her skirt. Pa [George III] is playing on the accordion with his eyes shut. Charles [Sarah's son, age 9] is a jabbering away about his valentine he is to send to Linda." She added ominously, "I hear there are cases of smallpox there. Be careful." The Fayerweathers may not have wanted to send their daughter Isabella to school in South Kingstown because the local public schools did not admit black children (which probably was not the case); they likely were disappointed with the quality of the Kingston public school.

It was not uncommon for the Fayerweathers to socialize with local white persons. One letter from George III to his wife Sarah, while Sarah was traveling, mentions that a local white woman "visited this evening and sends her love." In another letter, George III mentions sympathetically the illness of a white neighbor.

While the success of the Fayerweathers indicated an advance in race relations and equality, the Fayerweathers must still have felt that their skin color held them back from enjoying the benefits of full citizenship. Rhode Island had laws on its books prohibiting blacks from voting (1822) and prohibiting whites and blacks from marrying (1798). It was common to exclude blacks from serving on juries. It does not appear that any Fayerweather was selected as a juryman up to the 1880s. There is no record of any Fayerweather or other black person being extended a loan by the local Landholders Bank. It appears that black villagers were not welcome in the various private clubs that arose in Kingston, including the Kingston Musical Society. Black students were accepted at the Kingston Sabbath School Society, but no black adults were members of the society. Black children apparently could attend the public schools, but not the more elite Kingston Academy. Black persons were accepted as members of the Kingston Anti-Slavery Society, but their names generally were placed at the end of the list (with the exception of the name of George Fayerweather, which was a mark of respect for him). No black persons were selected as officers of the organization.

The Kingston Congregational Church

The Kingston Congregational Church is a symbol of continuity in the village. Villagers have been worshipping in the church since 1820. With its towering steeple, gently sloping roof, rectangular structure, small entry door, simplicity, and white paint, the church also symbolizes Kingston's arrival as an archetype New England village. Furthermore, its dominating presence at the crest of Kingston Hill represents its importance in village life.

Until 1820, members of the Congregational Church had no meeting house in Little Rest. When the court house and jail were removed from Tower Hill to Little Rest in 1752, a meeting house for Congregationalists was serving worshippers in Tower Hill. However, the minister, Dr. Joseph Torrey, stubbornly refused to move his church to Little Rest, despite the dwindling numbers of church members. Members of the Congregationalist Church in Little Rest suffered. They typically met on Sundays in the Court House, but that was not a satisfying experience for them.

Elisha Reynolds Potter, Sr. believed that Little Rest should have its own meeting house and minister. In 1803, Potter led a failed effort to obtain subscribers to build a church in the village. Upon his return to Little Rest after three terms as a representative in the U.S. Congress, he tried again. By 1819, the Tower Hill church was in such bad repair that the minister used an old school house in Tower Hill to hold services and he had only two local members remaining. Potter wrote to Congregationalist ministers in Boston, discussing with them the prospect of sending to Little Rest a minister who could also serve as a teacher for school children. The ministers granted the request, sending to Little Rest a talented pastor, the Reverend Oliver Brown. By the end of the year, Brown had established a Sunday school with 23 girls and 44 boys in attendance, representing many families in Little Rest.

In March 1820, an organization to construct a meeting house was formed in Little Rest, named the Presbyterian Society of the Pettaquamscutt Purchase. Thirty-one persons pledged themselves to contribute to the cost of building a church "to be called the Union Meeting House." Elisha R. Potter, Sr. led the way, as he donated the land for the church and subscribed for the most shares, 25. The next largest number of shares, four, were subscribed by Thomas Taylor, the successful storekeeper, and Thomas R. Wells, the cashier of the Landholders Bank. Not surprisingly, Potter was elected chairman of the building committee and Wells was elected its treasurer.

The building committee performed its work quickly. On March 18th, plans were adopted to build a church 35-by-48 feet in size, with 19 posts. By July 22nd, the frame had been prepared for raising. The men who assisted in the raising were rewarded with two and 3/8 gallons of spirits. In all, it appears that 17 men built the church, each averaging about 50 days of work.

By the end of 1820, the new meeting house was ready for use. In October 1820, the General Assembly granted a charter to the church, with 47 persons named as charter members (only two of whom were women, Mary Potter, wife of Elisha R. Potter, Sr., and Hannah Potter, wife of Asa Potter, Elisha's brother). On January 21, 1821, the church was formally organized by the public signing of the articles of faith and covenant by Reverend Brown, five men and two women. There were substantially fewer members than churchgoers, following Congregationalist tradition.

In 1823, the church purchased a bell weighing 490 pounds and hung it in the steeple. Within a year, however, Reverend Brown and his congregation decided that a larger bell, with a stronger voice, was needed. Another subscription for funds in the village was successfully undertaken, and a bell weighing 706 pounds was purchased. This bell had to be recast in 1831. The bell called the villagers to worship, announced weddings, and tolled sadly for funerals until 1857, when a fierce gale blew the steeple off the church. A new steeple and bell replaced the old ones. In 1860, a pipe organ was first installed in the church, a gift of Deacon Thomas R. Wells. In 1877, villagers donated funds for an outdoor clock to be inserted in the steeple.

One more element was needed to make the church a true village church – a burial ground for the deceased. In 1826, Elisha R. Potter, Sr. gave the church land on the north side of the road leading to West Kingston. Members of the church and the Society that owned the church, their families, and any persons living within one mile of the meeting house could be buried there. Many of the individuals mentioned in this book are buried there, now called Old Fernwood Cemetery.

Soon after the arrival of the Reverend Brown and the building of the church, Brown reported that "the change in the social and religious intercourse of Little Rest is great. The Sabbath is very much more regarded; meetings on that day are better attended; and, as to harmony and good neighborhood, it seems like another place." Brown served as church minister until 1835 when he moved to Connecticut.

The Kingston Congregational Church was open to white and black persons alike. Several members of the Fayerweather family became members of the church. Black children attended Sunday schools held at the church.

The Presbyterian Society of the Pettaquamscutt Purchase continued to serve as the secular arm of the church. Its role included holding in trust the land and meeting house, raising funds for the pastor's salary, managing the rents from the Ministerial lands, and repairing the meeting house. Members of the Society did not have to be members of the church. Indeed, influential members Elisha R. Potter, Sr., and later his son Elisha R. Potter, Jr., served on the Society, but never became members of the church. The church and Presbyterian Society operated side-by-side (as they still do today).

Kingston Congregational Church, 1820. Detail of map of South Kingstown by Henry F. Walling, 1857. *Rhode Island Historical Society,* RHi X42 84.

As well as serving the spiritual needs of the village, the Kingston Congregational Church enriched the social life of the village. Church and Presbyterian Society members, as well as the pastor of the church, were important in creating a circulating library in 1824, a Sunday school in 1825, the Kingston Musical Society in 1825, and a temperance society in 1829. The Reverend Brown led the Sunday school and the library, and Deacon Thomas R. Wells was president of the local temperance society.

The South Kingstown Sabbath School Society (later renamed the Kingston Sabbath School Society) was formed by village residents in 1825. It was a branch of the Rhode Island Sunday School Union. The Kingston Sunday school met each Sunday at the meeting house from 9:30 to 11 a.m. It started with 32 students and four adults as teachers, but each year grew in size. By 1829, the school had increased to 76 students and six teachers, with an equal number of male and female students and teachers. By 1833, the school had grown to 169 "scholars" and 26 teachers. Of the scholars, there were 103 white males, 5 black males, 48 white females, and 13 black females. A number of the white male students were from the Kingston Academy, as the society felt the pressure to properly instruct these students, many of whom would become state leaders. Society members also helped to establish Sunday schools at Mooresfield and Rocky Brook. Women played important roles as teachers and organizers. Still, a pessimistic Thomas P. Wells expressed disappointment in the society's annual report for 1834 that for all of the labors of the teachers, no student had been converted to church membership. Wells complained that the teachers "do not pray enough."

An interesting element of the Kingston Sabbath School was the establishment of a library. The library served as an incentive for students to recite catechisms and verses in the Bible. In 1827, the society's annual report indicated that students had recited a total of 9,510 answers in catechisms and 4,244 verses in the scriptures. Memorization of religious texts at the time was considered an act of religious devotion. Students who helped meet this goal as a prize were entitled to borrow library books from the society. The society emphasized that in order to keep the students interested in winning prizes, new books had to be added each year. Accordingly, each year, villagers contributed sufficient funds so that about 30 books were added to the library. By 1838, the library had grown to 263 volumes. Many of the books while instructive in nature were not solely religious in content, were appropriate for children, and were quickly worn out by use.

The church would play a role in the village's moral reform activities, including antislavery and pro-temperance activities. But efforts by pastors to control the conduct of villagers would lead to disputes involving two important village institutions, the Kingston Academy and the Kingston Free Library and Reading Room.

The Rise of the Bank and General Store

In the early part of the 19th century, there were indications that the commercial life in Little Rest was increasing in sophistication. This was a common occurrence in other Rhode Island and New England villages in the years of the early Republic as well. In Little Rest, this transformation was reflected by the establishment of a bank and modern general stores.

The Landholders Bank

Beginning in 1813, "Nailer Tom" Hazard mentions his dealings with the Narragansett Bank, which was established in 1805 in Wickford as the first bank in Washington County. At different times, Nailer Tom gave villagers John Nichols, Timothy Peckham and Elisha Potter cash for them to carry to Wickford to repay interest and principal on loans borrowed by Nailer Tom. Both the presence of the bank, which made cash transactions more common, and the charging of interest on notes, were indications that commercial transactions in Little Rest were increasing in complexity and becoming more modern. With the arrival of banks, Nailer Tom was able to reduce his barter transactions and deal in cash more frequently. The bank, however, was inconveniently located in North Kingstown.

In 1818, circumstances arose that enabled Little Rest to attract its own bank. In 1818, there was a rush to obtain state bank charters due to an impending change in the state's laws. After 1818, all newly chartered banks were to be denied the privilege of "bank process," a power unique to Rhode Island under which banks were given the right to obtain a judgment against a debtor without a trial and the right to seize a defaulting debtor's property even though that property may have been pledged earlier to secure a non-bank loan. The General Assembly was spurred to charter sixteen banks, with most awarded one to each rural town. In South Kingstown's case, the bank charter came under the control of the most powerful politician in southern Rhode Island, Elisha Reynolds Potter, Sr.

Elisha Potter obtained a charter for the Landholders Bank of South Kingstown. It was chartered in 1818 with capital of $150,000. Realizing the importance that a bank might have for Little Rest, Potter also made sure that the bank had its office in Little Rest. The bank's sparsely furnished office was located in the heart of Little Rest, in what is now known as the Helme House. The present building originally was two separate buildings. They were joined and the dividing road between them was eliminated in 1818 in order to provide the offices for the Landholders Bank. The bank leased the space from John Nichols for $400 per year in perpetuity. The bank vault, said to have been built at the carriage factory in Biscuit City, was an iron cage protected by a thick granite encasement. The iron doors had three locks.

The bank was organized as a corporation, which had a separate and distinct legal identity from its shareholders, then a relative novelty. The bank had unique rights, including the right of process. Dividends could be paid with respect to bank stock. Potter, of course, was the bank's largest shareholder. Many villagers invested their earnings to purchase dividend-paying stock of the Landholders Bank. It was one of the few investments that ordinary villagers could make in a business.

Potter was the bank's first president and he held that office until his death in 1835. Thomas R. Wells served as cashier from 1827 until his death in 1853. Wells ran the bank with good business sense. While some of the state's banks that were chartered in 1818 either floundered or failed, the Landholders Bank served Little Rest and the town effectively for many years.

The bank made obtaining credit for local villagers easier and increased the availability of cash in the pockets of ordinary persons. Bank records indicate that it lent money to a wide variety of borrowers, from Elisha Potter borrowing $2,000 at a time, to John Nichols borrowing $60 at a time. The bank helped local farmers and others throughout South Kingstown. Daniel Stedman, an ordinary farmer residing between Little Rest and Wakefield, noted numerous times in his journal traveling to Kingston either to obtain cash from the bank or to pay down his note to the bank. Stedman mentioned Wakefield's new bank in 1835, but on one occasion the bank could not buy his note due to credit problems that the bank had with a Providence bank. Stedman preferred to deal with the reliable Landholders Bank.

In addition to increasing the commercial possibilities for Little Rest villagers, the bank connected Little Rest to the larger national commercial market. For example, in 1839, the Landholders Bank held notes payable in the aggregate amount of $21,710 from banks in New York, Boston, New Orleans, and Norwich, Connecticut. The bank even held some foreign notes. In addition, the bank held in its vault gold and silver reserves, making it interested in the prices of those commodities. Notes issued by the Landholders Bank were held by other banks as well.

In 1855, the Kingston Savings Bank was organized to hold the deposits of villagers and others in the surrounding area. With Nathaniel Peckham as its president, and Thomas P. Wells as its secretary and treasurer, the bank did a good business in Kingston for many years. The savings bank was located in the same building as the Landholders Bank, and both institutions tended to have the same officers.[24]

---

[24] The Landholders Bank later merged into the Kingston Savings Bank. Unfortunately, the savings bank closed in 1920, after embezzlement by a bank employee was discovered.

General Stores

In addition to the arrival of modern financial institutions in Little Rest, modern general stores appeared. In 18th century rural New England towns, most transactions were conducted by means of a complicated barter exchange. A shoemaker would sell his wares to a carpenter in exchange for furniture; the carpenter would exchange with a blacksmith for horseshoeing services; each of them might trade for farm produce. Sometimes, the barter exchanges were simple. For example, in 1800, Nailer Tom Hazard, in exchange for having his hat "bound and brusht" by Cyrus French of Little Rest, made French a knife blade in his blacksmith's forge. Small merchants, such as Samuel Casey, Joseph Perkins, James Helme and Immanuel Case of Little Rest, did appear in some villages and towns. But due to the shortage of cash and manufactured goods, they also often engaged in barter transactions, which limited the growth of their businesses. In addition, because many of their goods were handmade by local tradesmen, their stores did not have a wide variety of goods. Little Rest storekeepers obtained some goods from Newport merchants by trading them cheese and other produce obtained in barter trades from local farmers. Newport merchants imported alcohol, cloth and a few manufactured goods from overseas, but the selection in their warehouses was limited. Farmers often relied on "long credit" with general stores and other shopkeepers, as they typically sold their cheese, butter and pork once a year (in the fall and winter), but purchased goods from general stores year-round.

John Nichols, the saddlemaker, often engaged in barter transactions with his customers. He converted farm produce into cash by also operating a boarding house, serving the produce at meals. Most village shops did not have this ability.

In the 19th century, with the increased availability of credit and cash from banks, improved transportation, and the increased availability of cheap manufactured goods, the business of storekeepers grew. Storekeepers became intermediaries between city merchants and manufacturers on the one hand, and farm households on the other hand. They were able to provide their rural customers with inexpensive manufactured dinnerware, cloth, hats and other goods. With the increasing availability of cash and credit for their customers, the storekeepers were able to insist on being paid in cash. Rural customers were able to buy goods at general stores that previously they had obtained from the personal labor of neighbors or not at all. Humble households could acquire goods that only wealthy elites could afford in colonial times.

In the early part of the 19th century, Little Rest attracted one of these new types of general stores, owned and operated by Thomas S. Taylor. Taylor first opened a store in Little Rest in 1807. In 1817, Taylor married

Elisa Potter, sister of Asa Potter, who was the brother of Elisha R. Potter, Sr. Taylor moved his store into the former school house on main street next to the Landholders Bank building. Taylor also served as village postmaster from 1820 to 1837.

The surviving ledgers and other account books of the general store of Thomas Taylor indicate that he sold a wide variety of manufactured dry goods from his store. He sold dinnerware, furniture, locks, beaver hats, women's hats, shoes, men's and women's clothing, cloth, satin, silks, sewing needles, napkin holders and school supplies. He sold foodstuffs such as sugar, butter, coffee, tea and molasses. In addition, he sold large quantities of rum, wine, brandy, gin and other types of alcohol. Taylor sold a variety of medicines.

Surprisingly, the "goods bought" account books of Thomas Taylor indicate that he purchased goods primarily from merchants in major cities along the eastern seaboard, not just from nearby Providence and Newport merchants. He dealt with New York City, Boston and Baltimore merchant houses who specialized in supplying general stores with a wide variety of manufactured dry goods. Taylor's suppliers included Arthur Tappan, the wealthy New York merchant who became influential in the antislavery movement; Willis & White, a New York city merchant house; Lamson & Lane, another New York city merchant house; and Andrew Taylor & Son, a Baltimore firm that specialized in medicines. Taylor's ties with New York City and other eastern seaboard merchant houses reflected the growing commercialization of economic life in early America, including rural areas such as Little Rest, Rhode Island. The beneficiaries of these new commercial relationships were Little Rest villagers and other townsmen, who as a result had access to a wide variety of modern, manufactured relatively inexpensive goods. Taylor's few ties with Newport merchants demonstrated Newport's decreasing importance, after it had played such a key role in the lives of Narragansett planters in colonial times. Newport still had many distilleries that made rum and other spirits, which Taylor occasionally purchased. Taylor acquired goods for his store from only a few local townsmen; one was Cyrus French, who made beaver hats at his home in Little Rest.

Taylor decided to expand his store and begin purchasing more goods in 1819. He was able to accomplish this expansion by borrowing money from banks. He borrowed in 1819, for example, $900 from the United States Bank, which was the nation's first central bank and which had a branch in Providence. Taylor also borrowed $700 from the Narragansett Bank in Wickford (he did not borrow from the Landholders Bank, although he was a depositor of that bank). In addition, Taylor borrowed from his wife's uncle and wealthiest man in the village, Elisha R. Potter, Sr. Taylor was able to repay each of his creditors within a year.

In another sign of increasing modernity, Taylor kept meticulous records of his dealings with villagers and other townsmen who frequented his store. Taylor kept a "day" book from 1807 to 1839, in which he recorded on the page for the day each transaction with each customer. For example, Henry Eldred, who lived on North Road in Little Rest, one day purchased a small amount of coffee, some molasses and some muslin. Taylor recorded this transaction in his "day" book. Later, Taylor recorded the amount owed by Eldred for that transaction in his ledger book, on a page solely devoted to Eldred's transactions. A running tab was maintained of the amounts Eldred owed Taylor for goods purchased at his store (the debits), less cash paid by Eldred that reduced the amount Eldred owed (the credits). In most cases, customers paid Taylor cash, and not in-kind goods or services as in earlier years. Some of these running tabs were maintained for years. Taylor did not adopt the modern practice of charging interest on overdue accounts. In addition, Taylor kept a separate book of his purchases with New York City and other suppliers of goods, and a separate book of money that he borrowed.

Taylor had over two hundred customers, from the wealthiest villagers and townspeople to the poorest. Interestingly, in his account books, he does not label the account of a black customer as involving a black person, unless the name of a black customer was the same as a white customer. In that event, Taylor would label the account as follows, from an 1813 entry, "Samuel Potter (blk)."

The goods that Taylor purchased typically were transported by ship to Providence, where a South Kingstown sloop picked up the goods and sailed them to South Ferry. The goods would then be transported by wagon to Taylor's store in Little Rest. With his ties to shipping, Taylor naturally turned his attention to mercantile activities. In 1830, he invested with Elisha R. Potter, Sr. in building a sloop designed for east coast trade, the *Kingston*. On the *Kingston's* maiden voyage, it left South Ferry in 1830, sailing for Philadelphia with a load of South County potatoes and cheese. In 1831, it returned from a trip loaded with molasses, which Taylor advertised could be purchased from South Ferry and Newport. Taylor also invested in the sloop *Wickford* in 1830.

Another store in Little Rest was owned and operated by Thomas R. Wells. His store was located in the Tavern Hall Club, then known as the "red house on the corner" (the west side of South Road and main street). This store was stocked with groceries and dry goods. Wells also sold a considerable amount of alcoholic beverages by the bottle, as Nailer Tom Hazard's journal attests. There are fewer surviving records of this store as compared to Taylor's store. It appears that this store was well stocked with goods, but did not have the same variety and quality of goods as Taylor's store. Wells also served as village postmaster from 1809 to 1820.

In the late 1820s, Wells became a leader in the temperance movement in South Kingstown and stopped selling alcohol from his store, which must have hurt his profits. Wells supplemented his income by also serving as the cashier for the Landholders Bank commencing in 1818. His son, Thomas P. Wells, also operated a store, advertising in 1831 in the *Rhode Island Advocate* luxurious items such as imitation goat's hair, "common chamlets," "6 pieces circassians," "Bombazettes," and "satinetts." Wells also served as the postmaster of the village from 1837 to 1843.

The general stores and other shops in Little Rest provided farmers with, as one newspaper advertisement stated, "a good market for all kinds of farming [products]." One of Thomas R. Wells' sons recalled heaps of pork piled up at his father's store each fall, as local farmers brought their hogs to the store to be butchered. Thus, Wells became an important outlet for local farmers. Wells probably sold the pork and other foodstuffs (such as butter, cheese, poultry, and potatoes) in Providence. Another villager recalled that James Helme, who by 1816 was elderly and had scaled back his store's operations, "merely traded in flax seed taking in all raised by the farmers in the towns round about, exporting it, and receiving in return course salt, etc...."

The success of Taylor and Wells is reflected by the roomy and handsome new houses they built in the village. About 1827, Taylor had the colonial Joseph Perkins house moved to a right angle behind his new house on main street. The main house built facing the road was the first one in the village built in the new Federal style, with a hipped roof and columns on the portal entrance. There was a parlor and library in the first floor. (Shortly thereafter in 1829, Asa Potter built the other fine Federal-style residence on main street to the east of Taylor's house). In 1820, Thomas R. Wells built a comfortable residence on North Road.

Taylor and Wells became wealthy enough that they contributed the second highest amount for the construction of the Congregational Church. In addition, Taylor served in the General Assembly and on the South Kingstown town council, and Wells served as the town clerk from 1827 to 1853.

After Taylor's and Wells' successes, other general stores were opened in Kingston. In about 1820, John G. Clarke "put up quite a large store, and stocked it with a fine assortment of foreign and domestic goods, and had a large number of customers." His brother, George, joined him, who ran the store for many years afterwards. Another general store, known as Robinson & Anthony, was located next to the Court House in the former Peckham tavern. Both stores sold liquor by the bottle. John P. Case, a former sea captain, kept a store that "dealt out common groceries rather sparingly, liquid goods more freely." Later storekeepers included Benjamin Palmer, Job Watson, Albert Watson, George Robinson, John G. Perry, and Bernon and Nathaniel Helme. Alonzo Greenman operated the Kingston Hill Store at the turn of the century.

The Kingston Academy and Kingston Female Seminary

If Little Rest was going to secure its place as an important village in the future of South Kingstown, the village leaders knew that it had to improve its educational offerings. Elisha R. Potter, Sr., when he was a boy, had to travel to and attend the Plainfield Academy in Connecticut to receive a decent education. Others in Little Rest had not been as fortunate. Elisha Sr. must have become concerned about educational opportunities in Little Rest since his four sons (Elisha Jr., James, Thomas and William) were about to enter their teenage years. Elisha Sr. was keenly aware that a good education was a key for his sons to carry on the Potter legacy.

One of the first school houses in South Kingstown was built in Little Rest on main street in 1759. About a dozen families in Little Rest contributed funds for the purchase of land and for constructing the small schoolhouse. The school was supported by private donations from villagers and not the town government. In 1787, a young Elisha R. Potter, Sr. served as teacher at the school house, with 23 students, including two sons of silversmith and judge John Waite and the son of James Helme, Jr. The school was still operating in 1790, as five young students boarded with John Nichols, but apparently it did not last much longer.

Public schooling was not a concept that was accepted in the early 1800s in Rhode Island. Rhode Islanders generally did not want to be taxed to support schools for children who were not their own (Providence was a bright exception). Little Rest's white elites also probably preferred to have their children attend an exclusive school, instead of an open public school. Little Rest's leaders therefore turned their attention to forming a private school.

In 1695, Judge Samuel Sewall of Boston (a judge in the Salem witchcraft trials) conveyed 500 acres of land in South Kingstown in trust, the rent from which was to support a "learned, sober and orthodox schoolmaster." A schoolhouse was finally constructed on this land at Tower Hill in 1781. (Elisha R. Potter, Sr. started his teaching stint at this school house in 1785, with 24 students). As Tower Hill continued to decline and Little Rest continued to grow after the removal of the court house to Little Rest, pressure arose to move the school to Little Rest. In 1816, Elisha R. Potter, now an influential politician, used his influence to effect the move. He wrote to Congregationalist ministers in Boston proposing the move. They agreed on the condition that Little Rest provided "sufficient inducement to some qualified person to undertake the joint duties of both Schoolmaster and Pastor." Later in 1816, Potter traveled to Boston to secure the removal of the school to Little Rest and the appointment of an individual to serve both as schoolmaster and pastor of the Congregational Church. In 1819, the Reverend Oliver Brown arrived in Little Rest to fulfill those two duties. The

Sewall-funded school was moved from Tower Hill to Little Rest and Brown began supervising the school, with hired instructors.

Shortly after Brown's arrival, several of the village's notables, led by Potter, bought one-eighth of an acre of land on North Road for the purpose of building a new school house. In 1823, these men agreed to give this property "to aid in raising the present school into an academy, to be called the Pettaquamscutt Academy." In May 1823, these same men obtained a charter of incorporation from the General Assembly for the planned academy. The trustees were Elisha R. Potter, Sr. (also the first president), Oliver Brown, James Helme, Robert F. Noyes, John T. Nichols, and William P. Newell. In addition, they petitioned the General Assembly successfully to sell the land at Tower Hill from the Sewall gift and set aside the proceeds ($4,268) for the academy. A school house was constructed. The name of the school was changed to the Kingston Academy in 1825. As were most private schools that catered to the elite at this time, the Academy admitted only male students.

For more than a generation, the Kingston Academy served the needs of the area's elite, providing a traditional education emphasizing the classics and English. All of Elisha R. Potter's four sons attended the school, and three of them went on to attend Brown University and one attended Harvard University.[25] Many Academy graduates went on to have distinguished careers, including a future governor of Rhode Island. Students came from as far away as the Caribbean Islands, the Azores and Minorca. From 1819 to 1831, a total of 159 students attended the school. After an advertising campaign in 1832, 137 students enrolled for a single year. The building was then enlarged to accommodate the influx of students. Advertisements in the local newspaper, the *Rhode Island Advocate*, sought to induce parents to send their children to the Academy, stating that its Kingston Hill location was a "pleasant and healthful situation" (implying that schools located in urban areas were not always pleasant and healthful). Courses in Latin, Greek, Mathematics, natural philosophy, and "all branches of common English Education" were taught.

The school building was located next to the North Road residence of Christopher Comstock, the English instructor. Students roomed at Comstock's residence and the current Tavern Hall Club. The Comstock residence also served as the dining hall and laundry service. Students had to abide by a strict code of rules, including the rule that "No student shall on any pretense whatever visit, or be seen loitering about those places where ardent spirits are sold."

---

[25] There is no indication that Elisha Sr.'s daughter, Mary Elizabeth, received a formal education. She likely had some private tutoring lessons at home. She was sent to a finishing school in New York City in 1836 and 1837.

Elisha Reynolds Potter, Jr., after he returned from Harvard University, served as a trustee and as president of the Academy. When a classical teacher departed in 1832, the trustees selected him as a replacement. The Reverend Oliver Brown did not, however, approve of the selection of Potter. Under the terms of the Sewall fund, a teacher had to be "learned, sober and orthodox." Brown objected because Elisha Jr. was not a member of the Congregational Church and therefore was not in his view "orthodox." With an exchange of letters in late 1834, the dispute created tensions between Brown and the village's two most important men, Elisha Jr. and his father. Elisha Jr. served only one term as a teacher and Brown left Kingston in 1835, perhaps in part because of this dispute. It would not be the first time that Elisha Jr. would have a serious disagreement with the village's pastor.

In 1837, 147 students enrolled in the Academy, including 49 females. The trustees accepted female students probably in an effort to improve the school's finances and probably in part as a result of pressure from parents who wanted to see their girls receive a quality education.

Unfortunately, the Kingston Academy became embroiled in a controversy over the sale of the lands from the Sewall gift and control over the proceeds. In 1836, sufficient questions were raised about the Kingston Academy's use of the funds from the Sewall gift that the trustees at the time (led by Elisha R. Potter, Jr., Thomas R. Wells, and Thomas Taylor) felt compelled to publish a "Statement of Facts in Relation to the Funds of the Kingston Academy," with the hope that inhabitants of the area and Rhode Island "would not be prejudiced against the Academy, and that the Trustees may not be convicted, before the bar of public opinion, of *willfully and fraudulently* misapplying the funds entrusted to their keeping." The trustees felt that paying the cost of the pamphlet was worthwhile, as "Reputation for honesty and veracity is certainly worth defending." Despite the "Statement of Facts," a lawsuit was filed by parties who objected to the use of the proceeds of the sale of the lands from the Sewall gift by the Kingston Academy. In May 1840, the Rhode Island supreme court ruled against the Kingston Academy trustees and removed the Sewall Fund from their custody. The Kingston Academy trustees had difficulty working with the new trustees of the Sewall Fund. Without these funds, the Kingston Academy could not make ends meet; tuition from students was not sufficient. By 1844, the Kingston Academy had ceased to operate. The school building was sold to School District No. 3, the new public school district in Kingston.

The Kingston Academy trustees started a new school in 1853, calling it the Kingston Classical Seminary. The Kingston Seminary was progressive in that it accepted both male and female students. The trustees were responding to the interest parents had in educating their daughters as well as their sons. Most elite private schools at the time were exclusively for either male or female students. Only a few such schools opened their doors to both sexes, including the Lapham Institute in North Scituate. Perhaps the trustees felt that there was not sufficient demand to operate two independent schools, one for boys and one for girls. Hence, they made the school co-educational and hoped that parents would be enlightened enough to send their children.

A fine school building was constructed to house the Kingston Seminary on North Road just north of the old Kingston Academy school house. It was dedicated in a well-attended ceremony on August 31, 1853. The trustees included prominent villagers Elisha R. Potter, Jr., his brother James B. M. Potter, their cousin, Asa Potter, John G. Clarke, and Wilkins Updike, as well as prominent men from other parts of South Kingstown, Isaac P. Hazard, Isaac P. Rodman, and Rowland Hazard. Elisha R. Potter, Jr. was its president. The principal was male and four instructors were female. The school has 35 boys and 42 girls, most of whom were from South Kingstown and other parts of South County, with a few from Providence and Newport. Teachers were hired under yearly contracts. An 1854 catalogue was published to promote the school, probably authored by Elisha R. Potter, Jr., who at the time was state Commissioner of Education. It extolled the high elevation and cool summer breezes of Kingston Hill, and added that "the village is distinguished for its very intelligent and highly cultivated society, and is entirely free from the unhappy and dangerous influences peculiar to places devoted to Manufacturing." In addition to English, Latin and Greek courses, three pianos were provided for the Music department.

In this age of Victorian prudishness, the trustees were aware that some parents were concerned about male and female students mixing together. Accordingly, the trustees banned students from walking "abroad promiscuously in the evening," banned male and female students from writing to each other, and banned "all unsuitable familiarity between pupils of different sexes." Many parents were not ready, however, to send their sons to a school with female students and female teachers. The number of parents who sent their sons to the school declined. The co-educational experiment in Kingston failed. Due to the "general sentiment against mingling the sexes in our higher schools," to the feeling that single sex schools led to the best quality schools, and to the reality that the Seminary was losing money, the trustees in July 1855 arrived at the "painful conclusion" that the school should be exclusively for girls and renamed the Kingston Female Seminary. The idea was to model the Seminary after the successful Wheaton Seminary for girls at Norton, Massachusetts. (In Rhode Island, there were also the Young Ladies' High School in Providence and the Warren Ladies' Seminary.)

Even after the change to a single-sex female school, the school continued to lose money each year and struggled to pay teacher salaries. The trustees resorted to borrowing money from the Landholders Bank and

Kingston Savings Bank, using the school building as collateral. In 1863, plagued by operating losses and the lack of a trust fund, the Kingston Female Seminary closed down.

It appears that neither the Kingston Academy nor the Kingston Seminary ever had any black students. This was probably intentional. The Academy sponsored some "charity" students for several years, but apparently never selected a local black student.

Turning the Seminary into a female only school in 1855 left a gap in the village's private educational offerings. In 1857, J. Hagadorn Wells used an addition to the rear of the Wells house next to the Kingston Congregational Church to run a boarding school for boys. Wells had about ten students and conducted classes for about five years. When his wife died in 1862, he closed his school. By then, a taxpayer-supported public school had opened in Kingston and had been operating for eighteen years. As public schools improved in quality, private schools had more difficulty surviving.

Kingston Female Seminary, 1853. The building is now used as a residence on North Road. Detail of map of South Kingstown by Henry F. Walling, 1857. *Rhode Island Historical Society,* RHi X42 83.

Corporal Punishment in Little Rest

While Massachusetts and Connecticut by the early 1800s had instituted reforms reducing the severity of corporal punishment, Rhode Island had not. Consider the crime of perjury before a court. According to Rhode Island's criminal code, a convicted individual was to be punished, in the discretion of the judge, with any of the following punishments: standing four hours in the pillory; cropping of the ears; branding; imprisonment not exceeding three years; or a fine not exceeding $1,000.

Corporal punishment continued to be inflicted in Little Rest. A person found guilty of a petty theft crime typically was ordered to pay the victim money for losses suffered and to pay court costs. If the guilty person refused to or could not pay the amounts ordered, he or she would instead be subject to corporal punishment. For example, in 1796, in a justices court held in Little Rest, two white women, Mary and Rebecca Jones, were found guilty of stealing a few pewter plates, forks and knives. They were assessed fines to pay the victim, witness fees and court costs. If they failed to pay the assessed amounts, they were to "be whipped ten stripes each on the Naked Back." It appears they were whipped. Sometimes, the crime was deemed so serious that the convicted criminal could not avoid whippings by payment of fines. For example, in 1791, in another justices court session in Little Rest, for the dual crimes of forging a court order and stealing a horse, Caleb Church was ordered to be whipped by the Washington County sheriff an equal number of times on a Wednesday, Friday and the following Monday.

Many of the prisoners who could not pay their fines and were therefore subject to corporal punishment were black. In 1801, Bristol Gardner, a black woman found guilty of theft, was whipped at the end of a cart through the streets of Little Rest. In the same year, Jacob Lewis was whipped. In 1802, Plato Babcock was found guilty of theft, served at least five months in jail, and was whipped by jailer Robert Helme, which according to Helme "paid his fine for stealing." In 1807, Prince Watson, another black man, was convicted of theft; when he refused to or could not pay his fine of five dollars, he was whipped.

In the early 1800s, it appeared that crimes involving money and property were punished more harshly and were more likely to involve corporal punishment than violent crimes against persons. In 1808, George Northrop, a white man, was convicted of theft and whipped. In 1813, James Short, a white man convicted of forging a note, was sentenced to have a "piece of each of his ears cut off" while standing in the Little Rest pillory for an hour. In 1825, Palmer Hines of North Kingstown was convicted of setting fire to a barn filled with nine tons of hay, nine hogs and farming utensils. He was sentenced to pay a fine of $1,000, to be imprisoned in the Little Rest jail for four years, to have his ears cropped, and to be branded with the letter "R." In 1823, William Bowen of Charlestown, for forging a $5 bank note, was imprisoned for six months in the Little Rest jail. In 1818, Thomas James of West Greenwich stole about $45 in cash and goods from Thomas Taylor's general store in Little Rest. He was sentenced to six months in jail and to be whipped "39 stripes on the Naked Back." In 1826, Benjamin Church stole only about $7 of gin and brandy from the Reynolds tavern in Little Rest, but was sentenced, in addition to repay the amount and court costs, to be imprisoned in the Little Rest jail for two months. As will be explained in a later chapter, two men convicted of stealing substantial amounts from local shopkeepers were sentenced to die by hanging.

By contrast, violent crimes against persons were not punished as harshly. In 1814, a South Kingstown white man who was convicted of burning and choking to death a five-year old girl, was sentenced to pay a fine of $2,000 and to be imprisoned for six years. In 1827, four Exeter residents were convicted of beating a four-month old infant to death, but only received a six month prison sentence. In 1824, William Casey was convicted of beating and choking his wife, but he was sentenced only to remain in jail until his $30 fine and court costs were paid. In 1815, Jeremy Bradford stabbed a man with a knife, causing a four-inch gash, but was sentenced only to remain in jail until he paid a $50 fine and court costs. In 1825, two men who were convicted of beating a man "so that his Life [was] Greatly Dispaired of" received a sentence of only a fine and one month in jail.

Jonathan P. Helme, who was born in Little Rest in 1809, recalled from his boyhood two times when the pillory was used in Little Rest. In one case, a convicted forger was sentenced to be cropped and branded while being held in the pillory in front of the Court House. The sheriff carried out the sentence and, with blood running from his ears, the man was returned to the jail. In the second case, the victim was ordered to stand in the pillory for an hour. A crowd watched the punishment with "the boys throwing eggs, dirt, etc..., at the time he was exposed."

Newspaper commentators began criticizing the use of whipping as inhumane in the 1820s, but it had no effect on the conservative law-and-order types. In 1822, the General Assembly appointed a committee of three men, including Elisha R. Potter, Sr., to undertake a revision of the criminal code, with a view, according to a newspaper, "of multiplying the cases in which the punishment of whipping, cropping, and branding may be inflicted." This development caused alarm in neighboring Connecticut, where a New London newspaper lamented that Rhode Island "continues proof against the improvements of the age, and disgraces herself and the Union, by adhering to all these relics of feudal barbarism, not to be endured in a republic." Even though Potter favored expanding the crimes in which corporal punishment could be inflicted, the majority of the committee favored simply limiting the discretion of the court in applying corporal punishment. Christopher Bickford, in his *Crime, Punishment and the Washington County Jail, Hard Time in Kingston, Rhode Island*, writes:

> The problem for Potter, along with other law-and-order advocates, was his perception that the laws of Rhode Island were not being consistently applied. The apparent willingness of the Legislature to release convicts from jail and of judges to remit sentences of whipping, they thought, was breeding a disrespect for the law that they considered dangerous and unhealthy.

Part of the problem was that the state refused to create a single state penitentiary, a reform that had been adopted in many states. Until a proper prison was built to house prisoners on a long-term basis, corporal punishment would continue to be part of the penal system. When every prisoner in the Kingston jail broke out in January 1827, the *Providence Daily Journal* commented that "this is another proof of the necessity of erecting a states prison." Elisha R. Potter, Sr. became the most vociferous opponent of a state prison. In 1832, he stated bluntly that he was against the building of a state penitentiary and was "in favor of cropping, branding, and whipping." Potter believed (with little evidence) that only one in fifty convicts was native born and that public whipping would drive off foreign rogues. When 1,600 Rhode Islanders presented a petition to the General Assembly protesting such mutilation of prisoners and the lumping together of prisoners in small county jails, and supporting the construction of a state prison, Potter responded that the petitioners paid little in taxes and that the funding for the state prison would have to come from banks and the land – in other words, the taxpayers of Washington County. But a heavy newspaper campaign and circulation of a detailed report in January 1834 favoring reform finally won over public opinion. In a referendum in April 1834, Rhode Island voters supported the construction of a state prison 4,433 to 502. In 1838, a new state prison, with forty cells, opened in Providence.

The General Assembly also enacted legislation reforming the criminal code in 1838. The three punishments included in the new code were "separate confinement in the state prison at labor, imprisonment in a county jail, and pecuniary fine." As a committee report stated, "In substituting these for whipping, cropping, branding, and pillory, the committee believe they have carried out the intention of the General Assembly in the erection of a State Prison." Under the code, all those sentenced to imprisonment for a period longer than one year were to be placed in the state prison, not the Kingston jail or any other county jail. Rather than hold those convicted of serious crimes such as murder and rape, the county courts would only hold those charged of such crimes until the trial had been completed. The list of capital crimes was reduced to murder and arson. (A committee had proposed that Rhode Island "try another experiment" and become the first state to abolish the death penalty entirely, but the proposal was narrowly defeated.) Those convicted of serious property crimes were no longer subject to corporal punishment or death sentences. For example, in 1851, two men who broke into a bank in Westerly and stole $15,400 in bank bills were sentenced to eight years in the state prison in Providence "at hard labor."

One area that was not significantly reformed was imprisonment for debt. Much of the legal system in the county, starting from the local justices courts and ending in the jail in Kingston, was devoted to insuring that creditors were paid amounts owed to them. The sad story of many insolvent debtors is told in the hundreds of petitions for relief that jailed debtors submitted to the General Assembly, which granted only about half of them. In 1803, debtor John Phillips of Hopkinton said that he had spent a total of four years in jail, and in 1814 Simon Hazard of South Kingstown reported that he had been jailed three times for petty debts. On one occasion, the debt itself was only 48 cents but the jailer's fees had raised it to $3.25. Elisha R. Potter, Sr. did introduce and push through bills in 1830 in the General Assembly to exempt females from prison for debts, to forbid corporal punishment for debtors, and to abolish imprisonment for a debt of less than $5. But Potter led the opposition to passage of laws to abolish all imprisonment of debtors.

Historian Peter Coleman believes that reformers may have had difficulty rousing public opinion because the bankruptcy laws may have been viewed as being fairly lenient. For one, by posting a bond, jailed debtors had the "liberty of the yard" (the privilege of walking outside the jail cells) and could practice their crafts during the day. Debtors generally had two options. First, they could take the "poor man's oath," which "Nailer Tom" Hazard traveled to Little Rest in 1822 to inquire about for his son. This forced the creditor to choose between releasing the debtor's debts or holding him in jail at the creditor's expense. Holding a debtor in jail gave the creditor revenge, but was likely to cost him even more money. Alternatively, the debtor could petition for the benefit of the Act of June 1756, which required the debtor to make a full disclosure of his property, which was then distributed among creditors. If the debtor did not make an honest inventory, the General Assembly could send the debtor to prison until full disclosure was made. Thomas Potter, the tavern keeper and merchant, in 1769, and Samuel Casey, the silversmith, in 1770, and William Lunt, the Revolutionary War pensioner and barber, in 1813, used this option. Debtors could also be released if they signed notes promising payment at a future date.

Jonathan Helme recollected two shocking (and perhaps exaggerated) examples of local residents who were imprisoned for debt by their creditors in the Washington County jail. In one case, the debtor was a storekeeper in a neighboring village who was jailed after his business failed. His creditors kept him in jail by paying the jailer one dollar a week. Helme stated that "His wife came to see him once a fortnight, bringing him clean clothes, and something to eat (as he had the liberty of the yard) and kept 'old bachelor's hall' *for more than fifteen years.*" The man died not long after his release at the age of 76. In the other case, a Baptist minister was imprisoned for debt. He was a talented minister but had a weakness for rum and fell behind in his rent and grocery bills. Since he could not post a bond, he did not obtain the "liberty of the yard." He was confined with others in one of the cells "in the common jail." After his release from jail, another creditor sued him and sent him back to jail, "so that it was some time before the old minister could get home to his family or church." Writing in 1874, Helme wrote that "there have been a great many attempts to eradicate this barbarous law from the statute book, but it has as yet only been modified." Daniel Stedman, in his journal in June 1832, noted that a local debating society (possibly held in Kingston) debated the issue of whether imprisoning debtors should be abolished, and the consensus was that it should be abolished. Christopher Bickford found that the number of debtors in the county jails steadily decreased after the Civil War, but that the laws permitting imprisonment for debt remained on the books into the 20th century.

While the "warning out" of town of transients continued as a practice throughout the 19th century, there were some improvements in the harsh treatment of the poor. By around 1810, the practice of jailing adults who were the parents of illegitimate children had ceased. By the 1830s and 1840s, many towns, including South Kingstown, had "town farms" that housed the poor. The town farms provided shelter, food, clothing and work. While town farms were sometimes subject to severe rules, they were more humane than the system of "binding out" poor persons who were town charges to strangers.

Thomas R. Hazard, the author of *The Jonny-Cake Papers,* was the state's most important reformer of the poor laws. In a shocking report in 1850, he criticized the continuing use of "binding out" town charges, which had not been completely abolished in Rhode Island towns. He bluntly stated that Rhode Islanders would not put out their cattle as they let out their poor. He explained the benefits of town farms and asylums. He recommended the abolition of dark rooms, dungeons, chains, and corporal punishment in dealing with the poor, which the General Assembly quickly did.

In 1847, the Butler Asylum for the insane was opened in Providence due to the gifts of many benefactors, including the Hazard brothers. Beginning in 1855, the South Kingstown town council began paying the hospital for caring for a few townspersons.

The Village Changes Its Name to Kingston

Elisha Reynolds Potter, Sr. performed many great deeds for Little Rest. But he did a great disservice in leading the effort to change the name of the village from the colorful "Little Rest" to the dull "Kingston."

In 1825, at the request of the Little Rest inhabitants, the name of Little Rest was changed:

> At a meeting of the Citizens of the Village of Little Rest in South Kingstown, the 23rd of December, 1825, to take into consideration the propriety of altering the name of said village from its present to some other more agreeable and suitable name where Elisha R. Potter Esquire was chosen chairman and Matthew Waite, Secretary. Voted unanimously that the name of this place be forever hereafter called Kingston and that the inhabitants thereof will use all proper means in our power to carry the same into effect.

Villagers moved quickly to effect the name change. By January 6, 1826, the federal Post Office Department sent a notice to the Kingston postmaster confirming the name change on its books.

One can surmise why the "Citizens of Little Rest" wanted to select a more "agreeable and suitable" name. At this time, Little Rest was losing its position as the preeminent town in South Kingstown and Washington County. The villages of Peace Dale and Wakefield, in particular, with their new woolen mills attracting increasing numbers of working families, were challenging Little Rest. The future of South Kingstown lay in those towns and in the Narragansett Pier, not Little Rest. In order to compete with other towns, the "Citizens of Little Rest" sought to be taken more seriously by ridding themselves of the name "Little Rest."

Villagers were probably tired of outsiders poking fun at how the village became known as "Little Rest." The true origin of the village's name was likely to commemorate the "little rest" that soldiers reportedly took on the hill on their march to attack the Narragansett tribe in the Great Swamp in 1675. But that did not stop other observers from speculating as to the origin of the name. For example, in *The Jonny-Cake Papers*, "Shepherd Tom" Hazard writes,

> Some hold that it originated from the multitude of lawyers that used to reside and assemble there, who made it their chief business to involve everybody they came in contact with in quarrels and law-suits, that they might profit thereby, thus giving their clients Little Rest. Others say that the name was not

conferred on the village until after the General Assembly held its annual session, at which time the public accommodations were so limited, that the members of both houses were obliged to sleep four in a bed, heads and points, to make better stowage. Of course there could be little rest in such circumstances, and hence the name Little Rest. From all I can learn, I think, however, the name . . . grew out the fact that in olden time, Little Rest was the home and headquarters of a class of men who were peculiarly addicted to inflicting practical jokes not only on one another, but upon all temporary visitors to the village, and thereby giving their victims but little rest.

While the annoyance of villagers with such speculations was understandable, though regrettable, the "Citizens of Little Rest" showed remarkably little imagination in selecting the name "Kingston" as a replacement. Not only is the name dull, it has resulted in confusion for numerous persons in subsequent years, as a result of the need to understand the distinction between "Kingston village" and the "Town of South Kingstown."

The name of "Kingston" reportedly was suggested by an Englishman, who compared "Kingston Hill" in Rhode Island to Kingston Hill in the fashionable Richmond district outside London. Having visited both hills, the author can confirm that if the "Citizens of Little Rest" were comparing their village to Kingston in England, the comparison was not apt. In addition, the new name harkened back to the days when the English "King" ruled Rhode Island. Yet in December 1825 it had not yet been a full fifty years since Rhode Island had declared its independence from the English royals; indeed, the patriots Thomas Jefferson and John Adams still lived. In 1781, the General Assembly had changed the name of King's County to Washington County in order to rid itself of any connection to British royalty. The move to change the village's name to Kingston may be the earliest demonstration in our nation's history of its infatuation with all things English. One can imagine the fuss Little Rest villagers made when that particular English fop arrived in the village, threw his nose up at the name Little Rest, and suggested as a replacement name a proper English-sounding one.

The author does fervently wish that a movement would arise in Kingston to change its name back to Little Rest. Unfortunately, such a move would likely meet resistance by the University of Rhode Island, as such a change would be costly in terms of updating their written pamphlets and other materials. But imagine the horde of out-of-state students who would compete for the privilege of attending college in a village called Little Rest!

IV. KINGSTON IN THE

AGE OF INDUSTRIALIZATION AND REFORM,

(1826 – 1865)

Beaver Hat Made by William French, Made from Beaver Skin and White Rabbit Fur, and William French Hattery Label. The hat reportedly was owned by Elisha R. Potter, Sr. French's shop, located across from the Washington County jail, employed several apprentices, including women. *Pettaquamscutt Historical Society.*

Elisha R. Potter, Sr. and His Responsibility
for Causing the Dorr Rebellion

This is not a chapter about an influential politician demonstrating courage to act against constituents' pressures in order to do the "right thing" – in this case, extending the basic right of voting on a "one-man, one vote" basis to a class of urban men who had been denied the right. Rather it is about the opposite behavior, the protection of pure self-interest. It is about an influential man from Little Rest – Elisha Reynolds Potter, Sr. – and the role he played in Rhode Island politics to prevent the state from adopting a constitution based on a "one-man, one-vote" system.

In the early 1800s, the country underwent a steady progression toward more democratic government. By 1830, constitutions in many states had been amended to provide for universal white male suffrage. Rhode Island's failure to follow this movement led to a tragic and disgraceful episode in the annals of Rhode Island history, known as the Dorr Rebellion. The issue of constitutional reform was the key issue in Rhode Island politics during the first half of the 19th century. The events leading up to the Dorr Rebellion also had unfortunate overtones of prejudice against Irish immigrants. Little Rest men, beginning with Elisha Reynolds Potter, Sr., loom large in this story as they sought to protect the agricultural interests of Washington County. To be fair to Elisha R. Potter, Sr., initially he took a courageous stand to amend Rhode Island's constitution to liberalize voting rights. But once this effort was rejected by voters in agricultural towns, Potter ended his days leading counter-efforts against any extension of voting rights.

During the first half of the 19th century, Rhode Island politics were dominated by the state's agrarian interests. This influence contrasted sharply with the rapid transformation in Rhode Island's economy from a state formerly dominated by agrarian and mercantile interests to one dominated by industrialization and manufacturing. By the late 1820s, cotton mills displaced foreign trade as the backbone of Rhode Island's economy. The cotton mills were located largely in the northeastern part of the state along the Blackstone River and other river valleys. Providence rose as a major New England center of manufacturing. New turnpikes facilitated commerce in the northern towns. By contrast, the once-thriving South Kingstown and other agricultural towns in South County were declining. In 1790, South Kingstown's population was 4,131. But by 1800, the population had declined to 3,438. The population, stunningly, would not reach pre-war levels until the 1850s. Many townsmen moved upstate to take factory jobs, or they migrated to upstate New York or further west where they could acquire cheap land. A modern historian, Patrick Conley, has accurately written, "The woods of southern Rhode Island today harbor tangible evidence of the decline and exodus . . . . They are dotted with gaping cellar holes and interlaced by miles of stone walls that enclose neither pasture nor field, but rather stands of second-growth oak, red cedar, and pine."[26] The population of all of Washington County declined from 18,075 in 1790 to 14,324 in 1840. By contrast, Providence's population increased from 6,380 in 1790 to 23,172 in 1840.

As a result of the growing industrialization, urbanization and immigration, the city of Providence and the northern towns were becoming populated with families who worked in factories and who rented their homes. Despite these significant changes, Rhode Island's old royal charter that had been granted by the British Crown in 1663 remained in effect. It was faulty on two grounds. First, it gave disproportionate influence to the declining rural towns. In the General Assembly, representatives in the lower house were allocated as follows: Newport (6); Providence, Warwick and Portsmouth (4 each); South Kingstown and the remaining towns, which were all rural (2 each). At the time the royal charter was granted, this allocation gave due consideration to the preeminent position of the commercial towns, then Newport, and in part Providence and Portsmouth. This arrangement persisted into the 19th century despite the fact that Providence was a thriving, growing city; Newport had suffered a commercial decline from which it would never recover; and the number of rural towns established in Rhode Island had proliferated since 1663, but were in decline. In addition, one state senator was elected from each town, which gave the more numerous rural towns control of the senate. The problem was that there was no internal mechanism for reapportioning the number of representatives from Rhode Island towns based on population. Consequently, rural towns were assured of continued control of the legislature because the collective number of their representatives greatly exceeded those of the major commercial areas.

Second, the state's old real estate requirement for voting and officeholding was retained, even though it had been abandoned in all other states. The freehold qualification for men voting was set at $134 worth of land, which benefited rural landholders over urban, landless laborers. Furthermore, the charter allowed the first-born sons of freemen to vote upon coming of age, even if they did not meet the real estate qualification. This relic from colonial times also primarily benefited the rural interests. In 1775, democracy flourished in Rhode Island, with perhaps 60 to 75 percent of the adult white males in Rhode Island voting. By 1840, an astounding 60 percent

[26] Along a similar line, J.R. Cole in his *History of Washington and Kent Counties,* in 1903, when discussing the decline of the Narragansett planters, wrote "where once stood elegant mansions there are now only to be seen dilapidated walls, and loose boulders overgrown with briars and bushes. Such are the footprints of Time on this once fertile and beautiful farming country."

of the free adult white males in Rhode Island were disenfranchised. In Providence, with the increase in landless urban dwellers, including shopkeepers, firemen and factory workers, only one out of three white males had the vote. They saw the explosion of democracy in neighboring states with the end of voting barriers and participation of new voters. They became bitter when they could not participate in the same way in Rhode Island.

The rural politicians jealously guarded their powers under the Rhode Island charter and became very alarmed with the growing industrialization and prosperity of northern towns. They were very suspicious in particular of increasing numbers of Irish immigrants who began to fill factory positions in Providence and other northern towns. By 1850, there were more than 23,000 foreign born residents in the state, most of them Irish and most in Providence. Immigration was changing the face of Rhode Island. Historian Patrick Conley writes, "The outnumbered rural folk regarded reapportionment and 'free suffrage' as their political death knell." Rhode Island was totally out of step with the egalitarianism and democracy of the Age of Jackson in the United States. But the rural Rhode Island politicians paid little heed.

Rhode Island farmers resorted to an ideology of the moral superiority of farmers to justify their policies. One writer paid homage to "Agriculture, the most ancient and useful of the Arts, the inseparable companion, if not the parent, of civilization." Another writer, echoing Thomas Jefferson's writings, cited "the habits of industry, temperance, and reflection which agriculture produces." To this was contrasted the "rotten and hollow population" of the commercial and manufacturing towns.

With control of the General Assembly, Rhode Island farmers, led by the rising South County politician Elisha Potter, in 1793 were able to able to shift tax away from their lands and on to the commercial interests based primarily in Providence. In 1822, the legislature raised taxes on banks and imposed new taxes on corporations, money brokers and insurance companies. As a result, the tax rate on Rhode Island farmland was low.

As early as 1796, Providence merchant John Brown wrote to Elisha Reynolds Potter, Sr. suggesting that South County join with northern towns to support a state convention to revamp the state's constitution. Nothing came of this effort, despite the fact that South County towns had made the same calls for reform in 1782 and 1784. The difference now was that the tax burden had shifted away from the rural towns to the northern towns.

By 1822, by which time Elisha Potter had become the most influential politician in South County, Potter had come to accept that reform was inevitable. In this position, to his credit, Potter at the time was a moderate, in between the activists for reform in Providence and the agrarian conservatives of southern Rhode Island. Potter apparently tied voting reform to tax reform. He wanted to pass a bill that shifted even more of the state's tax load to the increasingly prosperous northern towns and away from the declining South County towns. But he realized that passing such a bill would not be acceptable in the northern towns unless the representation of the northern towns in the General Assembly was increased. Potter introduced in the General Assembly a bill that would give Providence seven representatives, South Kingstown and five other towns three representatives each, and the other towns two representatives each.

In suggesting this compromise, Potter perhaps was also thinking of his own statewide prospects. He wanted to run for the United States Senate in 1822, but he realized that his chances for support in Providence and other parts of northern Rhode Island would be dim if he was viewed as a parochial defender of South County's rural interests. Potter's tactics almost worked, as he was very competitive in the election against a popular incumbent.

Potter continued to advance reform efforts, to his credit, calling for a state convention to revise the state's constitution. He proposed that delegates be elected by each town in accordance with the current apportionment rules. In June 1824, the convention finally met. In addition to Potter, in attendance was Wilkins Updike, an influential attorney who had moved from his family's historic seat at Smith's Castle in Wickford to Little Rest in 1819. In recognition of his ability and efforts in organizing the convention, the delegates selected Potter as the convention's president. In the end, the delegates recommended to the Rhode Island voters a reasonable compromise, although it was far short of "one man, one vote."

Despite Potter's taking the lead in the reform effort, the agrarian interests continued to fear domination by "the manufacturers." Rhode Island voters in a referendum soundly rejected the proposed constitution. Predictably, South County and other declining towns had large majorities against the proposal, while northern towns strongly supported the proposal. Because many northern Rhode Island citizens were not permitted to vote in the referendum, the rural interests were able to win the day.

At this point, Potter hardened his stance against reforming Rhode Island's voting laws. In 1828, in typically colorful terms, he remarked to an associate that "if I had served my God with half the zeal that I have [served] the Landed Interests of this State, I should now almost be prepared to go to Heaven in the Flesh." In 1829, a future governor of Rhode Island, John Brown Francis, wrote Potter stating that he and his friends placed their "trust to your management in stopping the floodgate." In that year, due to opposition by Potter and Updike, memorials supporting the extension of voting rights that had been submitted to the General Assembly were withdrawn.

In 1833, activists in favor of reform were becoming more aggressive in their tactics. At one rally in Providence, a reformer blasted the "Duke of Kingston" (Elisha Potter) for his statements against free suffrage in the May

1833 session of the General Assembly. The "Duke," grumbled the reformer, has "about 100 freemen (so called) under his influence by means of mortgages," and yet talks about the danger of the manufacturer controlling votes. Elisha Reynolds Potter, Sr. and Wilkins Updike were identified as inveterate opponents of free suffrage in the state.

The rural interests continued to fear that if they lost control of the state, the heavy taxation of rural lands that they had suffered in the years during and after the Revolutionary War would return. One pamphleteer wrote, "when the landholders look back and consider hardships they were obliged to undergo, while the system of land taxes was in operation, and the oppressions which many of the country towns were subjected to, by means of a disproportionate valuation, it will make them careful how they run the risk of getting into the same difficulties again." In an 1829 pamphlet, Kingston's Wilkins Updike argued that increasing the number of voters would give manufacturers, bankers, merchants, and large capitalists control of the state which they would use to tax the land. An opponent of Updike argued that in fact manufacturing helped farming families, as it gave farmers' children the ability to obtain mill jobs nearby their families and to avoid having to migrate to the West. But this argument fell on deaf ears in South County.

Still, pressure to reform Rhode Island's system of government increased. After Virginia abandoned the requirement for white men to own land to vote in 1830, only Rhode Island continued to have this relic of colonial times. Yet Rhode Island by the 1830s was among the most urbanized and industrialized states in the country – precisely the kind of state in which a freehold requirement was inappropriate.

In 1834, another movement to hold a state constitutional convention gained momentum. The aging Potter resorted to the old argument that supporters of free suffrage wanted to tax the land and not the banks. In no mood to compromise, Potter insisted that the convention contain "the same number of representatives that we now have, and elected by the voters of the same qualifications as at present." This was not a recipe designed for reform. Potter again attended the convention. The proposal that was drafted was an improvement over the current system, but was again far short of the "one man, one vote" principle demanded by reform activists. Neither side was happy with the outcome. The reform effort died when a quorum failed to appear on the day the proposal was up for approval by the convention.

Elisha Reynolds Potter, Sr. died in September 1835, having acted as a bulwark against voting reform in his lifetime. The mantle of representing the rural interests of Washington County would pass to the able hands of his son, Elisha Reynolds Potter, Jr., with continued assistance from Kingston's Wilkins Updike. In 1842, on their watch, the frustration felt by supporters of reform would explode into the Dorr Rebellion, as told later in this book.

Efforts at Manufacturing in Kingston Fail

Ever since Little Rest's rise in the early 1700s, the village had been an important hub in South Kingstown and the Narragansett country. But this was during an era when agriculture and mercantilism dominated the local economy. By the 1820s and 1830s, it was clear that Rhode Island was heading in another direction. Providence businessmen invested large amounts of capital in cotton mills located in the Blackstone Valley and other areas mostly located in the northern part of the state. By 1832, the mills manufactured cotton for export and employed more than 9,000 workers. By the 1830s, due in large part to the rise in manufacturing, Rhode Island was the most urbanized and densely populated state in the country.

In South Kingstown, wool manufacturing became an important industry. Rhode Island's woolen industry was pioneered by Peace Dale's Rowland Hazard. In 1804, Hazard acquired full ownership of a water-powered mill in Peace Dale on the Saugatucket River. He began to focus on manufacturing. First, he brought hand weavers into the mill, where they produced wool woven onto cotton. Next, he mechanized spinning. In about 1813, he installed a power loom. Other wool mills powered by looms were established at brooks and rivers in South Kingstown. By 1832, the town had 120 workers, many of them women, employed in wool mills.

The journal of Daniel Stedman, the middling white farmer who resided in between Kingston and Wakefield, reflects the increasing importance of the mills. Daniel's daughters worked in several different mills in South County and in the northern part of the state, as did his two sons for a short time. Typically, the daughters would work for several weeks at a mill and then return home for a few weeks. Farming simply did not provide a future for these children. A woman who was abandoned by her husband boarded with the Stedmans and supported herself by working in the mills. Stedman's journal also notes the new dangers of increasing industrialization. In 1832, Stedman reported that the daughter of Philip Rose was killed at the Peace Dale factory. In 1839, he reported that the son of a local man was "Killed in the Gearing of Whitman Kinyon Factory" in Richmond. In 1840, he reported that a twelve or thirteen year-old boy "Got drawed over the drum in the Factory and tore him to peaces very bad and Broke his Leg. Shockingly hurt . . . he Died the Next day."

Kingston's leaders viewed the developments in manufacturing with alarm. They preferred the country life of the farmer, but they realized that they had to do something, or else Kingston would be left behind Peace Dale and other local areas. They looked to invest in small manufacturing enterprises in Kingston.

Since about 1792, Kingston had been the home of a successful, albeit small, manufacturing establishment. Cyrus French and his son, William, were noted manufacturers of beaver hats. Their hat factory was located in one section of their house across the street from the current Washington County jail. The store was located in another section of their house, operated by Cyrus's wife. In the basement were located the furnace and dye vats.[27] Women and girls trimmed the hats and applied the finishing touches. The hats were packed in boxes and delivered to stores in the South County area. (One of the French hats that purportedly belonged to Elisha R. Potter, Sr. is on display at the Pettaquamscutt Historical Society.) But this was a small, family-owned business. The Frenches had the additional services of a few apprentices (including Cook, a key figure in the "Cat Inspector" story in this book) and women and girls, but they did not employ the numbers of workers that were needed to operate the wool mills.

Little Rest men focused on the one area near the village that was a possible site for a new mill, the area around what is now known as Biscuit City Pond (formerly the Mill Pond), just off current Biscuit City Road down the hill from the Washington County jail. Land around Biscuit City Pond had been acquired as early as 1671 by William Knowles. Elisha Reynolds purchased this land around 1740. In 1788, Reynolds sold the land to John Larkin, who then apparently built the first grist mill at the site. In 1797 the mill was sold to Jonathan Babcock, who began to call himself a "Miller."

In 1808, Rhode Island had 16 cotton mills, with seven more under construction. As in many rural towns and villages in the state, local men decided to pool their extra capital to invest in a manufacturing venture. The Narragansett Cotton Manufactory Company was established and acquired the Biscuit City mill site with the intent of erecting the first cotton mill in South County. The president of the company was James Helme, Jr., the storekeeper in Little Rest, and included two other villagers on its Board of Directors, Cyrus French, the hatter, and William Peckham, a farmer and judge. Encouragingly, Rowland Hazard, the Peace Dale manufacturer, was also a member of the board. The 26 stockholders from South County (including the

---

[27] Even some of these small industries must have created environmental problems that were not then recognized as potential health hazards. In his reminiscences, Rev. J. Hagadorn Wells, in addition to recalling the French's basement "containing furnace and dye kettle" for the hat manufacturing business, he recalled as a boy playing in Joseph Stanton's yard with old tanning vats, which had stored powerful chemicals for tanning leather. Both of these businesses operated for most of the 19th century. These chemicals were likely dumped in a way that may have affected the village's water supplies.

men mentioned previously and Little Rest villagers John G. Clarke (storekeeper), Elisha R. Gardner (deputy sheriff), and John T. Nichols (saddlemaker)) formed a private corporation to own and operate the business, said to be one of the first corporations organized in New England. With contributions from stockholders, and with a $2,000 loan from the Narragansett Bank in Wickford, the Cotton Manufactory built a cotton mill at the site for the manufacture of cotton cloth. The mill, in one large three-story wooden building approximately 30 feet wide and 60 feet long, was surrounded by about six smaller buildings. Most of the workers were housed in the outer buildings. The mill produced usable cotton. Nailer Tom Hazard, in his journal, mentions traveling to the "cotton facktory" several times to purchase yarn in the years 1810, 1811 and 1812.

The Cotton Mill adopted the Waltham system, in which the daughters of farmers were typically employed and housed in well-ordered dwellings built near the mill and operated by the company. The female workers, including children, worked long hours. William Rathbun, writing in 1956, recalled the following:

> My grandmother, Mrs. Ann M. (Adams) Sherman, 1802-1900, often told of working in the cotton mill [at Biscuit City] during the winter of 1812 [Ann would have been 10 years old]. The mill, like most of the industries at that time, operated a boarding house for employees, and an older sister of my grandmother operated it. . . . The working hours in 1812 were: operations started at 5 in the morning, there was a stop for breakfast at 6 o'clock. Then operations continued until noon, and on to 6 o'clock at night when there was a stop for supper, after which work continued until 8 o'clock. The only method of lighting was tallow candles.

Rhode Island in this era employed the country's highest percentage of children in cotton mills. For unmarried women, the jobs were an opportunity to gain a measure of financial independence.

Despite Rowland Hazard's backing, the mill does not appear to have been a particularly large or successful venture. Hazard probably paid little attention to it, as he devoted most of his time to his growing wool mills in Peace Dale. The Biscuit City mill appears to have ceased operations in 1814.

Elisha Reynolds Potter, Sr. was not a stockholder in the Cotton Manufactory. It may have been because he and Helme were political rivals, or because he had an aversion to manufacturing (although Potter did list among his assets some "factory stock"). He did deed to "the copartners and proprietors of the Cotton Factory" a tract of land to be "used and occupied as a road or public highway across the lands of the grantor." In 1809, the town council approved the laying out of this road, which became Biscuit City Road.

The cotton mill may have created tension with local farmers. Prior to the construction of the mill, masses of herring swam up the brook leading to the Mill Pond. The mill dams ended this fish run. Some farming families may have relied on the fish run to provide them with food. But they could not stop the powerful interests who owned the rights to the brook and pond.

Biscuit City Mill in Ruins, circa 1890. The large 30 feet-by-60 feet building was originally constructed to house the Narragansett Cotton Manufactory Company. Water was transported to the water wheel by a raised wooden flume hundreds of feet long. *Pettaquamscutt Historical Society.*

In 1819, the mill was sold to Rowse Clarke. The $2,000 paid for the site repaid most of the loan that the Cotton Manufactory owed to the Narragansett Bank in Wickford. Clarke shut down the mill operations and established a factory for the construction of carriages and farm wagons. Clarke's one-horse carriages were in particular fashion with the wealthier set. This business succeeded for a time, but also failed to prosper in the long-term. One observer blamed the laziness of the owner. It was later sold in 1830 to Solomon Harley, who in a notice to townsmen, stated that he planned to continue "to manufacture and repair carriages of all descriptions." This business also failed. Joseph Harley then transformed the site back into a grist mill, which harked back to a time before the industrial revolution.

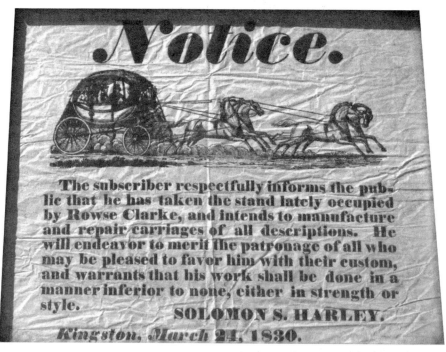

Solomon Harley Carriage Factory Shop Advertisement. Broadside, 1830. *Pettaquamscutt Historical Society.*

Attempts to establish a successful manufacturing mill at Biscuit City Pond had failed. It appears that no more than six houses and the mill were ever built around Biscuit City Pond. Fittingly, in the late 19th century, the ancient watering hole called the Great Spring, became a popular picnic area.

The water power produced by the brook at the Mill Pond may have been very limited, and this probably was a factor limiting the success of manufacturing operations at the site. The mill operators went to great lengths to work with the water power they had. The following is a description of the mill's water supply: "The water from the pond was carried by a flume some three or four hundred feet long to a ponderous over-shot water wheel, said to be the largest one of its kind in the state." Another description stated that the flume "was held high in the air by rough stone columns, and led the water to the top of a gigantic wheel." Thus, Little Rest lacked the key geographic advantage of a stream with enough rushing water to power a factory mill.

Other efforts at manufacturing were made in Kingston village. In 1831, the *Rhode Island Advocate*, the village's first and last newspaper, was published and printed in what is now the Tavern Hall Club. The proprietor of the newspaper relocated his business from Wickford to Little Rest in November 1831. But the newspaper arrived in financial difficulty, as the newspaper almost immediately began running advertisements for the sale of its printing press due to the failure of the proprietor to pay his debts. The newspaper shut down after one year and the press was sold.

A generation after the effort to establish the cotton mill at Biscuit City Pond, in 1837, Kingston residents made another major effort to bring manufacturing to the village with the establishment of the Kingston Boot and Shoe Company. The purpose of the new venture was to manufacture shoes and boots. Kingston residents agreed to capitalize the company with $10,000. Stockholders who agreed to contribute $1,000 each were Elisha R. Potter, Jr.; Thomas Taylor (storekeeper); William French (hatter); and Isaac Hazard (Peace Dale manufacturer). Stockholders who agreed to contribute $500 were Jesse Babcock (tavern keeper); Asa Potter (businessman); Christopher Comstock (school teacher); John G. Clarke (shopkeeper); John Nichols (saddler); Thomas R. Wells (bank cashier); Thomas P. Wells (storekeeper and accountant); Peleg Johnson (doctor); and Thomas Potter (military doctor). Four other men contributed either $200 or $300 each. Ultimately, the amount of $7,950 was actually contributed to the company, mostly by villagers. In March 1837, the company authorized William French, the hatter, and Daniel McCoon Stedman, a shoemaker by trade, to go to Grafton, Massachusetts in order to "procure all necessary information" relating to the manufacturing of footwear. The latter man was the son of the journal keeper, Daniel Stedman, the local farmer, who was also a part-time shoemaker. In his journal, Stedman described the purpose of the trip to Massachusetts "to Git some information or some one to go forward in the business." After French and Stedman's son made the trip, French reported back to the stockholders. Stedman in his journal next reported that in August 1837, French and Stedman's son purchased in New York "about 2000 Dollars worth of Leather." In March 1838, the company purchased for its manufacturing operations the current Tavern Hall Club from Elisha R. Potter, Jr. for $1,350.

As one villager observed, while the company stockholders and directors "hop[ed] to do much for Kingston," the business "soon collapsed." The company apparently produced some shoes, but it never really got off the ground. In 1841, company records indicate that the stockholders voted "to send the boots and shoes finished and such other things as can be sold there to advantage to New York to be sold at auction forthwith." The house on the corner was sold back to Elisha R. Potter, Jr. It is not clear why the business failed. It could have been due to a lack of expertise or a lack of outlets for the footwear. It does appear from company records that a firm in New Albany, New York (where former villager Asa Potter then resided) was intended to be the seller of shoes manufactured by the company, but that the firm had its own financial difficulties and failed to pay the Kingston company a substantial amount of money it owed. The Kingston men lost a considerable sum and did not join in any other village ventures.

Just east of Kingston in Mooresfield, a cotton mill was established in 1836. In 1841, the mill was purchased by Daniel Rodman, who gained expertise in the textile business operating cotton and woolen mills in South Carolina in the 1830s before returning to Mooresfield. The mill manufactured "slave cloth," which was sold to southern slaveholders to clothe their slaves. The mill prospered. Rodman grew wealthy and became president of the South Kingstown town council. Mooresfield gained a store, post office, a small church for black churchgoers, a one-room school and several houses.

At least one Kingston man had success in manufacturing. In 1835, James B. M. Potter inherited land at South Ferry and Usquepaug villages from his father, Elisha R. Potter, Sr. In 1837, at the age of only 21, James erected a mill in Usquepaug. It was named "Independence Mill" because it was raised on the fourth of July. It made Kentucky Jean Cloth, which was shipped to the South to be made into clothing for slaves. He also established a successful mill at South Ferry, on land inherited from his father.

With the establishment of successful mills, substantial communities arose in Usquepaug, Rocky Brook, Peace Dale and Wakefield. The kind of success that Daniel Rodman enjoyed in Mooresfield, and that James Potter enjoyed in Usquepaug and South Ferry, was not replicated in Kingston. Kingston had to face the reality that the industrial revolution would largely pass it by. As a result, the prominent position that Kingston held in South County and South Kingstown inevitably would come to an end.

The Railroad Comes to West Kingston

In 1837, dramatic improvements in transportation brought changes to Kingston. The Boston & Providence Railroad, chartered in 1831, was New England's first viable common carrier railroad. Construction began in Boston in 1832 and the line was completed to Providence in 1835. Passengers and goods from Boston to Providence, upon arrival in Providence, then had to be ferried to India Point, where a waiting ship took them to Newport, New York or other places. The trip was somewhat slow and occasionally dangerous as the ships to New York had to veer around Point Judith. Even before the completion of the railroad line to Providence, it was recognized that the line needed to be extended to the Connecticut coast, which would speed the trip and bypass the dangerous sea passage around Point Judith in favor of direct access to the relatively calm waters of Long Island Sound. The New York, Providence and Boston Railroad Company was chartered in 1832 to build and operate the line.

Almost immediately, discussions ensued as to where the railroad tracks of the extension should be laid out in Rhode Island. The *Rhode Island Advocate*, the newspaper published in Kingston for a year in 1831-1832, saw the railroad as the savior of the agricultural interests of southern Rhode Island. In 1832, when a route for the railroad to the west of Providence was discussed that would avoid southwest Rhode Island, the newspaper rose in protest. The newspaper stated that if instead the railroad came to South County, its residents would "have the facilities for traveling and for the transportation of country produce to Providence or New York markets greater than our forefathers ever dreamed of." The newspaper focused its anger on Benjamin Hazard of Newport, the powerful leader in the General Assembly, who was concerned that a route through South County, Newport's historic hinterland for its merchants, would reduce Newport's shipping trade. Hazard stalled consideration of the South County route. The newspaper warned:

> This is the way the country are always treated in the Assembly. The moment a project is proposed to benefit them, up jumps some cit or would be cit . . . and immediately discusses some objections to it. It is time the country folks began to look out for themselves and to see their rulers and keep their rights and privileges and interests from being trampled on, or transferred to those are who trying so hard to makes themselves masters and controllers of the fate of Rhode Island.

Ultimately, the decision was made to extend the railroad line through South County. In 1837, a line was extended from Providence to Stonington, Connecticut, thereby making the trip to New York quicker and safer. The tracks for the "Stonington line" were laid out across the northwest corner of South Kingstown. Building new grade and laying the tracks through the Great Swamp was an impressive engineering feat. A train station on the line was built about two miles west of Kingston, in what would become West Kingston. It was called "Kingston Station" or "Kingston Depot," because Kingston was the nearest village, despite the two-mile trip, part of it uphill. The trains were pulled by 4-4-4 steam locomotives (meaning that the locomotives had four wheels each in the rear, middle, and front). They must have made quite a racket chugging through the quiet South County countryside.

The arrival of the railroad to West Kingston speeded travel from Kingston to Boston, Providence and New York City, and eased the shipment of country produce to far away markets. Daniel Stedman's daughters, for example, frequently took the "Cars" in order to travel to northern Rhode Island mill jobs. Yet the railroad was one of the leading factors in Kingston's decline. Now those out-of-towners who visited the Court House at Little Rest – legislators, lobbyists, lawyers, judges, and parties to lawsuits – could easily arrive from Providence or Westerly for the day and return to their homes. No longer would Kingston be crowded for days at a time with meetings of the General Assembly and the county court. This development in particular hurt the taverns in the village. One keen observer noted that the coming of the railroad resulted in the "golden harvest" that Kingston tavern keepers had enjoyed being "transferred to the stockholders and employees of the Providence and Stonington Railroad."

The railroad ended many of the long stagecoach runs. There was no further need for Old Bill Nichols and his successors to spend two days in a wagon traveling to and from Providence to pick up and deliver federal mail. The mail for the area was delivered by railroad from Providence, with the stagecoach driven by villager John N. Taylor picking up the mail at the "Kingston Depot" and dropping it off at the Kingston Inn, then a tavern operated by Jesse Babcock. The mail was then sorted by the postmaster in one of Kingston's general stores and delivered to new post offices in Rocky Brook, Peace Dale and Wakefield.

In addition to picking up the mail, stagecoach drivers were needed to meet the train at Kingston Station and transport disembarking passengers on short runs – to Kingston, Peace Dale, Wakefield or Narragansett Pier (a difficult nine mile trip). Passengers traveling to points beyond Kingston occasionally spent the night at a Little Rest tavern or stopped for a refreshing drink. The Joseph Reynolds tavern, operated by Philip Taylor and later John N. Taylor, was a stopping place for passengers and a key depot for stagecoaches. It reportedly had 50 or more horses in the barns behind the tavern serving the stagecoaches in the busy summers.

Of course, now Kingston villagers could travel more easily to the growing metropolitan areas of Providence, Boston and New York. But the trip to New York and Boston was still not easy. Passengers arriving in Providence could continue the trip to Boston only by taking a ferry to another railroad line. On trips to New York City, passengers typically disembarked at Stonington and took a steam packet ship to complete their journey. By 1860, passengers could travel by railroad directly from Providence to New York City. During the Civil War, many Union soldiers from New England, traveling to the war front by railroad, passed through and sometimes stopped at the Kingston station.

Kingston's residents did not know it in 1837, but in 1876 the extension of this new railroad from Kingston Depot to the Narragansett Pier would be the catalyst for Kingston's rapid decline.

Stagecoach, with Driver Stephen Knowles, circa 1870. The John N. Taylor Tavern, formerly the Joseph Reynolds Tavern, in the background, reportedly kept 50 or more horses in its stables to help transport passengers from the Kingston Depot railroad station to points in southern Rhode Island during the busy summer months. *Pettaquamscutt Historical Society.*

Elisha Reynolds Potter, Jr.: Educator, Historian, Politician and Judge

In 1835, Kingston's most influential person in its history, Elisha Reynolds Potter, Sr., passed away. In his footsteps came his eldest son, Elisha Reynolds Potter, Jr. He was more than a worthy successor. If his father was Kingston's most influential person, he was its most illustrious.

Elisha Jr. was born at the Potter Homestead on June 20, 1811. His mother was Elisha Sr.'s second wife, Mary Mawney Potter. He attended the Kingston Academy and then entered Harvard University in 1826, graduating four years later. After graduation, he returned to Kingston, where he became an instructor in Classics at the Kingston Academy. In the meantime, Elisha Jr. studied for the bar, served as apprentice to an attorney in Providence, and was admitted to the bar in 1832. Thereafter, he practiced law in Kingston. He served as adjutant general of Rhode Island from 1835 to 1837. He served in the Rhode Island house of representatives from 1838 to 1840.

Elisha R. Potter, Jr.'s role in opposing the forces of voting reform led by Thomas Dorr, including his serving on a committee to meet with President John Tyler on behalf of the Law and Order Party supporters, is told in an upcoming chapter. In 1843, he was elected as a Law and Order Party candidate to the United States Congress. He was defeated, however, in his bid for reelection in 1845 by voters who apparently did not approve of his support to annex Texas as a state (which was seen by many antislavery northerners as helping the pro-slavery South). Potter was elected to the Rhode Island senate in 1847. As a Democrat, he ran unsuccessfully for state governor in 1858 and 1859. His failures were in part due to rising sectionalism; Republicans, viewed as promoting Northern antislavery views, were more popular than Democrats, who were viewed as supporting Southern slavery interests. But Potter was still popular locally. He served in the Rhode Island senate during the Civil War from 1861 to 1863.

Potter's party affiliations changed due to political turmoil in Rhode Island. He began political life as a Democrat, the same party as his father's at his death. When the leaders of the Democratic Party in the northern part of the state became supporters of the Dorr Rebellion, Potter along with many rural Democrats joined the Law and Order Party. The Law and Order forces were dominated by the Whig Party, and Potter accepted the Whig nomination to run for a seat in Congress in 1843 and again in 1845. In 1845, a friend wrote to him, "When you get tired of Whiggery you would gratify your old friends by coming home to the Democratic Party." With the issues of the Dorr Rebellion finally settled, Potter ultimately returned to the Democratic Party, and was that party's candidate for state governor in 1858 and 1859.

Potter performed valuable public service in the field of education. He first assisted the renowned public educator Henry Barnard, who in 1842

Elisha Reynolds Potter, Jr. (1811-82). He was Kingston's most illustrious resident in its history. Oil on canvas painting, Edward Dalton Marchant, circa 1845. *Rhode Island Historical Society,* RHi X3 5715. (There is a painting of an older Elisha Potter hanging in Potter Hall on the second floor of the Kingston Library.)

helped Rhode Island join the movement started in Massachusetts and Connecticut for public schools to adopt uniform standards. Following Barnard, Potter was then appointed as the second state Commissioner of Public Schools, serving from 1849 to 1854. It was said of Elisha Jr. that he ranked "second to his predecessor only in quantity of his labors not in their quality." He was instrumental in establishing a state normal school (teacher's school), which was the forerunner of the present Rhode Island State College.

Potter was one of the finest historians in Rhode Island's early history. He represented a new breed of historian who strived for accuracy and not merely romanticism. At the age of only 24, he published *The Early History of Narragansett* (1835). He provided an invaluable service by collecting and saving ancient original documents relating to the Narragansett tribe and the early settlers of 17th century Rhode Island. The Rhode Island Historical Society now possesses many of these documents. Two years later he authored a book on colonial Rhode Island's use of paper money.

Potter wrote historical studies relating to controversial topics of the day. In 1842, he published a pamphlet on the voting rights controversy, *Considerations on the Questions of the Adoption of a Constitution and Extension of Suffrage in Rhode Island*. As the crisis with the South and demands for the abolition of slavery increased, Potter gave a speech summarizing the history of slavery in Rhode Island to the Rhode Island senate in 1847 and to the Rhode Island Historical Society in 1851.

Potter also wrote about the oppressed elements in Rhode Island's history. In 1839, as a member of the Rhode Island house of representatives, he wrote a report on the treatment of the Narragansett tribe, including the encroachment of white neighbors on its lands. Potter recommended that severe punishments be imposed on these whites, but no one was ever punished. In 1842, he was appointed by the General Assembly as commissioner to settle claims made against the Narragansett tribe. In later years, perhaps in honor of his mother, Mary Mawney, whose family descended from French Huguenot settlers who settled in East Greenwich in 1686, he wrote *Memoir Concerning the French Settlement and French Settlers in the Colony of Rhode Island*. This book discussed the harsh treatment of the early French Huguenot settlement by Massachusetts Puritans.

Elisha Potter, Jr. was always fond of books and studies. A fellow-historian praised Potter's knowledge of surveying, history, religion and botany. He added:

> Virgil was his favorite Latin author, but his library is filled with the classics in many editions, both ancient and modern. He could read Dante and Tasso in their mother tongue, and with French he was as familiar as with English . . . .

Mr. Potter was an immense collector of books, but he was more than that; he was an immense reader of books, and which were read for the purpose of acquiring knowledge. A fact which he had once read never escaped from his tenacious memory, but years afterwards he could at once recall it for immediate use.

Elisha Jr. was described as having a gentle nature that was "almost feminine," but also as demonstrating a firmness in his beliefs. The latter point is demonstrated in his forceful speeches and writings. Elisha Jr. resided in the Potter Homestead all his life. He never married and never had children. His sister, Mary Elizabeth, ran the Homestead, supervising the house servants and organizing dinner parties.

Elisha Jr. presents a sharp contrast to his father. The differences may reflect the maturing Rhode Island countryside.

- Elisha Sr. was a large man with a blustering, domineering, "man-of-the-people" personality. He could swear at a black servant for not performing labor on his fields and haul him off to jail if he tried to leave without permission. He enjoyed frequenting taverns and mixing with ordinary villagers. By contrast, Elisha Jr. was slim, refined and scholarly, with a gentle nature. He never lost his temper even when engaged by a political opponent. No questionable anecdotes found their way into his speech.

- The portrait of Elisha Sr. in the Pettaquamscutt Historical Society shows a powerfully built, thick-necked man in a simple black coat. The portrait of Elisha Jr. in the Rhode Island Historical Society brings to mind a sharply-dressed, slim and dashing poet.

- While Elisha Sr. was well read for his day and his letters show that he was clearly literate, Elisha Jr. was on a higher level in that regard. Elisha Jr., the first of the Potter generation born after the American Revolution, was educated at the Kingston Academy and Harvard University, and he developed an active, intellectual frame of mind. He was part of a literary and cultural group that included the leading writers and politicians based in Providence.

- Elisha Sr. aggressively acquired land and invested in commercial enterprises, but becoming wealthy was not a goal of Elisha Jr.'s. It was said of him that "He never became a very rich man, but was always possessed of ample means and was known to the poor and distressed of a wide community as a generous benefactor and wide counsellor." One report stated that he "had a good many dependents in the town, who frequently went to him for assistance." He reportedly assisted his family's former black servants in their retirements.

- Elisha Sr. was a strong orator, but Elisha Jr. was not. Several times the *Congressional Globe* reported that Mr. Potter spoke but that the speech was inaudible.

- While the desire to produce heirs to continue the Potter dynasty was important to Elisha Sr., it apparently was not an important desire in Elisha Jr.

On the other hand, father and son had significant similarities: they both fought in political circles at the state and national levels to defend South County's agricultural interests. As did his father, Elisha Jr. worked to promote the interests of Kingston. In 1839, Potter made a considerable effort to rejuvenate the circulating library in the village, including incorporating the library society. He donated a large collection of books that was the basis of the initial collection of the Kingston Free Library. He was also a leading member of the Presbyterian Society of the Pettaquamscutt Purchase, the secular arm of the Kingston Congregational Church. As was his father, he was elected president of the Landholders Bank. Elisha Jr. also had close ties to the Kingston Academy. During his life, he was a student, teacher, trustee and president of the academy. He also was a trustee and president of the academy's successor, the Kingston Seminary.

Elisha R. Potter, Jr. was held in high regard by many South Kingstowners as well. He was often elected as moderator of the town meeting. He also served several terms on the town's school committee.

In 1861, Elisha and his brothers, James and William, suffered a severe financial reverse. James owned mills in Usquepaug and South Ferry, but by 1860 they were running losses. James mortgaged the mills and his other property, and apparently brothers Elisha and William did as well. In February 1861, James became insolvent and the banks foreclosed on his mills and other property. A Kingston villager wrote, "Elisha has not one cent he can call his own or a foot of land. William is involved for $35,000, all the help must come from Tom & Mary. Everything is to be sold the first of May, both factories, the homestead here all the land all the horses & everything else. I presume Tom will secure the homestead if possible. Elisha has opened a law office in Newport and is going to live there." Fortunately, Elisha was able to hold onto the Potter Homestead and somewhat recover financially.

In 1868, the Republican-controlled General Assembly elected Elisha Jr. as a Rhode Island supreme court justice. He served in that capacity for fourteen years. He was described as a hard worker and as "always gentlemanly and courteous in bearing, and considerate of the rights and of the feelings of others." Potter served on a three judge panel in one of the largest and longest cases in state history, involving the bankruptcy of the A. & W. Sprague Manufacturing Company. Potter usually issued dissenting opinions, which one historian believed would have resulted in a fairer outcome to creditors and to less embarrassment to the state than the majority opinions.

Elisha Potter, Jr. left his judicial office on Providence on Friday, April 7, 1882, but was struck by a sudden attack of pneumonia, which ended his life at the Potter Homestead on April 10th. His funeral at Kingston was attended by many state luminaries. A train from Providence carried the governor, General Assembly members, supreme court judges, state officials, and members of the Providence bar. The "major portion" of the residents of Kingston also attended the funeral, including "rich and poor, white and black alike." On the day of his funeral, his casket was draped in black cloth in the southeast parlor of the Potter Homestead. The casket was then lifted onto a bier and was carried by mourners slowly across the lawn, through the orchard, and down the hill to the Potter family cemetery. Potter was laid to rest in the vault next to his mother and father, with "the heavy door closed upon them." After the funeral, villagers treated out-of-towners to dinner in their houses.

Elisha R. Potter Homestead. Home of Potter family members from 1809 to 1938. The author lived in this house as a child. The scene has changed little from 1840 to today. Daguerreotype, circa 1840. *Pettaquamscutt Historical Society.*

Wilkins Updike: Politician, Historian, and Lawyer

Wilkins Updike was a contemporary of both Elisha Reynolds Potter, Sr. and Elisha Reynolds Potter, Jr. Updike as a politician generally supported both Potters, but he was an influential man in his own right. He had a more conservative, traditional frame of mind than either of the Potters.

Wilkins Updike was born in 1783 into one of Rhode Island's oldest families. The Updike family had lived in Smith's Castle (Cocumscussoc) in Wickford in North Kingstown for over 120 years. His forefathers were Narragansett planters. Updike had received private tutoring in his youth and he attended Plainfield Academy in Connecticut. When Updike was 23 years old, he became the heir to Smith's Castle. But the old plantation was no longer large or fertile enough to support Updike. Accordingly, Updike studied for and was admitted to the bar in 1807. Two years later, he married Abigail Watson, from a prestigious Narragansett planter family. During his apprentice years, Updike studied law under several attorneys, including Elisha R. Potter, Sr.

Updike appeared to have a bright future at Smith's Castle. Unfortunately, Updike made the decision to guarantee loans made to one of his brothers who had started a business in New York City. The brother's business failed, and in order to discharge his debt, Updike found it necessary in 1812 to sell Smith's Castle.

In order to promote his career as a lawyer, Updike moved to Kingston. In about 1819, Updike built a roomy house on main street in Kingston (next to the Kingston Hill Store) which he, his wife and twelve children inhabited. Updike had his law office in a one-room building, which he called "Big Enough." He moved the building to various locations on Kingston's main street.

For many years Wilkins was elected to represent South Kingstown in the General Assembly. He played an important role in the adoption of reforms in the state's judiciary system, in securing the removal of restrictions upon the rights of married women, and in supporting public education (his latter efforts are described in an upcoming chapter). As we have seen in a previous chapter, Updike was a leader representing the agricultural interests of Washington County in resisting "one man, one vote" voting reforms. As we shall see in upcoming chapters, Updike was a leader of the conservatives in suppressing the Dorr Rebellion.

Updike was a leader of South County's agricultural interests against the urban and commercial interests in the northern part of the state. In one typical affair, a Providence bank sought authority from the General Assembly to issue paper money on its own credit with no gold backing, something that became common but then was controversial. All waited for Updike to present

Wilkins Updike (1783-1867). As a politician, he was accused of insulting every important person in the state. Drawing, unknown artist, circa 1850. *Pettaquamscutt Historical Society.*

the case of the "country" party against the proposal and in favor of the gold standard, and Updike did not disappoint the onlookers. The proposal was rejected. Another heated issue involved whether Rhode Island should pay the holders of notes that the state had issued during the Revolutionary War. Speculators in Providence had purchased some still outstanding debt at prices substantially lower than face value, in the hopes that the state would redeem the debt at full face value. Updike was a leader against payment of the debt, which he saw as an attempt by urban, commercial interests to make country farmers subsidize invalid claims.

Updike spent most of his career with the Whig Party. In 1847, Updike was nominated as the Whig candidate for a seat in the U.S. House of Representatives, but he lost the election. A collection of broadsides issued on Updike's behalf during the election were acquired by the Smithsonian Institution and were included in a recent exhibit on classic American broadsides. Political broadsides and pamphlets were used frequently by Updike and other political leaders of the day. In an age before television and radio, broadsides and pamphlets were invaluable in communicating the messages of leaders to the mass of voters in order to recruit the maximum number of voters to their cause. They were not literary masterpieces, but they were effective in conveying messages to ordinary voters. These efforts showed the egalitarian nature of politics in that elites found it necessary to appeal to ordinary voters with persuasive written pieces.

The "rough and tumble" of election campaigns in the mid-19th century is demonstrated in broadsides issued in Updike's 1847 congressional campaign. Updike issued a broadside entitled "History of the Alleged State Debt of Rhode Island," which conveyed his views that the Revolutionary War debt held by commercial men in Providence was invalid, "pretended debt" that was held by greedy speculators. In an earlier broadside, Updike had written that the political supporters of payment of the debt were "an unprincipled band of politicians" and the holders of the debt were "an unprincipled knot of speculators." He called the "whole subject . . . a fraud, from beginning to end – a stupendous fraud." He caustically commented that the holders of the debt were "vultures who gyrate over our little State, to gorge themselves on the fetid carcass of this State debt." The opposition Democrats did not remain silent, but instead sought revenge and political support from voters in a pamphlet, entitled "Political and Moral Claims of Wilkins Updike." The following charges were leveled against Updike in the pamphlet:

- The pamphlet claimed that Updike switched parties, showing little allegiance to principles. He started out as a Federalist, but when that party's fortunes waned, he switched to the Republican Party. Then he switched back to the Federalist Party, and in the 1847 election was running as a member of the Whig Party.

- The pamphlet attempted to show division in Updike's relationship with his long-time ally, Elisha R. Potter, Sr. (Interestingly, in 1847, the elder Potter had been dead for twelve years.) The pamphlet stated that a Whig who lived near Potter said to him, "Mr. Updike is saying hard things of you, on every possible occasion." Potter was reported to have responded, "What of that? When I want to use him, I can have him, as easy as turn my hand." If it was not already clear to the reader, the pamphlet continued: "This meant, he could whip him in, at his own good pleasure. Mr. Potter knew 'every inch' of Wilkins Updike, and he knew precisely what office, or how many stripes, would keep him steadily pulling in the traces."

- The pamphlet made note of Updike's advanced years. "Wilkins Updike has not the physical energy to perform the arduous duties consequent to his position, should he be elected a Representative to Congress. He is laboring under PREMATURE OLD AGE." (Updike lived to be 84 years old and when the pamphlet was written in his 63rd year, he was still vigorous and even courted a young poetess.)

- The pamphlet noted that Updike had received support from the temperance movement supporters, but that he had been caught violating his temperance pledge. Updike had reportedly explained that his pledge was effective for Washington County, but not for Providence County.

- The pamphlet accused Updike of insulting practically every person of importance in the state during his career.

Only after leveling these charges did the pamphlet address the substance of the validity of the Revolutionary War debt claims.

Wilkins Updike was known for his witty and frank public speaking. As an example of his wit, Updike spoke in the General Assembly against the use of Latin phrases in legislation.

Mr. Speaker, there was a man in South Kingstown about twenty years ago, a perfect nuisance, and nobody knew how to get rid of him. One day he was hoeing corn and he saw the sheriff coming with a paper and he asked him what it was. Now if he had told him it was a writ, what would he have cared! But he told him that it was a *capias ad satisfaciendum,* and the man dropped his hoe and ran and has not been heard of since.

While Updike also had an acerbic tongue and has been described as a "sharp-tongued" lawyer, he also enjoyed life. A contemporary wrote that Updike "enjoyed himself, and so was a source of joy to all around him. He loved to eat and drink and laugh and work."

Wilkins Updike is remembered today for two historical works that he authored, *Memoirs of the Rhode Island Bar* (1842) and *A History of the Episcopal Church in Narragansett* (1847). The latter book is relied upon by historians as a source of information about life in the colonial Narragansett country. Updike's writing style is very modern in its clarity and lack of puffery. The book does establish that Updike believed in a traditional, hierarchical society in which the "better sorts" at the top of the social scale ruled and others below deferred to them.

Two letters from Wilkins Updike indicate that he and Elisha R. Potter, Jr. were part of a literary and social elite in the state. At the time the letters were written in 1847, Updike's wife Abbey had passed away and Updike was 63 years old. Updike wrote the letters to a talented young poet, Sarah Helen Whitman. Shortly after the letters were written, she engaged in a famous romance with Edgar Allen Poe. Updike himself courted Whitman, as he promised in the letter to "clear out" any of her suitors who may be supplanting him. Whitman never reciprocated his romantic interest and she did not accept his invitations to visit his Kingston home. Updike's two letters to Whitman reveal that his circle of friends included many the most prominent men in Rhode Island at the time: Potter, Francis Wayland (president of Brown University), Rowland G. Hazard, Henry Barnard, Judge Job Durfee and Albert G. Greene. The letters are full of references to books and poems. One historian notes that "these men comprised a distinguished part of a flourishing community of scholars and writers that existed in Providence at the time." A contemporary wrote that Updike was often the center of attention in these gatherings, some of them at Updike's house, as he provoked laughter in parrying the jests of these accomplished men.

While Updike did not work to promote his new home village with as much zeal as the Potters did (it was not Updike's hometown after all), Updike did make some substantial efforts. He was a trustee of the Kingston Academy and later of the Kingston Seminary, and served several terms on the town's school committee. He also pushed through bills in the General Assembly to make improvements to the Court House and jail.

Wilkins Updike reportedly never spoke again of his beloved Smith's Castle after he moved from there to Kingston. He died in Kingston on January 14, 1867 at the age of 84. His fine gravestone is in the cemetery surrounding St. Paul's Church in Wickford.

The Roles of Elisha R. Potter, Jr. and Wilkins Updike
in Suppressing the Dorr Rebellion

The reformers seeking a "one-man, one-vote" system of government and a fairer apportionment of legislators from the towns in Rhode Island had had enough of failed efforts to amend Rhode Island's constitution within the framework of the existing constitution. The problem was that the constitution itself did not allow for peaceful change within the system. Because only propertied voters could vote for a new constitution, and because the rural towns dominated the General Assembly, the rural interests continually voted to quash reform and protect their interests. The northern part of the state, particularly the many landless, urban dwellers in Providence, had virtually no voice in governing themselves. One historian has estimated that more than 90% of Providence's adult men were not entitled to vote.

Even though Rhode Island was the only state in the union with a property requirement to vote, conservatives felt no great push for reform. Accordingly, they failed to act in a way that would have prevented a threat to the legal government of Rhode Island and great embarrassment to the state.

In 1841, the reformers decided to bypass the General Assembly and convene a People's Convention, equitably apportioned and chosen by an enlarged electorate. A broadside called South Kingstown citizens to hold a town meeting at the Court House in Kingston on August 28, 1841 in order to elect town delegates to the People's Convention to be held in Providence in October 1841. South Kingstown was not a hot bed of suffrage activity, but an impressive 100 persons attended the meeting at the Court House. Thomas Wilson Dorr, a Providence attorney, assumed leadership of the movement in late 1841 and became the principal draftsman of the progressive People's Constitution, which was ratified in a popular referendum in December 1841. Although conservative forces abstained from the vote, Dorr claimed that a majority of freeholders even as defined under existing law had voted for the People's Constitution. A total of 144 South Kingstown voters voted for the People's Constitution, including Kingston villagers William French, Luke Aldrich, John Eldred, and John Larkin. While there was a dispute as to whether many of the Dorr voters fraudulently voted, Elisha Reynolds Potter, Jr. exclaimed to former Governor Francis, "Dorr's plan has succeeded beyond his most sanguine calculations." Dorr was elected governor under this document in April 1842. There were now two state governments.

In response to the call to draft the People's Constitution, the conservative forces in the General Assembly voted to call for a "legal" constitutional convention. At a meeting at the Court House in Kingston, Elisha R. Potter, Jr. and Wilkins Updike were selected as two of South Kingstown's three delegates. At this "Landholders Convention" in November

1841, Potter, Updike and others drafted a fairly liberal constitution. Potter was a leading figure at the convention. He was more liberal than most delegates, as he attempted on two occasions to place the choice of state officials in the hands of the people. The conservative forces, led in part by Wilkins Updike, defeated these efforts. The delegates as a whole were not liberal in extending voting rights to immigrant and black men. At the adjourned February 1842 session, the Landholders Convention agreed to allow all native-born white males to vote for or against ratification, without regard to property qualifications. So immigrant and black men continued not to qualify as voters (black men had been disenfranchised in the state in 1822; extending the vote to women was not considered). At a meeting at the Kingston Court House on February 28, 1842, Elisha Potter and Wilkins

Dorr Rebellion Broadside, 1841. Advertising a mass meeting of suffrage supporters at the Court House in Kingston. *Rhode Island Historical Society,* RHi X3 6946.

Updike met with South Kingstown voters to express support for the proposed constitution. But with Dorr supporters opposing the Landholders Constitution on the ground that reform did not go far enough, and with solid opposition to reform still in South County and other rural areas of the state, the Landholders Constitution was rejected by a vote of 8,689 to 8,013.

Immediately after the election, the General Assembly passed a law stating that it was an act of treason against the state to serve as an officer under any fraudulent constitution. This law was called the "Algerine Act." The conservative forces also formed a "Law and Order" party, which was a coalition of Whigs (including Wilkins Updike) and rural Democrats (including Elisha R. Potter, Jr.). With most Dorrite candidates withdrawing from the election after the passage of the harsh Algerine Act, the Law and Order Party swept the 1842 regular elections. Incumbent Governor Samuel Ward King was returned to office. Elisha R. Potter, Jr. was easily elected to the Rhode Island senate and Wilkins Updike and James B. M. Potter (Elisha's brother) were elected to the Rhode Island house of representatives.

Just prior to the April election, Governor King sought federal intervention by President John Tyler (a Whig) to suppress the Dorr forces. In April 1842, Governor King sent Elisha R. Potter, Jr. and two other men ("three of our most distinguished citizens") to confer with President Tyler in Washington, D.C. President Tyler was, however, hesitant to act in the face of the popular movement in Rhode Island. After the election, in May 1842, Governor King again sent Potter and two others to demand federal intervention to suppress the Dorrites. The three-man delegation met with conservative southern congressmen and explained that the Dorr supporters were seeking the equal and natural rights of all men and the iron rule of the majority, terms certain to arouse the fears of southern congressmen of a black slave rebellion. Potter, in a memorandum of his meeting with President Tyler he drafted after the meeting, wrote that "I mentioned once we leave the laws what is there . . . to prevent negroes from revolutionising the south?" "He [President Tyler] agreed." A number of the southern congressmen, who were lobbied with a similar message, became apoplectic at the prospect of free suffrage and the risk that black slaves could be given the vote. The Rhode Island delegation brought back a letter from President Tyler to Governor King, in which President Tyler expressed ambivalence and hope for changes that would satisfy the insurgents. In the end, President Tyler promised to support the Law and Order supporters with a federal military force if a true "insurrection shall exist against the government of Rhode Island."

Elisha Potter wrote the President that when the General Assembly convened in May 1842, "the subject of calling a convention immediately and upon a liberal basis was seriously agitated amongst us," but the "objection made was that they did not wish to concede while the people's party continued their threats." Potter suggested to President Tyler that the solution to end the legislative impasse was for Dorr to "allow himself to be arrested peaceably and give bail." Potter wanted Dorr simply to surrender, which Dorr would not do. Privately, Potter admitted to President Tyler that "in this country the majority doctrine has the appearance of at least being democratic and of course will carry with it the sympathies of the people of the other states which will react upon our own citizens. We on the other hand are subjected to the odium of being called aristocrats. . . ."

Matters came to a head when Dorr, seeking to exercise what he considered his valid authority as governor, seized artillery from a military academy in Providence. On May 12, 1842, with 204 men, he attempted to seize a state arsenal building in Providence but failed. His troops fled in a state of confusion. Fearing retaliation, most of his followers deserted the cause, and Dorr himself fled into exile. In South Kingstown, Elisha R. Potter, Jr. drafted a resolution that was passed at a town meeting held on June 11, 1842 with only one negative vote. The resolution reflected Potter's moderation, as it denounced all attempts to change the existing government by force, but agreed that the time for an extension of voting rights had arrived. Later in June, the General Assembly debated calling for a new constitutional convention, but most South County representatives continued to express anxiety about the threat to their agrarian interests.

On June 25, 1842, Dorr supporters and troops gathered in Chepachet in the northwest part of Rhode Island. Dorr returned in late June to inspect his troops and reconvene his so-called People's Legislature in Chepachet. Governor King declared martial law and a Law and Order army of 3,000 men gathered in Providence to face the threat. On the night of June 25th, 600 troops from South County arrived in Providence, and "they were received with cheers." These troops included the Third Brigade, a Washington County state militia unit, with Captain James B. M. Potter as a quartermaster. They also may have included the "Washington Cadets" based in Wakefield (later the name was changed to the "Wakefield Cadets" and finally to the "Narragansett Guards") and the Washington Grenadiers, chartered independent companies that had been organized in South Kingstown and Washington County in response to the Dorr Rebellion. Daniel Stedman, the local farmer and shoemaker, in his journal, reports that on June 25th the militia was "Called out to go to Providence to guard the Town against Dorr . . . ." The Law and Order army marched to Chepachet, resulting in the Dorr army disbanding, with some supporters being arrested. Dorr fled into exile a second time. On June 29th, two days after Dorr had departed the state, President Tyler ordered federal troops to intervene. The Dorr Rebellion was essentially over, but its fallout would be felt for years to come, including by Elisha Reynolds Potter, Jr. himself.

The Dorr supporters for free suffrage did not disappear. At a free suffrage clam-bake in August 1842, Benjamin Nichols (a relative of Kingston's John T. Nichols) was elected one of seventeen vice-presidents. In September 1842, at another free suffrage clam-bake, Alfred Updike (a relative of Wilkins Updike) was elected a vice-president. The Law and Order Party did not ignore Kingston. In late September 1842, Governor King traveled by train to Kingston and reviewed Colonel Hoxie and his militia troops in the Eleventh Regiment parading in the village.

Elisha Reynolds Potter, Jr.'s usual response to an important issue of the day was to write a history about it. In September 1842, Potter published a history of Rhode Island's constitutional development and a spirited critique of the Dorr uprising in *Considerations on the Questions of the Adoption of a Constitution and Extension of Suffrage in Rhode Island*. Even though it was published after Thomas Dorr had been jailed, he explained the need for a discourse on the Dorr controversy on the grounds that "the civil agitation of the controversy will probably be continued . . . ." He was correct in that conclusion. In satirical tones, Potter observed of the People's Convention, "A few persons get together, and call themselves *the people*. And then they ask, are not the *people* sovereign? Have they not the right to do whatever they choose? It was certainly a lucky thought." But as a moderate member of the Law and Order Party, Potter was among the state's influential men who pushed for a constitutional settlement.

Finally, the Law and Order forces consented to drafting a written state constitution, with the convention meeting on September 12, 1842. The draft constitution was presented to the public for a vote in late November 1842. With Dorrites abstaining from the vote, the constitution was adopted by a wide margin.[28] At the South Kingstown town meeting held at the Court House, the vote was 237 for adoption, 167 against, and 55 for reporting a constitution "allowing coloured persons to vote."

While the new constitution fell short of "one-man, one-vote," it increased the representatives from Providence and other northern towns. There were three classes of voters. Landholders needed only one year's residence in Rhode Island to vote on all matters. A native-born American

---

[28] Historians state, with small variations in numbers, that the vote by Rhode Island towns in November 1842 was 7,024 in favor of the constitution and 51 against. *See,* for example, Patrick T. Conley's *Democracy in Decline* at page 351. This would appear not correct based on the voting results at the South Kingstown town meeting alone. A table in Peter J. Coleman's *Transformation of Rhode Island*, at page 286, correctly counts the 237 "yes" votes, but not the 167 "no" votes. It may be that the 167 "no" votes related to a separate vote against permitting black males to vote.

who did not qualify as a landholder was subject to a two-year residency qualification, but if he paid taxes on $134 worth of personal property he could vote in all elections. A new class of voters did not have to meet the $134 net worth requirement if they performed at least one day of volunteer service in the militia and paid $1 in tax. However, this class of voters could not vote in local elections. The final category was reserved for immigrants who were naturalized citizens. They were still subjected to the old real estate restriction that was the most blatant instance of discrimination against immigrants found in any state constitution in the country.

Potter later explained to former President Martin Van Buren that the prevalence of manufacturing in Rhode Island necessitated restrictions against foreign workingmen who would soon inundate the state and possibly dominate its political fortunes. Surprisingly, black men, who had been disenfranchised in 1822, were given back the right to vote. Potter expressed the view in a letter to former Governor Francis that extending the vote to blacks was thought to be acceptable because black voters were more likely to follow conservative leaders than Irish leaders. On March 5, 1844, nearly a year after the new constitution went into effect, over 75 naturalized Americans, many of them prominent Irish-Americans, petitioned for redress to the U.S. Congress due to their continued lack of voting rights. As part of their grievance, they stated that "the *negroes* of this State [have] the right of suffrage, as freely as it is accorded to any native citizen of the United States, thereby degrading us below the negro population."

As a further check for the rural interests, a veto power was in effect given to rural towns in the state senate. There was one senator from each town, regardless of its population. The leading historian in this field of Rhode Island history, Patrick Conley, wrote: "South County had prevailed; the 'agrarian interest' was secure." In a broadside supporting Wilkins Updike's candidacy for a seat in the U.S. Congress in 1847, Updike was praised for his key role in enabling country folk "to hold a salutary check on many of the plans" of the their "more wealthy and aspiring neighbors."

Further reform would come much later in Rhode Island's history. The real estate ownership requirement imposed on immigrants was removed in 1888 for state and federal elections, but not for town meeting votes and town elections. The $134 net worth requirement continued to limit the voting of most city dwellers, many of whom were now immigrants of French and Italian extraction; they could not control their own local governments. This requirement was finally removed in 1928. The rural towns' stranglehold on the state senate remained until the "bloodless revolution" in 1935, when the urban areas finally gained power. Not until 1966 did the principle of one-man, one-vote prevail in its entirety in Rhode Island.

The Potter Brothers, Updike and the
Aftermath of the Dorr Rebellion

Continued Turmoil in State Politics

As 1842 came to a close, the political situation in the state had calmed down, but it was still unsettled. The state's Democratic Party, which had included many Dorr sympathizers, continued to support free suffrage principles. Elisha R. Potter, Jr., who had been a Democrat for many years, had fled to the Law and Order Party, the alliance of Whigs and rural Democrats, once it became clear that the Democrats were dominated by Dorr supporters. In a letter to newspapers, dated December 16, 1842, Potter expressed his desire to unite the Democratic Party, but he found that free suffragists continued to dominate the party and not recognize the new state constitution. He concluded that "it is now evident that such hope can be no longer entertained." Potter continued to be an outcast in the Democratic Party and for the time being remained with the Law and Order Party.

The Law and Order Party and Democrats prepared for the April 1843 elections. Elisha R. Potter, Jr. and Wilkins Updike held meetings in southern Rhode Island to shore up support for the Law and Order Party. On March 2, 1843, a meeting was held at the Court House in Kingston with leaders from throughout Washington County. Wilkins Updike called the meeting to order and Elisha R. Potter, Jr. was selected its president. The primary speaker warned of the dangers of the past Dorr Rebellion, which threatened to "break down all government both State and National." A newspaper sympathetic to Democrats accused the speaker of "feeding and exciting the jealousies of the south against his fellow citizens of the north." Similar Law and Order meetings, with Potter presiding, were held at the Kingston Court House on March 6th and March 10th. By contrast, free suffrage Democrats held meetings outside Kingston in towns populated by mill workers: a school house at Mooresfield and a house in Wakefield.

In the April elections, the Law and Order Party swept the field. Voters were still concerned about issues of anarchy and violence. Elisha R. Potter, Jr. received a strong majority in winning a seat in the state senate, and Wilkins Updike was elected to the state house of representatives. In May 1843, the old royal charter was supplanted by Rhode Island's new constitution. Potter and Updike served on committees to smooth the transition and to select the primary orator for the celebratory festivities.

As a reward for his firm support of the Law and Order Party, Potter was selected as its candidate for one of Rhode Island's seats in the U.S. House of Representatives. The election in the fall of 1843 proved to be another bitter one, as the coalition of Whigs and conservative and rural Democrats supported Potter, while Dorrite Democrats largely in the northern part of the state supported his opponent. Potter won the election handily and left for Washington, D.C. He was listed as a Whig in Congress and tended to support that party.

"Oration Delivered at Kingston, R.I., July 4, 1843"

The Dorr Rebellion was one of the seminal events in Rhode Island history. It divided the state as perhaps no other issue did in its history, including the American Revolution. No one could ignore it; everyone had to take one side or the other. Families were divided, including the Updike and Nichols families in Kingston. For years afterwards, the consequences of the Dorr Rebellion were felt. As the participants on the winning side of the Dorr Rebellion, men from Kingston, at least in the short term, continued to be involved in these events on a statewide scale, representing the conservative rural interests of Washington County.

The occasion of Independence Day was often a day of celebration in Kingston, with speakers addressing local crowds at the Court House. The occasion on July 4, 1843 was particularly special. The Law and Order Party had just defeated Dorrite Democrats in the April elections, the new state constitution was in effect, and Thomas Dorr himself was in prison, awaiting trial for treason. On this Independence Day, one of the brothers of Elisha R. Potter, Jr., James B. M. Potter, was asked to give an "oration."

James Brown Mason Potter was born in Kingston in 1818, was educated at the Kingston Academy, and graduated from Brown University in 1839. He demonstrated business acumen by establishing wool mills at Usquepaug and South Ferry. At South Ferry, he erected a church for any denomination that would occupy it and keep it in repair. The church stands today; its spire is one of the most visible markers on the west side of lower Narragansett Bay. In 1842, he served as a delegate in the Landholders Convention and was elected as one of South Kingstown's representatives to the state house of representatives. In May 1843 he appeared in a list published by suffragists of "renegade" Democrats who opposed the free suffrage cause. He had some military experience from 1841 to 1843, serving as quartermaster and inspector of Washington County's Third Brigade of Militia, with the rank of major. In the summer of 1843, at the young age of 25, James B. M. Potter was asked to make the keynote speech for the July 4th celebration in Kingston.

Most of Potter's speech, which was later printed at the request of townsmen, did not have much merit, being a rather sappy eulogy to the Revolutionary War "men of '76," and their Greek and Roman predecessors. Potter at the end of his speech got to the purpose of his speech – congratulating the local military personnel in attendance for their roles in suppressing the Dorr Rebellion. In attendance were members of the

Narragansett Guard, headed by Col. Whitford, and members of the Washington Grenadiers, headed by Col. Greenman, with all present in full uniform. These military outfits had been formed in South Kingstown and Washington County, respectively, to help defeat Dorr's army, and both outfits probably were among the South County militia that rushed to Providence in late June 1842 to defend against Dorr's army based in Chepachet. Potter himself had marched to Chepachet with his state militia outfit.

After praising Rhode Island's Revolutionary War heroes, Potter exclaimed that the "memory of their brave deeds inspired [the Kentish Guard regiment] as it stood upon Pawtucket Bridge." Potter was referring to an incident that occurred near Chepachet after Dorr's military forces had dispersed. The Law and Order army occupied the town, and at one point, the Kentish Guards were faced with a crowd of unruly and hostile civilians who blocked their path on a bridge to the Massachusetts side and who hurled sticks, stones and invective at them. In a scene that would foreshadow the killings by the Ohio National Guard at Kent State during the Vietnam War, the Kentish Guards fired a volley into the crowd, killing one civilian bystander and wounding two more. Potter ended his oration with the stirring words, "God grant that this land remain the inheritance of a free and virtuous people, till the last trumpet shall sound, and time be swallowed up in eternity."

Following the speech, the military companies, in full uniform, attended "exercises at church" (most likely the Kingston Congregational Church), and "the two companies, together with the citizens, sat down to a temperance entertainment" (alcohol-free, consistent with the temperance movement in the town) that was prepared by Philip Taylor, the tavern keeper at the former Joseph Reynolds tavern in Kingston. The event "was enlivened with speeches and toasts appropriate to the day." It is possible that the Potter brothers, in appreciation for the services of the soldiers, paid for the soldiers' dinners, and that Elisha was therefore in a position to suggest his brother James as the keynote speaker. Apparently, the soldiers enjoyed the occasion, and as a sign of thanks and respect, requested James Potter to publish the speech.

Members of the Narragansett Guards, Washington Grenadiers, and the Potters were pleased with themselves. In their view, they had helped to suppress the forces of anarchism and had upheld republican government and the ideals of the American Revolution by insuring that institutional change could only be accomplished through constitutional means. By contrast, the Dorr supporters thought that they were promoting republican government and the ideals of the American Revolution by advancing the cause of natural rights and popular sovereignty. While the Dorr supporters did not win their struggle in the 1840s, ultimately in the 20th century their views carried the day.

Elisha R. Potter, Jr. on the Defensive in Washington, D.C.

Elisha R. Potter, Jr. took his seat in the U.S. Congress in Washington, D.C., but he could not escape the aftermath of the Dorr Rebellion. After his election, Rhode Island Dorrites continued to assert their positions. Democratic members of the Rhode Island General Assembly sent to the U.S. House of Representatives a petition challenging the right of Potter to his seat, requesting the House to apply the U.S. Constitution as it related to a "republican form of government" in favor of the People's Constitution, and asking the House to inquire into the role of President Tyler in suppressing the Dorr movement. A select committee was appointed to consider these questions.

The arguments in favor of extending the vote to all male citizens regardless of property ownership and of basing representation in the General Assembly on each town's population were easy to make. Suffrage supporters merely had to quote from their forefathers in the American Revolution on the doctrines of the rule of the people. Making arguments against the suffrage movement was more challenging. As we have seen, crass arguments were made based on maintaining the dominance of the rural interests over urban interests. There was also the fear of change from the rise of urban centers and mill towns in the northeast part of the state. In addition, there was prejudice against the rising numbers of Catholic Irish immigrants among the dispersed, rural, landowning and Protestant country interests.

Potter's arguments against the suffrage movement were more moderate and thoughtful. As to the requirement to own land in order to vote, Potter wrote that it had been introduced in order "to secure the control of affairs to those who had a permanent interest in the prosperity of the colony." He added, "Those who possess [property] should possess the power to protect it." This was a conservative, traditional view with feudal roots. Potter apparently did not feel that a mill worker who rented a house in the state had a sufficient stake in society to merit granting him the vote. Part of the concern was that unpropertied men did not pay taxes. (However, a tenant does pay taxes indirectly; the tenant's rent is increased to help cover the landlord's cost of property taxes. This was also an age before the income tax.) Suffragists, by contrast, claimed that the right to vote was a "natural" right, which "attaches to the man, independent of the accidents of birth or fortune."

Potter argued that the will of the majority could only be expressed under the forms of law through legal procedures. He wrote in 1842, "A majority . . . of . . . voters can have no legal, constitutional or conventional rights, but such as the constitution or social compact gives them; and government being formed by the people for the protection of minorities as well as majorities, when once instituted it can only be changed by the whole people, or in such manner as they have agreed it shall be changed." Potter concluded, "Any irregular action, without legal authority, is no action at all . . . ." In his view and the view of other conservatives, sovereignty could only be exercised through valid institutions.

Elisha Potter spent three days in March 1844 addressing the House, giving the background of the controversy and urging the House not to vote in favor of the motion. His main argument was that revolution could only be accomplished legally within the framework of the Rhode Island constitution. Potter argued:

> We have been accused of denying the republican doctrine of the sovereignty of the people. Sir, we believe we hold to that doctrine in its only true and practical meaning – not that there is a sovereignty residing in every individual; that every man is sovereign; that the sovereign will is to be gathered from the wild and lawless passions of lawless factions, however large – but that, subject to the supreme sovereignty and laws of God, the political sovereignty resides in the community as an organized body, in the whole people as a State; and that this sovereignty can only speak and make itself known explicitly and authentically through the constitution and the laws.

A humorous moment occurred when Potter, questioning the legality of voters who voted in favor of the People's Constitution, stated "Why, sir, this House will hardly believe that on the list of voters in Newport is found the name of PETER SQUIRT." He criticized the hypocrisy of the Dorrites for excluding "the colored people entirely from voting! How they could consistently do this, after all their professions about natural equality, is rather strange."

Potter did concede that "I most freely admit, Mr. Speaker, that it would have been prudent and politic for us to have extended the suffrage long ago; and this not because I believe it a natural right, nor that I think we should be any better or more economically governed; but simply because it is in accordance with the prevailing public opinion" in the sister states. Potter added that Rhode Island would "sink or swim" with its sister states, "and even if free suffrage ruins them, we cannot expect to be saved from the general wreck." Potter was on dangerous ground here, as he was suggesting that laborers who did not own real property as voters could ruin government. He recovered somewhat, stating "Besides, I believe if there is not always as much intelligence and information, there is at least apt to be as much honesty and virtue among the middling class and the poor, as among the wealthier and more favored classes."

Potter's lengthy arguments were unsuccessful in stopping the congressional investigation. Potter and Rhode Island conservatives were riding against the traditions of the American Revolution of rule by the people and against a tide of egalitarianism in the Age of Jackson. Congressmen Edmund Burke, a Democratic member of the select committee, wrote a lengthy majority brief that supported Dorr's cause and questioned the role of President Tyler. But Congress did not take any action against the government of Rhode Island and Elisha Potter retained his congressional seat.

Elisha R. Potter, Jr. Loses His Bid for Reelection

By late 1843, cracks were appearing in the ranks of the state's Law and Order Party. Some argued that Thomas Dorr should not be placed on trial for treason. Politicians who had fled the Democratic Party to the Law and Order Party felt as if they were being pushed aside by the state's Whigs. John Brown Francis wrote Elisha Potter a letter complaining, "Why should I trouble to make this a Whig state and then be rode over" by the Whigs?

In June 1844, Thomas Dorr was put on trial, convicted of treason, and sentenced to life imprisonment at hard labor. The harsh sentence was a political blunder for the Law and Order Party. With the fear of civil war in Rhode Island subsiding with the acceptance of the new constitution, many Rhode Islanders grew sympathetic towards Dorr. Prior to the 1845 election, some Whigs bolted from the Law and Order Party and allied themselves with Dorr Democrats to field a "liberation" slate to free Dorr. The "liberation slate" included a prominent Whig from South Kingstown, former governor Lemuel Arnold, who ran for Potter's seat in the U.S. Congress. There were also Dorr Democrats who opposed Potter in South County. In October 1844, Daniel Stedman reported in his journal that the Democrats held a "great mass meeting at Kingston" and later raised a hickory pole at a supporter's house in Wakefield.

The Law and Order Party, the alliance of rural Democrats (called by Dorr Democrats "renegade" Democrats) and Whig Party members, was breaking apart. Key members of the Law and Order Democrats included Kingston's Elisha R. Potter, Jr., James B. M. Potter, William French, Judge William Peckham, and John G. Clarke. Key members of the Whig Party included villagers Wilkins Updike and Matthew Waite. The division between these two groups was dramatically illustrated at the Court House in Kingston in the fall of 1844. The unwritten understanding between South Kingstown Law and Order Democrats and Whigs was that a Law and Order Democrat would be nominated to run for the Rhode Island senate and that two Whigs would be nominated to run for the Rhode Island house of representatives. There were many "ultra" Whigs, however, who were not happy about sharing power with the Law and Order Democrats. The "ultra" Whigs circulated a notice in town for a meeting to be held at the Court House in Kingston of all those voters who were in favor of the Whig candidate for the President of the United States, Henry Clay. The many Law and Order Democrats in town feared that this was simply a pretext for Whigs to nominate their own slate of local officials to the General Assembly. Accordingly, Law and Order Democrats such as James B. M. Potter, William French and John G. Clarke attended the meeting, even though they were not Clay supporters. After the meeting was opened by Matthew Waite, William French introduced a resolution to the effect that the unwritten understanding between Law and Order Democrats and Whigs was still in place. This annoyed the Whigs, but they voted for the resolution. Then a wealthy Whig "in an ungentlemanly and uncourteous way, objected to the Hon. James B. M. Potter being present at the meeting; for Mr. Potter, he said, knew that they were the strongest, and ought to know that he had *no business* there." Potter, who up to that time had not spoken at the meeting, responded that he was attending merely to insure that the agreements at the state Law and Order Party convention were observed in South Kingstown and to determine "whether the men of South Kingstown would be the first to dissolve the Law and Order party" in the state. Despite passing the resolution, the Whigs then violated its spirit by voting for a Whig (mill owner Samuel Rodman) to be the nominee to run for the Rhode Island senate. The Law and Order Democrats, in disbelief, objected to this breach of faith; two of them, including John G. Clarke, moved to form a committee to reevaluate who should be nominated to the Rhode Island senate. But the "Whigs said they wanted no one to make a nomination, as they had men enough to do their own business, and voted down the call for a committee . . . ." The Whigs then nominated to run for the state lower house Whig Wilkins Updike and Law and Order Democrat Judge Peckham. The Law and Order Democrats left the meeting in disgust. The Law and Order alliance in South Kingstown had ended.

In addition to facing division within the Law and Order Party and the rising tide of the Dorr Democrats, Elisha Potter, Jr. spoiled his chances for reelection by a vote he made at the end of his first term in Congress. In January 1845, the General Assembly voted to instruct Rhode Island's representatives in Congress to work to defeat the proposal to annex Texas to the U.S. William Sprague, the powerful Rhode Island industrialist and politician, in a letter to Potter, urged Potter to vote against annexation. This issue was the primary national issue of the day, and served as a proxy for pro-slavery and antislavery interests. Sprague thought that a vote in favor of annexing Texas would alienate many Whig voters, who thought that annexing Texas would expand and support slavery in the South. But only a few days before the letter was written, Wilkins Updike had presided over the Law and Order meeting that had nominated Potter to run for his second term in

Congress. With the nomination in hand, Potter cast the vote according to his own conscience to admit Texas.

In the election, the "liberation" slate of Dorr Democrats and Whigs defeated the Law and Order candidate for governor and defeated Potter in his re-election bid. Potter lost by only 126 votes. He lost many votes from suffragists in the northern part of the state, but he also lost Whig votes due to his vote in favor of annexing Texas. For example, Westerly and Hopkinton were natural allies of the Law and Order Party, but they were also strongly against annexing Texas. Those towns voted heavily for Potter in the 1843 election, but in the 1845 election they voted for his opponent by the astounding margin of 504 to 9. It seems that memories of the Dorr Rebellion faded relatively quickly, while new issues dominated the minds of voters, namely the relationship of the North and South and the institution of southern slavery.

Elisha Potter wrote in a letter to his brother Thomas regarding the defection of the Whigs, "It is a piece of treachery unparalleled, I believe, in the history of our politics." Once elected, the Dorr Democrats freed Thomas Dorr from jail on June 27, 1845.

Elisha Potter, despite being one of the most talented public servants in the state, was never again a candidate for a congressional seat. Potter's active role in the Law and Order Party probably tainted him as a candidate who could garner statewide support. In addition, he lost support among the Whigs due to his lukewarm support of the antislavery cause. In 1847, the Whigs put forward Wilkins Updike of Kingston as a candidate for the congressional seat. Updike also lost this election.

The new Constitution resulted in an increase in eligible voters particularly from Providence, making it more difficult for Kingston and other South County men to be elected to a seat in Congress. Constitutional reform had resulted in their losing statewide influence, as they feared. But that was, after all, a just result flowing from the movement towards a "one-man, one-vote" system of government. The old fear that rural lands would be subject to increased taxation proved to be unfounded.

Murder Trials and the Abolition of the Death Penalty

The Gordon Murder Trial

Kingston men were involved in another statewide affair, this one involving a notorious murder and the resulting backlash by Rhode Island's native-born, conservative and Protestant establishment against the growing Irish Catholic immigrant community. It was the trial of the Gordon brothers, which was Rhode Island's equivalent to the Sacco and Vanzetti trial in Massachusetts early in the 20th century. Instead of the hysterical fear of Italian anarchism that resulted in the execution of Sacco and Vanzetti, in Rhode Island's case the trial was part of the anti-Irish hysteria that permeated the state after the Dorr Rebellion.

On New Year's eve in 1843, Rhode Island textile manufacturing magnate Amasa Sprague was brutally shot and beaten to death. Within two days, three Irish immigrant brothers were arrested, charged with murder, and scheduled for trial.

Amasa's powerful brother, U.S. Senator William Sprague, selected as one of the prosecutors of the Gordon brothers to assist the state Attorney General a Kingston man, William Harvey Potter. Potter at the time was an attorney serving as a junior partner in the law office of former Attorney General Albert C. Greene in Providence. Potter was the youngest of Elisha Reynolds Potter, Sr.'s four sons. He was, of course, the brother of Elisha Reynolds Potter, Jr., who played an important role in subduing the Dorr Rebellion and was a personal friend and political ally of Sprague.

William Potter was born in 1816 in Little Rest. He was educated, like his brothers, at the Kingston Academy. He graduated from Brown University in 1836, with distinction. He attended Harvard Law School for two years, and then moved to Providence to serve as an apprentice in Albert Greene's law office.

William Potter was an ideal selection as prosecutor for the conservative elements in Rhode Island. Like his brother Elisha, William had been active in the anti-Dorr movement. He had been a delegate to the Landholders Convention to frame a new constitution, and he had also served as an officer in the Providence Horse Guards, defending the state against Dorr's army in June 1842. In addition, he had prosecuted some Dorr supporters who had been charged with violating the "Algerine Act," which made it an act of treason to serve as an officer under an illegal constitution.

The first Gordon trial involved only two of the brothers, John and William Gordon, who were charged with actually committing the crime. William Potter gave the opening statement to the jury for the prosecution team. The trial was a large one for those days, lasting six days and involving 102 witnesses. Potter also made a persuasive summation to the jury.

At the end of the trial, on April 17, 1844, the jury found William Gordon not guilty, but found John Gordon to be guilty of murder. The authors of a modern book on the Gordon trial conclude that John Gordon was a victim of not very persuasive circumstantial evidence, a number of questionable rulings from the presiding judge, and bigotry against Irish Catholic immigrants. They concluded that John Gordon served as a scapegoat to appease a community outraged over the murder of its wealthiest citizen and worried about an uprising of Irish immigrants.

On April 18, 1844, the defense team sought to delay John Gordon's sentencing until after the trial of the third brother, Nicholas Gordon. His trial was crucial, as the theory of the case for the prosecution was that Nicholas had arranged for the murder of Amasa Sprague by his two brothers, with the motive that Sprague had persuaded the Cranston town council to reject a renewal of Nicholas' liquor license for his tavern near some of Sprague's mills (Sprague wanted to stop his workers from drinking on the job). The defense argued that a "not guilty" verdict in Nicholas' trial could have an impact on John's sentence. William Potter responded that John's guilty verdict was a "true verdict" after a full and impartial trial, and that "the penalty of the law [should be] followed quick upon its violation." The next day, John Gordon was brought before the court; the state Attorney General moved "that the sentence of death . . . be pronounced upon him."

The political atmosphere in Providence was tense. The Irish community became enraged by the guilty verdict against John Gordon and viewed the trial as an unjust one. In addition, just eight days after this verdict, the treason trial of Thomas Dorr began. On May 7, 1844, a jury found Dorr guilty of treason, and Dorr was sentenced to life imprisonment at hard labor. This enraged the Irish community yet again.

Six months later, on October 9th, John Gordon was sentenced to die by hanging on February 14, 1845. When asked if he had anything to say to the court, John Gordon spiritedly maintained his innocence and stated that his "prosecutors have wickedly and maliciously sworn away my life."

A petition to spare John Gordon's life was introduced in the General Assembly. Wilkins Updike of Kingston, representing South Kingstown in the state senate, led opposition to the petition. Updike was a descendant of white Protestants who had settled the Rhode Island countryside long ago. He was a conservative who had resisted efforts to abolish the death penalty. Updike declared that Gordon had had a fair trial and was found guilty and that he should be hung. Leniency could only lead to disregard for the law, Updike argued. "Nothing but the prompt enforcement of every law, and the inflexible opposition of the pardoning power, to every interference with the judgments of the Court, will save us from this calamity." To interfere would only be "opening a way of escape to the greatest criminals." Updike admitted that he "knew nothing about the prisoner. He had never read the evidence. Newspaper evidence was not to be relied upon. It was the appearance, the look of the witness which gave its force to testimony." Updike felt that the jury's opportunity to look at Gordon (an Irish immigrant) was reliable, not trial evidence summarized in newspapers. The state senate voted to deny the petition 39 to 21. On February 14, 1845, John Gordon was hanged by the state of Rhode Island.

William Potter also actively participated on the prosecution team in two trials of John's brother, Nicholas Gordon. In both trials, the jury could not agree on a verdict and Nicholas was freed. The lack of a jury verdict against Nicholas, who allegedly arranged for John to murder Amasa Sprague, undermined confidence in the verdict against John. In addition, new material evidence was uncovered after John's trial that under modern judicial standards probably would have merited John a re-trial.

William Potter and Wilkins Updike were part of the conservative, elitist and Protestant establishment that ruled Rhode Island. They were fearful of Irish Catholicism and that the state's numerous immigrants would overrun their traditional society. Many ordinary men and women in Rhode Island had the same fears from the influx of immigrants. Many of these men served in the 3,000-man Law and Order army raised to defeat the Dorr supporters, and many of them had voted against efforts to reform the Rhode Island constitution. Thus, not all the blame can be laid at the feet of the leadership. But leaders must share in any blame for their roles in creating an atmosphere of bigotry and mistrust, leading to "mob justice" in an individual circumstance. The anti-Catholic and anti-immigrant hysteria led to the brief rise of the "Know-Nothing" party in Rhode Island in 1855 and 1856. One of its leaders was Thomas R. Hazard, the author of *The Jonny-Cake Papers*. Typical of the conspiracy theorists, he once wrote that he saw the hand of the "Jesuits" behind the antislavery movement.

A revulsion of feeling followed the execution of John Gordon. Popular belief that an innocent man had been put to death spread rapidly. More than any other event, the trial and hanging of John Gordon led to Rhode Island's abolition of the death penalty.

Murder Trials in Kingston

With the memory of Thomas Mount's hanging for burglary in the not too distant past, South Kingstown residents were reluctant to support hanging for petty crimes. Moreover, the General Assembly demonstrated a willingness to overturn judicial death sentences for petty crimes and even serious crimes. It appears that some judges followed the letter of the harsh criminal code, expecting the General Assembly to overturn their harsh sentences.

In 1815, James Billington and William Smith of South Kingstown were found guilty of burglarizing a local shop, taking $82 in bank notes and cash and about $6.50 in goods. In county supreme court trials held in Little Rest, each man was found guilty by a jury and sentenced by a judge to die by hanging. Levi Totten, a Little Rest lawyer, prepared petitions to submit to the General Assembly that was meeting in Little Rest at the end of December 1815. Totten wrote of Billington, who was convicted merely of being an accessory, that "Horror & guilt are spread before him and unless relieved by your Honors, he shall be hurried out of this World into everlasting Despair." Smith also protested that the law made burglary a hanging offense, when he did not personally injure anyone. South Kingstowners also submitted a petition asking for leniency, stating that "life was a gift of God." They also made the practical argument that "confinement to hard labor for a given time, has lessened the number of offences, and in some instances, has entirely reformed the offender." The General Assembly took pity on the two men and commuted their sentences to life terms.

In 1826, Daniel Stedman, in his journal, reported that "The Court Condemned one John Robinson (man of Color) to be hung for Breaking in to Borden Hazard Store at Mumford Mills." The seventeen year-old Robinson was found guilty of stealing $900 in bank notes and $83 in coins. He submitted a petition for a reduced sentence to the General Assembly, which granted it, reducing his sentence to seven years in jail. One year later, he submitted another petition asking to be liberated, explaining that he had suffered confinement for 21 months, including in two cold winters. The General Assembly, meeting in Kingston, granted his request.

While the Gordon murder trial and hanging set the stage for the abolition of the death penalty in the state, the stage was set in South County with the trial of Daniel Harry. Harry, a Narragansett Indian, had been accused of stabbing a Narragansett tribal leader to death in Charlestown in a drunken brawl in 1839. Harry was incarcerated in the Kingston jail and brought to trial in the Kingston Court House, where he was defended by two of Kingston's premier lawyers, Nathan F. Dixon and Wilkins Updike. The trial gained much attention throughout the state. Harry impressed court viewers with his sincerity and humility. The jury brought in a guilty verdict, and the presiding judge, Job Durfee, sentenced Harry to die by hanging (Durfee would also sentence John Gordon to death in 1845).

As was customary, Harry was given the opportunity to petition the General Assembly for leniency. Prepared by attorney Dixon, Harry admitted his guilt and the justice of the sentence, but pleaded for the General Assembly to commute the sentence to life in prison. In the petition, Harry noted that after the jury had found him guilty, it "unanimously recommended your petitioner to the mercy of the General Assembly." More than 200 signatures were collected on additional petitions, which expressed the "opinion that the punishment of imprisonment would better comport with the principles of public justice than the infliction of death by public execution." The General Assembly agreed and sentenced Harry to life imprisonment at hard labor and separate confinement. Harry was taken from the jail in Kingston to the new state prison in Providence. Ten years later, Harry was pardoned. He returned to South County and lived out a quiet life.

The Abolition of the Death Penalty

While the Harry trial was important in leading South County residents to question the use of the death penalty, it was the Gordon trial that ultimately turned the tide. After Gordon's hanging, numerous mass meetings were held in Providence to protest the continuance of the death penalty. Several prominent national "anti-gallows" campaigners came to Rhode Island to speak against the death penalty. But the Law and Order Party, which controlled the state government in the 1840s, refused to listen. Once the Democrats regained power in 1851, the General Assembly quickly enacted several pro-Dorr laws. In 1852, the General Assembly voted to abolish capital punishment, making Rhode Island only the second state to do so (Michigan was the first in 1846). Life imprisonment replaced the death penalty as the state's severest deterrent. The reformers, however, in order to gain sufficient support, agreed to retain the death penalty for any person convicted of committing murder while serving a life sentence. This provision, which still exists today, has never been applied, making John Gordon the last man to be executed by the state of Rhode Island.

The man who has been described as the "leading figure" in the anti-gallows movement was Peace Dale's Thomas R. Hazard, the author of *The Jonny-Cake Papers*. He circulated many petitions and wrote many tracts supporting the anti-gallows movement on Christian principles.

Elisha R. Potter, Jr., Wilkins Updike and
the Public School Movement in Rhode Island

Today, we take public schooling for granted, including the need for towns to raise substantial taxes to support schools, the need to require children to attend school, and the need to train teachers. But it was not always so. Prior to the Civil War, Rhode Island did not have a good public school system, unlike its neighboring states. As a result, its illiteracy rate was considerably higher than that of Massachusetts and Connecticut. The state did not choose to support public education and few people held the concept that public school education should be provided and funded by state and local governments. Kingston's Elisha R. Potter, Jr. and Wilkins Updike sought to promote public schooling in the state, and they had admirable success.

In 1828, a bill was enacted by the General Assembly authorizing towns to collect a tax to finance public schools and to choose a school committee, and providing for a state permanent school fund, started with a meager $5,000. A bill to require towns to match money received from the General Assembly in order to receive the state funds was defeated after objections were expressed by Elisha R. Potter, Sr., who felt that voters would not accept compulsion to pay taxes. In 1836, the fund was increased by the state's share of surplus Federal government revenue, but funding was still woefully short. Only Providence made a serious effort to develop a decent public school system. Other towns in Rhode Island were reluctant to increase their taxes to support free, public schools.

The year 1843 was an important one for the public school movement in Rhode Island. Henry Barnard of Connecticut, one of the country's leading educators in the 19th century, visited Wilkins Updike in Kingston. Barnard and Updike discussed plans to improve Rhode Island's public school system.

In the October 1843 session of the General Assembly, Wilkins Updike introduced a bill authorizing the governor to appoint an agent to visit, examine and report on the public schools in the state. With arguments and statistics probably provided by Barnard, Updike argued his cause forcefully in the state senate. Updike noted that Rhode Island was behind other New England states in the quality of its public education. Updike complained that the state lacked any uniform standards of teaching, a uniform set of class books, a board of examination of teachers, a school for teachers (i.e., a "normal" school), and a state board of education. In addition, Updike argued that improvements in rural Rhode Island schools needed to be made in order to bring them up to the standard of the public schools in Providence.

The bill passed and Barnard was chosen to make the survey. Barnard helped to combat the popular perception that school was a private concern and not one for the government. In 1844, he wrote legislation designed to improve public education in Rhode Island, including the appointment of a state Commissioner of Education and detailing obligations for the state, towns and school committee to fulfill. One North Kingstown legislator objected to a provision requiring each town to raise at least one-third of the state funds received for public schooling. He complained that "my constituents . . . don't believe it constitutional to tax them to educate other people's children." But with Updike's leadership, the bill passed by a substantial margin.

Henry Barnard was selected to serve as the first state Commissioner of Education. One of Barnard's first tasks was to organize and hold institutes for the formal training of teachers where they could learn new methods of teaching and exchange ideas. In 1845, Barnard held four two-week institutes, including one in Kingston. In 1846, Elisha R. Potter, Jr. began assisting Barnard, notably by publishing a codification of the new school law, with remarks, commentaries, and standard forms.

In 1849, Barnard retired and Elisha R. Potter, Jr. was selected as the second Commissioner of Education. An historian described Potter as "the practical man of affairs needed to carry into effect the work planned by Henry Barnard." In 1852, Potter began to edit a publication, *The Rhode Island Educational Magazine,* which was filled with statistical information on the state of public schools, advice for teachers on how to teach and how to run a classroom, advice for administrators on how to manage a school, and standard forms. It is a fine testament to the movement to unify standards for teaching and administration. The magazine reportedly was funded primarily from Potter's own contributions. The magazines were condensed into two volumes, one for 1852 and a second for 1853.

One of the most serious problems Potter faced was the relatively small number of children who actually attended school. While the average attendance at schools in the state was 16,590 in 1849, the number of school-age children in the state exceeded 27,000. Potter placed some of the blame for this absenteeism on the practice of some towns charging the parents of students a fee to provide for the difference between state and town funding. A fee of up to $1 per student was permitted by the General Assembly in 1845. Potter recommended the abolition of the practice, stating

> there can be no doubt that the present . . . system is one great obstacle in the way of more general attendance. In several of the larger towns the schools are now made entirely free by town taxation, but in many of the towns the state and town appropriations are insufficient and the remainder is assessed on scholars . . . . [T]he greatness of the evil is apparent. It is for the wisdom of the legislature to devise a remedy.

It was not until 1868 that tuition was finally abolished.

Commissioner Potter also laid part of the blame for poor school attendance on the large number of children who were employed in factories during the day and thus were unable to attend classes. Potter did not blame the factory owners, such as Peace Dale factory magnate Rowland Hazard, who opposed mandatory attendance for children. Instead, Potter criticized those parents who lived "upon their children's earning, and maintain themselves in idleness and sometimes in dissipation." To help these children, Potter advocated the establishment of evening schools in manufacturing villages. Realizing that the children working in factories often had immigrant parents, he wrote in the 1853 state school report that "Our own safety, the prosperity of our country, the purity of our government, depend upon the education of all, rich and poor, native and foreigner." A few successful evening schools were opened in Providence. In 1853, the General Assembly partly addressed the problem by limiting the ability of factories to hire children who did not receive at least three months of schooling in the year.

A South Kingstown school report concluded that parental indifference was mainly responsible for poor school attendance: "We fear that all parents do not feel the importance of the regular attendance of their children both as it respects themselves and the school." Wilkins Updike acerbically complained that it would be "till doomsday" if they tried to wait until the ignorant came forward "to ask for an education for their children, the pleasures and advantages of which they are entirely unconscious of themselves."

Under Potter, teacher institutes continued to be held. In his 1851 school report, Potter boldly stated that "No teacher should be employed in any country district who has not attended one or more of them." The large number of teachers who attended these meetings was evidence that teachers thought they were worthwhile as well. Potter reported that a teacher generally left a session of an institute with increased pride in his profession:

> He begins to realize, too, that he belongs to a profession, one of the most honorable and influential in society, and that the honor and respectability of this profession depend in some measure upon his own conduct as a member of it.

The South Kingstown School Committee reported that female teachers' "readiness in adapting themselves to the condition, feelings, and capacities of children enables them to exert a happy influence over them." The report further found that female teachers were "as well, if not better informed in all the branches of study in our schools than males." Potter agreed, adding that teaching provided "a respectable and useful employment for the female sex."

While Potter believed that the key to good schools was good teachers, he also encouraged parental involvement. He advised parents to speak respectfully of the teachers in the presence of their children, so that the teachers would have an easier time with classroom discipline.

Potter felt that the best way of improving the quality of teachers was for Rhode Island to establish a normal (teachers) school. The *Providence Journal* agreed, noting that few of the teachers in the state's public schools were from the state and many of them were insufficiently prepared. An exasperated Potter noted in his 1852 report that in some towns the children "have been so long taught by the dunces who have been sent among us from abroad . . . that they have no idea of anything better than what they have been used to." In 1851, through Potter's efforts, the state's first normal school was established as a department at Brown University. The effort failed, however, in part because Brown at the time did not accept female students. In 1852, a private co-ed normal school devoted solely to the training of teachers was established in Providence. The school achieved some success, and the praise of a member of its examination committee, Elisha R. Potter, Jr.

In a speech to students at the normal school, Potter cautioned the prospective teachers against excessive use of corporal punishment since many parents objected to it. Instead of using force, he said, a teacher should achieve order by capturing the interest of students.

In his term as Commissioner of Education, Potter played a key role in quelling the controversial issue of religious teaching in school, which divided Protestants and Catholics. At the time in Rhode Island, an anti-Catholic and anti-immigration movement, whose supporters were known as "Know-Nothings," was at its height. Potter resisted the popular tide in this instance.

Potter believed in the separation of the public-supported schools and religion. In his magazine, Potter posed the question of "whether a teacher has a right to open a public school by reading of the Scriptures, if objected to." It was Potter's enlightened position that if a Protestant should not be forced to listen to the Roman Catholic version of the common prayer, then Catholics should not be forced to listen to the Protestant version of the common prayer. Potter concluded that "Our school system is a part of the machinery of the State . . . and no one has a right to use it as a means to enforce upon others his own religious views." One letter writer disagreed, arguing that the rights of the Protestant majority were being ignored. Potter responded that the idea of majority rule could be used by Catholics in certain public school districts to force Protestant children to attend Mass or learn Catholic doctrines. Potter also warned against any teacher or administrator using the school to promote his or her religious philosophy, stating "The public school is supported, and the house built, by money collected from people of all religions, and from people of no religion."

Potter took the position that reading the Bible in class was permitted to promote moral and religious instruction, but that if a student objected, the student could be excused from class. While this was also an enlightened view for the day, under current U.S. Supreme Court law, the reading of the Bible in a public school class is generally not permitted, on the ground that it is a violation of the constitutional doctrine of separation of church and state.

Potter lacked a spirit of reform in a crucial area: legislation that would make school attendance mandatory. Many strong proponents of the public school system pushed for mandatory attendance. Some pointed to the high illiteracy rate among Irish immigrants. One newspaper observed that "Parents should not have the exclusive control over their children, but as in Athens, should be considered Public property." Potter responded that persuasion rather than compulsion should be used to combat parental lack of interest in education. He believed that in "a republican government, founded on the basis of the right of the people to govern themselves, every person should be permitted to manage his own concerns . . . ." Potter also viewed the push for mandatory school attendance as part of an effort to stop Catholic parents in Providence from sending their children to private Catholic schools. Potter firmly believed that once parents fulfilled their obligation to provide education to their children, the parents had a right to choose the school. An historian writing on public education in Rhode Island praised Potter for his foresight, leadership and hard labors in working to improve Rhode Island's public schools, but also criticized him for being too conservative in failing to promote compulsory attendance of children at schools.

In 1855, Potter sent a bill to the General Assembly for the creation of a state board of education to strengthen the state's commitment to public education. Potter resigned to clear the way for a new board of education. This reform was finally adopted in 1870.

In South Kingstown, in 1821, there were only seven school houses, none built with public funds. The 1828 law divided the town into school districts and spurred more interest in public schools. By 1832, the town had twelve public schools. In 1834, the town council began requesting the town treasurer to certify that all state funds available to be spent on public schooling had been spent by the town. But such funding likely was not sufficient and families of students had to pay fees as well. In Kingston, evidence indicates that a public school was opened in 1828, with a young Thomas P. Wells serving as the teacher. The school was probably housed in a private home in the village and apparently did not survive for long.

In conjunction with the state law of 1843 to promote public schools, and a state law in 1844 permitting school districts to purchase land and build schools, a public school was opened in Kingston in 1844. School District No. 3 was created, which included all of Kingston and the surrounding area, extending north to the North Kingstown line, south to Rocky Brook, and west to Larkin's Pond. Meeting in the Court House in Kingston on July 31, 1844, a majority of the "legal voters" in the school district met for the first time to address the school district. The voters decided to spend $275 to lease the former Kingston Academy schoolhouse for twenty years and to repair it. To pay for the lease and repairs, the voters imposed an annual tax on the property owners in the school district. Finally, villagers were willing to tax themselves to fund public schools. This tax revenue allowed the district to meet expenses not covered by state and town funds, and funds from the Sewall School Fund. Consistent with Elisha R. Potter, Jr.'s vision, the voters voted not to assess scholars for any of the cost of the repairs. But in subsequent years (for example in 1855 and 1856), the voters broke down and assessed a tax on the families of students in order to make up for the school budget's shortfall.

At the town level, a school committee was formed, which was elected annually at the town meeting. Elisha Potter, Jr. served on the town's first school committee in 1846, and would serve several other terms. But initially, the local districts wielded most of the influence with teachers and students. Kingston developed a new bureaucracy, with school district tax assessors, tax collector, treasurer, and auditor. Many of Kingston's men served in these positions, including Wilkins Updike, William French, Dr. Peleg Johnson, Thomas R. Wells and Nathaniel Peckham.

In a report of South Kingstown's public schools in 1851, the statistics regarding Kingston's public school were as follows:

- The number of school-age scholars in the district was 88, with 47 girls and 41 boys;
- The number of school-age children who attended school for at least three-quarters of the school session was 53;
- Average daily attendance was 66;
- The length of the school year was only four months.

The 75% average daily school attendance was considerably higher than the state average. The schoolhouse, on North Road, while small, did have a blackboard, globe of the world and a small school library. It appears that South County public schools from their inception were integrated.

Rhode Island as a whole was successful in educating native white children, but it was less successful in educating black children and immigrant children. In 1865, only one in 78 native-born white adults was illiterate. By comparison, one in 6.5 black adults was illiterate, and one in 3.7 Irish-born adults was illiterate. This discrepancy is explained in part by the fact that many Irish immigrants came to Rhode Island as adults; but it may also be due to immigrant and black families being less inclined to send their children to public schools, in an age when school attendance was not compulsory.

Kingston in the Temperance Movement

Between 1790 and 1830, Americans had a serious drinking problem. President Washington complained that alcohol was "the ruin of half the workmen in this Country." His successor, John Adams, worried that Americans were exceeding the rest of the world in "this degrading, beastly vice."

In Kingston, the drinking of alcohol was common, and South County as a whole was described as "notoriously bibulous." We know from Charles Comstock's *History of South Kingstown*, which is summarized earlier in this book, that alcoholism was a problem in Kingston in the early 1800s. Drunk persons slept on door steps and off nearby roads. The deputy sheriff, Elisha Gardner, played practical jokes on drunkards in the hope of keeping them out of the village. Elisha Gardner himself, after two friends watched over him as he lay ill one evening, woke up the next morning feeling better and promptly ambled over to Thomas R. Wells' general store to buy rum for his sleep-deprived friends.

Gatherings in Little Rest such as town meetings and militia musters were often followed by drinking alcohol. For example, after a town meeting in the Court House in April 1800, Elisha R. Potter, Sr. and four other men bought for their supporters 170 gills of rum and 104 gills of brandy.

Since colonial times, general stores in Little Rest sold alcohol by the bottle and even by the glass. From the late 18th century to the mid-19th century, alcohol was a substantial part of the inventory of the general stores operated by Thomas R. Wells, Thomas Taylor, the Clarke brothers, John P. Case and others. Reverend J. Hagadorn Wells, in his memoirs of Kingston, described Case's store in the 1820s as selling "groceries rather sparingly, liquid goods more freely." He described John G. Clarke's store as an "inveterate and incorrigible drink-making concern." Of course, there were also the taverns. Kingston generally had three to four taverns that dispensed alcohol by the glass. In 1796, Little Rest villagers obtained six licenses to sell liquor by the glass. The "best of liquors" could be obtained at the Joseph Reynolds tavern. An establishment run by Benjamin Palmer, next to the church meeting house, had a grocery store on the first floor and a bar on the second floor. The Reverend Wells and Jonathan Helme, in their memoirs of the early-to-mid 1800s, wrote that they were aware of five or six establishments in Kingston that sold rum at the same time. Not only was the drinking of alcohol a common leisure activity in private and public affairs, up through about 1830 it was often expected that employers would supply their laborers with a daily dose of spirits. Even in the construction of the Kingston Congregational Church in 1820, workmen were supplied with alcohol.

Excessive drinking began to be viewed as a problem at the same time that religion in the United States was experiencing a revival, known as the Second Great Awakening. Baptists and Congregationalists led the state's temperance movement. The movement had its beginnings in Rhode Island in the 1820s. In 1822, the sale of alcohol within a mile of any church meeting was prohibited. In 1827, the first Rhode Island mass meeting in opposition to the sale of alcohol was held in the First Baptist Meeting House in Providence. In 1828, delegates from around the state met in Pawtucket to form a state temperance organization.

By 1829, the temperance movement had reached Kingston and rural South Kingstown. The interaction between the religious revival and the need to combat alcoholism became a powerful force in rural South Kingstown. On November 27, 1829, the South Kingstown Temperance Society was established in Kingston. Members who signed the constitution, and thereby pledged not to partake of any intoxicating liquors, included 24 men and 27 women. The names of the men were listed first, with the women following. Members included male villagers Thomas R. Wells, John G. Clarke, Dr. Peleg Johnson, the Reverend Oliver Brown, Thomas P. Wells, and Christopher Comstock. Some of the female members, such as the Aldrich and Peckham women, were members, but their male family members were not. Notably absent as members: Elisha R. Potter, Sr. and Jr., and Wilkins Updike.

The constitution of the temperance society required that a meeting be held on each July 4th. On July 5, 1830, Thomas R. Wells gave a major temperance speech at the Kingston Court House. Wells had owned a dry goods store in Kingston that had once sold alcohol in substantial quantities, but he ceased this practice in 1822. He served as cashier of the Landholders Bank, as town clerk for many years, and as the Kingston Congregational Church's first deacon from 1827 until his death in 1853. In his speech, Wells focused on the evils of drinking alcohol:

> What occasions most of the poverty, misery and distress, of the individuals and families of your own acquaintance? Can you not trace it directly or indirectly to intemperance? What occasions a greater part of the pauperism of those who are sent to our poor-houses, to be supported on public charity? Intemperance! What occasions the bloated faces and swelling eyes of so many of the unhappy youth of our beloved country, who have been insensibly drawn into this vortex? Intemperance! What occasions a great part of the jarring, contention, litigation and angry feeling which we are constantly witnessing among individuals around us? I answer again, Intemperance!

Wells criticized "professing Christians" who were "deeply involved in the guilt" by selling alcohol. In a personal reference to his own role, Wells admitted, "I dare not withhold the truth, fellow-citizens, though it prove a dagger in my own breast." At this point, in a footnote in the pamphlet containing the speech, it states, "The author was once a retailer of ardent spirits." (Thomas R. Wells' son, the Reverend John Hagadorn Wells, who became minister of the Kingston Congregational Church in 1862, recalled his father's deep regret that he had once sold alcohol in Kingston. Until his death, Thomas R. Wells "bewailed and condemned the blindness that had so perverted that part of his business life.")

After Wells' speech, the South Kingstown Temperance Society held its annual meeting, with about 65 members. Wells was selected its president, with Christopher Comstock, a teacher at the Kingston Academy, selected as its secretary. Each year on or around July 4th, the society met at the Kingston Court House or church meeting house to listen to a speaker promoting temperance.

The temperance movement permeated all levels of society and many religious groups. One well-known speaker, John W. Hawkins, traveled more than 100,000 miles in ten years and delivered more than 2,500 temperance lectures. In 1841, he came to Wakefield, stirring impressive support for the movement. At about the same time, a Seventh Day Baptist minister in South Kingstown was leading a revival movement so powerful that all business was stopped for about ten days while people worshipped and prayed in hope of salvation.

Daniel Stedman, an ordinary farmer and shoemaker who lived between Wakefield and Kingston, noted in his journal that he attended his first temperance meeting in January 1832. In December 1832, after attending a lecture on the evils of alcohol, Stedman and his wife joined the South Kingstown Temperance Society, with six other persons. From 1832 to 1844, Stedman reports of his attending thirteen temperance lectures and events, either at his Baptist meeting house or in Kingston. In February 1841, Stedman attended a two-day debate held on the issue of what was the greater evil, intemperance or slavery. After "a great number of arguments on Both Sides," the president of the debate ruled that intemperance was the greater evil. Stedman also grimly noted in his diary men who had alcohol-related deaths.

The Kingston Congregational Church eventually took a strong stand supporting abstinence. At a meeting held at Thomas R. Wells' house on December 4, 1841, church members adopted the following resolution:

> Whereas intemperance has been the cause of great and overwhelming evil in and out of the church; Therefore resolved

> unanimously that we deem the use of intoxicating drinks except for medicinal purposes, as destructive to moral and religious character and as opposed to the heavenly principles of the gospel, and must hereafter consider any member of this church who uses them as a drink except as aforesaid or encourages their use, sale, or manufacture by others as violating his or her church obligation.

The Kingston Congregational Church charged member John Larkin with violating its temperance pledge. For this and other infractions, Larkin's church membership was rescinded.

The temperance movement must have created tensions in Kingston. Thomas Taylor, the successful general store owner, continued to sell alcohol by the bottle, even though he attended the Kingston Congregational Church (he was not a member). Tavern keepers in the village continued to sell alcohol, which was an important source of their earnings. Even though Taylor and the tavern keepers had respectable occupations and performed services in addition to selling alcohol, they were probably denounced by temperance supporters as purveyors of evil spirits. There is no evidence that Elisha R. Potter, Sr., before his death in 1835, or his son, Elisha R. Potter, Jr. supported temperance (indeed, Elisha Sr. enjoyed frequenting the village taverns). Wilkins Updike, in a mark of the power of the temperance forces, made a temperance pledge in an election campaign for a General Assembly seat, but apparently he was caught violating the pledge in Providence (Updike's response was that his pledge was good for Washington County, but not Providence County).

The temperance supporters had some success in the General Assembly. Sunday sales and sales to habitual drunkards were forbidden by the General Assembly in 1839, and sales to minors and intoxicated persons were prohibited in 1841. A local option law, enabling each town to determine if it would be "wet" or "dry," was in effect from 1838 to 1841 and from 1845 to 1852. Statewide prohibition was in effect from 1842 to 1845.

As a result of the General Assembly's prohibition law, South Kingstown temperance supporters applied pressure on the town council to enforce prohibition. Philip Taylor in the 1840s was the tavern keeper of the prominent Joseph Reynolds tavern in Kingston. Philip Taylor was the son of Thomas Taylor, who sold liquor for many years in the village general store. In January 1842, Philip Taylor and Wakefield tavern keeper Willard Hazard each were granted licenses to operate a tavern and sell alcoholic beverages, consistent with the practice in the town for over 100 years. But Philip Taylor may have seen the writing on the wall. Daniel Stedman noted in his journal on February 7, 1842, that "Philip Taylor, Kingston, had his Temperance Sign put up." On February 10th, Stedman spent the entire day in Kingston on temperance activities. In the afternoon, he listened to temperance lectures by prominent visiting speakers at the Court House. In the evening he attended more temperance lectures at the Congregational meeting house. Afterwards, the "friends of Temperance had a Splendid Supper at the New Temperance hotel . . . after Lectures. (Mr. Taylor formerly kept a Rum Establishment)." Stedman concluded that "The Temperance Cause goes well." When Willard Hazard sought to renew his license to sell alcohol in July of 1842, the council denied the request. The town council allowed alcohol to be sold by Kingston's Dr. Thomas Hazard for medicinal purposes only, consistent with state law.

The year 1843 saw a struggle by the town council and temperance supporters to enforce prohibition in the town. The town council authorized the prosecution of all violations. Daniel Stedman reported in his journal in March 1843 that "The Rumsellers that Sold Contrary to Law tried at the Court and fined." In April 1843, Wakefield tavern keeper Willard Hazard spoke at the Baptist meeting house and said that he would give up selling alcohol if Wakefield storekeeper Sylvester Robinson would pledge to do the same. But Robinson refused to make this pledge as long as others in the town were selling alcohol.

Meanwhile, Philip Taylor benefited from his decision to cooperate with the temperance cause. On July 4, 1843, after the speech of James B. M. Potter at the Court House praising the soldiers in attendance who helped quell the Dorr Rebellion, Philip Taylor served a "temperance" meal to the soldiers and citizens in attendance. In December 1843, the town council met at Taylor's tavern. For the next several years, Taylor was granted a license to operate a tavern, but not the privilege to sell "ale or strong liquor."

Why was the temperance movement so popular in rural South County and New England? Of course, there was the legitimate concern about the adverse effects of excessive drinking on the lives of individuals and society as a whole. It also has been suggested that the temperance movement was an outgrowth of growing paranoia at the growth of urban society and increasing immigration. It has further been suggested that the movement was the logical outgrowth of modernizing commercial farming and manufacturing. If farmers and mill owners wanted their laborers to work productively and safely, it was best if they did not drink during work hours. Mill owner Rowland Hazard was satisfied with the accomplishment of temperance efforts, especially on the "lower orders " of society in South County, who though honest, were previously given to drink.

In 1852, a statewide prohibition law was passed, subject to confirmation or repeal by referendum. The referendum confirmed prohibition by a vote of 9,280 to 8,228. Thomas P. Wells, a temperance man, wrote in 1855 in his new newspaper, the *Narragansett Times,* that the passage of the prohibition law had caused "consternation in Providence," but pointed out that the law was the same as in Massachusetts, Connecticut, Maine and other states. No doubt that certain tavern keepers and store owners in Kingston were unhappy with this development, but no doubt most members of the Kingston Congregational and nearby Baptist churches were pleased. Observance of the law, however, was lax. Thomas P. Wells, then serving as editor of the *Narragansett Times,* complained about drunken men walking the streets of Wakefield. But as one historian noted, with the long, boring and tiring hours spent at the mills, it was not realistic for the "best people" to expect mill workers to avoid alcohol as a release in their off-hours.

The prohibition law was repealed in 1863, as a war measure to raise revenues. Kingston's own Elisha Reynolds Potter, Jr. led the repeal movement. The General Assembly reenacted prohibition in 1874.

Kingston residents, after the Civil War, continued to press the cause of temperance. J. Hagadorn Wells, the pastor of the Kingston Congregational Church from 1862 to 1877, and villager Bernon Helme in the following decades, played important roles in the local and state temperance movement. A state temperance convention was held at the Court House in 1871. Two reminiscences of Kingston, one written in 1874 and one written in about 1880, state that no alcohol was for sale in the village. In 1886, Rhode Island voters agreed to statewide prohibition. But violation of the law apparently was widespread and cases were rarely pressed. In June 1889, after a vote by the General Assembly to repeal the prohibition law, Rhode Island voters concurred by a vote of 28,315 to 9,956. At the first graduation of the agricultural college in Kingston in 1889, a local young graduate gave a speech excoriating the legislators in attendance for the political deal that repealed prohibition. The *Westerly Sun* wrote that the incident confirmed the editor's suspicion that "Kingston College was one of the rallying points for South Kingstown Prohibitionists."

The Kingston Anti-Slavery Society
and Other Antislavery Activities

Between 1833 and 1836, Rhode Islanders began to send numerous petitions to the General Assembly concerning black slavery in the South. Many of the petitions sought the immediate abolition of black slavery in the South. Some had more limited goals, such as banning slavery in the nation's capitol, Washington, D.C. Of course, the controversy surrounding slavery and the abolitionist movement centered on the national government – the U.S. Congress, the Presidency and U.S. Supreme Court. But state and local antislavery efforts were also important in building the groundwork for a national movement against slavery.

Rhode Island Anti-Slavery Convention in Providence

By 1836, antislavery efforts in Rhode Island had picked up steam. In addition to the antislavery petitions, antislavery literature was disseminated in the state. Attention was also focused on the slavery issue in 1836 when the General Assembly, encouraged by the increasing numbers of Southern planters visiting Newport, considered banning antislavery literature, speeches, organizations and meetings. Initially, men and women regarded their antislavery efforts as an extension of their religious commitment to benevolent societies. But soon efforts were made in the state to establish organizations solely devoted to the antislavery cause.

In February 1836, the first Rhode Island convention of abolitionists was held in Providence. The delegates believed that "AMERICAN SLAVERY is a heinous sin against God" and sought the "immediate emancipation" of the slaves. This was a radical position to take, as many northerners supported gradual emancipation so as to not alienate the South.

By February 1836, 20 local societies had been formed in Rhode Island, most of them in the northern part of the state. In total, 850 delegates from every town in the state attended the convention, including out-of-state abolitionist leaders such as William Lloyd Garrison, the editor of the Boston abolitionist newspaper, *The Liberator*, and Henry Stanton. Delegates who attended included old and young, "lawyers, judges, legislators, ministers, . . . mechanics, 'unbought farmers,'—members of all political parties and religious denominations." The reference to "unbought farmers" suggests that wealthy landowners (perhaps even Elisha R. Potter, Jr.) pressured farmers who worked on their lands not to support the antislavery movement. Despite the active participation of women in the antislavery movement, only men served as delegates. It was still not acceptable in society for women to take such an active political role, although many women did attend the meetings in the audience. When abolitionist leader Henry Stanton asked the convention audience to promise to work against slavery, regardless of loss of reputation, property, or life, the president of the convention asked all in favor of Stanton's resolution to signify their pledge by standing. The official proceedings recorded that the audience "stood up through the whole house, man and woman, one living and enthusiastic mass." Thus, as historian Deborah Bingham Van Broekhoven noted, the women made it into the official record of the meeting.

Thirteen delegates from South Kingstown attended the convention, of whom seven resided in Kingston. They were John G. Clarke (storekeeper), William P. Newall (attorney), John H. Clarke (unknown), Luke Aldrich (cabinetmaker), Asa Potter (attorney and former state official), Thomas P. Wells (bank cashier) and Charles Grosvenor (minister of the Kingston Congregational Church). On the first day of the convention, John G. Clarke served as a vice-president of the convention and William Newall organized the rules committee for the convention. The second day of the convention was presided over by John G. Clarke, with Thomas P. Wells as a vice-president. That evening's session was opened with a prayer by the Reverend Grosvenor. Asa Potter served as a member of the society's board of directors. All of the Kingston men were solidly middle class. John G. Clarke had a thriving general store on main street. His father was Judge William Clarke, who lived in a house down South Road. In 1836, John G. Clarke purchased a house on North Road from fellow delegate Luke Aldrich. The Reverend Grosvenor was a Yale graduate who had become minister at the Kingston Congregationalist Church in 1835. South Kingstown residents who could not attend the convention in person, including Kingston villager William French, sent a letter supporting the convention's goals.

In the midst of the excitement generated by the meeting, the delegates agreed to form the Rhode Island State Anti-Slavery Society. A constitution for the state society was written, approved and signed the delegates.

Notable in their absences in the convention were Kingston villagers Elisha R. Potter, Jr. and Wilkins Updike. They opposed slavery, but did not promote immediate emancipation out of concern of alienating the South and destabilizing the Union. In Elisha Potter's papers is a document in Potter's distinctive handwriting dated 1836, but there is no indication that it was sent or published. The document criticizes the abolitionists for trampling on the property rights of southern slaveholders and for leading the country into a possible "war of extermination." It states that immediate liberation of the slaves, before they were prepared for freedom, would be "injurious to the slaves themselves." Thomas R. Hazard, the author of *The Jonny-Cake Papers,* in a pamphlet stated that antislavery men were intemperate and that the slave question should not be allowed to disrupt the union. Potter and Hazard expressed the views of many conservative Democrats in Rhode Island.

The Kingston Anti-Slavery Society

On June 20, 1837, the Rhode Island State Anti-Slavery Society met in the Court House in Kingston. John G. Clarke presided over the meeting. Two speakers at the meeting inveighed against the evils of slavery and the need for immediate emancipation. One of the speakers was William L. Chapin, an agent of the American Anti-Slavery Society, whose task was to organize local antislavery societies. After a "full and free discussion," a number of antislavery resolutions were adopted, the first one boldly stating that "the system of American slavery is one of legal robbery, murder, licentiousness, and oppression, which has no parallel on the page of history – that it is to be immediately and forever abolished." At this meeting, and another society meeting in East Greenwich on the following day, $115 was raised from collections. The meetings and resolutions adopted were the subject of an article in the June 30, 1837 edition of *The Liberator,* the leading abolitionist newspaper edited by William Lloyd Garrison.

The primary purpose of the state society's meeting at the Court House was to form a local antislavery society, which initially was called the Kingston Anti-Slavery Society. Dr. Peleg Johnson was selected as chairman of the meeting and, as usual, Thomas P. Wells was selected as secretary to keep the minutes. The minutes of the Kingston Anti-Slavery Society are the only ones surviving of an antislavery society in Washington County. The antislavery traveling agent, William L. Chapin, suggested that the antislavery supporters form separate auxiliaries for men and women. But the Reverend Grosvenor spoke against the idea, and the villagers supported him in forming one society for both men and women, and white and black persons. No women or black persons were listed as officers of the society, but the men wisely selected two white women to serve on a six-member committee charged with soliciting money and recruiting members.

The Reverend Grosvenor read the constitution for the society that had already been prepared. It read, in part, as follows:

> The objects of this Society shall be to endeavor, by all means sanctioned by law, humanity and religion, to effect the immediate abolition of Slavery in the United States – to improve the character of the free people of color – to inform and correct public opinion in relation to their situation and rights – and to obtain for them equal civil and political privileges with the white inhabitants of the land.

Accordingly, the society's purpose was not only to promote the immediate abolition of slavery in the South, it was to promote free blacks in Rhode Island obtaining civil and political privileges equal to those enjoyed by whites. The meeting ended, with the members singing hymns and perhaps antislavery songs together.

After the adoption of the society's constitution, 25 persons in attendance signed as members. In later months in 1837, 23 additional persons signed as members. Of the 48 members of the society, 22 were men (including Kingston villagers Reverend Grosvenor, William French, Dr. Peleg Johnson, John G. Clarke, Thomas P. Wells and Powell Helme) and 26 were women (including Kingston villagers Emma P. Wells and Elizabeth Rose). There were three male "coloured" members: Kingston blacksmith George Fayerweather (George II), one of his sons, William Fayerweather, and William Harris. There were five female "coloured" members: Nancy Fayerweather (George's wife), Isabella Fayerweather, Sarah Brown, Sarah Wood and Martha Robinson. (A full list of the members is attached at Appendix C). Once members from outside Kingston joined, the members voted to rename their organization as the South Kingstown Anti-Slavery Society. William French was elected as president of the society.

Interestingly, the Kingston Anti-Slavery Society, along with the Newport Anti-Slavery Society, were among the few abolitionist societies in Rhode Island to permit the mixing of whites and blacks. This may have been because of the low numbers of members in the Kingston and Newport societies. On the other hand, it may have been because the whites in Kingston and Newport were simply more comfortable in the presence of blacks than whites in the northern part of the state. In contrast to Washington County and Newport, the northern part of the state did not have a history of slavery and a high percentage population of blacks, and was populated increasingly by white immigrants. In addition, during and after the Dorr Rebellion, tension between urban blacks and white Dorrite supporters (especially among the Irish immigrants, who viewed blacks as competitors for scarce jobs) limited cooperation among whites and blacks in the northern part of the state. Even so, the list of Kingston Anti-Slavery Society members is separated as follows: white men, black men, white women, and black women. The only exception was for George Fayerweather, whose name was in the middle of the white men's names, which was a sign of the respect in which he was held.

It is interesting to compare the white members of the Kingston Anti-Slavery Society and attendees at the Rhode Island Anti-Slavery Society convention with the South County white families who held slaves in colonial times. The comparison indicates that most of the antislavery proponents came from families who owned no or few slaves in colonial times, including the Wells, Helme, French, Clarke, Aldrich, Eldred, Rose, Larkin, Stedman and Smith families. In colonial times and in the 1830s, these families were largely middling shopkeepers and farmers. The families in South County who held the most slaves in colonial times were the Hazard, Robinson, Gardner,

Updike, Potter, Niles, Watson, Brown, Perry, Champlin and Babcock families. Few members of these families were antislavery proponents. An exception was Asa Potter, who served as a leader in the Rhode Island Anti-Slavery Society convention. He was the grandson of Little Rest slaveholder Thomas Potter, Jr. and cousin of Elisha R. Potter, Jr. Other exceptions were Martha and Mary Robinson, and Dorcas Gardner. Dorcas was probably a descendant of Caleb Gardner, one of Little Rest's most substantial slaveholders. For the most part, however, descendants of slaveholders stayed away from antislavery organizations.

At some time after the organizational meeting, on the list of members, a "#" sign was marked next to the names of most of the female members. The minutes state that "The females having this # mark against their names are members of the female society." It is not clear why this step was taken. The active participation of women in the abolitionist movement in New England was criticized in the Congregational Church and other circles.

Other than organizing, the only project reflected in the minutes was requiring candidates for elective office in upcoming Fall 1837 elections to state their positions on whether the slave trade should be immediately abolished, whether slavery should be outlawed in the District of Columbia, and whether Congress should support annexing Texas as a slave state. (There was no question on whether Congress should vote to abolish immediately slavery in the South, probably because the prevailing view at the time was that Congress did not have that power absent a constitutional amendment.) A series of written questions was sent to five candidates, including Elisha Potter, Jr. All of the candidates responded. Each one agreed that slavery was an "enormous evil." William Hazard was honest enough to state that while he opposed slavery, in light of the constitutional rights of slaveholders, the need to support the slaves once freed, and in the interest of peace, he did not support immediate abolition. Elisha Potter answered to the satisfaction of the antislavery members, but he did add the qualification that immediate abolition of slavery should be accomplished "as soon as can be done without interfering with the Constitutional rights of those states in which it exists." These were code words for the same position that William Hazard took. (While Potter said that Texas should not be admitted to the United States, when he was a congressman in 1845, he voted to admit Texas as a slave state.)

The reading of Elisha Potter's response in August 1837 was the last recorded activity in the Kingston Anti-Slavery Society minutes. The society appears to have disbanded shortly thereafter. It is not clear why this was the case. The disappearance of the society reflected a general decline in Rhode Island antislavery efforts after 1837. By then, the attention of Rhode Islanders was increasingly focusing on the looming Dorr Rebellion. The Dorr supporters for the most part excluded black participation, so there was little

- 237 -

sympathy among Dorrites for supporting abolition of slavery in the South. Alternatively, the members may have been uncomfortable with being associated with such a radical group. Furthermore, many of the members were Congregationalists, yet the church drew back from the abolitionist movement that was increasingly dominated by those promoting the immediate end of slavery in the South. The members may have felt social pressure from church members not to promote immediate abolitionism.

Other Antislavery Activities

Despite the decline in formal antislavery societies in Kingston and Rhode Island generally, individual men and women continued to work informally for the cause by circulating antislavery literature and discussing the issue with friends. Speakers regularly came to South Kingstown, some probably to the Court House in Kingston and local churches. Daniel Stedman, the ordinary farmer who lived between Kingston and Wakefield, and who was a Baptist, mentions antislavery speakers lecturing at his Baptist meeting house on two occasions in 1844.

From a detailed account of newspapers received by Kingston villagers in the period from 1837 to 1843, it can be determined that a number of villagers subscribed to antislavery newspapers. Five villagers subscribed to the radical newspaper *The Liberator*: John G. Clarke, Jeremiah Sherman (the jailer), George Fayerweather, Edwin Brown, William French, and Elisha R. Potter. Edited by abolitionist William Lloyd Garrison, *The Liberator* espoused the uncompromising position of immediate emancipation of southern slaves. Potter was not a radical abolitionist; he was interested in being informed of the arguments used by them. In addition, twelve villagers subscribed to *The Emancipator*: Arnold Sherman, John Larkin, William French, Thomas R. Wells, Luke Aldrich, William Nichols, Orpha Rose, Christopher Comstock, Robinson Rose, Job Watson, Thomas P. Wells, and the Reverend Charles Grosvenor. *The Emancipator* was an abolitionist newspaper sponsored by the American Anti-Slavery Society, but it was not as radical as *The Liberator*. George Fayerweather and the Reverend Grosvenor also subscribed to the *Coloured American,* a Philadelphia newspaper with black editors. All of these newspapers typically were passed to friends and neighbors. One can imagine that *The Liberator* editions obtained by the Fayerweathers were well worn by other black persons in Kingston, Biscuit City and nearby Mooresfield.

The informal antislavery network, speaking tours, and antislavery newspapers helped to create the environment in Rhode Island society that accepted abolitionism as a just cause. For example, in 1855, the *Narragansett Times* reported that William Wells Brown, black agent of the Anti-Slavery Society, spoke effectively at the Wakefield Baptist Church. The success of these efforts is evident in the 1847 campaign literature to elect Wilkins Updike to the U.S. Congress, as described in the next chapter.

On an evening in December 1841, the Kingston Congregational Church took a step in support of the antislavery movement. Congregational Churches in New England would have seemed to have been likely allies of William Lloyd Garrison, Theodore Weld, Wendell Phillips, Angelina and Sarah Grimke, and other abolitionist leaders. But a schism arose in the antislavery ranks. These abolitionist leaders argued for the immediate end of slavery in the South. A group of Massachusetts Congregationalist ministers, however, preached against the concept of immediatism, believing that it would alienate the South. In addition, they expressed concern about the participation of women in the ranks of the radical abolitionists, calling the mixing of males and females in the same audience "promiscuous." The clergymen argued that Christians could best address the issue of slavery within their own congregations, without the distraction of the radical agenda.

On the night of December 4, 1841, members of the Kingston Congregational Church met in Thomas R. Wells' home in Kingston to discuss whether the church should take a position on slavery. Christopher Comstock, longtime member of the church and instructor at the Kingston Academy, recorded the resolutions. The members of the Kingston Congregational Church decided to follow the moderate path of the Massachusetts ministers. They adopted the following statement:

> Resolved, unanimously, that we deem slavery, or the involuntary holding of human beings in bondage, as a great sin against God, having originated in selfishness, oppression and power and continued and sustained through a long course of years by the same unholy principles, as entirely opposed to the fundamental principles of the gospel of the blessed Savior, which breathe a spirit of love, and as requiring the rebuke of the Church as it must ultimately be visited with God's avenging judgments. Hence we cannot consistently with the great principles of our holy profession extend the hand of fellowship to any who participate in its guilt or encourage or abet the holding of slaves in any way whatever.

The statement focused only internally at its own members and was not an assertive call to join other groups in working to end slavery immediately. Attendees of the Rhode Island State Anti-Slavery Convention and members of the Kingston Anti-Slavery Society, both of which took strong stands in favor of immediate emancipation, must have been disappointed with the church's moderate stance. The moderate stance is explained in part due to the departure from his post as minister in 1838 of the Reverend Grosvenor, who had been a strong immediate abolitionist. Thomas R. Wells, the influential church deacon, was also apparently a moderate. He was an active member of the temperance society and Kingston's other organizations, but he never joined the Kingston Anti-Slavery Society. The church's statement was, nonetheless, a definite statement against slavery. It was perhaps impressive that this statement was made by a congregation some of whose parents and grandparents had held slaves. It was also in line with other mainstream Congregational and Baptist churches in New England – immediate emancipation was simply not as popular at this time as support of temperance.

In general, the temperance movement appeared to spur more enthusiasm than the antislavery movement in South Kingstown. Between 1832 and 1844, Daniel Stedman attended thirteen temperance lectures and events, while he attended only three antislavery lectures and events. He also attended a two-day debate held on the issue of what was the greater evil, intemperance or slavery. After "a great number of arguments on Both Sides," the president of the debate ruled that intemperance was the greater evil. In 1841, Stedman reported in his journal that an antislavery speaker was turned away from his Baptist meeting house because some parishioners objected to the message and antislavery supporters did not want to offend them.

Some of the lukewarm support for the antislavery cause in South Kingstown may have been due to the fact that many of the local mills produced clothing that was purchased by southern planters for their black slaves. Mill owners Rowland and Isaac Hazard, Samuel Rodman and James B. M. Potter manufactured "Georgia Kerseys" and "Washington Jeans" that were shipped to the South. Each man had business contacts in South Carolina, Georgia and other southern states. Thomas P. Wells, while he resided in Wakefield, had a printing business and he printed tags for the clothes manufactured by Rodman and Potter. Moreover, South Kingstown's most valuable crop was potatoes, which primarily were shipped to markets in the South. In 1839, South Kingstown's potato harvest was 75,000 bushels. The end of slavery meant the end of much of that trade. Yet by and large, South Kingstowners and other South County residents seemed to have separated this economic issue from the moral issue of slavery, and they generally were antislavery in outlook. Rowland G. Hazard finally went on the record as opposing slavery in the South in a speech in the General Assembly in 1850; and Thomas P. Wells was a member and secretary of the Kingston Anti-Slavery Society. Yet they did not go as far as immediately cutting off their economic ties to the South in protest of slavery.

Biscuit City reportedly was an "underground railroad" stop for escaped southern slaves on their way to freedom in Canada. While this report is impossible to confirm, Biscuit City was an ideal location, as it became a neighborhood populated by black families beginning around the 1860s.

The Restoration of Black Voting Rights in Rhode Island

The constitution of the Kingston Anti-Slavery Society set as a goal the acquisition by black persons of "equal civil and political privileges with the white inhabitants of the land." White Rhode Islanders by 1837 and thereafter during the Dorr uprising were forced to look not only at slavery in the South, but at their own treatment of blacks.

In 1822, the General Assembly had enacted legislation providing that only white males could vote. Why black males were disenfranchised is not clear. Rhode Island likely was influenced by the bordering states in New England and New York, which after the War of 1812 revised their constitutions with similar racial restrictions. For example, Connecticut eliminated black suffrage in 1817 and New York raised discriminatory property qualifications in 1821.

What happened to the attitudes of white Rhode Islanders after the heady days of emancipation following the Revolutionary War? In *Disowning Slavery*, historian Joanne Pope Melish explains that after emancipation of black slaves following the Revolutionary War, abolitionists thought that freeing blacks from the institution of slavery would solve their problems. But black slaves understandably took time to adapt successfully to their new-found freedom. Black farmers did not have the key advantage of whites who inherited farms from their parents. Many had to serve as temporary hired hands on farms. Black men interested in starting a trade typically did not receive either a proper education or vocational training, and due to discrimination were not likely to receive loans from local banks to start businesses. Melish believes that whites, viewing the struggle of free blacks to succeed and their continued degraded condition, came to the conclusion that blacks were somehow innately inferior. The solution was to remove them from white society, starting with the right to vote. Because recently freed blacks were not yet well organized, politically they were too weak to protest effectively.

While the law banning blacks from voting was an insult to black citizens' dignity, in practice, it may not have had much of a practical impact in South County. The state's $134 real estate ownership requirement for obtaining the vote still existed in 1822 and had kept most blacks from becoming freemen able to vote in town and state elections. In Kingston, George Fayerweather, the successful black blacksmith, had not been listed on the town's voting rolls prior to 1822. With the house he built in the village in 1820, he probably met the $134 real estate requirement, but if he did, he chose not ask the town to have his name placed on the voting lists, perhaps out of concern of creating a controversy. After 1822, some white villagers may have wondered whether it was proper that a man of George

Fayerweather's obvious abilities was not permitted to vote. They saw his success at blacksmithing, must have commented on his well-organized ledger book, were aware that he joined the Kingston Anti-Slavery Society, and knew that he subscribed to newspapers such as *The Liberator, The Coloured American*, and the *Courier Journal,* a Providence daily newspaper. In a few New England towns, black men who paid town taxes filed suit against the towns and claimed that they should be exempt from tax, on the ground that if they could not vote, they should not be required to pay taxes. While George Fayerweather paid his town taxes, he did not take the aggressive move of bringing suit against the town.

In the struggle to adopt a new constitution in Rhode Island in the early 1840s, black voting rights again became an issue. The People's Constitution adopted by the Dorr supporters restricted the vote only to white males. Dominated by Irish and other immigrants, who competed with blacks in northern Rhode Island for jobs, and who strove to be viewed as socially superior to black persons, the Dorr party generally was hostile to black voting rights. The Landholders Constitution, the alternative proposal at a compromise adopted by conservative delegates on March 8, 1841, also limited the vote to "white males." Antislavery forces protested the exclusion of blacks from voting and they scheduled meetings in several towns in the state to organize opposition, including one in Kingston. The Rhode Island Anti-Slavery Society voted to oppose the Landholders Constitution and any other constitution that limited the right of black men to vote.

In a letter published in the *Providence Journal* on March 18, 1842, Kingston's William French pleaded with the Rhode Island Anti-Slavery Society to support the Landholders Constitution. In the letter, French described himself as an abolitionist (he was the former president of the Kingston Anti-Slavery Society and subscribed to *The Liberator*). He argued that abolitionists should vote for the Landholders Constitution, as it expressly outlawed slavery. He also pointed out that by voting down the Landholders Constitution, "you deprive the white man of his right of suffrage." He questioned whether abolitionists wanted to be counted with Rhode Islanders who opposed the proposed constitution – those who would bring "anarchy and disorder to government" (i.e., the Dorr supporters) and "those who mobbed your lecturers through the state in December last" (several antislavery meetings in Providence had been interrupted by hecklers and mobs opposed to black voting rights). While the state antislavery society stood its ground, other former members of the Kingston Anti-Slavery Society agreed with French. Of the thirteen former Kingston Anti-Slavery Society members who voted (white males who met the property qualifications), twelve voted to approve the constitution. To them, resolving the voting controversy with Irish Catholic immigrants was more of a priority than addressing the continuing wrong of prohibiting blacks from voting. Nonetheless, the Landholders Constitution was rejected. With the margin of defeat only 676 votes, the votes against the constitution by members of the state's antislavery society helped to decide the vote.

Providence blacks became increasingly organized and vocal on the issue of the re-enfranchisement of blacks. Seeing the hostile reaction to blacks in the Dorr party, they turned to the conservative Law and Order Party for support. Rhode Island blacks helped their cause when many of them joined Law and Order militias that helped to quell the Dorr uprising in June of 1842. Black voting rights again became an issue as the Law and Order forces began framing the new state constitution that was ultimately adopted in 1843. Conservative Protestant whites saw blacks as their natural allies against the influx of Catholic immigrants. The perceptive Potter noted in a letter, "there is not so much scolding about letting the blacks vote as was expected," explaining that "they would rather have the negroes vote than the d---d Irish." Potter added in another letter that Rhode Island blacks were "conservative and go with the wealthy part of the community." Rhode Island blacks, Frederick Douglass, the black abolitionist, later said, "cared nothing for the Dorr Party on the one hand, nor the 'law and order' party on the other. What we wanted, and what we labored to obtain, was a constitution free from the narrow, selfish, and senseless limitation of the word *white*."[29] Some whites agreed, seeing the hypocrisy of supporting the freedom of slaves in the South while at the same time denying Rhode Island black men the basic privilege of voting.

Late in the constitutional convention, delegates voted 45-15 to drop the term "white" from the voting clause. Black leaders persuaded white Law and Order leaders that a referendum should be held on whether voting should be restricted only to white males. Rhode Island voters voted against restricting blacks from voting, 4,031 to 1,798. This vote was in sharp contrast to failed efforts in Connecticut, New York, and New Jersey between 1840 and 1860 to eliminate discriminatory voting restrictions. Due to Rhode Island's unique struggle between native and immigrant whites over voting rights, the state was actually advanced in permitting black males to vote.

In Kingston, the men of the black Fayerweather family became eligible voters. In 1856, for example, George and Solomon Fayerweather, and two of George's sons (David and Isaac) were listed on town records as eligible voters.

---

[29] While in Rhode Island at this time, Douglass reported that he was sometimes discriminated against on the Stonington railroad line. "The Stonington route was a 'hard' road for a colored man 'to travel' in that day. I was several times dragged from the cars for the *crime* of being colored."

Elisha R. Potter, Jr. and Wilkins Updike:
Rationalizing the Slaveholding of Their Forefathers
with Pre-Civil War Opposition to the South

When the northern states after the Revolutionary War gradually abolished slavery, America became divided into two societies, North and South. The northern states came to view the continuation and expansion of the southern slave system as grossly inconsistent with the ideals of the Declaration of Independence and U.S. Constitution. In the Narragansett country, more than any other place in New England, elites from families that formerly held slaves had to rationalize the new antislavery views with their families' relatively recent history of slaveholding. In South County, this task was performed by two of its most important persons, Kingston's Elisha Reynolds Potter, Jr. and Wilkins Updike.

Both Potter and Updike had relatives who had held slaves in the Narragansett country in colonial times. The will for Daniel Updike, Wilkins' great-grandfather and a prominent Narragansett planter who had his estate near Wickford at Smith's Castle, indicates that he held 19 slaves at his death in 1757, tied for the highest number of slaves recorded in the probate records of North and South Kingstown. Daniel's son and grandson also held slaves at Smith's Castle. In addition, Wilkins' father, Lodowick, apparently was involved in investing in ships that engaged in the slave trade. Elisha R. Potter, Jr.'s grandfather, Colonel Thomas Potter, is recorded as holding three black slaves in the 1774 census. Elisha Jr.'s grandmother, Elizabeth Reynolds, was the daughter of Little Rest slaveholder Elisha Reynolds. Elisha Jr.'s father, Elisha R. Potter, Sr., held Kingston's last slave, who was freed in 1810.

An election broadside in support of the campaign of Wilkins Updike for a seat in the United States House of Representatives in 1847 is revealing regarding the strong antislavery views of the day. The broadside begins,

> ELECTORS OF THE WESTERN DISTRICT! READ AND CONSIDER! At a meeting of gentlemen of the Whig Party, and citizens generally, favorable to the election of Hon. Wilkins Updike, to Congress, held at Kingston Court House, Aug. 11, 1847. The meeting was called to order by Elisha R. Potter, Esq.

Two speakers, well known politicians from Providence, addressed the crowd. Each address was firmly antislavery. The theme of each address was that the recent Mexican War had as its primary object the odious "EXTENSION OF SLAVERY!" One speaker stated that the South's aim was "to acquire new territory, and to make that territory into new slave states to increase their power in Congress." The speaker inveighed, "Were the freemen of the north

ELECTORS OF THE WESTERN DISTRICT!
READ AND CONSIDER!!!

At a meeting of gentlemen of the Whig Party, and of citizens generally, favorable to the election of Hon. WILKINS UPDIKE, to Congress, held at Kingston Court House, Aug. 11, 1847.

The meeting was called to order by Elisha R. Potter, Esq. and on motion of Sylvester G. Sherman, Esq. the Hon. George D. Cross, of Westerly, was chosen Chairman.

Gen. Samuel Ames of Providence being present, attending Court, was invited to address the meeting. We give the substance of his remarks as follows.

Mr. Ames began by remarking on the great importance of the present election. In ordinary times, when the majority in Congress was large for either party, it might not be of so much consequence who was elected. But at present, when the whigs had been gaining in all the recent southern and western elections, there was a great probability that the two parties in Congress would be very nearly tied, and one vote might decide the great questions of peace and war and slavery, and more remotely the presidential question itself.

Of the two candidates personally he should say but little. They were both men whom he respected and who were estimable in the relations of private life. But the present is no time to indulge our personal preferences, or to gratify our private jealousies or resentments. Higher considerations should govern us.

If Mr. Updike was elected he would support the measures of the party which elected him. If Gen. Thurston is elected, he too must support the measures of the democratic party which elects him. However much he may profess to dislike war and slavery, he must, if he goes to Washington, act with his party.

What then are the measures of the democratic party, which you vote for and endorse by giving a vote for Gov. Thurston?

Do you not by so doing approve of the present unjust and wicked war with Mexico, a war begun by President Polk alone without the sanction of Congress, and which Congress were afterwards reluctantly brought to vote the supplies for? A war begun by the President for the purpose of getting possession of the treasures of the government, and of increasing the number of officers to enable him to distribute fat jobs and contracts among the followers of his party. And thus millions of the people's money were spent every month in increasing the patronage and power of the party. And members of Congress were threatened and abused into voting the money for this war, and those who conscientiously opposed it were denounced as Mexicans and traitors!!

But it was not merely the amount of public money squandered in this war, it was not even the great danger to the liberties of the country from the enormous and unconstitutional powers claimed by the President, and from the system of corruption which prevailed in the administration—there was a more momentous consideration than even all these—that was the object for which the war was carried on—the EXTENSION of SLAVERY!!

This was the avowed object of the southern politicians who controlled the administration, to acquire new territory, and to make that new territory into new slave states to increase their power in Congress, and to enable them to keep that control of the offices and patronage which they have always hitherto held through the submissiveness of northern demagogues.

Consider the history of this question—formerly they acknowledged slavery to be an evil and professed to desire to get rid of it, but now since the extension of the cultivation of cotton and since slavery has become profitable to them—they justify it as a natural blessing!—Were the freemen of the north ready to sanction such a doctrine as this? To protect this southern interest, to enable them to put money in their pockets by the extension of the trade in human flesh, was the great object of this war. The war was entirely for the interest of the South—the money was expended there, the offices were distributed there, and its whole effect was to enrich and strengthen the power of the South at the expense of the free people of the North.

Hon. Albert C. Greene was next called upon and addressed the meeting.

Gen. Greene said he agreed with Mr. Ames that the question now before the people was of far greater consequence than the election of any particular individual. He agreed with him in speaking highly of the character of both candidates as individuals and in private life. But whigs—lovers of liberty—should consider that the election of Gov. Thurston, however brought about, whether from personal esteem for him or misrepresentation of his opponent, and however it might be considered here, would be hailed abroad as the triumph of his party—it would be claimed as a victory of those who supported and justified the President in all his measures for carrying on the war and extending slavery. No doubt some of the party here might profess to be against slavery—some might be sincere, but if Gov. Thurston was elected he must support his party, and that party throughout the union—are and in this State too!!! justified this war and denounced those who opposed it. The columns of the Republican Herald every week prove this. It is filled with praises of the President and his whole policy. There is not one of his measures they have disapproved of. This is the party paper, taken and read by all the democrats in the State. And this party which supports this paper is the party which is trying to elect Gov. Thurston, and which he must support if he is elected.

It was idle talk for any of the democratic party here to profess to be against slavery and yet to support the present administration, whose avowed object in carrying on this war was to extend slavery and to perpetuate it. Do not all the newspapers of their party every where support the war? Do not all their swarms of office holders in Providence and elsewhere justify it? And can any man see it clearly—party, with a party which he knows will, if it succeeds, adopt such measures and not expect to be held responsible for the consequences of those measures?

Gen. Greene spoke impressively and eloquently of the obligation and sacred duties of every freeman in relation to these questions. Every elector should consider his vote as a sacred trust to be used not for his own advantage, not for the advantage of any particular candidate, but for the good of the whole country and for the advancement of truth and justice.

Fellow citizens, we have given a brief account of the proceedings of this interesting meeting. Consider before it is too late. The democrats—the friends of the war—rely on succeeding by your indifference and apathy. They are secretly and quietly taking measures to ensure a full attendance of their own party. Let us disappoint them. If we do our duty we have the strength and can elect Mr. Updike. If defeated, it is not Mr. Updike's defeat, it is the defeat of the party which supports him; it will be considered as the triumph of the southern policy, the triumph of those who follow the lead of President Polk and his clique of office holders in Providence, the triumph of the party who support war, extravagance, corruption and slavery.

Voters! you who are not quite ready yet to sanction this inhuman system of slavery, you who are not willing to have your labor and industry degraded to the level of the slaves of the South, awake, attend the polls and rebuke the men who dare to insult the intelligence and virtue of northern freemen, by asking them to support a party which was against all the principles of justice, against all the best interests of humanity.

When Mr. Calhoun was told by some of the apologists of the President that this would be a cheap war and a short one, he answered that it would continue at least three years, and would cost at least one hundred millions of dollars. The recent estimate of the Secretary of the Treasury shows that we are now spending at the rate of ONE HUNDRED MILLIONS A YEAR, and if Mr. Calhoun's estimate shall prove as much too short in the duration as it was in the cost, we may calculate upon a war of nine years, and a cost of nine hundred millions. The annals of invasion and conquest scarcely furnish an example of such enormous and prodigal expenditure. The necessary expenses of such a war, enormous as they are, are augmented by the wastefulness, the wrecklessness, and more than either by the ignorance which prevail in the purchasing departments, and by the absurd arrangements which are made at Washington.

The war with Great Britain cost but trifle in comparison with this, and scarcely any war in ancient or modern times can show such an enormous expenditure in proportion to the men engaged and the means employed. Thousands of contractors and agents, the favorites of the administration, are growing rich upon the spoils not of Mexico, but of our own country; and the people must pay for it all. A national debt is now piling up which will oppress the treasury for years to come. Every man must pay his part of it; every citizen must contribute of his substance and his earnings this share of the millions which are wasted in a foreign war, in which success or defeat is alike disastrous. And what is all this? What is to pay us—we will not say for the loss of human life, the corruption of public morals, and the thousand other evils of war—but for the bare pecuniary sacrifice which we are making? How are we to get our money back, or our money's worth? In the annexation of more territory? In the extension of the institution of slavery? In the incorporation of an indolent, degraded, and superstitious people with our own republic? Such remedy is even worse than the original evil.

Considering the wealth and prosperity of this State, and its large consumption of dutiable articles, it is not too much to say that its proportion of the money already spent in this war exceeds HALF A MILLION OF DOLLARS. For every cent of this sum, sooner or later, directly or indirectly, in some form or other, the people of THIS STATE MUST PAY, and every year that the war continues adds an equal amount to the swelling sum. Will the people of the Western District elect as their Representative a man who will support the administration in this war, or one who will hold the President to an account for his unconstitutional usurpation?

The following are the appropriations which have already been made, and for a large portion of which the country is, at this moment in debt. Future taxes must be relied upon to discharge this debt.

Appropriations at the last Session.

For support of the army and volunteers	$32,178,461 88
For support of the navy	9,307,958 10
For concluding peace with Mexico	3,000,000 00
	$44,486,419 98

Appropriations at the previous Session.

For prosecution of existing war	$10,000,000 00
For support of the army	6,873,062 67
For volunteers and other troops	11,957,342 00
For support of the navy	7,449,703 53
For reg'm't mounted riflemen	81,900 00
For sappers, miners & pontoniers	23,500 00
	$36,396,645 02

War appropriations since the war begun.

Last year	$36,396,645 02
This year	44,486,419 98
Total of war appropriations	$80,873,065 00

The appropriations for the same objects at the next session of Congress, should the war continue, will exceed rather than fall short of Fifty Millions of Dollars.

Wilkins Updike Campaign Broadside, 1847. Note the symbol for run-away slaves. Displayed by the Smithsonian Institution in an exhibit on classic American broadsides. *Library of Congress, Rare Books and Manuscripts Division.*

ready to sanction a doctrine as this? To protect this southern interest, to enable them to put money in their pockets by the extension of the trade in human flesh, was the great object of the war." The next speaker argued that while the Whig opponent, Democratic Governor Thurston, professed to be against slavery, a victory by the Governor's party, the Democratic Party, would be "hailed abroad as the triumph of his party – it would be claimed as a victory of those who supported and justified the President in all his measures for carrying on the war and extending slavery." The speaker roused the crowd with an emotional finish:

> Voters! You who are not quite ready to sanction this inhuman system of slavery, you who are not yet willing to have your labor and industry degraded to the level of the slaves in the South, awake, attend the polls and rebuke the men who dare to insult the intelligence and virtue of northern freemen, by asking them to support a party which was against all the principles of justice, against all the best interests of humanity.

The broadside demonstrates that antislavery views had so permeated Rhode Island by 1847 that the two main parties, the Whigs and Democrats, vied with each other for the mantle of most antislavery. In addition, an interesting aspect of the broadside is that at a major rally held at the Kingston Court House on behalf of Wilkins Updike, with Elisha R. Potter, Jr. presiding, neither Updike nor Potter spoke at the meeting. This was probably because the Whig crowd wanted to hear firmly antislavery speeches. While they opposed slavery, neither Updike nor Potter was an ardent abolitionist or wanted to alienate the South. Indeed, Potter had some southern sympathies. While serving as one of Rhode Island's representatives in the U.S. Congress in 1845, Potter was faced with the decision of whether to vote in favor of annexing Texas, which among Rhode Island voters was viewed as a proxy for supporting or opposing the extension of slavery by the South. In a letter to his brother Thomas in 1845, Elisha wrote, "Southern institutions are now the only check upon our northern demagoguism." He told his brother that the annexation of Texas was inevitable. Potter ended up voting in favor of annexation (which was also inconsistent with his pledge to the Kingston Anti-Slavery Society in 1837). In the next election later that year, Rhode Island voters had responded by throwing him out of office.

While Potter and Updike were against slavery, they were conservative in their approaches. In an 1840 General Assembly committee report authored by Potter, the committee opposed liberation of the handful of remaining slaves in Rhode Island, on grounds of humanity. Potter thought that any remaining slaves were old and infirm and would not be able to care for themselves outside their masters' homes. Potter expressed disbelief that while the southern slavemasters used to argue that they knew slavery was wrong but they did not know how to rid themselves of it, southern slavemasters were now arguing that slavery was "a blessing." Still, the committee report concluded that "any attempt on the part of any persons, to interfere with institutions in the southern states, by any other than peaceable and legal means" would be "resolutely opposed by the great body of the people of the North . . . ."

How did Potter and Updike rationalize the slaveholdings of their relatively recent forefathers in the Narragansett country with the current antislavery and anti-Southern sentiments that prevailed in Rhode Island? As noted by historian Robert Fitts, in his thorough study of slavery in the colonial Narragansett country, *Inventing New England's Slave Paradise, Master/Slave Relations in Eighteenth-Century Narragansett, Rhode Island*, Potter and Updike had several alternative approaches. They could ignore the past. Potter and Updike were both historians and intellectually honest men, so they could not do this. Alternatively, they could break with their past and declare that what their forefathers did was immoral and wrong. This they chose not to do; they simply lacked the courage to take this stand. Instead, they chose to "soft pedal" the conditions of slavery in the Narragansett country, arguing that slavery in the Narragansett country was relatively benign.

Elisha Reynolds Potter, Jr. authored the first study of slavery in the Narragansett country in an address to the Rhode Island lower house in 1840; he expanded on this work in an address to the Rhode Island Historical Society in 1851. In his 1840 speech, Potter stated: "It is believed that while slavery existed in Rhode Island, the slaves were always treated with humanity, and that they were generally rather a burden than a source of profit to their owners." This argument was repeated in Potter's 1851 address, in which he stated that "public opinion would not sanction over-work or ill treatment" of slaves in the Narragansett country. While both addresses were antislavery in nature, they attempted to free the Narragansett planters from blame while rejecting the ability of the southern slavemasters to use the same argument. While it may have been true that slavery in the Narragansett country was less brutal than slavery in the South, it was still the case that white Narragansett planters had held black people in bondage against their will, that white slaveowners were supported by laws to instill terror in blacks if the blacks considered running away or resisting their slave status, and that there were instances of cruel treatment of black slaves.

By 1863, Potter no longer tried to differentiate between northern and southern slavery. Instead, he argued that each new generation should not be held accountable for the sins of their forefathers. Interestingly, he made this argument in the context of discussing slavery in colonial Massachusetts, not in the colonial Narragansett country of his forefathers. In an 1863 address to the Rhode Island senate, in arguing that the North should not take a harsh post-Civil War stance against the South, Potter states,

> if a southern slaveholder is a robber and a murderer now, then were these old Puritan slaveholders, robbers and murderers, and all the people were accessory to these crimes for permitting such laws to exist . . . . If it is not right to hold the present Massachusetts people responsible for the acts of their ancestors, then it is not right to hold the southern people responsible for the acts of theirs.

In discussing slavery in colonial Massachusetts, which was substantially less important than in the Narragansett country, Potter may have sought to use a device to deflect the emotional burden of his own forefathers in holding black slaves. By implication, Potter was arguing that slavery as practiced by his forefathers was wrong, but that his generation should not be assigned guilt for the sins of his forefathers. Alternatively, he may have selected Massachusetts because of its strong abolitionist heritage, which annoyed Potter. In a letter to his brother James discussing prospects for the U.S. House of Representatives to vote to annex Texas, Potter wrote that "Massachusetts will act like fools as a matter of course," meaning that its House representatives would take a strong antislavery stand and oppose the annexation of Texas.

In 1847, Wilkins Updike wrote a *History of the Episcopal Church in Narragansett,* which became an influential history of the colonial Narragansett country. Updike's vision of slavery in the Narragansett country was one of mildness, benevolence and paternalism. It was a romanticized world where white slavemasters were at the top of the social scale, and black slaves were content with their position at the bottom of the social scale. Updike writes romantically of black corn huskings, weddings and the Negro Elections, but he spends little time on the working conditions of a slave on a Narragansett plantation or the laws that kept the slaves in bondage. Historian Robert Fitts accurately states that Updike's book played an important role in establishing in the minds of future historians and the public that Narragansett slavery was mild, harmonious and different from its counterpart in the South. He writes that Updike's interpretation "suggested that racial strife developed in the South and was not a Northern problem. As a result, Northern whites believed they had few, if any, racial problems."

Sarah Harris Fayerweather: Heroine and Abolitionist

Kingston is fortunate to have been the home of a heroine and antislavery activist in the pre-Civil War period, Sarah Harris Fayerweather. Born Sarah Harris in 1812, she was one of 12 children. Her family resided in Canterbury, Connecticut, a town in the northeast part of the state. Her father, a local farmer, was a literate black man who sold copies of *The Liberator*, the abolitionist newspaper edited by William Lloyd Garrison. Garrison was the leading proponent among abolitionists of the immediate end to slavery in the South.

When she was 20-years-old, Sarah felt the urge to improve her education. At the time, public schools in Connecticut were not well developed; and free black students such as herself faced additional problems because of discrimination by white teachers. Sarah had the goal of becoming a teacher in the black community of her former hometown, Norwich. She was aware that Prudence Crandall operated a private school for white girls in Canterbury. Sarah's older sister was a servant in Crandall's house, so Sarah was not a stranger to Crandall. Indeed, through Sarah and her sister, the abolitionist arguments had first come to Crandall's attention.

Sarah approached Prudence Crandall in the fall of 1832 and courageously informed her that she "wanted to get a little more learning." If Miss Crandall admitted Sarah to Miss Crandall's school, Sarah would forever be obliged, "but if such action might be a means of injury, she would not insist upon the favor." Sarah asked the right person in Crandall. Crandall was raised as a Quaker. She was appalled at the conditions of black people in the country, both slave and free, that she read about in *The Liberator*. Crandall knew that there would be opposition among white families in the town to her admitting Sarah Harris as a student. But she was a strong-willed person who believed in doing the right thing. She admitted Sarah Harris to her school.

The week following Sarah's acceptance, several prominent white townspeople called at the school. Their message was that if Sarah Harris was not dismissed, they would withdraw their own daughters from the school. Crandall refused, and some, but not all, white students were withdrawn. Knowing that the school could not survive with only a few white students, Crandall dismissed the remaining white students and reopened it in April 1833 as a school for "young ladies and little misses of color" from New England and New York. With Garrison's contacts, black girls from New England and New York signed up to attend Crandall's school. Crandall's neighbors in Canterbury became enraged. On May 24, 1833, the Connecticut General Assembly passed a law making it illegal to establish any school for "colored persons who are not inhabitants of this State." Crandall was arrested and imprisoned for a night. She endured three court trials. The town made the extreme argument that black people were not citizens under the U.S. Constitution and therefore that they were not entitled to freedom of education. Garrison and other abolitionists hoped to take the case to the U.S. Supreme Court to resolve the issue of black citizenship. This plan, however, was sidetracked by a campaign of harassment. The school building was pelted with stones, eggs and mud. In January 1834, someone tried unsuccessfully to burn the school building, which also served as the residence of the students. On the night of September 9, 1834, a mob attacked the school building, breaking more than 90 window panes. Fearing for the safety of her students, Crandall closed the school the following day. A Connecticut minister from a nearby town who had supported Crandall wrote, "I felt ashamed for Canterbury, ashamed of Connecticut, ashamed of my country." Crandall's noble effort had ended.

Before the attempted burning of the school, Sarah Harris had withdrawn from the school. On November 28, 1833, Sarah, at the age of 21, married George Fayerweather III of Kingston. After remaining in Canterbury a short while, they moved to New London where they lived until 1855. George carried on the family trade of blacksmithing. Their first child, born in 1834, was named, fittingly, Prudence Crandall Fayerweather.

In 1855, the Fayerweathers moved from New London to George's home village of Kingston. George, Sarah, and their five children moved into the eastern half of the rambling old Helme House (across from the current Kingston Hill Store). Sarah Harris Fayerweather had purchased this real estate in 1853, in a deed witnessed by Elisha Reynolds Potter, Jr. George's widowed mother continued to live in the Fayerweather Cape Cod cottage. George III joined his brother Solomon in running the local blacksmith shop.

Sarah Harris Fayerweather continued her support of the abolitionist movement. Over the years, her home became a center of antislavery activity. Sarah reportedly hosted many antislavery lecturers at her home in Kingston. She also circulated antislavery tracts and newspapers to local families.

Sarah did not became a member of the Kingston Anti-Slavery Society in 1837, probably because she resided in New London at that time. By the time she had moved to Kingston in 1855, the society had disbanded. Sarah did not become a member of the Kingston Congregational Church. This decision may have been influenced by her support of the immediate end to slavery in the South, and not the more moderate stance adopted by the church in 1841. Sarah also apparently decided not to cause controversy in Kingston by pushing for the integration of the village's elite academic institution, the Kingston Academy. Given her experience in Canterbury, one cannot blame her.

Sarah corresponded with William Lloyd Garrison and his wife, Helen. Sarah was a subscriber to, and avid reader of, *The Liberator*. (In the Fayerweather papers at the University of Rhode Island is a receipt made out to her for *The Liberator*, dated January 1, 1862). Sarah's intimacy with Garrison, the tower of strength in the abolitionist movement, and his wife, Helen, was reflected by Sarah's custom to send the Garrison family a cake for the holidays. (The fact that she could afford this luxury indicates the level of her financial security).

Sarah frequently traveled outside of Kingston to attend antislavery meetings. A letter written in 1863 from Helen Garrison states that her husband enjoyed seeing Sarah in New York and accompanying her to an antislavery lecture by Wendell Phillips, one of the leaders of the antislavery movement. In another letter from the daughter of the husband of Prudence Crandall (by his first marriage), the daughter describes her meeting with Sarah in Boston at a meeting of the Massachusetts Anti-Slavery Society in 1863. She wrote that she met "a colored woman of very pleasing manners and appearance," and was intrigued to learn that she was the Sarah Harris of her "Mother Crandall's" school. She wrote:

> I invited her to come and pass the afternoon with me, which she did yesterday, and I wish you could have been here to hear her talk of the days of Mother's persecution, and also to her many things about Mother, for whom she entertains the warmest love and gratitude . . . . I do not know when I have enjoyed an afternoon better than in this woman's society. She is very intelligent and lady-like, well informed in every movement relative to the removal of slavery and converses very well . . . .

With Union victory in the Civil War drawing near, the abolitionists who had worked so hard all those previous years basked in glory as the emancipation of all slaves in the South was drawing near as well. After the fall of Charleston in February 1865, the Lincoln administration decided to make the recaptured Fort Sumter the place for a dramatic pageant to commemorate the symbolic end of the war. At President Lincoln's suggestion, William Lloyd Garrison was invited as a dignitary. Sarah Harris Fayerweather was thrilled for Garrison, writing to him:

> I praise the name of the Lord that he has prolonged your precious life to see this day. My joy is full when I think of your being at Charleston, South Carolina, having those very slaves for whom you have tolled a persecuted lifetime bowing down at your garment . . . I can say that it is glory enough for our century.

Sarah Harris Fayerweather (1812-78), circa 1860. During her years in Kingston, she traveled to antislavery meetings, met its leaders, and corresponded with William Lloyd and Helen Garrison. *Prudence Crandall Museum, State of Connecticut.*

Still basking in the glow of success, Garrison's daughter was married in March 1866. Sarah Harris Fayerweather sent the Garrison family a huge wedding cake by express from Providence.

In her later years, Sarah Harris Fayerweather resumed her correspondence with Prudence Crandall, who had moved to the West and was living a difficult life. In an 1869 letter, Crandall wrote to Sarah, "I have no friend on earth I would be more rejoiced to see than yourself." They promised to see each other again and share their antislavery and family experiences, but they were not able to meet in person again.[30]

George Fayerweather III died in 1869. Buried in the Old Fernwood Cemetery, his headstone reads, "he won the respect and esteem of the community, and those who knew him best respected him most." Sarah continued to reside in the old Helme House, and she began attending Sunday school classes at the Kingston Congregational Church. Sarah passed away in 1878 at the age of 66. She was buried next to her husband in the Fayerweather plot in Old Fernwood Cemetery. Upon her death, William Lloyd Garrison sent Sarah's children a poem in remembrance.

In 1970, the University of Rhode Island named a newly constructed residence hall in honor of Sarah Harris Fayerweather. The University of Rhode Island library possesses a collection of Sarah's papers, as well as the Fayerweather family papers. In 1965, the Fayerweather house was acquired and restored by the Kingston Improvement Association, led by the efforts of Carl Woodward and Lucy Tootell.

[30] Unfortunately, four of the original five letters written to Sarah Harris Fayerweather by Prudence Crandall and Helen Garrison were stolen recently from the University of Rhode Island Library (Special Collections). The letters had been stored in the archives building next to the Kingston Free Library and Reading Room since about the 1950s. Several years ago these letters were transferred to the college library. Fortunately, copies of the letters still exist.

Kingston During the Civil War

A Civil War Send-Off in Kingston and a Sad Return

   With the failure of the North and South to resolve the issue of slavery, the threat of Civil War loomed. War fears were heightened when, after the election of Abraham Lincoln, southern states seceded from the Union. In response, military preparations began in various northern towns, including South Kingstown.

   The chartered company that had been organized in 1842 in response to the Dorr Rebellion, first called the Washington Cadets, then the Wakefield Cadets and finally the Narragansett Guards, was revived. On April 19, 1861, a meeting of the outfit was held at the Court House in Kingston at 10 a.m. While the meeting was held in Kingston, men from Peace Dale, Wakefield and Rocky Brook dominated the event.   Prior to the meeting, 94 men assembled in Peace Dale and marched through Rocky Brook to Kingston. A total of 130 men enlisted in the company, including two from Kingston. Isaac P. Rodman of Rocky Brook was chosen as Captain. After an hour of drilling, the company was dismissed and enlisted men were requested to meet for drill every evening at Peace Dale, Wakefield and Rocky Brook.

   Isaac Peace Rodman would become South Kingstown's greatest war hero. He was a partner with his father and brother in owning and operating textile mills at Rocky Brook. He also served as president of the Wakefield Bank, and he had served for several years as president of the town council and a representative in the General Assembly. Rodman had been the colonel of the Narragansett Guards in 1846 and was the driving force behind its revival in 1861. At the time of the muster in Kingston, he was serving his second term in the Rhode Island senate.   He was a close friend of Governor William Sprague and he had married Sally Lyman Arnold, the daughter of a former governor. Many of the recruits in the Narragansett Guards worked in his mills.   Even though the Civil War would injure his family's business of making "slave cloth" for black slaves in the South, Rodman (as well as many of his mill workers) eagerly supported the Union cause.

   On May 4, 1861, meeting at the Court House in Kingston, the South Kingstown town meeting passed resolutions supporting President Lincoln in the full conduct of the war. Elisha R. Potter, Jr. moderated the meeting. The town meeting pledged that the town would assist the families of the men who enlisted and would pay enlistees $1 for every six hours of drilling. That same day, Captain Rodman received word that the Narragansett Guards would become Company E of the 2nd Rhode Island Volunteer Infantry, then organizing in Providence.

On June 2, 1861, orders arrived requiring Company E to depart the Kingston railroad station for Providence on the afternoon of June 4th. Hearing that the troops would march through Kingston, Thomas P. Wells and his wife Mary offered to host a farewell party for them on the spacious lawn between their home and the Kingston Congregational Church. The officers of Company E accepted the offer. After marching to Kingston, the men of Company E relaxed on the lawns of Kingston's houses on main street, drinking punch and eating food brought to them by villagers. Music filled the air, and women and girls had one last dance with their beaus. The minister of the Kingston Congregational Church, as well as Thomas P. Wells, gave reassuring speeches. Captain Rodman then announced that it was time for the soldiers to depart for the train. Wakefield's new newspaper, the *Narragansett Times*, reported that

> About 3 o'clock the volunteers formed in front of the Court House, and escorted by the Home Guards marched to the depot. A long train of vehicles proceeded and followed the companies, and the roads were thronged with people on foot. The procession occupied the whole slope of Kingston Hill extending nearly half a mile. Good judges estimated two thousand persons were at the station. There were many women and children who had come to say farewell to husbands, fathers and brothers. There were many parents, past the prime of life, who had come to bid their sons Godspeed. There were many moist eyes and quivering lips, but the moist eyes and quivering lips bespoke an emotion which did honor to the heartbeating beneath.

As the men of Company E rested in their tents, after fighting in the Battle of Bull Run and other horrible battles in the South, they must have reminisced longingly for the time that they enjoyed relaxing on Kingston's lawns.

Early in the Civil War, Captain Isaac Peace Rodman quickly became a favorite of the highest ranking Rhode Islander in the Civil War, General Ambrose Burnside of Cranston. Burnside was impressed with the conduct of the 2nd Rhode Island Volunteers in the Battle of Bull Run. Burnside detached Rodman from Company E and promoted him to Colonel of the Fourth Rhode Island Regiment. Rodman distinguished himself at the battle of Roanoke on February 8, 1862. On March 15, 1862, at the battle of New Bern, in North Carolina, at the crucial moment, Colonel Rodman on his own initiative ordered his troops to make a bayonet charge, which routed the surprised Confederates. Rodman was promoted to the rank of Brigadier General.

After helping Union troops capture Fort Macon, Rodman was struck down with typhoid fever. He was sent home to South Kingstown to recuperate. On his arrival at the Kingston Depot, he was met by a large delegation of local citizens, militia companies and a music band. Elizabeth Hagadorn, daughter of Kingston's Thomas R. Wells, wrote in a letter dated July 9, 1862 that when Rodman visited Kingston, he informed her that he "feels as well as ever save his strength" and that he was "anxious to be at his post." But she noted that Rodman was "still very thin and his limbs tremble very much when he walks." When Rodman's health was only partially restored, General Burnside wrote to him, asking that he return to the field in anticipation of a great battle. Rodman responded to the call and was placed in command of a division in the Ninth Corps of the Army of the Potomac as it marched towards Antietam. Rodman led his troops in the Battle of South Mountain. Sadly, on September 17, 1862, in the bloodiest single day of the war in the Battle of Antietam, Rodman was mortally wounded while sitting in the saddle on his horse. Rodman's body was brought to Providence where it lay in state with full honors given to him as New England's first general to be killed in the war.

Rodman's body was brought by train to the Kingston Depot, and then by horse-drawn funeral coach through Kingston to his home at the corner of Kingstown and Saugatucket Roads. Many mourners came to pay their respects; the procession that passed through Kingston extended the full two miles from the railroad station. This occasion was in sad contrast to the high hopes that townsmen felt on June 4, 1861 when Company E stood in front of the Court House before departing for war.

War Opposition in Kingston

Not everyone in Kingston village or the town of South Kingstown enthusiastically supported Union war efforts. South Kingstown was a strong Democratic town, and many former Democrats, including the Potter brothers, were angry that Republicans had, in their view, goaded the South into war.

Elizabeth Hagadorn, the daughter of Landholder Bank cashier Thomas R. Wells and a marvelous letter writer, commented on the lukewarm war support in her correspondence in 1861 with her brother, Amos Wells. Elizabeth noted that the Company E soldiers were mostly "operators in the factories and mechanics – some of whom were foreigners [Irish and other immigrants]," and that there "was not a farmer in the company." Most of the farmers, and the shopkeepers in Kingston, were rural Democrats who initially did not strongly support Union war efforts.

The Union loss at the Battle of Bull Run shocked northerners and helped to galvanize support for the war. Hagadorn achingly wrote of her acquaintances and townsmen who had been killed in the battle. In the case of one soldier from Company E who had died, Hagadorn had seen the soldier's mother on the day Company E departed Kingston "in a flood of tears." Hagadorn noted that the Battle of Bull Run had "wrought quite a change in the minds of some of our secessionists here – Elisha Clarke says now, he is ready to go and fight with all his might. Even John Larkin says he is ready to fight for law and government."

Divisions in the village broke out in the open when James B. M. Potter sought a position in the Union army, while at the same time publicly criticizing the Union cause. The younger brother of Elisha R. Potter, Jr., James had established textile mills at South Ferry and Usquepaug. Potter suffered "heavy losses on his goods" for several years and in February 1861 was forced to turn over his two mills and his interest in the South Ferry to the Landholders Bank and Kingston Savings Bank. At the age of 43, he was forced to find a new career. With the coming of the Civil War, he decided to seek a post as paymaster with the Union army. Elisha Potter was a close ally of Democratic Governor William Sprague's and he persuaded Governor Sprague to write a letter of recommendation for James to bring to Washington, D.C. But before he departed, James, a die-hard Democrat, shocked Kingston villagers with his anti-Union statements. Elizabeth Hagadorn, the daughter of Thomas R. Wells, wrote in a letter that Potter's "last wishes, before leaving home, were strongly expressed for the success of the rebels and denouncing the [Lincoln] administration in the severest language possible." This conduct was particularly hurtful to many villagers, as they had recently heard the news of the Union loss at the Battle of Bull Run. Hagadorn wrote that before July 4, 1862, someone had sent a letter to the proper authorities in Washington, D.C. alerting them of Potter's sentiments. The rumor was that villager John G. Clarke, Jr. had sent the missive. Clarke denied it to Hagadorn, but "felt sufficiently indignant to do so." Hagadorn concluded, bitterly, "I think we are in more danger from such traitors in the Cause than from the rebels." Potter ended up securing the job.

While Elisha Reynolds Potter, Jr. was not a military man, he played an important role in the state legislature. In some ways consistent with President Lincoln, Potter emphasized bringing the South back to the Union instead of emphasizing the defeat of the South and eliminating slavery. As a member of the Rhode Island senate at a special session on August 10, 1861, Potter introduced a resolution calling for the "full and sincere union of all political parties." While he spoke about the hope of restoring peace and the Union, he was enough of a realist to recognize that that was unlikely to occur and was prescient enough to recognize that Union goals in the war could change. At this early time in the war, most Union soldiers fought to preserve the union of the states. They did not want to see the country forged in the

Revolutionary War as an experiment in democracy become split into pieces and become like Europe, constantly fighting. Potter pledged the "entire resources" of the state "for the preservation of the Union." In his speech, Potter argued that the resources of the South, and the reasons that had led it to secession, were such that the North must expect a difficult war. Speaking only a few weeks after the Union's loss at the first Battle of Bull Run, Potter expected that the war would be a "bloody one." He noted, "compromise is for the present out of the question. Since the last battle, the South will not, and the North cannot with self-respect, offer terms of peaceable re-union." Yet Potter saw that the vision of why Union soldiers fought would eventually be transformed. He stated that "it seems to me" that "we are inevitably drifting" into "an anti-slavery war." Potter also expressed disbelief that the South would resort to a war which would have as its likely end result the destruction of slavery. The *Narragansett Times* reprinted Potter's entire speech on its front page.

Potter, to his credit, sponsored a bill in the state senate to give equal voting rights to naturalized citizens who fought in the Union forces. This would have included many Irish male immigrants who had been excluded from the voting rolls under the 1843 state constitution that Potter helped to draft. Wilkins Updike, however, helped to block the measure, which led to his being the target of a vitriolic attack in a Providence newspaper. At a town meeting held in June 1862, with Wilkins Updike serving as moderator, voters instructed their representatives to oppose legislation that would extend voting rights to native born citizens who did not otherwise satisfy legal requirements, on the ground that "no person ought to be allowed to vote in questions of taxation unless he is himself taxed."

Potter also pushed forward a state senate investigation as to whether an amendment to the state constitution was "necessary to prevent slaves who have escaped, or who may escape, from the Southern States into this State, from voting without proper restrictions." Potter was supported in this effort by Thomas P. Wells, a former abolitionist. Both men were concerned that slaves, lacking in education and experience being free, would not be informed voters. One former Virginia slave, John White, did settle in Kingston, where he died in 1895.

Raising Troops and Fighting Battles

Kingston men served in various military units. Charles Aldrich, son of Kingston cabinetmaker Luke Aldrich, in August 1861 joined as a second lieutenant the 3rd Regiment, Rhode Island Heavy Artillery. This regiment saw service on the South Carolina coast. Aldrich then served as first lieutenant in the 14th Regiment, Heavy Artillery. This regiment was primarily manned by black troops with white officers. As in the American Revolutionary War, local black men enlisted in military ranks as well. In August 1863, Samuel Potter, a black man from South and North Kingstown, worked to enlist 20 black men for the 14th regiment. The *Narragansett Times* noted that because Potter was drafted, he did not receive the $300 bonus that the 20 enlistees received. The *Narragansett Times* spoiled the compliment to Potter, writing that "Although a colored man, and belonging to an inferior race, he has shown himself more patriotic than his white superiors." This regiment garrisoned forts in Texas and Louisiana. South Kingstown black enlistees Charles Weeden, James Rooms, John Charles, Daniel Wamsley and James Wamsley died of disease. Frederic Potter, probably a relative of Samuel Potter's, died of combat wounds. Samuel Potter rose to the rank of sergeant.

In the 8th Regiment, Third Brigade, Kingston had four officers, including Major John G. Clarke, Jr. But this regiment never completed its formation.

Amos P. Wells, a son of villager Thomas R. Wells, served as a cashier of the Landholders Bank in Kingston for about three years from 1853 to 1856, and later served as an officer with the 20th New York Regiment of Colored Infantry. He frequently wrote letters to his relatives in Kingston about his war-time experiences, especially to Elizabeth Hagadorn. He contracted an illness in the army that led to his premature death in 1866. Storekeeper William Helme Case had twin sons who were raised in the old Helme House, both of whom enlisted in Rhode Island regiments and were killed in combat. A third son, John Peck Case, survived the army in a Connecticut regiment and returned to Kingston in 1869. In 1862, the *Narragansett Times* reported that Carroll H. Potter, the son of former Kingston attorney Asa Potter, Jr., had been killed in combat. Captain Potter was happy to correct that error and he also lived to retire to his birthplace, Kingston village.

A "home guard" outfit that consisted mostly of Kingston men was the Pettaquamscutt Light Infantry. It was led by Kingston's Colonel Elisha C. Clarke, who served as county court clerk and would serve after the Civil War in the General Assembly. Shortly before its assignment to the South, in May 1862, Kingston celebrated the outfit. The day started with the company going through drills on the lawn in between Thomas P. Wells' house and the Kingston Congregational Church. In the afternoon, the company, "with spirit-stirring fife and drum," demonstrated its marching technique in the village's streets. In the evening, the "ladies of Kingston" feted the company at the Peace Dale armory. A beautiful silk flag was brought into the room. With piano accompaniment, a choir of women sang the Star-Spangled Banner. A woman representative, dressed in red, white and blue, then stepped forward to give an impressive speech and to present the silk flag to the company. After Colonel Clarke accepted the flag, the call "choose partners for cotillion" was made and responded to by the soldiers and guests.

Unfortunately, the service of the Pettaquamscutt Light Infantry did not match the day's celebration. Forty-seven recruits agreed to join a Rhode Island regiment, in reliance on the recruiter's promise that they would have their full proportion of officers and non-commissioned officers. When they arrived in Washington, D.C., however, they were given only one position as officer and one as non-commissioned officer. It appears that some of the men became discouraged and returned to Kingston. Others joined another outfit, an artillery company in the 9th Regiment of Rhode Island volunteers. This outfit served primarily to man defenses approaching Washington, D.C. before their enlistments expired in three months. Enlistees included Alonzo Greenman, son of grocer Job Greenman, and John Taylor, Jr., son of the tavern keeper with the same name. In August 1863, the Pettaquamscutt Light Infantry joined with several other town companies to form the First Battalion of the 13th Regiment of Rhode Island militia. Elisha Clarke was unanimously elected as the battalion's major. This regiment did not see active service.

While it appears that only a few Kingston men fought in the Civil War as front-line soldiers, villagers heard and talked about stories of the many South Kingstown and other South County men who met horrible fates during their service in the Union army. One South County regiment, the 7th Regiment of Rhode Island Volunteers, fought in several major and minor battles from 1861 through 1864, and lost many men to battle and disease. For example, at the Battle of Bull Run near Manasses, Virginia in July 1861, Stephen Holland, a weaver from South Kingstown, was killed in the battle. Henry L. Jacques, a 43 year-old fisherman from South Kingstown, was wounded and taken prisoner, and later died in prison. At a camp at Pleasant, Maryland, Joseph Weeden Burdick of Hopkinton had his first assignment, but he soon contracted measles. While sitting in the hospital talking with his doctor, he suddenly fell backward and died. The cause was suspected to be heart disease aggravated by the "Yazoo fever." At another major battle at Fredericksburg, Virginia in December 1862, Charles Knowles, a wheelwright in South Kingstown, was killed on the field of battle. He left a wife and two children. Nicholas Mattewson was a mill worker in North Kingstown. While his regiment was standing at rest in the streets of Fredericksburg, Confederate artillery found its range. One of the shots struck Mattewson, taking off both of his feet. He died soon afterwards, leaving a wife and two children. In the searing heat of Mississippi, the 7th Regiment fought a battle on July 13, 1863. Jonathan R. Clarke, a South Kingstown farmer, was killed in the battle; he left a wife and twin boys, aged five years. John K. Hull of Tower Hill was killed before the battle while on picket duty. Hull wrote many thoughtful letters to family members that survive to this day. Captain Thomas Greene of North Kingstown helped to raise 30 men to enlist in the regiment. He fought in all of the regiment's battles, until he contracted a fever in Mississippi and was discharged. He became an invalid as a result of the fever's effects. The 7th Regiment fought in several small battles in Virginia near the end of the war in

September 1864. Stephen R. Clark, a Richmond cotton mill carder, was killed at the Battle of Pegram House. His brother, next to him in the battle, described his death: "A flying bullet broke Stephen's arm, and, in about five minutes, another bullet went through his heart, when he fell out of my arms dead."

1864: The Peace Party Versus the War Party in South Kingstown

As the war dragged on, and more Union soldiers were killed or suffered wounds in horrible battles, sentiment against the war increased in the North. This was particularly true in Democratic strongholds, such as rural South Kingstown. The appearance of Internal Revenue Service agents at the John N. Taylor tavern in Kingston to collect federal taxes (newly imposed to support the war) from local townsmen added to the anger of Democrats.

In March 1863, Elisha R. Potter, Jr., a leading Democrat, created a controversy, as a result of his relatively sympathetic view of the South. In the state senate, he introduced a resolution calling for the "settlement of our present national difficulties upon the basis of a restoration of the constitutional rights of all the States, as soon as it can honorably be done." Potter was calling for an end to the war and a return to the status quo permitting slavery. The resolution failed to pass. For most Rhode Islanders, the war had gone too far merely to return to the status quo.

Anti-war sentiment reached its pinnacle during the 1864 presidential election. In October 1864, at a crowded meeting of South Kingstown Democrats in the Kingston Court House, Elisha Potter delivered a speech in favor of General McClellan, President Lincoln's Democratic opponent who wanted to end the war. In response, on November 4, 1864, a large crowd of Republicans met at the Court House in support of Lincoln for President. Peace Dale's Rowland Hazard inveighed against the "Peace Party" and asked the crowd whether it wanted to "succumb to the South and give up all that we have conquered from it." Women were prominent at both gatherings. Elizabeth Hagadorn, a strong Republican supporter, in a letter to her brother Amos, wrote of the election's results. According to her, the Democrats (she called them "Copperheads," a derogatory term for Northerners who wanted to end the war immediately) expected that a majority of town voters would support McClellan. On election day, Hagadorn wrote with disgust that there were Democratic leaflets plastered on the village's trees and in the Court House, where the town voting took place, claiming that a second Lincoln administration would increase prices and taxes. To Hagadorn's great pleasure, a majority of South Kingstown voters voted for Lincoln (by only 26 votes). She wrote that while she was "ashamed that I live in a town that could give so *small* a majority against traitors, and rebels, I rejoice that the town has not been blackened by giving her votes in favor of them." Hagadorn mentioned the increasing popularity of the Republican Party "in our Coppery town."

Two of Elisha R. Potter, Jr.'s brothers served honorably in the war. The U.S. military gave them an honorable career, as it did many younger sons of well-born families. One brother, Dr. Thomas Mawney Potter (1814-1890), was educated at the Kingston Academy and Brown University, graduating from the latter school in 1834. He received training as a medical doctor with a Providence doctor. He then obtained a medical degree from the University of Pennsylvania in 1838. Thomas joined the U.S. Navy as an assistant surgeon in 1839, and later participated in the Mexican War. He served on many ships and sailed around the globe, including on one ship that became ship-wrecked on the Cape Verde Islands in 1850. He became a full surgeon in 1854 and served throughout the Civil War.

Elisha's brother James B. M. Potter served as a paymaster in the Union army, rising to the rank of lieutenant-colonel by war's end. In 1861, he personally met with President Lincoln in the White House in seeking the job. Lincoln, seeing the recommendation from Governor Sprague, signed his request, commenting that Rhode Island troops had responded well to his call for troops in early 1861. While stationed in Washington, D.C., Potter sometimes played cards with General Ulysses S. Grant.

James B. M. Potter also witnessed the tragic assassination of President Lincoln at Ford's Theatre in Washington, D.C. in April 1865. In the afternoon of the fateful day, newspapers advertised that President Lincoln and General Grant would attend Ford's Theatre that evening. Potter's view of Lincoln and the Union cause had likely shifted by war's end and he wanted the thrill of seeing in person these two men who had played such key roles in the Union victory. At the theatre that evening, Potter sat near the front row, with a good view of President Lincoln and his wife, Mary Todd Lincoln. President Lincoln rested his elbow on the railing of his theatre box, with his hand to his face, sometimes "turning around to look at the audience." During the performance, Potter heard the crack of a pistol and saw a man jump from the President's box. Potter yelled that the President had been shot and yelled for Dr. Morely, a friend of Potter's. Potter was asked to assist escorting Mary Lincoln out of the theatre and across the street to the home where President Lincoln had been taken. Potter said that Mary Lincoln kept exclaiming, "Oh why did they let him do it?" Potter also attended to Major Henry Rathbone, who had been in the box with the Lincolns and had been stabbed with a knife by the assassin, John Wilkes Booth, after Lincoln was shot. Potter wrote these recollections in a letter in 1890 to John Hay and John Nicolay, the authors of a famous Lincoln biography.

V. KINGSTON IN DECLINE;

KINGSTON SAVED,

(1866-1900)

Main Street, Kingston, Rhode Island (looking westward), circa 1890. The street was so little used that flowers could thrive right next to it. The elm trees survived until the 1938 hurricane destroyed them. *Pettaquamscutt Historical Society.*

Post-War Public School Developments

When the General Assembly first passed a law in 1800 providing that each town establish a public school, it limited the law's application to "the instruction of all the white citizens of said town between the ages of six and twenty years." Thus, there was no mandate for the towns to educate black persons or Native Americans. Providence finally established two black-only schools in 1838. Newport and Bristol followed Providence's lead in establishing separate schools for blacks.

While not clear, it appears to have been the case that public schools in South County were integrated in the 1800s. It was probably the case in colonial times that black children were not permitted to attend the Little Rest and Tower Hill school houses, which were one-room quasi-public schools. This policy probably changed after the Revolutionary War and the gradual emancipation of Rhode Island slaves. Thomas R. Hazard, in *The Jonny-Cake Papers,* recalled having attended the one-room school house at Tower Hill (around 1810) "with black Suke Watson on one side of me . . . ." Records indicate that the Kingston Sabbath School Society permitted black children to attend Sunday School at the Kingston Congregational Church. In 1833, out of at total of 169 children in attendance in the Sunday School, 18 were black (5 boys and 13 girls).[31] Since many of Kingston's adults attended the Congregational Church, this may be an indication that the local Number 3 School District also held integrated classes. There is also no record of a dispute or decision to permit black children to attend the Kingston public school. In the subsequent battles to enact a bill to desegregate public schools, only Providence, Newport and Bristol were mentioned as having segregated schools. The Fayerweathers sent a few of their children to schools in New Bedford, probably because they believed that the New Bedford schools were superior to the Kingston public school, and not because the Kingston school excluded black students. If the Kingston public school and other rural South County public schools accepted black students in the early 1800s, it was probably in part due to the desire among the rural towns to avoid having to pay additional taxes to support a separate school for black children.

During the 1850s, the General Assembly was pressed by African-American businessman George Downing and other reformers to eliminate the "separate but equal" education that kept black children in separate (and usually inferior) city schools. But fear of Providence segregationists prevented any movement on the issue. With the Civil War came the

---

[31] The percentage of black Sunday School children, just under 10%, probably is a fair indication of the percentage of black persons who resided in Kingston and the surrounding area in 1833.

realization of the hypocrisy of Rhode Islanders fighting to free black slaves in the South, while at the same time denying free blacks full rights at home. This was another example of a cataclysmic event involving democracy and freedom forcing the white majority to liberalize policies in the treatment of blacks (the first event was, of course, the American Revolution, which led to the emancipation of Rhode Island blacks from slavery). In 1865, Wager Weeden of Westerly delivered an impassioned speech in the General Assembly demanding that blacks be given their full rights as citizens, including the right of black children to attend schools with white children. Rowland Hazard of South Kingstown, then running for Lieutenant Governor, also supported desegregation. Finally, in 1866, the General Assembly passed a statute providing that no person could be excluded from a public school "on account of the race or color of the applicant." A photograph of a class in the Kingston public school in 1884 shows five black students out of 18 students.

In general, public schools were reducing the rate of illiteracy, but problems persisted, particularly in the Irish and black communities. In 1865, 8% of Rhode Island adults could neither read nor write. But most of the illiteracy was centered among immigrants, with a 21.73% illiteracy rate for all immigrants and a 27% rate among those with Irish parents. Blacks had a 15.3% illiteracy rate. The illiteracy rate among whites who had non-immigrant parents was down to 1.3%.

Tensions arose between Kingston and the growing villages of Wakefield and Peace Dale when the Hazard family sought to improve the education of the latter two villages by erecting the town's first stand-alone high school. In 1874, the Hazard family offered to give land to erect a high school building in Peace Dale and to provide some funds for operations, on condition that South Kingstown taxpayers support a portion of funding the school with taxes. Kingston residents opposed the plan. A farmer wrote in the *Narragansett Times,* "we are already taxed to support a common school, which make our taxes high enough. The farmers work hard for their money, and have but little after their bills are paid, and when the cold weather comes on, they deny themselves many of the comforts and luxuries of life."

Elisha R. Potter, Jr., the former Commissioner of Education in Rhode Island, found himself in the awkward position of opposing the building of a stand-alone high school in the town. Understandably, in an age before the automobile, Kingston residents did not want to pay taxes for a school that their children could not attend due to transportation limitations. What was needed was a special school district tax in Peace Dale and Wakefield, but this was not seriously considered. In a letter published in 1875 in the *Narragansett Times,* Elisha R. Potter, Jr. wrote,

> I suppose a great many of the people of Peace Dale have been made to believe that we are opposed to their having a high school there. We are indeed opposed to being taxed to support a school there . . . There is wealth enough in Peace Dale to endow a school without anybody there having a teaspoonful less of anything for breakfast, and without taxing the distant and poorer portions of the town for it. They have a splendid church, which is a credit to the place and to those who built it; a high school would cost a great deal less.

Neither the General Assembly nor the South Kingstown town meeting voted to support the high school. Finally, with donations from Edward Robinson and Rowland Hazard, the town's first high school was established in 1880.

Up North Road in Kingston, the public schoolhouse for District Number 3 (the former Kingston Academy building built in 1823) fell into disrepair. In 1879, public school was held in a private home in Kingston. In 1882, School House No. 3 finally burned down. The next year, a 2 1/2 story schoolhouse was built for $3,000. It was owned and operated by the town of South Kingstown as a public school, with some funding from the Sewall fund. In the 1890-91 school year, average attendance was only 17 students, which was described as "very poor" in an official report. There were continual complaints about the quality of the teaching. It was decided that the best teachers for the money were women, and a number of women were hired. The town superintendent of schools wrote, "The Kingston district has found that a higher grade of teacher can be obtained for the same amount of money by employing a woman rather than a man, and a considerable advance has been made there during the year." In other words, female teachers of high quality could be paid the same as male teachers of poor quality.

Bernon Helme of Kingston became superintendent in the 1894-95 school year, and he promoted the end of the district system and the adoption of a town system of managing schools. Helme reported that under the current district system, "the teachers are responsible to the district not the school committee." By contrast, the town's school committee and superintendent "are a tolerated legal invasion." Accordingly, Helme wrote, the "quality of any particular school depends upon the ability of its teacher." Helme's recommendation was finally adopted in 1902.

Another problem was the length of the school year. The few districts that imposed a school tax kept school open for nine months. Other school districts kept school open only for the legally required six months. Kingston's school, which imposed taxes on school district residents, had an eight-month school year.

The Opening of the Narragansett Pier Railroad

After the Civil War, Peace Dale and Wakefield continued to thrive. The Hazard family's Peace Dale textile mills employed hundreds of workers. Narragansett Pier rose to become a premier vacation spot, with its superlative beach and cool summer winds.

Pressure began to build for the construction of a new railroad line from the Kingston Station to Narragansett Pier. Passengers disembarking at the Kingston Station found the stagecoach ride to Peace Dale, Wakefield and Narragansett Pier uncomfortable. While a new road opened in 1850 from Kingston to Wakefield and Peace Dale (current Kingstown Road or Route 108) helped, the journey was still inconvenient. The growth of summer visitors to Narragansett Pier was limited due to this inconvenience. The *New York Herald* wrote of Narragansett Pier, "Heaven has many attractions but is unpopular because of the difficulty of getting there." Significantly, the Hazards of Peace Dale began to consider the benefits that a railroad line could bring to their mill business. They shipped to their mills huge amounts of raw materials (raw cotton and wool) and coal to generate steam for their mills. They also shipped their finished products to national commercial markets. At the time, they were largely using wagons to transport raw materials, coal and finished products to and from Narragansett Pier, which had some docking facilities. The Hazards saw that having a train stop next to their mills to deliver the raw materials and coal, and to pick up the finished products and carry them to the Narragansett Pier, would reduce their operating costs and make their business more efficient.

In the 1860s, Rowland G. Hazard attempted to raise interest in constructing a railroad line from Kingston Station to Narragansett Pier. On June 22, 1868, Hazard and the powerful A. & W. Sprague Company were granted a charter to build the line, to be called the Narragansett Pier Railroad. Later that summer, a survey was completed for the route of the railroad. Ominously for Kingston villagers, the route avoided Kingston Hill and instead skirted around Larkin's Pond and Teft's Hill to the south of the village. Efforts to build the railroad line then slowed, as competing charters to build other railroads in South County made investors skittish about investing in the Narragansett Pier Railroad. The collapse of the Sprague commercial empire in 1872 meant that financing the railroad would be left to the Hazard family and a few Wakefield investors and Narragansett Pier hotel owners. In April 1875, with the charter about to expire, Rowland G. Hazard led a meeting in Peace Dale that established the railroad company.

On June 15, 1875, at a meeting in Peace Dale, the members voted to order two separate surveys to be made – one with the Larkin's Pond and Teft's Hill route, and the second passing through Kingston village. Kingston villagers fought hard to have the route pass through their village, even though it was the more expensive and difficult route since the railroad would have to climb up steep Kingston Hill and pass through a settled community. But Kingston villagers realized that if the railroad bypassed their village, so would economic development. Throughout New England, along railroad depot stops, manufacturing centers arose and development occurred.

The railroad dispute was particularly difficult for Kingston residents due to the driving force behind the railroad, Rowland G. Hazard. He was well known to Kingston residents, as he had been a member of the Kingston Congregational Church for many years. In 1857, he had the church's blessing to depart and start the Peace Dale Congregational Church.

Elisha R. Potter, Jr. took the lead in promoting the Kingston route. He helped Kingston residents raise a fund of $13,500 to meet the additional expenses of the Kingston route, plus $1,500 for a depot in Kingston. Potter and Hazard engaged in contentious negotiations. It did not help Potter that the two had tangled previously when Potter had publicly opposed Hazard's idea of imposing a town tax to support a public high school in Peace Dale.

On January 22, 1876, at a meeting of all stockholders held in Peace Dale, more debate ensued over the location of the line. The pastor of the Kingston Congregational Church, J. Hagadorn Wells, promoted the Kingston route, and Rowland G. Hazard promoted the Larkin's Pond and Teft's Hill route. With the Hazard family and their allies controlling a large majority of the shares in the company, the issue was never in doubt. As a gesture of "friendship with the Kingston people," Rowland Hazard permitted his personal shares to be voted by William Potter in favor of the Kingston route. When the final vote was taken, 492 shares were voted in favor of the Larkin's Pond and Teft's Hill route and 180 shares were voted for the Kingston route. Only 30 shares in addition to those owned by Rowland Hazard were voted in favor of the Kingston route. Kingston villagers were dispirited.

After the vote, Potter and Hazard engaged in an ugly exchange of letters published in the *Narragansett Times*. Potter pointed out the many lawsuits that Hazard was involved in, as an indication of his character. Potter wrote that Hazard "complains that I urged him to adopt the Kingston route. In answer to his professions of goodwill, I did say that the road would be made just where he wanted it to be. He observed in reply, that he was obliged to *consult his partners.* I did not laugh in his face, but I began to think he was growing old and disposed to give up the concerns of this world, excepting of course his lawsuits." In turn, Hazard excoriated Potter for threatening in negotiations "lawsuits and injunctions" against the railroad and asserting that the charter for the Narragansett Pier Railroad Company was void. Hazard questioned Potter's judicial ethics, as at the time these threats were made Potter was a justice on the Rhode Island Supreme Court and would profit from the route being laid through Kingston.

After this exchange, the Potter family of Kingston developed a grudge against Rowland G. Hazard's family. At Elisha Potter's funeral in 1882, a newspaper reported that "Several gentlemen on reaching the house to attend the funeral were requested to leave the premises, which they did. The reason stated was the signing of a certain paper against the Judge a few years ago." The "gentlemen" may have been Rowland Hazard, his brothers and his sons.

After the failure of the vote to have the Narragansett Pier Railroad pass through Kingston, Kingston villagers met at the Court House to form a committee to analyze the feasibility of building a railroad line from Kingston Station to Kingston and on to South Ferry. These "Kingston Branch" plans, along with several others, were not financially viable and failed to materialize.

On July 18, 1876, a new locomotive named the "Narragansett 2" started out from Kingston Station with two new cars filled with members of the South Kingstown town council, railroad officials and prominent citizens. The train, decked out in flags and bouquets, made its initial run on newly-built railroad tracks to Narragansett Pier in twenty minutes and made the return trip in a quick fourteen minutes. Rowland Hazard was able to take a train from Peace Dale in the morning, arrive in Providence for a meeting less than two hours later, and return home that afternoon.

A new station house was built near the old Kingston Station and opened on June 1, 1875. Still in use today, the station shared a platform with the Stonington line. Other stations were built in Peace Dale, Wakefield and Narragansett Pier. By September 1, 1876, an estimated 20,000 passengers had traveled on the Narragansett Pier Railroad.

The impact on Kingston was immediate. The John N. Taylor tavern (the former Joseph Reynolds tavern) had provided stagecoaches for passengers disembarking at Kingston Station and seeking to travel to Wakefield, Peace Dale and Narragansett Pier. Wealthy tourists often stopped for refreshment at the Taylor tavern on their way to the seashore. With the coming of the Narragansett Pier Railroad, the stagecoaches were no longer needed, except if a passenger wanted to go to Kingston or its surroundings. Only a trickle of transient travelers stopped at the Taylor tavern. Kingston was also no longer needed as a depot for the stagecoaches and horses. The last trip of the mail stagecoach from West Kingston to Narragansett was made on February 28, 1877. After that date, the mail was delivered by the railroad to each of the town's depots, not just to Kingston Station. In addition, a marble cutting shop that was operated by Charles Aldrich on the site of the current Kingston Hill Store, and that had two other employees (one white and one black), was moved to West Kingston, with the hope that the proximity to the railroad would increase business. With the railroad extension, more changes would be coming to Kingston.

The Removal of the Town Hall and Court House from Kingston

The General Assembly enacted a law requiring that it meet only in Providence. The last session of the General Assembly held at the Court House in Kingston was in October 1853. No longer would the state's politicians travel by train, stagecoach or horse to Kingston for General Assembly sessions. This was another blow to the village's pride and to the business of the taverns. Still, Kingston continued to be the seat for the Washington County courts, the seat for South Kingstown's town council meetings and town meetings, and the location of the town clerk's office.

County court day continued to be an exciting time in Kingston. The *Narragansett Times* reported that at the August 1859 county court term, "an extraordinary large number of people were in attendance . . . and the usually quiet village has presented quite a lively and stirring scene." Rather than meet in one of Kingston's taverns, the South Kingstown town council began meeting in the Court House in 1858. The town clerk's office was also in the Court House. By 1855, the local justices court began meeting in the Court House. Arnold and Hoag, authors of a *History of Rhode Island*, wrote of Kingston, "Some considerable business is transacted here, and the place, from its peculiar position as the seat of the county government, bears an importance surpassed by no other village in the town."

Efforts were made to improve the Court House. In 1858, a small, stone building next to the Court House was built to store county court records. Called the "archives," it purportedly was one of the first fireproof buildings in the region. In 1855, the ornamental iron fence, which still surrounds the grounds, was put in, and the lawn was graded. Prior to that time, it was not uncommon to see stray farm animals grazing in front of the Court House. In 1861, the massive stone steps at the entrance to the building were put in place and a year later the railings at the side were added. In 1870, the town voted to purchase a fireproof safe in which to store town records in the town clerk's office. In 1875, a new weather vane in the shape of an eagle was placed on the roof. In 1876, the Court House was substantially altered, from the colonial, barn-like structure it had been for 100 years. The present ornamental mansard roof and tower were added.

In 1858, the Washington County jail in Kingston also benefited from an overhaul. Daniel Rodman and Edward Hazard reported to the General Assembly that the sixty year-old structure was "not only unsafe, but uncomfortable, and dangerous to the health of those who may be confined therein." There had been a number of escapes and "any person of ingenuity could easily break out of it." They urged the General Assembly to fund the construction of a new jail. The General Assembly agreed, and the current granite jail house was built in 1858. Eight cells measuring six by eight feet were constructed. The outside was built of solid granite walls. The local blacksmiths, the Fayerweather brothers, made and installed the iron bars for the windows. In addition, as a result of a resolution introduced by Wilkins Updike in the General Assembly, a new jailer's residence was built onto the front of the jail in 1861. John Eldred of Kingston won the contract for excavation, masonry, plastering and obtaining the granite locally. The new jailer moved his wife and family into the new residence, living in much greater comfort than his predecessors.

Despite the efforts to upgrade the Court House, because of Kingston's failure to keep pace with industrial and transportation developments in Peace Dale, Wakefield and Narragansett Pier, Kingston was destined to lose the last functions of the Court House as the town hall and county court. In 1875, the patrons served by local post offices were Kingston – 267; Peace Dale – 855; Rocky Brook – 210; Wakefield – 406. Kingston had less than one-sixth of the total. In the *Narragansett Times,* most of the advertisements were by Wakefield stores. The contrast between Kingston and Peace Dale was reflected in part by their congregational churches. In 1857, Rowland Hazard and others financed the construction of a modern, limestone church edifice, with large and beautiful stained glass windows. By comparison, the staid, wooden and white Kingston meeting house was old-fashioned.

Emboldened by the opening of the Narragansett Pier Railroad, South Kingstown town council members, and persons having business with the town council from Peace Dale, Wakefield and Narragansett Pier, began to complain that Kingston was too far removed from their homes. This sounded like the argument that Elisha Reynolds made to persuade the General Assembly to remove the Court House from Tower Hill to Little Rest in 1752. But it was true that most of the business of the town council concerned the expanding areas of Wakefield, Peace Dale and Narragansett, and not Kingston.

In January 1877, a petition signed by a number of South Kingstown citizens was presented to the town council proposing that a special town meeting be called on March 10th to act on a proposal to purchase a lot and erect a building for the use of the town. The town council voted to support the petition. All parties understood that what was at stake was the removal of the town hall from Kingston to Wakefield. At the March 10th town meeting, held at the Court House, the voters supported the acquisition of a lot and the construction of a new town hall in Wakefield. Prominent Peace Dale and Wakefield citizens were appointed to purchase a lot and erect a building for the use by the town. Shortly thereafter, a lot in Wakefield was acquired and construction of a new town hall was begun, all at private expense.

By January 1, 1878, a new town hall had been built in Wakefield and was ready for occupancy. On January 28, 1878, the town council met for the first time in the new building. As one of the first items of business, the town council considered a resolution regarding the new town hall building to direct the town clerk "to take possession of said building and remove all town and probate records, and all property, books and documents to said building without delay." The Kingston villagers, however, did not go down without a fight. The Kingston supporters on the town council voted against acceptance (thereby disregarding the town meeting vote). But the Kingston supporters were outvoted, 4-3, with the result that the town hall was removed to Wakefield. Feelings must not have run too hot, as the town council voted unanimously to purchase twenty spittoons for use by the public when visiting the new building.

The town council meetings, town meetings, and town clerk's business, which had been conducted in Kingston since 1752, would now be conducted in Wakefield. By the early 1890s, the local justices court (renamed the District Court in 1886) would move to the Wakefield town hall as well.

Significantly, Kingston still was the county seat for sessions of the Washington County common pleas and supreme courts. But some county residents viewed Kingston's position as vulnerable after the extension of the railroad in 1876 and the vote to remove the town hall in 1877. Westerly residents complained about having to travel to Kingston for county court sessions. In 1877, and for several years thereafter, a serious but unsuccessful effort was made to make Westerly a co-county seat. County residents from the Westerly area were annoyed having to make the inconvenient trip to Kingston. Judge Elisha Potter rejected a request to remove 56 cases to Westerly, even with the parties' consent, on the disingenuous ground that the court could not insure that fraud would be avoided in Westerly.

By 1890, lawyers and judges from Providence and other places who had to use the Kingston Court House were complaining about enduring the stagecoach ride from Kingston Station to Kingston. In 1891, the General Assembly appointed a commission to consider removing the court house to a more suitable location. Wickford and Westerly lobbied to be selected. Accepting the commission's recommendation, the General Assembly voted to build a new court house in West Kingston, within walking distance of the "Kingston Depot" railroad station. In 1894, the new granite Romanesque-style building was completed and the county court was removed from Kingston to West Kingston.

The county jail, owned by the state, was kept in Kingston, hardly an honor. The jail's use declined with the advent of the railroad and the arrival of the automobile. Prisoners could be kept more securely in the state facilities at Cranston. The jail continued to be used for holding prisoners during county court sessions, even after the court was removed to West Kingston. Still, prisoners escaped from the jail, one in 1878 and one in 1879. In hard times, the jail was used to shelter "tramps" who jumped off trains at Kingston Depot.

The Kingston Free Library: Its Proud Founding and a Bitter Feud

As neighboring Wakefield, Peace Dale and the Narragansett Pier began to overshadow Kingston, Kingston villagers turned inward and began to squabble among themselves. This was reflected in a struggle for control of one of the village's proudest institutions, the Kingston Free Library and Reading Room, and over church control of villagers' lives.

The beginnings of the Kingston Free Library and Reading Room went back to 1824, when a group of villagers met at the Court House to discuss establishing a library. At the meeting, forty-nine men founded a "social Library to be kept at Little Rest." The men included many of the same families who signed their names to establish the church: Potters, Taylors, Wells, Peckhams, Hazards and Watsons. In addition to Elisha R. Potter, Sr., thirteen-year-old Elisha R. Potter, Jr. signed his name. The Reverend Oliver Brown was elected president of the library society and was its first librarian. With subscriptions from the founders and fees and donations, Reverend Brown collected about 150 volumes. The founders signed up to purchase shares in the library society, but a number failed to follow through with their commitments. Of the original 49 founders, by 1827 fifteen had paid up on time, twenty-five were delinquent, and nine had not paid. Elisha R. Potter, Sr. did not pay for his shares until 1834. By that year, interest in the library among villagers had waned.

In 1839, Elisha R. Potter, Jr. took steps to revitalize the village library. Potter was aware that the General Assembly was preparing a law to permit the incorporation of libraries. In anticipation of this change, he purchased additional shares, bringing his ownership to eight of the outstanding twenty-three shares. Potter and the remaining fourteen shareholders successfully petitioned the General Assembly to incorporate the Kingston Library Society. Potter then added a great number of his books to establish a circulating library. He prepared a catalogue of books and a recommended reading list for his fellow villagers. By 1848, the circulating library had about 400 volumes in four large bookcases. The bookcases were circulated in Kingston and other town villages. In 1856, Thomas P. Wells printed a catalogue containing a list of about 1,300 books. While the library previously had rotated among the homes of villagers, by 1852 its volumes were stored in what is now the Tavern Hall Club, which at the time was owned by Elisha R. Potter, Jr. By 1873, the library had again declined, and its volumes had reverted back to Potter.

In 1873, villagers expressed an interest for informal gatherings other than in the small stores in the village. This time, the organization of the library was accomplished under the auspices of the Kingston Congregational

Church. At a church meeting held in the home of Reverend J. Hagadorn Wells on February 17, 1873, three villagers were selected to develop a plan for a reading room. Soon thereafter, formal committees were elected by the church for the management of what would soon become known as the Reading Room and Circulating Library. The committee for the management of the library was selected by the church. Elisha R. Potter, Jr. deeded hundreds of volumes to the Presbyterian Society, the secular arm of the Kingston Congregational Church, to start up the library. A small building that stood just west of the Court House on what is now Upper College Road was rented by the Presbyterian Society as the location of the Reading Room and Circulating Library. When the building was dedicated for its new use on the evening of May 8, 1873, the Reverend Wells presented the keys to the first president, Henry T. Braman, "charging him to see that a good use be made of them, and that nothing foul or unclean pass over the threshold." As the committee for the Reading Room and Library made its first formal entry into the newly-dedicated building, fireworks were set off at the side of the road in celebration by villagers.

The catalogue for the library issued in 1877 shows 1,481 volumes. Hoag and Wade's *History of Rhode Island*, published in 1878, devoted most of its paragraph on Kingston on the library:

> It has a library and public-reading room, and contains a fine collection of literary works, the greater number of which were the contribution of Judge Potter. This library receives from the State an annual appropriation of $25 for every five hundred volumes. The reading-room is open every day, with the exception of Sunday, when it is open for a few hours in the afternoon. The reading-room is sustained by voluntary contributions. This, indeed, is a worthy institution, and is highly prized by the citizens of Kingston.

Kingston villagers were rightfully proud of their library when Hoag and Wade visited the Library and Reading Room, probably before 1878. Shortly thereafter, however, a bitter feud over the control of the library and reading room broke out in the village. The feud shook the foundations of the village's two most prized institutions, the Kingston Library and Reading Room and the Kingston Congregational Church.

A key role in the feud was played by the Reverend J. Hagadorn Wells, who began serving as pastor of the Kingston Congregational Church in 1862. He was the son of Thomas R. Wells, the first deacon of the church, who kept a general store in the village for many years and later became cashier of the Landholders Bank. J. Hagadorn Wells' mother, Maria Potter Robinson, was the daughter of Asa Potter, who was the brother of Elisha R.

Potter, Sr. J. Hagadorn Wells attended the Kingston Academy and graduated from Amherst College in 1837. He then studied law under Elisha R. Potter, Jr. in Hopkinton, Rhode Island. In November 1842, in the midst of the Dorr Rebellion, the 25-year old Wells was elected by Hopkinton as a Law and Order Party delegate to the Landholders Convention to form a new constitution. After his father passed away in 1853, J. Hagadorn Wells returned to Kingston. In 1857, he opened a small school for boys in the rear of his house next to the church. When his wife died in 1862, Wells found it necessary to close the school. But by then he had turned to the ministry and was selected as pastor of the Kingston Congregational Church in 1862.

The Reverend Wells had some initial success. After a short service in the Kingston meeting house on Sunday, June 14, 1868, the whole congregation traveled to Larkin's Pond where the Reverend Wells baptized thirteen men and women by immersion. In the next month, twenty new members joined the church. New members included the African-American village blacksmiths, Solomon and Daniel Fayerweather, and their wives. Solomon Fayerweather served as sextant of the church for many years.

The Reverend Wells promoted moral reform in the church. Throughout his pastorate, he was an ardent supporter of the temperance movement, serving as a member of the board of the Rhode Island Temperance Union and as secretary of the Washington County Temperance Society. This may have put him in conflict with his former mentor, Elisha R. Potter, Jr., who led a movement in the state in 1863 to repeal prohibition. In 1870, the Kingston Congregational Church adopted a resolution condemning gambling and pledging that none of its members would participate in gambling or lotteries. In addition, at about this time, church members voted that "the sisters of this church have an equal right with the brethren to deliberate and vote on all questions that come before them." Women would not have the right to vote in federal and state elections until the 19th Amendment to the U.S. Constitution was adopted in 1920.

The village feud began when, in an attempt to assert control over the Kingston Free Library and Reading Room, Reverend Wells called for certain changes in its management. He may have wanted the church to control the content of the library's offerings. This can be gleaned from his admonition at the opening ceremony in 1873 to permit nothing "foul or unclean" to enter the library.

Reverend Wells' power play produced a sharp reaction in the village. While villagers were willing to have church control over certain areas of their lives (for example, the drinking of alcohol), they drew the line when it came to control over the books they could read. Villagers split into two factions. One faction, led by the Reverend J. Hagadorn Wells, asserted that the church should manage the library. The other faction, led by James Rose, believed that the library should be independent of church control. Rose was probably the front man for Elisha R. Potter, Jr., who never became a church member. In the end, Elisha R. Potter, Jr. withdrew from the library his numerous books and newspapers that he had contributed to its collection and transferred them to an independent, secular committee. On March 12, 1877, the church committee for the library, after a bitter debate, voted twelve to eight to transfer the remainder of the library to the new committee. With Potter's help, the library was reopened as a free library.

The trauma from the library feud, however, was not over. After the committee meeting, Herbert J. Wells began to interrogate the Reverend Wells, his cousin, about certain statements he had made in a recent sermon. This led to an extension of the feud. On April 6, 1877, church members gathered in the house of Deacon Thomas P. Wells, the Reverend Wells' brother, and passed a resolution calling for the resignation of the Reverend Wells as pastor of the Kingston Congregational Church. When the Reverend Wells refused to resign and failed to appear at the pulpit the next two Sundays, the church members met again at Deacon Thomas P. Wells' house and voted to request the Reverend Wells' resignation. The Reverend Wells refused to recognize the authority of the church members. The members then voted to remove him from his position. The Reverend Wells bitterly told his sister that Kingston "ought not to have a Church here or any minister." A new minister was selected, but he found it very difficult to do his job as J. Hagadorn Wells remained in the village, and continued the feud for several years afterwards. J. Hagadorn Wells held his brother Thomas P. Wells primarily responsible for his removal. William D. Metz, the historian who authored *The History of the Kingston Congregational Church*, wrote that "so intense was his [Reverend Wells'] bitterness that he refused to speak to his brother again, although he lived almost directly across Kingstown Road from the bank where his brother was cashier."

In 1891, the General Assembly adopted an act to incorporate the Kingston Free Library and Reading Room. In May 1894, all the books in the library were transferred to the new not-for-profit corporation. Once the county court was removed to West Kingston in 1894, the Court House sat unused. The old Court House was the logical place to house the library's growing collection. In that same year, the state of Rhode Island agreed to lease the court house building to the Kingston Free Library and Reading Room, where it remains today. The expenses of the library were for many years funded by a one dollar tax on certain village residents and the proceeds of a village fair.

Bucolic Kingston: A Future "as Bright as Pewter"

Bypassed by the industrial revolution and the age of transportation, and losing its status as the county and town seat of government, Kingston fell into a decline. It became a quiet, introverted, bucolic village. South County historian Oliver H. Stedman wrote that after the failure of the Narragansett Pier Railroad to pass through Kingston in 1876,

> Kingston people went into sort of a decline and for years following seemed to avoid any interest in the lower villages. Even when I was growing up, Kingston and its inhabitants were felt to be a group apart and there arose a popular saying throughout the State that the village of Kingston was only known for "its beautiful elm trees and dead broke aristocracy."

While Stedman claimed that the saying was "most unfair," it probably contained more truth than not. The "dead broke aristocracy" probably was a reference to the financial troubles of the Potter brothers.

Part of Kingston's problem was beyond its control. It was a hub of the agricultural community in South Kingstown, but the decades from 1870 to 1900 were miserable years for most New England farmers. With the large and productive farms in the Midwest producing bumper crops that were transported relatively cheaply by railroad to eastern markets, crop prices in New England fell drastically. At the same time, Providence had become the manufacturing, financial and political center of the state.

In 1875, at a meeting of the Kingston Lyceum, a debating and social club in the village, J. M. Aldrich gave the following toast regarding "The Future of Kingston":

> As I look back into the dim future
> I see a prospect as bright as pewter.
> As down the long vista the vision expands
> I see old Kingston just where it stands

Kingston village was lovely, charming and timeless. A classic picture of main street, later made into a postcard, shows an unpaved road lined with elm trees, white picket fences, and granite posts for tying up horses. A flower-strewn stretch of lawn and moss encroaches onto the street. The street was so little used that flowers could thrive right next to it. The old village well sits snugly within the moss.

Kingston attracted a few vacationers who enjoyed the quiet beauty of the village and the cheap prices at the Taylor tavern and other boarding houses. The current Tavern Hall Club from 1872 to 1875 was the summer home of Madame Pauline Lucca, a famous Viennese Opera singer who was then performing in New York City. But Kingston lacked the obvious advantages of Narragansett and other places along South County's ocean shores and never became a vacation destination.

Fittingly, at Biscuit City Pond, where unsuccessful efforts had been made at manufacturing in an attempt by Kingston villagers to keep pace with developments in the industrial revolution, the Great Spring became a favorite picnic ground. The path to the run-down mill site became a lover's lane.

Thomas P. Wells wrote to a son in Kansas in 1874, "Our village does not grow much and probably never will. But since I have been living here (about 14 years) there have been four new houses built where there were none before . . . ." Some of the new houses up North Road and down South Road were built in the Victorian style. But growth was slow compared to the manufacturing centers of Peace Dale and Wakefield and the resort village of Narragansett Pier. By 1895, with 409 inhabitants, Kingston was only the fourth largest village in South Kingstown.

Potter Homestead, Farm Scene, circa 1880. *Pettaquamscutt Historical Society.*

The old Court House, although no longer used for official town business after 1877 and county business after 1894, was still an important building for the village. After 1895, the first floor housed the Kingston Free Library and Reading Room. In post-Civil War Kingston, the Court House was used for music concerts, dances, lectures and political party meetings. Its use was controlled by the state, through the office of the county sheriff, who in 1871 caused a stir by refusing to permit a band to give a concert in the Court House. In 1874, the Washington County Agricultural Society was established and the Washington County Fair had its beginnings on the second-floor meeting room in the Court House. On the day before the Washington County Fair (held near the West Kingston railroad depot), herds of cattle and sheep on foot, and hogs and chickens in wagons, would be driven through Kingston on the way to the fair grounds. In 1888, an estimated 20,000 to 30,000 persons attended the fair.

Many of Kingston's talented men found it necessary to leave the village to pursue their careers. Elisha R. Potter, Jr., as the eldest son of Elisha R. Potter, Sr., inherited the Homestead and was able to reside their for the remainder of his life. But after experiencing financial troubles in 1861, he had to practice law in Newport and from 1868 to 1882 he served as a justice on the state supreme court in Providence. His younger brothers had to leave Kingston, with two finding careers in the military. William Potter became a successful attorney in a Providence law firm. From the Mexican War, to the Civil War and afterwards, Dr. Thomas Mawney Potter served in the U.S. Navy, traveling around the world. He became a medical director in 1871 and retired in 1876. James B. M. Potter inherited land in Usquepaug and South Ferry, and showed initiative in building successful factories in those locations. But after those business failed in 1861, he joined the Union army as a paymaster, and remained in the army after the war, serving in New Mexico, California, and other posts, until he retired in 1882.

Elisha Potter's brothers all retired to a quiet life in Kingston village. William Potter, who retired early due to a medical condition, lived in the fine Federal house on main street built by Asa Potter. Thomas resided in the house built by his great-grandfather Elisha Reynolds, in what is now the Tavern Hall Club. Dr. Potter became an early collector of colonial furniture, including several fine pieces made by the famed Newport cabinetmakers, Townsend & Goddard. James also retired to a small house on South Road.

Thomas P. Wells, the talented son of storekeeper and banker Thomas R. Wells, struggled to find profitable employment in Kingston and the local area. Wells started out, after graduating from the Kingston Academy in about 1825, teaching at a public school in Kingston in 1828, reportedly the first one in the village. He then served as a clerk in the general stores of Thomas Taylor in Kingston and Governor Thurston in Hopkinton. In 1829, he was hired as cashier of the Narragansett Bank in Wickford. After health problems, he returned to Kingston, built a fine house next to the church in 1832, and opened a general store in the eastern part of the building. In 1835, he moved to Wakefield, serving as the first cashier of the Wakefield Bank. Wells shortly later returned to Kingston, entering into partnership with aging general storekeeper Thomas Taylor. This partnership did not last, so he opened his own village store that had previously been operated by Benjamin Palmer. He also served two years as clerk of the Washington County supreme court. He resigned in 1843, returning again as cashier of the Wakefield Bank. He became interested in publishing, and in 1855 issued the first editions of *The Narragansett Times.* In 1856, due to low numbers of subscribers, he shut the paper down. He later hired editor Duncan Gillies, who reissued the newspaper in 1859. Finally, in 1861, Wells sold the paper and returned to Kingston, assuming the position of cashier of the Landholders Bank, succeeding Asa Potter. Wells remained in this position until his death in 1884. Most of Wells' sons left Rhode Island to pursue careers in Kansas, Chicago, and the U.S. army. One son, Herbert Johnson Wells, was elected in 1883 as President of the Rhode Island Hospital Trust Company, serving for more than 25 years. He managed to commute from Kingston to his office in Providence on the train.

On April 10, 1882, Elisha Reynolds Potter, Jr. passed away. He was the last of the members of the Reynolds and Potter families from Kingston to have significant influence on a statewide basis. Starting with Elisha Reynolds, who was the driving force in moving the court house from Tower Hill to Little Rest in 1752, a Reynolds or a Potter from Little Rest or Kingston had influence on a colony or statewide basis – Elisha Reynolds, Elisha Reynolds Potter, Sr. and Elisha Reynolds Potter, Jr. Elisha Jr. willed the Potter Homestead to his younger brother William, who died there in 1908. William bequeathed the Homestead to his niece, Mary LeMoine Potter, daughter of James B. M. Potter.

Black persons continued to live in the heart of Kingston village, with a small African-American community developing in Biscuit City. The blacksmith shop of Solomon Fayerweather continued to be a favorite gathering place for villagers to trade stories and gossip. Upon the shop's huge doors were posted advertisements, notices, and news of public interest. Henry Thomas had the jobs of lighting and dousing Kingston's street lamps (using a ladder) and maintaining the Court House. John White was known for, after finishing a hard days work at the marble shop in the village, sitting down and reminiscing about his days as a slave in pre-Civil War Virginia. Jane Hull, in Biscuit City, sometimes entertained local white children, telling them of her family's past as African royalty. In the 1880s, Kingston's black residents saw some of the last official bastions of racial inequality finally fall in Rhode

Island. In 1881, the General Assembly repealed an old law that made it a criminal offense for a white person to marry a black or Indian person. In 1885, the General Assembly enacted legislation that provided that no person was to be denied the facilities of any licensed inn or place of public amusement "on account of race, color or previous condition." The act also made it an offense to disqualify any citizen for jury service on account of color. This last law affected the operations of the county court in Kingston before it was moved to West Kingston in 1894. Unofficially, discrimination against blacks continued in some quarters. In the 1880s, several black families in Matunuck reportedly had their houses burned down in a race riot.

Kingston villagers continued to form new groups to improve their lives. The Kingston Lyceum was established in 1865. Villagers met periodically in the Court House to hear two villagers debate different sides of pressing political and social questions of the day. The Kingston Improvement Association was formed in 1884. Its purpose was to "promote good fellowship" and to improve the village's streets, sidewalks and other aspects.

Biscuit City House and Unknown African American Woman, circa 1890. The woman may be Jane Hull, who used to talk about her African royal ancestry, or Nabby Potter, a former servant of Elisha Potter, Jr.'s. Biscuit City became a community populated by African Americans. *Pettaquamscutt Historical Society.*

Kingston villagers generally resisted the encroachments of modern improvements. The first hard, macadam road in South Kingstown was laid in 1889. By 1895, hard surfaced roads were laid from Wakefield (Dale Carlia Corner) to Kingston to Kingston Station. Laying the road in Kingston was delayed by protests from villager William Potter. The mossy streets of Kingston village became a part of the past. Yet even as late as 1937, Kingston's "quiet" main street was described as "untouched by commercialism, and lined with elm trees, some of which are from 150 to 200 years old." In his diary, Nathaniel Helme wrote excitedly on July 26, 1888, that "the telephone company put in a long distance transmitter today, so we are able to communicate with Boston, New York or Philadelphia as easily as any place." In October 1889, however, as a result of resistance by villagers to placing the unsightly telephone wires on main street, Helme reported that "all the telephone wires were taken away today." In 1893, Kingston villagers again forced the telegraph company to remove the telegraph poles from the village's main street. Oliver Stedman wrote that "Although electric lights came to Wakefield in 1890, they did not reach Kingston Hill until 1916, 26 years later and then only after violent protests for fear of damage to the trees. The telephone company arrived a little sooner by running poles and wires through the back lots and thus avoiding the village street." Sadly, the hurricane of 1938 uprooted many of the huge elm trees in spectacular fashion.

The Kinneys of Kingston, in 1897, were the first villagers to own an automobile. The advent of the automobile, of course, would change the face of Kingston forever. It also led to the decline in Kingston's stores, as villagers and others in the surrounding area could easily travel to Wakefield and other places for shopping. Modern marvels were often exhibited at the county fair held in West Kingston. In 1912, Ruth Law, one of the few barnstorming female airplane pilots, created a sensation at the fair and village when she flew her Wright biplane for about 18 minutes circling over Kingston and the College.

Kingston did have in its midst an enthusiastic participant in the age of invention. He was inventor John G. Perry, who also served twenty years as town clerk. Perry invented meat cutters that won medals at the World's Fair in London in 1851 and at the World's Fair in New York in 1853. He also invented a mower, which won prizes at various state fairs and in Paris in the 1860s. If he had been born earlier and made his inventions in the 1830s, Kingston might have developed a manufacturing factory to produce his products. But by Perry's time, manufacturing was centered in cities and towns with railroad depots. A factory in Worcester, Massachusetts obtained the contract to manufacture the mowers.

Bernon Helme and the Founding of the University of Rhode Island:
An Idea to Save Kingston and Farming in Rhode Island

In early 1888, as 30 year-old Bernon Helme was sweeping the floor of his general store in Kingston with an old stub broom, he contemplated the decline of two institutions important to him: agriculture in Rhode Island and Kingston village.

Bernon Helme thought about such weighty matters, as he had assumed the mantle of Kingston's most important resident with the death of Elisha R. Potter, Jr. Helme operated a general store in the village, at the same location, in the old school house, in which Thomas Taylor had operated his general store from the early-to-mid 1800s. Helme was also the village postmaster. His family had deep roots in Kingston. One relative, James Helme, Jr., had operated a store in Kingston from 1777 to 1823, and had served as town clerk of South Kingstown from 1779 to 1812, as well as the jailer of the county jail from 1807 to 1812. Bernon's grandfather, Samuel Helme, and his father, Powell Helme, served as county court clerk for many years (Powell also served as town clerk from 1853 to 1858). Bernon Helme inherited the general store from his father. Bernon Helme was described as inheriting his father's "mercantile, clerical, and mathematical abilities." Helme attended the Friend's School (now Moses Brown) in Providence; he did not attend college. Helme was a clerk of the Kingston Congregational Church, a trustee of the Kingston Savings Bank, and a leader in the local temperance association.

Bernon Helme was justified in his concern about the decline of farming in Rhode Island. The numbers told the story. In 1865, Rhode Island had 10,754 farmers operating 6,280 farms. By 1885, only 2,175 farmers and 783 farms had been added since 1865. By comparison, Rhode Island had 36,993 manufacturing workers in 1865 and 63,349 manufacturing workers in 1885, an increase of 26,356 workers. In 1885, the value of the state's agricultural products was only $7.2 million compared to the value of the state's manufacturing products at $95.4 million.

In rural South County itself, the number of farm workers in 1885 – 2,424 – was not much more than the number of wool and cotton mill workers in 1885 – 1,811. In 1885, in South Kingstown, there were 757 farmers and 405 woolen mill workers (mostly at Hazard-owned Peace Dale mill). The small mills in rural villages such as Usquepaug and Mooresfield that had supplemented the income of farm families also had disappeared. Because they were not on railroad lines and not near a large, renewable, cheap workforce (such as immigrants in Providence), they were at a competitive disadvantage and closed down.

The years from 1870 to 1900 were poor years for New England farmers. The fact that much of Rhode Island's soil was full of boulders and was acidic was also not helpful for farmers. In addition, while it was hoped that the coming of the railroad to West Kingston in 1837 would be a boon to South County farmers, permitting them to transport their goods to new markets, the opposite was true. The railroad permitted agricultural produce from the Midwest's large, rich and productive farms to be shipped to the east coast. The introduction of refrigerated rail cars exacerbated the problem. Wheat, corn, hogs, beef, cattle, and sheep were not profitable in light of western competition. Rhode Island farmers focused on dairy farming, with milk, butter and cheese as the main sources of income, and on raising potatoes. A life of farming was simply not a path to riches and comforts in Rhode Island. Instead, it was hard work, with little hope for financial gain. Rhode Island farm boys, facing little future in farming, felt the lure of the city and left farms in droves.

A Rhode Island demographer in 1865 observed that Rhode Island's agricultural towns "have almost exclusively, a farming population, without any large villages. The population is almost entirely native American. There is nothing in these towns especially calculated to induce immigration to them; and not sufficient inducement in them to keep their young people at home." The demographer concluded that "a community, or town which depends exclusively for its progress upon agriculture, cannot be expected, as a general rule, to sustain itself as to numbers, or at least cannot increase to any great extent."

With the decline of agriculture in Rhode Island also came the decline of Kingston. Kingston had risen as a village to meet the needs of farmers in the Narragansett country in colonial times. It had served as the location of the county seat for Washington County, the most important agricultural county in the state, and as the location for the town hall and town meetings in South Kingstown, the richest agricultural town in the state, for over 125 years. Kingston men, from Elisha R. Potter, Sr. to Wilkins Updike to Elisha R. Potter, Jr., had served in public offices at the state level defending the agricultural interests of town and county. But changes in transportation, industrialization and urbanization had had a significant impact on Kingston. In general, these forces increased the power and influence of Providence and other northern towns and reduced the influence of the southern rural towns. As a result, even if Kingston had maintained its standing as the key South County village, its influence would have been substantially reduced in the state. But Kingston could not even maintain its standing in South County. As a result of the coming of the Narragansett Pier Railroad in 1876 and the failure of the railroad to run through Kingston, Kingston had lost its town hall to Peace Dale and its stagecoach taverns had seen their businesses dramatically reduced. It was only a matter of time before the county seat in Kingston would be removed to West Kingston, closer to the railroad depot. The population of Kingston had fallen behind Wakefield, Peace Dale and the Narragansett Pier, which had all benefited from the rise of mills and industrialization.

As Helme swept the floor of his general store, he had to wonder whether Kingston would go the way of Tower Hill. In colonial times, as the county seat, Tower Hill had been a thriving village; but when the county seat was moved to Little Rest (now Kingston) in 1752, Tower Hill fell into a decline from which it never recovered. Its dilapidated houses reflected the decline. More recently, after the loss of their mills, South Ferry and Mooresfield virtually disappeared as villages.

As Helme continued to sweep the floor of his general store, he had an idea. At the time, in 1888, the state was contemplating where to locate a state agricultural college. Helme thought, why not Kingston? The 140-acre Oliver Watson farm to the northwest of the village was for sale for $5,000. Helme thought he could help to raise money from donors to purchase the Watson farm, which would induce the state to select the farm as the location for the state's agricultural college. Kingston would reap benefits from having a college located next to it, and the college would produce graduates trained in the latest scientific agricultural methods who would rejuvenate farming in Rhode Island.

The Morrill Act of 1862

The story behind the founding of the University of Rhode Island began in 1862, when the U.S. Congress enacted the Morrill Act. This legislation granted a substantial amount of land to each state as federal aid to education. In a state like Rhode Island, which had a limited amount of public land, public land in another state or rights to buy the land in another state could be sold, with the proceeds invested in safe securities yielding not less than 5%. The funds were required to be used to endow at least one college where the primary aim was to teach "branches of learning as are related to agriculture and the mechanic arts."

Brown University was then Rhode Island's only college. The state did not want to lose the opportunity to use the federal funds, and Brown saw an opportunity to receive funds that it could use to extend free scholarships to Rhode Island students. But Brown was not an agricultural school and it had no intention of developing one. Both Brown and the state went along with the arrangement of Brown serving as the state's land grant university: Brown received $50,000 from the sale of lands in Kansas and income from the fund amounted to about $3,000 each year; Brown granted scholarships each year to Rhode Island students on the basis of need; but no student ever enrolled in an agricultural studies program at Brown.

The Hatch Act of 1887

In 1887, the U.S. Congress passed more legislation intended to encourage educational efforts to spur scientific farming methods. The Hatch Act granted each state $15,000 annually for the establishment of an agricultural experimental station to help in the acquisition and diffusion of "useful and practical information on subjects connected with agriculture." The experimental station in each state was to be established by the college that had been or would be created as a result of the Morrill Act of 1862. In Rhode Island, that apparently meant that Brown University would receive the funding under the Hatch Act.

With the possibility of substantial federal funds made available to help agriculture, Rhode Island farmers began to organize and protest the use of any of the funds from the Hatch Act by Brown University. At a meeting of the Rhode Island State Grange, the most important state and local organization for farmers, a resolution was passed calling for both (1) the establishment of a new state supported agricultural college that would be supported in part by Hatch Act federal funds, and (2) Brown's transfer of the Morrill Act funds to the proposed college.

In public hearings held in Providence in February 1887, Rhode Island farmers spoke out in favor of the Grange's resolution. Nathaniel Peckham, a state senator from South Kingstown, said that boys going to Brown University with free scholarships got Latin and Greek when what they needed was a more practical education to promote farming. He guaranteed that no professor at Brown "could tell the difference in the periods of gestation in a cow and in a rabbit." As Brown had done nothing to support farmers, Peckham demanded that the state reclaim the Morrill Act funds. Thomas G. Hazard, a prominent South Kingstown farmer who was then Master of the Rhode Island Grange, agreed that farmers ought to have the use of the Morrill Act funds, which the federal government had appropriated for their use. Arthur Brown, a West Kingston farmer, ridiculed the single agricultural course at Brown. He commented sarcastically about the type of men Brown produced, including "the professor who used to take off his hat to himself," and compared them to a talented Newport laborer. Other farmers complained that most of the free scholarships granted by Brown went to urban students and not to students from rural towns.

With the issue of federal funds to support agriculture resonating among Rhode Island farmers, members of the General Assembly took notice. It helped supporters of an agricultural school that under Rhode Island's constitution, the state senate continued to be dominated by agricultural towns. In March 1888, the General Assembly passed a law appropriating $5,000 for the establishment of a state agricultural school. The school would be called the Rhode Island State Agricultural School. The legislation did not say where the school would be located.

The Selection of Kingston for the State's Agricultural School

It was in this environment that Bernon Helme thought of locating the state's new agricultural school in Kingston. Helme was aware that the 140-acre Oliver Watson farm, to the northwest of the village on a sloping hill leading to a flat plain below, was currently for sale for $5,000. Helme wanted the offer to locate the college in Kingston to be attractive to the state, so he went about seeking donations from villagers and local farmers to fund the private purchase of the land. Helme raised about $2,000 from 30 individuals, mostly Kingston residents. Five Helme family members contributed $225 and Herbert G. Wells contributed $500. In addition, Helme persuaded Jeremiah Peckham, Jr., a Kingston farmer with a house on North Road and the new Master of the Rhode Island State Grange, to approach the South Kingstown town council. At a town council meeting held on February 20, 1888, by a bare 3-2 vote, the town council agreed to advance $2,000 toward the establishment of a college, on the condition that it be located in South Kingstown. Thomas G. Hazard, the former Master of the state Grange, supported Helme and Peckham.

The General Assembly committee entrusted with selecting the site for the new college received offers from Cranston, Coventry, Scituate and Portsmouth, in addition to Kingston and a new offer from West Kingston. On April 4, 1888, the *Narragansett Times* reported that on "Monday morning the committee met . . . in Providence to hear further proposals and suggestions. A large delegation from South Kingstown was present and the claims of South County were strongly urged." Bernon Helme noted that South Kingstown had always led the state in agriculture, including organizing the first grange, building the first creamery, and restoring the county fair to a healthy condition. Arthur Brown of West Kingston added that because the bulk of the farm property was in the southern part of the state, the school ought to be placed there. He hoped that, in any case, Cranston would not be selected, as with its state facilities, Cranston "was a sort of District of Columbia of Rhode Island." Bernon Helme recommended the 140-acre Watson farm. He commented on its fine soil and the money that had already been raised toward the $5,000 purchase price. Arthur Brown recommended the 130-acre Robinson farm in West Kingston, touting its proximity to the railroad station. But Thomas G. Hazard of South Kingstown objected to the Robinson farm, as its owner wanted to rent the land to the state, and Hazard thought that the state should own the land. After this meeting, Helme continued his efforts, traveling to Providence to meet with committee officials and joining committee officials when they inspected the Kingston site on May 8, 1888.

On June 26, 1888, the committee decided that Kingston was the superior location. Wanting to acquire the Watson farm as quickly as possible in order to start receiving federal funding, the committee sought to pay for the farm in July 1888. But at the closing, it was realized that the state statute did not authorize any person to draw funds from the state treasury to purchase the land, and the General Assembly was not scheduled to meet again until January 1889. Governor Royal Taft saved the day by digging into his own pockets and paying the $1,000 portion owed by the state (he was later reimbursed). The state received the deed for the land on September 27, 1888.

Surprisingly, in February 1889, members of the county's Grange objected to the selection of Kingston. In a meeting of about 100 Grange members representing every corner of Washington County held in Hopkinton, the criticism was made that the Watson farm was located two miles from the West Kingston railroad depot. It was felt that many students who could not afford to live on campus would find it difficult to afford the carriage fare to ride to Kingston. Would the railroad again deprive Kingston? Another criticism was that the Watson farm was accessible only by a path which when wet was said to be the worst in the county. Arthur Brown expressed his desire for the state to buy land in West Kingston near the railroad depot to serve as the site for the school. (Needless to say, Brown's farm fit this description.) An Exeter man expressed astonishment at the notion that the $2,000 contribution by the "capitalists of Kingston Hill" gave them license to dictate the location of the school. He complained that the only practicing farmers who had contributed to the fund were Jeremiah Peckham, Jr., who had succeeded Thomas G. Hazard as Master of the state Grange, and Peckham's father. The younger Peckham, ever the politician, rose to confess that he had strongly favored the West Kingston railroad depot location, but had been talked into contributing to the Kingston site by the persuasive Bernon Helme. The $2,000 contribution by the South Kingstown town council was also available to a West Kingston site, as well as to the Kingston site, as it was conditioned on the college being located in the town.

With his plans and reputation under attack, Bernon Helme did what his Kingston predecessors had done: he authored a spirited defense in a newspaper (the *Narragansett Times*) and in a broadside. Helme wrote that the Kingston site offered a greater variety of soil than did the land near the station, thus permitting more experimentation. He also claimed that the climate on the hill was more hygienic, citing as evidence the longevity of Kingston residents. In the *Narragansett Times*, Arthur Brown penned a sarcastic reply in which he rebutted Helme on twenty-four points.

On March 14, 1889, Washington County Grange members voiced their displeasure at the decision to select Kingston as the site for the state's agricultural school to the school's Board of Managers. But the arguments must not have been persuasive, as the next day the board entered into a contract for the construction of a road from main street in Kingston village north to the Watson farm. With the dispute still simmering, the *Providence Journal* pronounced the hygienic and moral surroundings for the school the very best in the state and the land ideally suited to the purposes for which it had been bought. Finally, the General Assembly closed the matter by releasing $5,000 to start construction on the new school in Kingston. Some of the school's first acquisitions were farming tools, wagons, two horses and a cow. In January 1889, the college hired Lorenzo Kinney as horticulturalist and botanist. Construction of academic and boarding halls began in earnest. By mid-1889, a *Providence Journal* reporter, while finding Kingston village itself to be "the picture of a county seat asleep on a summer afternoon," found that the Watson farm was being "metamorphosed" into an agricultural school. Bernon Helme had prevailed.

The school's first buildings were impressive granite buildings built from native stones. The granite for the walls was taken from a quarry at the base of the hill and hauled by ox team to the summit of the hill on a narrow-gauge track built specially for the purpose. Experiment Station, later renamed Taft Laboratory, was completed in June 1890. College Hall, the predecessor of Davis Hall, was completed one month later. A less impressive wooden boarding hall was opened to students in December 1890. Legislators from farming towns did not want to make the surroundings at the school too opulent, for fear that the students would become dissatisfied with the humble surroundings at their home farms. The first twenty-six students (two of whom were women) enrolled in September 1890. The college's report stated that "The requirements for admission to the College are necessarily low, on account of the deplorable condition of our district schools."

Transfer of Status as State's Land-Grant College

Rhode Island farmers continued to complain about Brown University keeping the $50,000 of Morrill Act funds. Brown University was about to give up the funds, but the matter was complicated when Congress passed a second Morrill Act. This legislation appropriated $15,000 from the sale of public lands to each state and an additional annual stipend of $1,000 for ten years for the benefit of agriculture and mechanic arts. But the legislation expressly permitted a broader range of courses, including English and various scientific courses. To make matters even more difficult for the farmers, the Rhode Island Supreme Court, in an advisory opinion, ruled that Brown University was the only institution in the state that could receive the new federal grant.

At a General Assembly hearing in the Court House in Providence, members of the Grange promoted the idea of transferring the Morrill Act funds to the new Rhode Island State Agricultural School in Kingston. Farmers crowded into the hearing room. Bernon Helme, the Reverend A. L. Clarke (pastor of the Kingston Congregational Church), Thomas G. Hazard and even Arthur Brown, Helme's antagonist from West Kingston, found common cause to support the Agricultural School. Hazard pointed to all of the farmers who had left their work to visit the legislature and compared them to Brown's lawyers and "men of education" in attendance. Hazard asked, "which represents the people?" He argued that the scholarships that Brown had granted with the old Morrill Act funds had benefited every class of people except farmers, a misuse of the money that he called "robbery." The Reverend Clarke, showing more restraint, praised the pastoral simplicity of the Agricultural School and made the valid point that most of the students enrolled at the school would not qualify to be admitted to Brown or other schools of similar quality. The historian of the University of Rhode Island, Herman Eschenbacher, wrote that this and subsequent heated debates,

> disclosed that the agriculturalists regarded the Kingston School as their own institution, governed by farmers, supposedly staffed by farmers, and recruiting students almost wholly from the farm areas. To them, it was the recognition of the importance, the value of agriculture as a way of life, educationally expressed. That it might become the captive of Brown University seemed yet another betrayal that must be beaten down at all costs. . . . The farmers saw there an alien culture indifferent to their plight and scornful of their values. Brown was the paneled library, leather chairs, fine wines, and white linen. Its graduates became doctors, lawyers, dilettantes, or worse; but never practicing farmers.

The General Assembly reached a legislative compromise. It passed a bill to incorporate the College of Agriculture and the Mechanic Arts at Kingston and to create a governing body. The college was granted the use of the second Morrill Act funds, but Brown was permitted to retain the first Morrill Act funds.

The supporters of the Agricultural School felt that they had won a great victory. Helme and Charles Flagg, the head of the school, both of whom had spent the week in Providence steering the bill through the General Assembly, received a tumultuous welcome from Agricultural School students who met their train at the West Kingston railroad depot on the night the bill passed. Eschenbacher writes colorfully,

> The boys carried their champions to a waiting carriage which they drew up the hill to the village in a torchlight procession. Helme

was permitted to leave the parade at his house after enduring a brief serenade . . . the students saluted the occasion by firing twenty-five rounds from a Civil War cannon donated for the purpose by a Captain Kenyon of the village. So vigorous was the crew manning the canon that they burst the gun with an excessive charge on the final shot and, sobered by the near disaster, they retired for the night, to the apparent relief of the villagers.

Surprisingly, Brown University would not give up its struggle to obtain the funds from the second Morrill Act. In May 1892, it sued the state, claiming that as Congress awarded the second Morrill Act funds to the land grant college that received the first Morrill Act funds, Brown was the rightful recipient of the second Morrill Act funds, not the Agricultural School in Kingston. A federal judge ruled against Brown, but Brown appealed its case to the U.S. Supreme Court. The appeal threatened to tie up the funds from the second Morrill Act for years. Fortunately, the parties reached a compromise. The state paid Brown $40,000 as compensation for Brown agreeing to transfer the $50,000 from the first Morrill Act to the state and to dismiss its appeal pending in the Supreme Court. Bernon Helme lobbied General Assembly members, attempting to persuade them that this was a good deal for the state. The deal was closed in May 1894. Again, the college students celebrated, this time by lighting a bonfire and marching through Kingston village "burning colored fire as they went along." The *Westerly Sun* pronounced the settlement a "happy conclusion" to an ignoble affair and looked forward to a bright future for the state college.

A prominent Providence attorney, who had represented the interests of the Agricultural School (despite his being a Brown graduate), wrote Bernon Helme,

> I most heartily congratulate you and your associates upon the successful outcome of your protracted and well sustained efforts on behalf of your Agricultural School and trust, now that the state has spoken so emphatically, that wiser counsels will prevail in the government of the University [Brown], and that you will not be further antagonized in obtaining the moneys . . . . With best wishes for the future progress and success of your, and may I say . . . our 'State College.'

In retrospect, Rhode Island had missed an opportunity to develop a true agricultural school for thirty years, from the time the funds from the first Morrill Act were made available in 1862. But both the state and Brown University had been satisfied with the arrangement in which Brown would grant free scholarships to needy Rhode Island students, providing the children of workers with possibilities for social mobility. Many of these students did indeed move up the social scale to become lawyers, doctors and other professionals. But Herman Eschenbacher writes, "When it became clear that social mobility was the least part of what the farmers wanted from the Federal act, that they wanted economic competence for their children as farmers, not as professional people, and when its was made plain that they were capable of exerting political pressure to achieve their ends, the issue of agricultural education gained an importance it had not formerly enjoyed."

Of course, the college in Kingston (renamed Rhode Island College in 1909 and the University of Rhode Island in 1951) would become much more than an agricultural school. Even providing an agricultural education applying the most scientific farming principles could not stave off the decline of agriculture in Rhode Island. The children of farmers in South County and other rural areas in Rhode Island needed to be trained in vocations that would provide other opportunities for useful employment. In addition to books entitled *Harris on Pigs* and *Practical Farm Chemistry,* students read books on regular chemistry, math and science. As early as 1897, the catalogue for the college announced a wholesale new offering of courses. Degrees would be offered in five areas: agriculture; mechanical arts; physics and mathematics; chemistry; and biology and preparatory medicine. The college in Kingston would also provide opportunities for the children of immigrant families. In addition, the college made available new opportunities, as well as the same courses, for women. In 1895, the college opened a dormitory for the exclusive use of women, with Kingston villager and college professor Anna Peckham having been appointed to the position of "preceptress, having full charge of the young women at all times."

Town and Gown

From the beginning, there was a symbiotic relationship between Kingston and the Agricultural School. In September 1890, the first 26 students arrived on campus, twelve of them from South Kingstown, prior to the completion of the boarding hall. Kingston residents took students into their homes and several eating clubs were established in the village. Even after the boarding hall was opened in December 1890, students attended church at the Kingston Congregational Church in pews rented by the college for that purpose and shopped at village general stores.

In 1895, the college suffered a calamity: College Hall burned on a Sunday morning in January. The fire was discovered in the chimney at a time when almost all of the students and faculty were in the village attending services at the Congregational Church. A student interrupted the service and students, faculty and villagers attempted to combat the blaze. But strong winds and a lack of water supply resulted in the fire destroying the building in less than an hour. The loss of the building amounted to $45,000 and the loss

Rhode Island College, Its First Three Buildings, circa 1890. Taft Laboratory on left, College Hall in center, Boarding Hall on right. *Pettaquamscutt Historical Society.*

Rhode Island College, 1898 Scene. Lippitt Hall, with Davis Hall to its left. *Pettaquamscutt Historical Society.*

of the newly-completed laboratory and other equipment amounted to $12,000. Whether the college could continue was in question. But the college and village pulled together to meet the challenge. A meeting was held at the Kingston Congregational Church and citizens threw open their doors to students who had lost their dormitory rooms. The county sheriff offered the use of the old Court House in the village for temporary use as an academic hall. On the day after the fire, the college was back in operation.

The college was a boon to Kingston village as well. If Kingston could no longer be an important political, legal and commercial center, it could serve as an educational and cultural center. With the availability of faculty and administration jobs in Kingston, and the increasing enrollments of students, money flowed into the village. Professors and administrators purchased many of the pre-Civil War houses in Kingston and kept them in good condition. As it would turn out, Kingston would not go the way of Tower Hill. The houses and public buildings of Kingston would survive the 20th century.

Faculty and administration personnel rejuvenated the Kingston Congregational Church, the Kingston Free Library and Reading Room, and the Kingston Improvement Association. In addition, new clubs arose for social recreation. In 1895, women established the "Every Tuesday Club," which served as a social and intellectual outlet for the wives of new college professors and women from families with long ties to the village. They held meetings each Tuesday at 3 p.m., at which papers prepared by members on classic literature and controversial social and political issues of the day were read and discussed. The Tavern Hall Club was started in 1913 by young male professors who boarded in the old Elisha Reynolds house at the corner of main street and South Road. Bernon Helme made a bequest of his home and a trust fund in 1937 that helped the South County Art Association to survive. All of these organizations exist today, continuing a long tradition of Kingston villagers coming together in voluntary associations to improve their lives and improve the village itself.

Appendix A

Museum Holdings of Silver
Made by the Silversmiths of Little Rest

Pettaquamscutt Historical Society
Kingston, Rhode Island

Samuel Casey. A teaspoon, currently on display. [32]

Newport History Museum
Newport, Rhode Island

Samuel Casey. A lovely teapot (circa 1760) with fine engraving at the top, currently on display. The owner is the Redwood Library. Initials on the teapot are those of Sarah S. Pope (1742-1819), who married William Redwood in Newport in 1757.

Redwood Library and Athenaeum
Newport, Rhode Island

Samuel Casey. A porringer (circa 1750). The original owners were Christopher and Patience Townshend of Newport.

Museum of Art, Rhode Island School of Design
Providence, Rhode Island

Samuel Casey. Sugar tongs donated by William Davis Miller. A pair of cups donated by Mary LeMoine Potter. A caster, which is currently on view. A beaker, which is currently on view. Two cream jugs, one of which is currently on view. A cann. Two porringers one with "James Robinson" on front. A tankard. Numerous tablespoons, donated by William Davis Miller and Mary LeMoine Potter, one of which is currently on view.

Joseph Perkins. Six spoons (circa 1772) donated by William Davis Miller. Three spoons donated by William Davis Miller. A pair of shoe buckles.

John Waite. A cream jug donated by William Davis Miller. Another cream jug. A tankard, which is currently on view. A porringer donated by William Davis Miller. A porringer donated by Mary LeMoine Potter. A pair of tablespoons donated by William Davis Miller. Serving spoon donated by William Davis Miller. Another two serving spoons.

---

[32] All pieces marked "currently on display" are as of the publication of this book. Museums frequently change their displays. Pieces not so marked are not currently on display as of the publication of this book.

Rhode Island Historical Society
Providence, Rhode Island

Samuel Casey. A cann with S-shaped handle (circa 1760). Another similar cann, with initials of TE (possibly Thomas and Eunice Hazard). Another similar cann, with flaring lip and foot. A tablespoon. A porringer (circa 1750). A punch ladle (circa 1760). A porringer with M*G engraved on it. A porringer with F*N engraved on it. (All prior items from the collection of Conrad Ham, who was a descendant of Casey). A small cream pot with a slim neck and spout. A porringer with leaf scroll. A milk pot with pear-shaped body. A porringer with a short neck.

Joseph Perkins. A dessert spoon (circa 1770-1780), with engraving of J.H.L., which may be John and Hannah Larkin.

John Waite. Dessert spoon, with upturned handle and engraved P.G. (probably for Patience Gardner, mother of John Larkin). Pair of serving spoons with fiddle handles, one engraved AJ the other AAW. Silver serving spoon with magenta felt case (circa 1770).

Museum of Fine Arts
Boston, Massachusetts

Samuel Casey. A tankard (circa 1767). The original owner was Job Almy (died 1767). Image is on museum website. A teaspoon. A gold button donated by Bernon Helme.

John Waite. A cann donated by Bernon Helme.

Clark Art Institute
Williamstown, Massachusetts

Samuel Casey. A cream pot, currently on display.

Historic Deerfield Museum
Deerfield, Massachusetts

Samuel Casey. A cream jug, with lovely curves. Currently on display and image is on museum's website.

John Waite. Pair of salt shakers.

Yale University Art Gallery
New Haven, Connecticut

Samuel Casey. From the Mabel Brady Garvan Collection: A tankard (1755), originally owned by Rev. Ezra Stiles, the talented Newport Congregationalist minister and later President of Yale University. A beaker (circa 1750-60), with its twin held in the RISD Museum. Pair of salt shakers (circa 1750-70). Pair of sauceboats (circa 1750-70), which is the only item of the museum's collection that is currently on display. Pair of tablespoons (circa 1750-60). Another tankard. A gold button (circa 1750-60). Gifts of the Kossack family: several teaspoons and tablespoons. From other collection: A Cann (circa 1750-60).

Gideon Casey. A pair of tablespoons (circa 1755-65). Two tablespoons (1760).

Joseph Perkins. Three teaspoons (circa 1770-80) (Mabel Brady Garvan Collection). Two tablespoons (circa 1755) (Kossack family gift).

Nathaniel Helme. Teaspoon (circa 1785) (Kossack family gift).

John Waite. Sugar scissors (circa 1765-75) (Mabel Brady Garvan Collection). From gifts of the Kossack family: Four teaspoons (circa 1770); three tablespoons (circa 1770); teaspoons (circa 1770); tablespoon (circa 1795); seven tablespoons (circa 1795). Four tablespoons (circa 1785).

Metropolitan Museum of Art
New York, New York

Samuel Casey. From the Judge Clearwater Collection, a tankard, and a creamer and porringer.

Smithsonian Institution
Washington, D.C.

Samuel Casey. A fine teapot, similar to the one displayed by the Newport History Museum. Originally owned by Abigail Robinson, a daughter of a Narragansett planter. Remained in Robinson family until 1979. Image is on museum website by typing on Google, "Samuel Casey".

Winterthur Museum
Wilmington, Delaware

Samuel Casey. A beaker (circa 1760-67), currently on display in the Chestertown Room. "Ester Helme" is engraved on the piece. Gold necklace, with clasp of a winged Phoenix (circa 1760). A spoon (circa 1760).

Gideon Casey. A beaker, currently on display in the SimsburyRoom; made of pewter. Spoons (circa 1760-67).

Nathaniel Helme. A spoon, worn by use (circa 1782-89). A teaspoon (circa 1782-89).

Joseph Perkins. A tablespoon (circa 1770-80).

John Waite. A spoon (circa 1770-80). A tablespoon (circa 1763-70).

Appendix B

The Full Description of the Negro Elections in "Recollections of Little Rest (Now Kingston) Hill, and its Surroundings Some Fifty Years Ago" by Jonathan P. Helme, *Providence Journal*, October 31, 1874; see also Manuscript in the Pettaquamscutt Historical Society and Kingston Free Library, pages 17-18.

Among the servants of the late E. R. Potter, was one by the name of John Potter. In those days it was the custom of the colored population of the State to elect each year a governor, and on one occasion John was the elect. The governor was installed in June and the headquarters were at Fulling Mills, as it was then called, now Apponaug. On the occasion of his installation, Mr. Potter told his servant John to take the best horse in his stable, as he had a number, among them a fine span of large bays, for his journey to Apponaug, about twenty miles. He selected one of the span, a noble large horse, and with the assistance of Mr. John T. Nichols,* his horse was beautifully caparisoned. Early on the morning of the day, the governor elect, mounted on his splendid steed, dressed in fine style, viz., blue coat, short waist, swallow tail, with a profusion of guilt buttons, red sash, black pants, put inside of a pair of boots, with white tops, and a handsome pair of silver-mounted spurs, together with a white hat, a large black plume with a red top, completed his regimentals. There were quite a number of our citizens assembled to see the governor elect start for the capital. He was met by a very large delegation of his colored fellow citizens about half way between Greenwich and Apponaug, with a band of music, consisting of three drums and two fifes (in those days the French horns, key bugles, etc..., were not known.) As soon as his appearance was noted, the band struck up "Hail to the Chief;" both sides of the road were lined with spectators, the ladies waving their 'kerchiefs, and the gentlemen their hats, while the governor with hat in hand bowed to the populace, his head nearly touching his horse's head. On his entrance to the village, the band played "Washington's March." If any one had told the governor on this occasion, as a slave once told a heroic Roman general, that with all this pomp and show he "was nothing but a man," he would have spurned him from his sight.

. . . . About this time Mr. E. R. Potter was urgently solicited to accept the nomination for Governor of this State. He declined, stating as one of the reasons, that one Governor in a family was sufficient.

*John T. Nichols was a respected saddlemaker (sadler) with his shop in Little Rest.

Appendix C

Members of the Kingston Anti-Slavery Society
(From Minutes of the Kingston Anti-Slavery Society)

Date Joined	Name	Voting Status	Sex	Race
June 20, 1837	Daniel M.C. Stedman	Fh	male	white
	Jeremiah S. Sherman	Fh	male	white
	William French	Fh	male	white
	John H. Clarke	Fh	male	white
	Job W. Watson	Fh	male	white
	George Fairweather	Nfh	male	colored
	Peleg Johnson	Fh	male	white
	Christopher Comstock	Fh	male	white
	John G. Clarke	Fh	male	white
	Charles P. Grosvenor	Fh	male	white
	Thomas P. Wells	Fh	male	white
	Luke Aldrich	Fh	male	white
	William Harris	Nfh	male	colored
	William Fairweather		male	colored
	Emma P. Wells #		female	white
	Harriet Johnson #		female	white
	Hannah G. Wells #		female	white
	Jane P. Sherman #		female	white
	Harriet Wells#		female	white
	Dorcas W. Gardner #		female	white
	Elisabeth Smith #		female	white
	Sarah Brown #		female	colored
	Sarah Wood #		female	colored
	Martha Robinson #		female	white
	Isabella Fairweather #		female	colored
	Nancy Fairweather #		female	colored
	Mary W. Robinson #		female	white
	Sarah P. Wells #		female	white
	Elisabeth M. Wells #		female	white
June 21, 1837	Henry Eldred, Jr.	Fh	male	white
	Cynthia Whitings #		female	white
	Elizabeth P. Comstock #		female	white

Date Joined	Name	Voting Status	Sex	Race
June 27, 1837	Powell Helme		male	white
July 4, 1837	Caroline Whitings #		female	white
	Elizabeth Rose #		female	white
	John G. Larkin	Fh	male	white
	Elizabeth B. Larkin		female	white
	Mary Ingraham		female	white
	Emeline D. Sherman #		female	white
	Mary E. Kenyon		female	white
	Joseph Marchant		male	white
	Electra Coon		female	white
	Catharine Marchant #		female	white
	John Aldrich		male	white
	Lydia Aldrich		female	white
	Amira D. Clarke #		female	white
August 26, 1837	Elisha F. Watson		male	white
August 28, 1837	Amos C. Wilbur	Fh	male	white

In the fifth column, "Fh" stands for freeholder (eligible to vote), and "Nfh" for non-freeholder over 21 years of age. "Those females having this # against their names are members of the female society." This seems to have been added in later, as it is in pencil and is squeezed in after the names. Immediately following this membership chart is a age of vowel markings for singing   lessons.

Bibliography

Unpublished Sources

Baker Library (Harvard Business School)
    Thomas S. Taylor Collection

John Hay Library (Brown University)
    John Hay Correspondence
    Charles Comstock's *History of South Kingstown*
    Broadsides relating to Elisha Reynolds Potter, Sr. and Wilkins Updike

Library of Congress (Manuscript Division)
    Papers of Tench Tilghman

Kingston Free Library and Reading Room
    Vertical file on local history

Pettaquamscutt Historical Society
    Elisha Potter Account Book
    Kingston Boot and Shoe Manufacturing Company Minutes
    Kingston Musical Society Minutes (Wells Papers)
    Kingston Post Office Records, 1837-40 (Wells Papers)
    South Kingstown Temperance Society Records (Wells Papers)
    South Kingstown Sabbath School Society Records (Wells Papers)
    Thomas P. Wells, Account Books (Wells Papers)
    Miscellaneous Records (Wells Papers)

Rhode Island Historical Society
    Elisha Reynolds Potter, Sr. Papers
    Elisha Reynolds Potter, Jr. Papers
    Thomas Mawney Potter Papers
    James Brown Mason Potter Papers
    Hagadorn-Wells Papers
    Elisha Reynolds Papers
    Joseph Perkins Papers
    Records of the Landholder's Bank, Kingston, R. I., 1818-1858
    William Davis Miller Papers
    Rhode Island Society for the Abolition of the Slave Trade Minutes
    Providence & Kingston Mail Stage Record Book of Trips, 1844-46
    Beriah Brown Papers

Rhode Island Judicial Archives
    King's County Inferior Court of Common Pleas Records
    Washington County Court of Common Pleas Records
    King's County Superior Court Records
    Washington County Supreme Court Records

Rhode Island State Archives
    Petitions to the General Assembly

South Kingstown Town Hall
        Town Land Evidence Records
        Town Meeting Records
        Town Council Records
        Town Probate Records
        Town Tax Records
        Town Voting Lists
        Justices Court Records

University of Rhode Island Library (Special Collections)
        Kingston Anti-Slavery Society Minutes
        Fayerweather Family Papers
        Carl R. Woodward Papers (Boxes 26-28)
        Elisha Reynolds Potter Papers
        Miscellaneous Manuscripts Collection
        Records of the Pettaquamscutt Academy (Kingston Academy)
        Records of School District No. 3, South Kingstown
        William Davis Miller Papers

Newspapers

Connecticut Courant (Library of Congress)
Narragansett Chief, 1842-43 (Library of Congress)
Narragansett Times, 1859-1900 (Kingston Free Library; U.R.I. Library (Special Collections); Peace Dale Library; Rhode Island Historical Society)
Newport Mercury, 1758-1820 (Library of Congress)
Providence Gazette, 1770-1820 (Library of Congress)
Providence Journal (Library of Congress)
Rhode Island Advocate 1831-32 (U.R.I. Library, Special Collections)
South County Journal, 1858 (U.R.I. Library, Special Collections)
The Liberator (Library of Congress)

Published Primary Sources

Acomb, Evelyn M. (ed.). *The Revolutionary Journal of Baron Ludwig Von Closen, 1780-1783.* Chapel Hill, N.C.: University of North Carolina Press, 1958.

An Abridgment of the Case of Gardner and Potter vs. Hannah Gardner and Others. Providence: Walter R. Danforth, 1826. (Copy at the Rhode Island Historical Society.)

Barrett, Shirley L. (ed.). *Voices from the Civil War, Letters and Journal Excerpts of South Kingstown Men in the Union Army, 1861-1863.* Kingston, R.I.: Pettaquamscutt Historical Society, 1992.

Bartlett, John (ed.). *Census of the Inhabitants of the Colony of Rhode Island and Providence Plantations, Taken by Order of the General Assembly, in this Year 1774.* Providence: Knowles, Anthony & Co., 1858.

Bartlett, John (ed.). *Records of the Colony of Rhode Island and Providence Plantations.* 10 vols. Providence: Knowles, Anthony & Co., 1858-62.

Bowditch, Franklin Dexter. *The Literary Diary of Ezra Stiles, D.D., LL.D.* 2 vols. New York: Charles Scribner's Sons, 1901.

Bureau of the Census. *Heads of Families at the First Census of the United States Taken in the Year 1790, Rhode Island.* Washington, D.C.: GPO, 1908.

Catalogue of the Trustees, Instructors and Students of Kingston Academy, for the Term Ending October 5, 1833. Kingston, R.I.: 1833. (Copy at Pettaquamscutt Historical Society.)

Catalogue of the Trustees, Instructors and Students of Kingston Academy, for the Term Ending April 20, 1837. Providence, R.I.: Knowles, Vose & Co., 1833. (Copy at Pettaquamscutt Historical Society.)

Catalogue of the Officers and Students of Kingston Classical Seminary, Kingston, R.I. for the Academic Year, 1853-54. *Providence: Knowles, 1854. (Copy at Rhode Island Historical Society.)*

Catalogue of the Library at Kingston, R.I. Wakefield, R.I.: Thomas P. Wells, 1855. (Copy in author's possession).

Chamberlain, Mildred (ed.). *The Rhode Island 1777 Military Census.* Baltimore: Genealogical Publishing Co., 1985.

Chappell, Virginia (ed.). "The Diary and Account Book of William Gould, Jr." *Rhode Island Genealogical Register.* V. 3, no. 2: 97-108 (Oct. 1980) & v. 3, no. 3: 227-237 (Jan. 1981).

Commerce of Rhode Island, 1726-1800. Massachusetts Historical Society Collections, LXIX-LXX. 2 vols. Boston: By the Society, 1914-15.

Comstock, Charles. *A History of South Kingstown; with a Particular Description of the Hornet's Nest Company, and the Cats Let Out of the Bag.* Newport: 1806. (Copy in the John Carter Brown Library, Brown University) (also reprinted with a forward by William Davis Miller, Kingston, Rhode Island: 1934).

Cook, Edward M., Jr. (ed.). "Jeffrey Watson's Diary, 1740-1784: Family, Community, Religion and Politics in Colonial Rhode Island." *Rhode Island History* 43: 79-116 (Aug. 1984).

Cotner, Robert C. (ed.). *Theodore Foster's Minutes of the Convention Held at South Kingstown, Rhode Island, in March, 1790.* Freeport, N.Y.: Books for Libraries Press, 1970.

DeSimone, Russell J. (ed.) *The Broadsides of the Dorr Rebellion.* Providence: Rhode Island Supreme Court Historical Society, 1992.

Field, Edward. *Diary of Colonel Israel Angell Commanding the Second Rhode Island Continental Regiment during the American Revolution, 1778-1781.* Providence: Preston and Rounds, 1899.

Gardiner, Thomas, A. "The Early Postal Services of South Kingstown." *The Reporter* (journal of the Pettaquamscutt Historical Society) (Winter 1988-89).

Hazard, Caroline (ed.). *Nailer Tom's Diary, Otherwise The Journal of Thomas B. Hazard of South Kingstown, Rhode Island 1778 to 1840.* Boston: Merrymount Press, 1930.

Hazard, Thomas R. *The Jonny-Cake Papers of "Shepherd Tom."* Boston: Merrymount Press, 1915.

Hazard, Rowland (ed.). *Important Correspondence Between Judge Elisha R. Potter and R. G. Hazard, Esq.* Providence: E. L. Freeman & Sons, 1876. (Copy at Rhode Island Historical Society; also published in the *Providence Journal,* April 18, 1876.)

Helme, Jonathan. "Recollections of South Kingstown. Reminiscences of Little Rest (now Kingston) Hill and Its Surroundings, Some Fifty Years Ago." *Providence Journal,* October 31, 1874.

Jackson, Ronald (ed.). *Rhode Island 1800 Census.* Salt Lake City: Accelerating Indexing Systems, 1972.

Goodwin, Daniel (ed.). *A Letterbook and Abstract of Our Services, Written During the Years 1743-1751, by the Revd. James MacSparran.* Boston: Merrymount Press, 1899.

Oatley, Henry Clay, Jr. (ed.). *Daniel Stedman's Journal, 1826-1859.* Greenville, R.I.: Rhode Island Genealogical Society, 2003.

Pearce, Cato. *Brief Memoir of the Life and Religious Experience of Cato Pearce a Man of Color.* Pawtucket: 1842. (Copy in the John Hay Library, Brown University.)

Pease, John C. and John H. Niles. *A Gazetteer of the States of Connecticut and Rhode Island.* Hartford: William Marsh, 1819.

Perry, Amos. *Rhode Island State Census, 1885.* Providence: E. L. Freeman & Son, 1887.

Potter, Elisha R., Jr. *Speech of Mr. Potter, of Rhode Island: on the Memorial of the Democratic Members of the Legislature of Rhode Island: Delivered in the House of Representatives, March 7, 9, and 12, 1844.* Washington, D.C.: Globe Office, 1844. (Copy at Library of Congress.)

Potter, Elisha R., Jr. *An Address Delivered Before the Rhode Island Historical Society, on the Evening of February Nineteenth, 1851.* Providence: George H. Whitney, 1851.

Potter, Elisha R., Jr. (ed.). *The Rhode Island Educational Magazine.* v. 1. Providence: Sayles & Miller, 1852.

Potter, Elisha R., Jr. (ed.). *Reports and Documents Upon Public Schools and Education in the State of Rhode Island.* Providence: Knowles, Anthony & Co., 1855.

Potter, Elisha R., Jr. *Speech of Hon. Elisha R. Potter, of South Kingstown: upon the Resolution in Support of the Union, with an Additional Note.* Providence: Cooke & Danielson, 1861. (Copy at Rhode Island Historical Society.)

Potter, Elisha R., Jr. *Speech of Hon. Elisha R. Potter of South Kingstown, March 14, 1863. Upon the Present National Difficulties.* Providence: Cooke, Jackson & Co., 1863. (Copies at the Rhode Island Historical Society and Library of Congress.)

Potter, James Brown Mason. *Oration Delivered at Kingston, R.I., July 4, 1843.* (Copies at Library of Congress and John Hay Library, Brown University.)

Reasons Why the Hon. Elisha R. Potter Should not be a Senator in Congress. Providence: 1834. (Broadside in John Hay Library, Brown University.)

Rhode Island Acts & Resolves. 4 vol., 1790-1800. (Copy in University of Rhode Island Library (Special Collections).)

Rhode Island Anti-Slavery Society. *Proceedings of the Rhode Island Anti-Slavery Convention.* Providence: H.H. Brown, 1836.

Rhode Island School Report, 1895. Providence: Rhode Island News Company, 1895.

Richmond, John Wilkes. *Facts Relative to the Political and Moral Claims of Wilkins Updike, f or the Support of the Whig Electors of the Western District.* Providence, 1847. (Broadside at the John Hay Library, Brown University.)

Schunke, Marjorie. "Potter Family Bible." *Rhode Island Genealogical Register.* 7: 341-43 (April 1985).

Smith, Joseph Jencks (ed.). *Civil and Military List of Rhode Island, 1647-1800.* Preston & Rounds, 1900; *Civil and Military List of Rhode Island, 1800-1850.* Preston & Rounds, 1901.

Snow, Edwin M. *Report Upon the Census of Rhode Island, 1865.* Providence: Providence Press Company, 1867.

Snow, Edwin M. *Report Upon the Census of Rhode Island, 1875.* Providence: Providence Press Company, 1877.

Stutz, Jean C. (ed.). *South Kingstown, Rhode Island Town Council Records 1771-1795.* Kingston, R.I.: Pettaquamscutt Historical Society, 1988.

S-K Publications. *1800 U.S. Census, Washington County, Rhode Island.* Wichita, Kansas.

Taylor, Maureen Alice. *Runaways, deserters, and notorious villains from Rhode Island Newspapers.* Camden, Maine: Picton Press, 1994.

Trustees of the Academy. *Statement of Facts, in Relation to the Funds of the Kingston Academy.* Providence: E.A. Marshall, 1836.

Updike, Wilkins. *Hints to the Farmers of Rhode Island. By a Freeman.* Providence: 1829. (Broadside at the John Hay Library, Brown University.)

Updike, Wilkins. *An Address to the People of Rhode-Island: Proving that More than Eight Millions of the Public Money has been Wasted by the Present Administration.*

By a Landholder. Providence: 1828. (Broadside at the John Hay Library, Brown University.)

Updike, Wilkins. *History of the Alleged State Debt of Rhode-Island.* Kingston, R. I.: 1846 (Broadside at the John Hay Library, Brown University.)

Updike, Wilkins. *An Address to the People of Rhode Island, Upon the Claims of Wilkins Updike, to a Seat in the Congress of the United States.* Providence: 1847. (Broadside at the John Hay Library, Brown University.)

Wells, Thomas R. *An Address Delivered at Kingston, R.I., July 5, 1830, Before the South Kingstown Temperance Society.* Newport: 1830. (Copy at Rhode Island Historical Society.)

What a Ploughman Said About the "Hints to Farmers," Made Last April, by Men of "Trade." Kingston, R.I.: 1829. (Copy at John Hay Library, Brown University.)

White, Virgil D. (ed.). *Genealogical Abstracts of Revolutionary War Pension Files.* 3 vols. Waynesboro, Tennessee: The National Historical Publishing Company, 1991-92.

Published Secondary Sources

Adamson, Thaire Congdon. "They Left Rhode Island, Part Two, Followers of Jemima Wilkinson to Yates Co., N.Y." *Rhode Island Genealogical Register.* 1: 103-12 (Oct. 1978)

Allen, Thomas S. "Landed Versus Paper Property in Rhode Island, 1781-1790." *Rhode Island History* 53: 3 (Feb. 1995).

Arnold, James. *Narragansett Historical Register.* 9 volumes. Providence: Narragansett Publishing Co., 1882-91.

Atkinson, Amaila Inge. "Captain Rathbun's Last Voyage." *The New England Historical and Genealogical Register.* V. CXV. Boston: By the Society, 1961.

Baker, William Spohn. *Itinerary of General Washington from June 15, 1775, to December 23, 1783.* Philadelphia: J.B. Lippincott Co., 1892.

Barnard, Henry. "Elisha Reynolds Potter, 1811-1882." *Harvard University Memoirs.* Boston: Rockwell and Churchill, 1886.

Bartlett, Irving H. *From Slave to Citizen.* Providence: Urban League of Greater Providence, 1954.

Bartlett, John (ed.). *Memoirs of Rhode Island Officers Who Were Engaged in the Service of Their Country During the Great Rebellion of the South.* Providence: Sidney S. Rider & Brother, 1867.

Beckley, Gail. *American Patriots, The Story of Blacks in the Military.* New York: Random House, 2001.

Beers, J. H. *Representative Men and Old Families of Rhode Island.* Chicago: J. H. Beers & Co., 1908.

Bickford, Christopher. *Crime, Punishment, and the Washington County Jail: Hard Time in Kingston, Rhode Island.* Kingston, R.I.: Pettaquamscutt Historical Society, 2002.

Bidwell, Percy W. and John I. Falconer. *History of Agriculture in the Northern United States, 1620-1860.* Clifton: Augustus M. Kelley, 1973 (reprint of 1925 edition.)

Biographical Cyclopedia of Representative Men of Rhode Island. Providence: National Biographical Publication Company, 1881.

Brennan, Joseph. *Social Conditions in Industrial Rhode Island: 1820-1860.* Washington, D.C.: The Catholic University of America, 1940.

Bronson, Walter, C. *The History of Brown University, 1764-1914.* Providence: Brown University Press, 1914.

Carpenter, Esther. *South County Studies.* Boston: The Merrymount Press, 1924.

Carroll, Charles. *Rhode Island: Three Centuries of Democracy.* 4 vols. New York: Lewis Historical Publishing, 1932.

Carroll, Charles. *Public Education in Rhode Island.* Providence: E.L. Freeman Company, 1918.

Cole, J.R. *History of Washington and Kent Counties, Rhode Island.* New York: W.W. Preston, 1889.

Coleman, Peter J. "The Insolvent Debtor in Rhode Island, 1745-1828." *William & Mary Quarterly.* 22: 413-34 (1965).

Coleman, Peter J. *The Transformation of Rhode Island, 1790-1860.* Providence, R.I.: Brown University Press, 1963.

Conley, Patrick T. *Democracy in Decline: Rhode Island's Constitutional Development, 1776-1841.* Providence: Rhode Island Historical Society, 1977.

Conley, Patrick T. (ed.). *Liberty and Justice, A History of Law and Lawyers in Rhode Island, 1636-1998.* East Providence: Rhode Island Publications Society, 1998.

Conley, Patrick T. *An Album of Rhode Island History, 1636-1986.* Norfolk, Va.: Donning Co., 1986.

Conroy, David W. *Public Houses: Drink and The Revolution of Authority in Colonial Massachusetts.* Chapel Hill: University of North Carolina Press, 1995.

Cotter, Betty J. *Kingston.* Images of America Series. Charleston, S.C.: Arcadia Publishing, 1999.

Cowell, Benjamin. *Spirit of '76 in Rhode Island.* Boston: A.J. Wright, 1850.

Creech, Margaret. *Three Centuries of Poor Law Administration, a Study of Legislation in Rhode Island.* Chicago: The University of Chicago Press, 1936.

Crofut, Florence S. Marcy. *Guide to the History and the Historic Sites of Connecticut.* v. I. New Haven: Yale University Press, 1937.

Daniels, Bruce C. *Dissent and Conformity on Narragansett Bay: The Colonial Rhode Island Town.* Middletown, Conn.: Wesleyan University Press, 1983.

Dearden, Paul F. *The Rhode Island Campaign of 1778: Inauspicious Dawn of Alliance,* Providence: R. I. Bicentennial Foundation, 1980.

Douglass, Frederick. *Life and Times of Frederick Douglass, An Autobiography.* New York: Gramercy Books, 1993.

Eschenbacher, Herman F. *The University of Rhode Island, A History of Land-Grant Education in Rhode Island.* New York: Appleton-Century-Crofts, 1967.

Federal Writers' Project. *Rhode Island, A Guide to the Smallest State.* Boston: Houghton Mifflin Company, 1937.

Fensternmaker, Joseph Van. *The Development of American Commercial Banking, 1782-1837.* Kent, Ohio: Kent State University Press, 1965.

Field, Edward (ed.). *State of Rhode Island and Providence Plantations: A History.* 3 vols. Boston: Mason, 1902.

Field, Edward. *Revolutionary Defences in Rhode Island.* Providence: Preston and Rounds, 1896.

Fitts, Robert K. *Inventing New England's Slave Paradise, Master/Slave Relations in Eighteenth-Century Narragansett, Rhode Island.* New York: Garland Publishing, Inc., 1998.

Freeman, Douglas Southall. *George Washington, a Biography.* New York: Scribner, 1948-57. v. 5.

Gilkeson, John S., Jr. *Middle-Class Providence, 1820-1940.* Princeton, N.J.: Princeton University Press, 1986.

Grant, Philip A. "Party Chaos Embroils Rhode Island." *Rhode Island History* 26: 113-25 (Oct. 1967) and 27: 24-33 (Jan. 1968).

Grossman, Lawrence. "George T. Downing and Desegregation of Rhode Island Public Schools, 1855-1866." *Rhode Island History* 36: 99 (Nov. 1977).

Haley, John Williams. *The Old Stone Bank History of Rhode Island.* 4 vols. Providence: Providence Institution for Savings, 1929-1944.

Haley, John Williams. *George Washington and Rhode Island.* Providence: Haley & Sykes Co., 1932.

Hazard, Thomas R. *Recollections of Olden Times.* Newport: John Sanborn, 1879.

Helme, Bernon. *The Old Court House at Kingston . . .* Providence: E. L. Freeman & Son, n. d. (Copies at Kingston Free Library and University of Rhode Island Library (Special Collections)).

Heitman, Francis B. *Historical Register of Officers of the Continental Army During the War of the Revolution.* Baltimore: Genealogical Publishing Society, 1967.

Henwood, James N. J. *A Short Haul to the Bay, A History of the Narragansett Pier Railroad.* Brattleboro, Vermont: Stephen Greene Press, 1969.

Hoag & Wade. *History of the State of Rhode Island.* Philadelphia: Hoag & Wade Co., 1878.

Hoffman, Charles and Tess Hoffman. *Brotherly Love: Murder and the Politics of Prejudice in Nineteenth Century Rhode Island.* Amherst, Mass.: University of Massachusetts Press, 1993.

Hopkins, William *The Seventh Regiment of Rhode Island Volunteers in the Civil War, 1862-1865.* Providence: Snow & Farnham, 1903.

James, Sydney V. *Colonial Rhode Island: A History.* New York: Charles Scribner's Sons, 1975.

Jones, Daniel *The Economic & Social Transformation of Rural Rhode Island, 1780-1850.* Boston: Northeastern University Press, 1992.

Johnston, Elizabeth Bryant. *George Washington Day by Day.* New York: Cycle Publishing Company, 1895.

Kaminski, John. "Political Sacrifice and Demise – John Collins and Jonathan J. Hazard, 1786-1790." *Rhode Island History* 35: 91 (Aug. 1976).

Kozlowski, Kazimiera and David A. Porter. "...To Get A Little More Learning", Prudence Crandall's Female Boarding School." *Cultural Resource Management* 20, 3: 40-43 (1997).

Leach, Douglas Edward. *Flintlock and Tomahawk, New England in King Philip's War.* New York: W. W. Norton & Co., 1966.

Lemons, Stanley J. & Michael A. McKenna. "Re-enfranchisement of Rhode Island Negroes." *Rhode Island History* 30: 5-13 (Winter 1971).

Lepore, Jill. *The Name of War, King Philip's War and the Origins of American Identity.* New York: Vintage Books, 1999.

Leslie, James W. "The Key to URI's Beginnings." *Horizons.* URI Alumni Association, Feb. 1988.

Lovejoy, David S. *Rhode Island Politics and the American Revolution, 1760-1776.* Providence: Brown University Press, 1958.

MacKenzie, Louise. *Strolling Through Kingston Formerly Known as Little Rest.* Westerly, R.I.: Narragansett Graphics, 1986.

Malone, Dumas. *Dictionary of American Biography.* New York: Charles Scribner's Sons, 1935.

Marsis, James L. "Agrarian Politics in Rhode Island, 1800-1860." *Rhode Island History* 34: 13-21 (Feb. 1975).

McCabe, Martha. *The Kingston Train Station, A History.* West Kingston, R.I.: Kingston Prints, 2000.

McBurney, Christian M. *Kingston: A Forgotten History.* Kingston, R.I.: Pettaquamscutt Historical Society, 1975.

McBurney, Christian M. "The South Kingstown Planters: Country Gentry in Colonial Rhode Island." *Rhode Island History* 45(3): 81-94 (Aug. 1986).

McLoughlin, William. *Rhode Island.* New York: W.W. Norton, 1978.

Melish, Joanne Pope. *Slavery Disowned: Gradual Emancipation and "Race" in New England, 1780-1860.* Ithaca, N.Y.: Cornell University Press, 1998.

Metz, William D. *History of the Kingston Congregational Church.* Kingston, R.I.: Kingston Congregational Church, 1996.

Metz, William D. "The Fortunate Village." *Rhode Island Alumni Bulletin* 5-10 (July/August 1972).

Meyer, Henry. *All on Fire: William Lloyd Garrison and the Abolition of Slavery.* New York: St. Martin's Press, 1998.

Miller, William Davis. *The Silversmiths of Little Rest.* Boston: Merrymount Press, 1928.

Miller, William Davis. "The Removal of the County Seat from Tower Hill to Little Rest, 1752." *Rhode Island Historical Society Collections* 11 (Jan. 1926) & 46 (April 1926).

Miller, William Davis. "Thomas Mount." *Rhode Island Historical Society Collections* (April 1927).

Miller, William Davis. "The Samuel Sewall School Land and the Kingston Academy." *Rhode Island Historical Society Collections* 4-10 (Jan. 1930) & 42-50 (April 1930).

Miller, William Davis. "Some Ancient Roads in the Pettaquamscutt Purchase." *Rhode Island Historical Society Collections* (July 1931).

Miller, William Davis. "George Washington at Little Rest." *Rhode Island Historical Society Collections* (April 1932).

Miller, William Davis. "Biscuit City." *Rhode Island Historical Society Collections* (July 1933).

Miller, William Davis. "An Early Rhode Island Collector." Reprinted from the Walpole Society Note Book, 1935. (Copy at the Pettaquamscutt Historical Society.)

Miller, William Davis. "The Narragansett Planters." *Proceedings of the American Antiquarian Society* 43 (1933).

Mitchell, Broadus. *Alexander Hamilton, Youth to Maturity, 1755-1788.* New York: Macmillan Company, 1957.

Mowry, Arthur May. *The Dorr War or The Constitutional Struggle in Rhode Island.* Providence: Preston & Rounds, 1901.

Myers, John L. "Antislavery Agencies in Rhode Island, 1832-1835," *Rhode Island History* 29: 82-93 (Summer 1970); "Antislavery Agents in Rhode Island, 1835-1837," *Rhode Island History* 30: 21-31 (Winter 1971).

Nickels, Cameron C. *New England Humor From the Revolutionary War to the Civil War.* Knoxville: University of Tennessee Press, 1993.

Payne, Abraham. *Reminiscences of the Rhode Island Bar.* Providence: Tibbitts & Preston, 1885.

Pettaquamscutt Historical Society. *Historic Buildings of South County.* Kingston, R.I.: Pettaquamscutt Historical Society, n.d.

Polishook, Irwin H. *Rhode Island and the Union, 1774-1795.* Evanston, Ill.: Northwestern University Press, 1969.

Potter, Charles, E. *Genealogies of the Potter Families and Their Descendants in America to the Present Generation, with Historical and Biographical Sketches.* Salem, Mass.: Higginson Books Co., 1990.

Potter, Elisha R., Jr. *The Early History of Narragansett.* Collections of the Rhode Island Historical Society, III. Providence: Marshall, Brown & Co., 1835.

Potter, Elisha R., Jr. *Considerations on the Questions of the Adoption of a Constitution and Extension of Suffrage in Rhode Island.* Boston: Thomas H. Webb & Co., 1842.

Reidy, Joseph. "Negro Election Day and Black Community Life in New England, 1750-1860." *Marxist Perspectives* 3:102-117, 1978.

Rhode Island Historical Preservation Commission. *Historic and Architectural Resources of South Kingstown, Rhode Island: A Preliminary Report.* Providence, 1984.

Rider, Hope S. *Valor Fore & Aft, Being the Adventures of America's First Naval Vessel.* Annapolis: United States Naval Institute, 1978.

Rider, Sydney S. *An Historical Inquiry Concerning the Attempt to Raise a Regiment of Slaves by Rhode Island During the War of the Revolution.* Providence: S. S. Rider, 1880.

Rider, Sydney S. *Historical Research and Educational Labor Illustrated in the Work of Elisha Reynolds Potter, Late Judge of the Supreme Court of Rhode Island.* Providence: The Franklin Press Co., 1901. Copy at Library of Congress.

Rosenfeld, Alvin. "Wilkins Updike to Sarah Helen Whitman: Two Letters." *Rhode Island History* 25: 97-109 (Oct. 1966).

Russell, Howard S. *A Long, Deep Furrow, Three Centuries of Farming in New England.* Hanover, N.H.: University Press of New England, 1976.

Saunders, Laura S. "A Glimpse of South Kingstown's Maritime Past." *The Reporter* (quarterly journal of the Pettaquamscutt Historical Society) 1 (Autumn 1986).

Schantz, Mark S. *Piety in Providence, Class Dimensions of Religious Experience in Antebellum Rhode Island.* Ithaca, N.Y.: Cornell University Press, 2000.

Scott, Kenneth. *Counterfeiting in Colonial America.* Philadelphia: University of Pennsylvania Press, 2000.

Scott, Kenneth. *Counterfeiting in Colonial Rhode Island.* Providence: Rhode Island Historical Society, 1960.

Simister, Florence Parker. *The Fire's Center: Rhode Island in the Revolutionary Era, 1763-1790.* Providence: Rhode Island Bicentennial Foundation, 1979.

South County, the Yearbook of Southern Rhode Island. Wakefield, R.I.: Narragansett Times. Various editions.

Stachiw, Myron O. "'For the Sake of Commerce': Slavery, Antislavery, and Northern Industry." *The Meaning of Slavery in the North* (David Roediger and Martin H. Blatt, editors). New York: Garland Publishing, 1998.

Stedman, Oliver H. *A Stroll Through Memory Lane.* 2 vols. West Kingston, R.I.: Kingston Press, 1999.

Sweet, John Wood. *Bodies Politic, Negotiating Race in the American North, 1730-1830.* Baltimore: Johns Hopkins University Press, 2003.

Taylor, Philip Kittredge. "Little Rest." *The New England Magazine.* v. XXVIII No. 2, April 1903.

Thompson, Peter, *Rum, Punch & Revolution: Taverngoing & Public Life in Eighteenth-Century Philadelphia.* Philadelphia: University of Pennsylvania Press, 1999.

Thresher, John C. "More Information about the Eldred Family." *The Reporter* (the quarterly journal of the Pettaquamscutt Historical Society) (Summer 1998).

Thresher, John C. "Education in Kingston, Part One – Kingston Academy." *The Reporter* (the quarterly journal of the Pettaquamscutt Historical Society) (Spring 1998).

Thresher, John C. "Education in Kingston, Part Two -- Kingston Grammar School." *The Reporter* (the quarterly journal of the Pettaquamscutt Historical Society) (Summer, 1998).

Tootell, Lucy R. (ed.). *Driftways into the Past (Richmond, Rhode Island).* Westerly, R.I.: The Utter Company, 1977.

Tootell, Lucy R. "Shipwright Saunders' Shipshape Ships." *The Reporter* (the quarterly journal of the Pettaquamscutt Historical Society) 29 (May 1963).

Tyrell, Ian R. *Sobering Up: From Temperance to Prohibition in Antebellum America, 1800-1860.* Westport, Conn.: Greenwood Press, 1979.

Updike, Wilkins. *A History of the Episcopal Church in Narragansett, Rhode Island.* Boston: Merrymount Press, 1907 (2d ed.).

Updike, Wilkins. *Memoirs of the Rhode Island Bar.* Boston: Thomas Webb, 1842.

Van Broekhoven, Deborah Bingham. *The Devotion of These Women: Rhode Island in the Antislavery Network.* Amherst, Mass.: University of Massachusetts Press, 2002.

Wade, Melvin. "Shining in Borrowed Plummage: Affirmation of Community in the Black Coronation Festivals in New England, 1750-1850." *Western Folklore* 40: 211-31 (July 1981).

Walker, Anthony. *So Few the Brave, Rhode Island Continentals 1775-1783.* Newport, R.I.: Seafield Press, 1981.

Weeden, William. *Early Rhode Island: A Social History of the People.* New York: Grafton Press, 1910.

White, Shane. "'It was a Proud Day': African Americans, Festivals, and Parades in the North, 1741-1834." *Journal of American History* 81: 13-50 (June 1994).

Whyte, J. Bruce. "The Publick Universal Friend." *Rhode Island History* 26: 18-24 (Jan. 1968) & 27: 103-12 (Oct. 1968).

Wiecek, William M. "Popular Sovereignty in the Dorr War: Conservative Counterblast." *Rhode Island History* 32: 35-51 (May 1973).

Wisby, Herbert A. *Pioneer Prophetess: Jemima Wilkinson, the Publick Universal Friend.* Ithaca, N.Y.: Cornell University Press, 1964.

Woodward, Carl R. *Plantation in Yankeeland.* Chester, Conn.: Pequot Press, 1971.

Woodward, Carl R. "A Profile in Dedication: Sarah Harris and the Fayerweather Family." *The New England Galaxy.* V. XV, No. 1 (Summer 1973).

Unpublished Manuscripts

Balch, Lewis. "Old Kingston Folk; Solomon Fayerweather; in Kingston Library; Journeys Back to Little Rest; Old Folks in Little Rest; A Sketch of Old Kingston." Undated, probably around 1910. (Manuscript at Pettaquamscutt Historical Society.)

Drery, Leo. "Union Regimental Histories and Rosters of the Kingstown, R.I. Area." Undated, around 2004. (Manuscript at Pettaquamscutt Historical Society.)

Flaherty, Thomas Francis. "The History of the Public School Movement in the State of Rhode Island and Providence Plantations from 1827 to 1857." Doctoral Thesis, Boston College, 1973.

Faella, Betty and Connie Fitzelle. "The Every Tuesday Club, Kingston, Rhode Island, The First Hundred Years, 1896-1996." 1998 Revised Edition. (Copy at the Kingston Free Library.)

Freeman, Donald McKinley. "South County Reaction to the Dorr Rebellion as Illustrated by Elisha Reynolds Potter." Masters Thesis, University of Rhode Island, 1955.

Helme, Jonathan. "Recollections of South Kingstown. Reminiscences of Little Rest (now Kingston) Hill and Its Surroundings, Some Fifty Years Ago." Undated. (Copies at Pettaquamscutt Historical Society, Kingston Free Library and Peace Dale Library.)

Helme, Nathaniel. *Diaries of Nathaniel Helme, 1886-1935*, 32 vols. (Typed summary manuscript at Pettaquamscutt Historical Society.)

Herndon, Ruth Wallis. "Governing the Affairs of the Town: Continuity and Change in Rhode Island, 1750-1800." Doctoral Thesis, American University, 1992.

Hunt, Annie M. "Industries, Stores, Lawyers, Etc. in Little Rest, Later Kingston." 1927. (Copies at the Pettaquamscutt Historical Society and Kingston Free Library.)

Langer, Kenneth Thomas. "Elisha Reynolds Potter, Sr., Politician." Master's Thesis, University of Rhode Island, 1957.

McBurney, Christian M. "The Rise and Decline of the South Kingstown Planters, 1660-1783." BA Honors Thesis, Department of History, Brown University, 1981. (Copies at South Kingstown libraries, Pettaquamscutt Historical Society, University of Rhode Island (Special Collections), Brown University Library, and Rhode Island Historical Society.)

Miller, William Davis. "A Brief Account of the Original Landholders and Their Lands in the Vicinity of Little Rest Hill in the Pettaquamscutt Purchase, 1657-1700." (Manuscript in the Rhode Island Historical Society, William Davis Miller Papers.)

Potter, James B. M. "Recollections of a Paymaster of the Army During the Civil War 1861-1882." Feb. 1896. (Manuscript in the Rhode Island Historical Society, James B. M. Potter Papers, Mss 629 SG 6, Box 1, Folder 6.)

Quinn, Catherine Harvey. "Rowland Hazard of Peace Dale, Rhode Island." Master's Thesis, University of Rhode Island, 1960.

Sweet, Edward F. "The Origins of the Democratic Party in Rhode Island, 1824-1836." Doctoral Thesis, Fordham University, 1971.

Titus, David K. "The Kingston Free Library and Reading Room, 1824-1893; a Revised History." University of Rhode Island term paper. August 8, 1975. (Copy in Kingston Free Library.)

Tootell, Lucy R. (ed.). "Kingston, Old Houses, Dates and Builders." (Manuscript in the Pettaquamscutt Historical Society.) (Excerpts from South Kingstown Land Evidence Records.)

Tyler, E. M. "History of Kingston." Undated. (Manuscript at the Pettaquamscutt Historical Society.)

Wells, Herbert G. "A Restful Corner of Rhode Island." Approx. 1880. (Copy at the Pettaquamscutt Historical Society.)

Wells, John Hagadorn. "Biographical Sketches of Distinguished Citizens of South Kingstown." Not dated. (Copy at University of Rhode Island Library (Special Collections).)

Wells, John Hagadorn. "Kingston Annals, Reminiscences of Little Rest." 1897. (Copies at the Pettaquamscutt Historical Society and Kingston Free Library.)

Zuckerman, Michael B. "The Political Economy of Industrial Rhode Island, 1790-1860." Doctoral Thesis, Brown University, 1981.

Notes to Chapters

Little Rest's Beginnings

For the Narragansett tribe and King Philip's War, *see* Leach, Douglas Edward, *Flintlock and Tomahawk*, 128-35; Lepore, Jill, *The Name of War, King Philip's War,* 88-89; Metz, William D., *History of the Kingston Congregational Church,* 16-17. In 1894, while digging a cellar for a house behind the Court House, the remains of four persons were found. They were thought to be Indians and have been buried for at least two hundred years. Two of them apparently were buried in a sitting position. *Narragansett Times,* Sept. 28, 1894, p. 1, c.5. For the early white settlers, *see* Hazard, Thomas R., *Recollections of Olden Times,* 44 (Knowles); McBurney, Christian M., "The Rise and Decline of the South Kingstown Planters, 1660-1783" (BA Honors Thesis) 15 & 32-33; Miller, William Davis, "A Brief Account of the Original Landholders and Their Lands," *passim;* MacKenzie, Louise, *Strolling Through Kingston,* 4 & 8; Bartlett, John (ed.), *Records of the Colony of Rhode Island,* v. III, 59 ("desolate wilderness"). For the naming of Little Rest to commemorate the Great Swamp Fight, *see* Taylor, Philip K., "Little Rest," *The New England Magazine* (April 1903) 129-30; *South County Yearbook* 35 (5th ed. 1952); Federal Writers' Project, *Rhode Island, A Guide to the Smallest State,* 370; McBurney, Christian M., *Kingston: A Forgotten History,* 11. For the history of early Kingstown, *see* James, Sydney, *Colonial Rhode Island,* ch. 6-7; McBurney, Christian M., "The Rise and Decline of the South Kingstown Planters, 1660-1783" (BA Honors Thesis) ch. I; Potter, Elisha R., *The Early History of Narragansett,* 106 (name change of Kingstown to Rochester in 1686). For a modern example of confusion over names, see Carl Bridenbaugh, in his *Fat Mutton and Liberty of Conscience* at 59, where he referred to "Rochester (Kingston)," when he meant Kingstown. For landholdings of the Pettaquamscutt Purchasers, *see* Miller, William Davis, "A Brief Account of the Original Landholders and Their Lands," *passim*; MacKenzie, Louise, *Strolling Through Kingston,* 4 & 8. For the laying out of roads, *see* Miller, William Davis, "A

Brief Account of the Original Landholders and Their Lands," *passim*; Miller, William Davis, "Some Ancient Roads in the Pettaquamscutt Purchase," *Rhode Island Historical Society Collections* (July 1931) 105-117; Potter, Elisha, R., Jr., *Early History of Narragansett,* 110, 223, 290 & 305; Bartlett, John R. (ed.), *Records of the Colony of Rhode Island,* v. III, 480-81 (1703 highway). For surveying done by Robert Hazard, see Potter, Elisha R., Jr., *Early History of Narragansett,* 290. For early land transfers in Little Rest, *see id.* at 292 (William Knowles acquires land in 1671 that would later be acquired by Elisha Reynolds and include the Elisha Potter homestead farm). For the Moore/Perkins house, see South Kingstown Land Evidence Records, v. 3A, 111 (Henry Bull to John Moore, Feb. 9, 1710); v. 3, 109-110 (John Moore to Abraham Perkins, July 11, 1715); v. 4, 727 (Abraham Perkins to Nathaniel Perkins, Nov. 2, 1744, including blacksmith shop and dwelling). For the Reynolds house, see *id.*, v. 4, 170 (Henry Knowles to Elisha Reynolds, 200 acres with a dwelling house, May 19, 1738); v. 4, 297 (Henry Knowles to Elisha Reynolds, 470 acres with dwelling house, on March 17, 1739). This house was called the "mansion house" in a 1752 land sale. See *id.*, v. 5, 364 (Elisha Reynolds to John Douglas, 1752). For the Robert Potter tavern, see *id.,* v. 3, 580 (Robert Potter, Sr. to Elisha Reynolds, ½ acre lot, Oct. 15, 1733); v. 4, 342 (Elisha Reynolds to Stephen Mumford, dwelling, stable and other buildings, March 4, 1740); v. 4, 739 (Stephen Mumford "shopkeeper" to Elisha Reynolds, same tract as previous one, April 13, 1745). For the Joseph Case land, see *id.*, v. 3, 259 (Joseph Case, Sr. to Joseph Case, Jr., 15 acres, Sept. 16, 1728); South Kingstown Probate Records, v. 3, 395 (Joseph Case, Sr. to Joseph Case, Jr., 1733); see also John Moore to Abraham Perkins transfer, *supra,* which states that that land was bounded on the east by land owned by Joseph Case; Potter, Elisha R., Jr., *Early History of Narragansett,* 309 (location of Joseph Case homestead east of Updike house); Thomas M. Potter's handwritten notes on Joseph Case, Wells Papers, Pettaquamscutt Historical Society. For the Robert Potter house, see South Kingstown Probate Records, v. 3, 418 (Robert Potter, Sr. to Robert Potter, Jr., 40 acres to begin 10 rods from house of Robert Potter, Sr.). The town meeting records, in addressing the topic of repairing town highways, mention in 1731 Abraham Perkins' shop and in 1741 Perkins' shop and nearby Joseph Case's land. South Kingstown Town Meeting Records, v. I, 52 & 120. For early probate records, see South Kingstown Probate Records, v. 1, 32 (Oct. 14, 1706) (Robert Hannah); v. 3, 34 (Feb. 14, 1736) (Robert Hannah, Jr.); v. 3, 127 & 131-32 (Jan. 11,1739) (Joseph Case); v. 4, 132 & 149 (Sept. 8, 1746) (Robert Potter, Sr.). For Reynolds as shopkeeper, see King's County Inferior Court of Common Pleas Records, v. A (1731-1741) 246, Rhode Island Judicial Archives (Elisha Reynolds of South Kingstown shopkeeper pla vs Samuel Clarke) (June 29, 1736). For the genealogies of the Robert Potter and Elisha Reynolds' families, see Potter, Charles, E., *Genealogies of the Potter Families*, Part 4, 1 & 20. For additional information on early Little Rest, see; MacKenzie, Louise, *Strolling Through Kingston,* 8-12. See also inventories of Henry Knowles of Little Rest, v. 3, 140 (May 12, 1740) (39 hogs; 6 horses; "old Negro Harry;" and "an Indian woman" who was probably an indentured servant); Abraham Perkins, v. 4, 218 (Feb. 10, 1746) (includes two silver spoons). For background on the Six Principle Baptist Church in Rhode Island, see Jones, Daniel, *The Economic & Social Transformation of Rural Rhode Island,* 17-22. For background on religious life in the Narragansett country, see McBurney, Christian M., "The Rise and Decline of the South Kingstown Planters, 1660-1783" (BA Honors Thesis) ch. IV. For information on the Baptists in Little Rest, see *id.* at ch. V; Potter, Charles, E., *Potter Family and Their Descendants in America,* 851; Potter, Elisha R., *The Early History of Narragansett,* 118-19 (letter in 1731 from Little Rest Baptists to Providence Baptists mentioning the "new Meeting House" in South Kingstown). The town council records in 1777 also refer to "the meeting House on Little Rest Hill," which may have meant a Baptist meeting house, but probably meant the Court House. See Stutz, Jean C. (ed.), *South Kingstown Town Council Records,* 83. For the first court house built in King's County in 1731 at Tower Hill, see Bickford, Christopher, *Crime, Punishment, and the Washington County Jail,* 5.

Little Rest: Rising Hub of the Narragansett Country

For the history of the Narragansett planters, see McBurney, Christian M., "The Rise and Decline of the South Kingstown Planters, 1660-1783" (BA Honors Thesis) ch. II-V; McBurney, Christian, "The South Kingstown Planters: Country Gentry in Colonial Rhode Island," *Rhode Island History* 45: 81-94 (Aug. 1986); Fitts, Robert K., *Inventing New England's Slave Paradise, passim;* Miller, William Davis, "The Narragansett Planters," *Proceedings of the American Antiquarian Society,* 43 (1933); Bidwell, Percy W. and John I. Falconer, *History of Agriculture in the Northern United States, 1620-1860,* 70, 105-13 & 116. For the backgrounds of Caleb Gardner, William Potter, Benjamin Peckham, Elisha Reynolds and Robert Potter, see Elisha Reynolds Papers, Rhode Island Historical Society, Mss 629, SG1 and McBurney, Christian M., "The Rise and Decline of the South Kingstown Planters, 1660-1783" (BA Honors Thesis) 75-76 (Reynolds as merchant); Bartlett, John (ed.), *Census of the Inhabitants of the Colony of Rhode Island, 1774* (South Kingstown); Updike, Wilkins, *A History of the Episcopal Church in Narragansett,* 235 (William Potter); Potter, Charles, E, *Genealogies of the Potter Families,* Part 4, 4 & 28-31 (William Potter); South Kingstown Town Council Records, v. 4, 89-90 and *passim* (Caleb Gardner, member of town council); South Kingstown Probate Records, v. 4, 132 & 147 (Robert Potter, Sr. will); v. 6, 263, Dec. 7, 1790 (Benjamin Peckham will); Elisha Potter's Account Book, 2, Pettaquamscutt Historical Society (Caleb Gardner's purchases) & 11, 32 (purchases by Robert Potter and Elisha Reynolds). For the tradesmen in Little Rest, see South Kingstown Land Evidence Records, v. 4, 455 (William Robinson to Nathaniel Helme, Mar. 27, 1741, shoemaker); v. 5, 180 (Caleb Gardner to Samuel Casey, Mar. 18, 1750, silversmith); v. 4, 727 (Nathaniel Perkins from Abraham Perkins, Nov. 2, 1744, "a certain blacksmith shop"); v. 4, 170 (Henry Knowles to Elisha Reynolds, 1738, storekeeper); v. 5, 364 (John Douglass from Elisha Reynolds, 1752; land mentioned in next entry); v. 7, 117 (John Douglass to George Teft, a "blacksmith shop," 1772); King's County Inferior Court of Common Pleas Records, Aug. 1760 Sess. 389 (John Douglass, blacksmith). See also chapter on Little Rest silversmiths. Elisha Reynolds brought numerous suits in the King's County inferior court of common pleas in his capacity as both "storekeeper" and "merchant" from 1736 until his death in 1791, with most cases being filed in the 1750s and 1760s. At Reynolds' death in 1791, a newspaper obituary described

Reynolds as "an honest Man, a good Citizen, and for many Years a very respectable Merchant." *Providence Gazette,* Nov. 11, 1791.

The *South County, the Yearbook of Southern Rhode Island,* Wakefield, R.I., Narragansett Times (6th ed. 1953), contains a short article summarizing a purported book by B. S. Silliman, *A Memorial to the Village, Being a Monument to the Providential Habitation and Prosperitie of Little Rest in the South County.* The book was purportedly published in Boston in 1747. The summary states that Silliman, apparently a Newport attorney, surveyed Little Rest village in 1743. He identified and described locations of the village church, the tavern, the village well and a dozen or so prominent buildings. The book describes some of Little Rest's earliest businesses. Among them was a blacksmith shop operated by Joseph Wetherby, who apparently achieved considerable fame for "most giant like" lifting "tenne bunches of haye all bound" above his head. Wetherby's brother, Carter, was a wheelwright who operated a wagon and wheel repair shop. The article states that the book was discovered by a Lester V. Plotkin of Wickford and New York. This book, if it ever existed, is lost. The author and the publisher believe that either the article or the book was a prank, in the tradition of Little Rest practical jokers described later in this book. It has been suggested that perhaps William Davis Miller was the author, as he was a knowledgeable person who could have achieved the subtle feat of passing off such a book as authentic. In addition to the book not being found and not being on any list of published books of which the author is aware, other features suggest the book is not authentic. First, the purported title of the book uses the term "the South County," which by all accounts was not being used at this time. Second, land evidence records do not indicate that a Joseph or Carter Wetherby resided in Little Rest. South Kingstown town council records and probate records do not mention any Wetherbys. Third, town council records do not indicate that a person in Little Rest kept a tavern during the indicated time period. In addition, it does not appear that a church existed in Little Rest in 1743. Finally, the pronunciation of the purported author's last name – silly man – suggests a prank. If anyone discovers an existing copy of the book (perhaps the only one!), please notify the Pettaquamscutt Historical Society and me.

The Removal of the Court House and Jail from Tower Hill to Little Rest

For the removal of the county seat to Little Rest, see Miller, William Davis, "The Removal of the County Seat from Tower Hill to Little Rest, 1752," *Rhode Island Historical Society Collections* 11 (Jan. 1926) & 46 (April 1926); Petitions to General Assembly, Petitions by Little Rest Inhabitants and Tower Hill Inhabitants, Feb. 1752, Mss 629 SG1, Box 1, Folder 5, Rhode Island Historical Society; see also Bickford, Christopher, *Crime, Punishment, and the Washington County Jail,* 7-9; Bartlett, John (ed.), *Records of the Colony of Rhode Island,* v. V, 349-50 (act authorizing removal); South Kingstown Town Meeting Records, v. I, 230 (51-21 vote approving removal). For the transfer of the land for the first court house and jail, see South Kingstown Land Evidence Records, v. 5, 395-97 (Elisha Reynolds) and v. 5, 397-99 (Robert Potter). For Robert Potter and John Potter taverns, see South Kingstown Town Council Records, v. 4, 217 (R. Potter's first license in July 1753);

v. 4, 225 (town council meeting at R. Potter tavern in 1753); v. 4, 240 (R. Potter reimbursed for dinners); v. 4, 229 (J. Potter issued first license to sell liquor "in the Dwelling House that he hired on Little Rest Hill"); v. 4, 237 (town council meeting at J. Potter tavern, September 10, 1753); v. 4, 240 (town council meeting at J. Potter tavern, December 10, 1753). For land sales by Elisha Reynolds and Robert Potter, and new buildings in Little Rest, see South Kingstown Land Evidence Records, v. 5, 364 (Elisha Reynolds to John Douglas, 1752); v. 5, 451 (Elisha Reynolds to William Caswell, 1752); v. 5, 460 (Elisha Reynolds to John Potter, 1755, land next to Caswell that Potter was renting to operate a tavern, and land at the corner of main street and Biscuit City Road); v. 5, 444 (Robert Potter to Daniel Weeden, Dec. 11, 1754, land 10 rods from the jail); v. 6, 20 (Elisha Reynolds to William Weight, 1757, land to west of first court house); see also Mackenzie, Louise, *Strolling Through Kingston,* 16-20. For the school house, see South Kingstown Land Evidence Records, v. 6, 110 (Robert Potter to Elisha Reynolds, James Rogers, George Gardner, Daniel Carpenter, Caleb Gardner, Nathaniel Helme, John Douglas, Benedict Helme, Thomas Cottrill, Oliver Helme, and John Weeden, Oct. 20, 1759). For some of occupations of Little Rest residents, see notes in this paragraph and to prior chapter; notes on chapters on silversmiths and tavern keepers; King's County Inferior Court of Common Pleas Records, Aug. 1760 Sess. 389 (John Douglas, blacksmith); Aug. 1771 Sess. 342 (Caleb Wescott, "housewright"); Aug. 1782 Sess. 585 (Abel Cottrell, tailor). For new purchases and building construction in the 1770s, see *id.*, v. 6, 489 (Elisha Reynolds to John Waite "silversmith," 1769); v. 6, 553 (Elisha Reynolds to Benjamin Barker of Newport, land with a dwelling house and a well of water, Nov. 11, 1770) (location of current Elisha R. Gardner house and presumably the village well); v. 7, 254 (Robert Potter to Joseph Perkins, April 25, 1774); v. 7, 289 (Robert Potter to John Weeden, June 28, 1775); v. 7, 312 (Robert Potter to Thomas Potter, 1775). See also Cook, Edward, M. (ed.), "Jeffrey Watson's Diary, 1740-1784," *Rhode Island History* 43: 79, 98 (Aug. 1984) (Reynolds raising a large house in Little Rest four corners lot in June 1760); South Kingstown Land Evidence Records, v. 8, 112 (Elisha Reynolds sells lot in Little Rest to Robert Helme, 1786). For Immanuel Case's store, see advertisement in the *Newport Mercury,* Aug. 26, 1771. This store apparently was located near the location of the Kingston Hill Store. See South Kingstown Land Evidence Records, v. 5, 559 (Nathaniel Perkins transfers the Moore/Perkins house to James Rogers, which is described as bounded to the east by land owned by Immanuel Case, Feb. 7, 1755). For Samuel Casey's store, see South Kingstown Land Evidence Records, v. v. 5, 180 (Caleb Gardner to Samuel Casey, including dwelling house and stable, Mar. 18, 1750); later chapter on Little Rest silversmiths and notes thereto. For James Helme's store, see South Kingstown Land Evidence Records, v. 7, 406 (former Samuel Casey property, with "store house" and "smoke house," transferred to James and Powell Helme, Dec. 26, 1777; see also later chapter on general stores in Little Rest. For information on the Baptists in Little Rest, see notes to previous chapter; Cook, Edward, M. (ed.), "Jeffrey Watson's Diary, 1740-1784," *Rhode Island History* 43: 79, 98 (Aug. 1984); Woodward, Carl R., *Plantation in Yankeeland,* 129 (Rev. Fayerweather services); Bartlett, John R. (ed.), *Records of the Colony of Rhode Island,* v. VI, 176 (Reynolds appointed to court martial board). For the role of the Little Rest Baptists in the founding of Brown University, see Bronson, Walter, C.,

The History of Brown University, 493-503 (petitions in Appendices); Bartlett, John R. (ed.), *Records of the Colony of Rhode Island,* v. VI, 385-86 (articles of incorporation). For Reynolds' grant of land to the Baptist church, see South Kingstown Land Evidence Records, v. 5, 473 (March 10, 1755) ("near ye lot on which ye Court House stands"); Wells, J. Hagadorn, *Kingston Annals,* 60-61. For Congregationalists, see Metz, William D., *History of the Kingston Congregational Church,* 35. For Anglicans and Quakers, see McBurney, Christian M., "The Rise and Decline of the South Kingstown Planters, 1660-1783" (BA Honors Thesis) ch. V. For the 1774 census, see Bartlett, John (ed.), *Census of the Colony of Rhode Island, 1774* (South Kingstown). For Royzell Smith serving as the jailer of the King's County jail in 1774, see Bickford, Christopher, *Crime, Punishment, and the Washington County Jail,* 29. Royzell Smith's name is misspelled "Roswell Smith" in the census. "House carpenter" Caleb Wescott and cordwainer John Weeden moved to Little Rest shortly after the 1774 census was taken. Wescott is credited with building the Joseph Reynolds tavern in 1774. Rhode Island Historical Preservation Commission, *Historic and Architectural Resources of South Kingstown,* 49. He purchased land from Robert Potter at the location of the tavern in April 1774. South Kingstown Land Evidence Records, v. 7, 244 (April 25, 1774). Both Weeden and Wescott are missing from the 1774 census, but are present in the 1777 military census, which was taken in the order of villages. See Chamberlain, Mildred (ed.), *The Rhode Island 1777 Military Census,* 100.

The Court House: The Heart of Little Rest

For the history of the first and second court house buildings in Little Rest, see Miller, William Davis, "The Removal of the County Seat from Tower Hill to Little Rest, 1752," *Rhode Island Historical Society Collections* 11 (Jan 1926) & 46 (April 1926); Helme, Bernon, "The Old Court House at Kingston"; Bickford, Christopher, *Crime, Punishment, and the Washington County Jail,* 7-9; Pettaquamscutt Historical Society, *Historic Buildings of South County,* 34-36; *South County Yearbook* (12th ed. 1959) 11 (repairs to court house; solid construction); Stedman, Oliver H., *A Stroll Through Memory Lane,* v. II, 6-8; depositions relating to land border dispute mentioning first court house, Timothy Peckham v. Cyrus French, Aug. 1818, Elisha R. Potter, Jr. Papers, Series 3, Box 4, Folder 35, Rhode Island Historical Society (includes Pollack statement that land for first court house was used as a "race ground"). For Potter's appointment and reimbursement for building expenses, see Bartlett, John R. (ed.), *Records of the Colony of Rhode Island,* v. VIII, 245-46 (appointment) & v. VIII, 24 (£231 and 9 shillings "for cash advanced, and materials provided for building the court house in King's county") & 158 (£14 and 11 shillings "for priming the sashes and glazing the windows of the court house in King's county"). Potter financed the court house and owned the land and building until he was finally reimbursed for all of the amounts and transferred ownership to the state in 1785. South Kingstown Land Evidence Records, v. 8, 57 (Nov. 3, 1785). For background on the colony level government, see Conley, Patrick T., *Democracy in Decline,* 36-54; Pettaquamscutt Historical Society, *Historic Buildings of South County,* 34-38. For background on the Ward-Hopkins controversy, see Lovejoy,

David S., *Rhode Island Politics and the American Revolution,* ch. I-VII. For election activities in Little Rest, see Cook, Edward M., Jr. (ed.), "Jeffrey Watson's Diary," *Rhode Island History* 43: 79, 103 (Aug. 1984); McBurney, Christian M., "The Rise and Decline of the South Kingstown Planters, 1660-1783" (BA Honors Thesis), ch. VI; Lovejoy, David S., *Rhode Island Politics and the American Revolution,* 129. For the act abolishing the slave trade enacted in Little Rest, see Bartlett, John (ed.), *Records of the Colony of Rhode Island,* v. X, 262. For the act changing the name of King's County to Washington County, see *id.,* v. IX, 484 (Oct. 1781). For villagers serving as waiters and messengers at General Assembly meetings, see, e.g., Bartlett, John R. (ed.), v. VIII, 24, 385, 572 & 617 & v. IX, 343; *Rhode Island Acts & Resolves,* Oct. 1791 Session, v. I, 34 & Oct. 1793 Session, v. II, 20 (to Douglas for attending as a waiter and providing candles); *Rhode Island Acts & Resolves,* Oct. 1791 Session, v. I, 36. For William Potter providing wood for use during General Assembly sessions, see *id.,* v. VIII, 192 (one cord, March 1777); v. VIII, 211 (half a cord, April 1777); v. VIII, 385 (March 1778); v. VIII, 477 (three cords, Oct. 1778). For Caleb Gardner providing wood, see *Rhode Island Acts & Resolves,* Oct. 1791 Session, v. I, 34 & March 1794, v. II, 4. For background on the county level government, see Field, Edward (ed.), *State of Rhode Island and Providence Plantations, A History,* v. III, 103-05; Conley, Patrick T., *Democracy in Decline,* 40-44. For the cases brought by Little Rest shopkeepers in 1762, see King's County Inferior Court of Common Pleas Records, Feb. 1762 Sess. 44-127. For the Potter-Hazard court case, see Cook, Edward M., Jr. (ed.), "Jeffrey Watson's Diary, 1740-1784," *Rhode Island History* 43: 79, 102 (Aug. 1984). For cases filed by Newport merchants against Narragansett planters, see, e.g., King's County Inferior Court of Common Pleas Records, Feb. 1755 Sess. 121 (Abraham Redwood, Newport merchant, sues Benjamin Hazard of South Kingstown); Aug. 1756 Sess. 685 (Godfrey Malbone, Newport merchant, sues Westerly man for £1,000). For cases filed by merchants outside King's County, see, e.g., King's County Inferior Court of Common Pleas Records, Aug. 1753 Sess. 291 (Elias Bland, merchant of London, sues John Chaloner, merchant of Newport, for £6,000); Aug. 1754 Sess. 1 (Thomas Hutchinson, merchant of Boston, sues Benjamin Belknap, trader of Providence); 41 (Andrew Oliver, merchant of Boston, sues John Holmes Gardner, merchant of Newport); Aug. 1760 Sess. 365 (Alexander McDougal, merchant of New York City, sues a Newport merchant). For background on the town level government, see Daniels, Bruce C., *Dissent and Conformity on Narragansett Bay, passim*; Herndon, Ruth Wallis, "Governing the Affairs of the Town," *passim.* For the right of freemen to instruct their deputies, see South Kingstown Town Meeting Records, v. 2, 165 (Apr. 17, 1783). For percentage of white males eligible to vote in Rhode Island, see Daniels, Bruce C., *Dissent and Conformity on Narragansett Bay,* 105 (42% in South Kingstown in 1767; range in various towns is from 41% to 82%, with an average of 61%); Lovejoy, David S., *Rhode Island Politics and the American Revolution,* 16 (79% in five towns, not including South Kingstown); Conley, Patrick, *Democracy in Decline,* 49 (75%); Crane, Elaine Forman, *A Dependent People,* 97, n.48 (believes 60% figure is more accurate than 75%). For exclusions of blacks, women, Jews and Catholics from voting, see Conley, Patrick, *Democracy in Decline,* 33-35.

For colony and county level military and civil offices, see Smith, Joseph Jencks (ed.), *Civil and Military List of Rhode Island, 1647-1800.*

The King's County Jail

This chapter relies heavily on Bickford, Christopher, *Crime, Punishment, and the Washington County Jail,* 3-12. For Helme's being released from prison for indebtedness, see King's County Superior Court Records, Jan. 1765 Sess. 26-27. For Helme's petition to run a lottery, see Bartlett, John R. (ed.), *Records of the Colony of Rhode Island,* v. VI, 316-17. For an example of the state paying jailers for feeding "poor Prisoners committed at the Suit of the State," see *Rhode Island Acts & Resolves,* Feb. 1791 Session, v. I, 20 & Feb. 1797 Session, v. III, 16. For Reynolds' escape and capture, see Scott, Kenneth, *Counterfeiting in Colonial Rhode Island,* 48-49. For the trials and sentences of Reynolds, other counterfeiters and accomplices, see King's County Superior Court Records, April 1754 Sess. 137-40. For the General Assembly restricting the jailer from allowing prisoners to roam at large, see *Rhode Island Acts & Resolves,* Sept. 1790 Session, v. I, 11. For the General Assembly's approving of the purchase of the lot and building a new jail, see Bartlett, John R., *Records of the Colony of Rhode Island,* v. X, 368-69. For the General Assembly paying for the construction of the new jail, see *Rhode Island Acts & Resolves,* Feb. 1794 Session, v. II, 18-19; see also *Rhode Island Acts & Resolves,* Oct. 1791 Session, v. I, 36; June 1792 Session, v. II, 17; October 1792 Session, v. II, 18. For the sentences of corporal punishment, see King's County Superior Court Records, Oct. 1770 Sess. 269-70; Oct. 1784 Sess. 76-80; Oct. 1787 Sess. 166; Apr. 1788 Sess. 208. For the 1788 order for stock and pillory, see South Kingstown Town Meeting Records, v. 2, 267 (Sept. 20, 1788).

"Three Good Taverns"

For militia muster references, see Bartlett, John R. (ed.), *Records of the Colony of Rhode Island,* v. VI, 78 (1757 muster); Hazard, Caroline (ed.), *Nailer Tom's Diary,* 25 (Oct. 27, 1781) & 150 (April 29, 1793); Wells, J. Hagadorn, "Kingston Annals," 66 ("drumming and fifing"). For the Robert Potter tavern, see South Kingstown Town Council Records, v. 2, 10 (Robert Potter license in 1723); v. 4, 217 (July 13, 1752) (first liquor license since 1723; Potter may have continued his tavern keeping business, but not obtained a license for it); v. 4, 225 (town council meets at tavern in 1753); v. 4, 232 (same); v. 4, 240 (same); Tootell, Lucy, *Kingston, Old Houses, Dates and Builders,* 32-33 (list of property owners and transfers among Potters); MacKenzie, Louise, *Strolling Through Kingston,* 8-12. For the Kingston Inn, see South Kingstown Town Council Records, v. 4, 229 (John Potter's first license in March 22, 1753), v. 4, 234 (license renewed, in July 9, 1753), v. 4, 237 (town council meets at tavern in 1753), v. 4, 240 (same), v. 4, 247 (same); Pettaquamscutt Historical Society, *Historic Buildings of South County,* 39 (general, including 1911 restoration); Tootell, Lucy (ed.), *Kingston, Old Houses, Dates and Builders,* 26 (including purchase by J.P. Rathbun); MacKenzie, Louise, *Strolling Through Kingston,* 8-12. In court cases brought by John Potter, he is sometimes identified as "innholder alias tanner." In one case, Immanuel Case, a general storekeeper in Little Rest, successfully ejected "John Potter the third . . . Innholder alias Tanner" from the shoemaker's shop just below the county jail. See King's County Inferior Court of Common Pleas Records, Feb. 1766 Sess. 113. This was probably Nathaniel Helme's old shoemaker's shop. Robert Potter and John Potter are the only taverns listed in Little Rest until Thomas Potter obtained his first license in 1770. For Thomas Potter tavern and merchant business, see South Kingstown Town Council Records, v. 5, 229 (first license, in July 1770); *Commerce of Rhode Island, 1726-1800,* Massachusetts Historical Society Collections, LXIX-LXX, v. I, 347 (letter to Lopez); Elisha R. Potter, Sr. Papers, Series 8, Box 2, Folder 33, Rhode Island Historical Society (T. Potter's account with A. Lopez, dated Feb. 5, 1770; also account with Newport merchant John Mawdsley, dated May 22, 1771; account with Elisha Reynolds, 1782); Stutz, Jean C. (ed.), *South Kingstown Town Council Records,* 303 (T. Potter's bankrupt estate); South Kingstown Land Evidence Records, v. 6, 217 (Reynolds mortgage, Dec. 10, 1767); Cook, Edward, M. (ed.), "Jeffrey Watson's Diary, 1740-1784," *Rhode Island History* 43: 79, 98 (Aug. 1984) (Reynolds 1760 house raising); Bartlett, John R. (ed.), *Records of the Colony of Rhode Island,* v. VI, 396 & 522 (Potter as deputy in lower house of General Assembly in 1762, 1764 and 1767); numerous cases brought by Potter in his capacity as storekeeper and merchant in the King's County Inferior Court of Common Pleas Records, from 1759 through 1791; notes to later chapter, The British Occupy Newport. After Thomas Potter's death, his wife Elizabeth Potter ran the tavern for several years, see South Kingstown Town Council Records, v. 6, 231 (July 11, 1796 meeting issuing licenses). For town alcohol licenses and meetings of the town council, see South Kingstown Town Council Records, v. 1-3, *passim.* For the quote on a tavern keeper entertaining Indians and blacks, see South Kingstown Town Council Records, v. 5, p. 224 (Feb. 12, 1753). For taverns in colonial America generally, see Conroy, David W., *Public Houses: Drink and The Revolution of Authority in Colonial Massachusetts;* Thompson, Peter, *Rum, Punch & Revolution: Taverngoing & Public Life in Eighteenth-Century Philadelphia.*

Samuel Casey and the Other Silversmiths of Little Rest

This chapter relies heavily on Miller, William Davis, *Silversmiths of Little Rest.* For the valuation of Rhode Island silver "ounces of plate," see Bartlett, John R. (ed.), *Records of the Colony of Rhode Island,* v. VIII, 169. For the location of Casey's house, see South Kingstown Land Evidence Records, v. v. 5, 180 (Caleb Gardner to Samuel Casey, including dwelling house and stable, land bordering Caleb Gardner's land to the northeast, Mar. 18, 1750) and list of owners of the land in Tootell, Lucy (ed.), *Kingston, Old Houses, Dates and Builders,* 9-14 (including James Helme). In addition, in a court case involving the county's sale of Samuel Casey's property in Little Rest by auction in 1772, the property is described as fronting main street at this site in Little Rest. The property is described as having a "Dwelling House, ware house, stable and outhouses." See King's County Superior Court Records, Oct. 1772 Sess. 341-42. For Samuel Casey, see also *Boston News-Letter,* Oct. 11, 1764 (house burned); Haley, John Williams, *Old Stone Bank History of*

Rhode Island, v. II, 86-88; Smithsonian Institution website "Legacies" (Abigail Robinson teapot). For court cases, see, e.g., King's County Inferior Court of Common Pleas Records, Feb. 1755 Sess. 231 (as storekeeper, with Gideon, against a Newport man); Aug. 1755 Sess. 449 (as a "goldsmith" against a Newport man); Aug. 1756 Sess. 522 (two cases, as a shopkeeper, one against a North Kingstown man and one against a Westerly man); Aug. 1761 Sess. 463 (as "goldsmith") and 479 (as "silversmith"); Feb. 1762 Sess. 82-84 (eight cases as "goldsmith" and two cases as "shopkeeper"). The term "goldsmith" was used interchangeably with the term "silversmith." Casey may have extended his business to money lending, as in later years he is described as a "merchant." See, e.g., King's County Inferior Court of Common Pleas Records, Aug. 1759 290; Aug. 1760 Sess. 376 & 378; Feb. 1761 Sess. 413-14 (seven cases, as "shopkeeper" and "merchant"); Aug. 1765 Sess. 80 (Casey as "merchant" sues North Kingstown man for nonpayment of note). The newspaper excerpt quoted in the following chapter, with the references to "European goods, with Drugs, Medicines, etc.," indicates that Casey also operated a store from his house. For recent evaluation of Casey's work, see *Boston Globe,* Jan. 28, 1999, F-1; *New York Times,* Feb. 11, 1999, D-1. For Gideon Casey, see also Scott, Kenneth, *Counterfeiting in Colonial Rhode Island,* 54-55; Scott, Kenneth, "Gideon Casey, Rhode Island Silversmith and Counterfeiter," *Rhode Island History* 50-54 (April 1953); Goodwin, Daniel (ed.), *A Letter Book and Absract of Out Services,* 47; South Kingstown Land Evidence Records, v. 5, 401 (Samuel Casey sells ½ interest in his Little Rest land to Gideon, June 1, 1753); v. 6, 194 (Gideon sells back the ½ interest to Samuel, May 14, 1762); King's County Inferior Court of Common Pleas Records, Feb. 1754 Sess. 436 & 440 (Gideon the "goldsmith" sues North Kingstown men for debts owed); Aug. 1754 Sess. 55 (same, suing Richmond man); Aug. 1755 Sess. 451 (Gideon sues as "shopkeeper"). For Joseph Perkins, see also South Kingstown Probate Records, v. 6, 215-16 (Oct. 28, 1789) (will of farms and notes receivables); inventory of estate of Joseph Perkins (in Pettaquamscutt Historical Society); South Kingstown Town Meeting Records, v. 1, 389 (Oct. 1775 meeting); King's County Inferior Court of Common Pleas Records, Aug. 1774 Sess. 44 (first case, as "goldsmith); Aug. 1782 Sess. 590 (goldsmith); Feb. 1783 Sess. 702 (goldsmith); Feb. 1789 Sess. 409, 429, 432, & 437 (first as merchant); South Kingstown Justices Court Records, George H. Peckham Justice, 1782-92 book, *passim* (as merchant, innkeeper and goldsmith); South Kingstown Land Evidence Records, v. 7, 254 (transfer of land from Robert Potter to Joseph Perkins, April 25, 1774); Joseph Perkins Papers, Box 1, Folders 7 & 9, Rhode Island Historical Society, Mss 629, SG 9 (including excerpts of store receipts and account books for sales of silver, alcohol and other goods; excerpts of receipts of amounts owed to Newport merchants for supplies; and excerpts of receipts of amounts owed to Narragansett planters for sales of cheese and corn to Perkins; correspondence with Hannah Potter in 1789 regarding commission sales). The town meeting later changed its mind about sending Perkins to New York City to purchase guns. For John Waite, see also South Kingstown Land Evidence Records, v. 6, 489 (transfer of land and dwelling from Elisha Reynolds to John Waite "silversmith" in 1769); Bartlett, John R. (ed.), *Records of the Colony of Rhode Island,* v. VIII, 16 (Waite exhibits two sets of printing plates for new state bills to General Assembly at 1776 session); chapter on Little Rest preparing for the Revolutionary

War. Waite also refused a seat on the state's supreme court that was offered to him. For Nathaniel Helme, see also *Newport Mercury,* Nov. 25, 1789 (death notice); South Kingstown Probate Records, v. 6, 90-94 (June 9, 1777) (James Helme, Sr. in will directs son Powell to make an apprentice of son Nathaniel). For Jeremiah Niles Sands, see South Kingstown Land Evidence Records, v. 8, 465 (Aug. 30, 1791) (lease of land on which Sands was to build a "clock and watchmakers shop;" the land is where the current Asa Potter law office now stands) & v. 9, 16 (Nov. 12, 1794) (sublease by Sands for two years of "goldsmith shop;" South Kingstown Justices Court Records, George H. Peckham Justice (1793-98 book) p. 99, Oct. 13, 1794 (in a suit by him to collect on a debt owed for services rendered, Sands is described as a "clock and watchmaker"); *Newport Mercury*, Jan. 6, 1795 (notifying public of his move from Little Rest to Wickford); South Kingstown Justices Court Records, Levi Totten Justice (1793-98 book), September 7, 1797 ("Jeremiah N. Sands of South Kingstown residing in North Kingstown" brings suit to recover money); *Newport Mercury,* Oct. 2, 1798 (Sands petitions the General Assembly for relief of debts by declaring himself a Newport goldsmith and an insolvent debtor); *Independent Chronicle,* July 23, 1801 (Sands advertises in Boston newspaper for journeyman silversmith to assist him in Boston); Washington County Court of Common Pleas, Feb. 1809 Sess. 288 (John T. Nichols v. Jeremiah N. Sands "of Portland, Maine," watchmaker); Feb. 1809 Sess. 292 (Levi Totten v. Jeremiah N. Sands, "Gold and Silversmith").

Samuel Casey: Master Silversmith and Smalltime Counterfeiter

See authorities on Casey brothers in notes to prior chapter. For the Casey brothers' counterfeiting activities prior to 1770, see Scott, Kenneth, *Counterfeiting in Colonial Rhode Island*, 49 & 54-56. For the burning of Casey's house, see *Boston News-Letter*, Oct. 11, 1764. For insolvency notice, see *Newport Mercury*, April 23, 1770. For his petition of insolvency to the General Assembly, see Petitions to the General Assembly 1770-72, No. 9, Rhode Island State Archives. For the trials of Casey and his four accomplices, see King's County Superior Court Records, Oct. 1770 Sess. 263-70. For the trial of William Carlisle, see id., April 1771 Sess. 289-90. For newspaper death sentence and penalties notice, see *Providence Gazette*, Oct. 13-20, 1770 and *Connecticut Courant*, Oct. 30, 1770 (also list of counsel, Wilson's trial and "defraud the public" quote). For details on Casey's counterfeiting activities, his capture, trial and jail break, see Scott, Kenneth, *Counterfeiting in Colonial America*, 229-35; Scott, Kenneth, *Counterfeiting in Colonial Rhode Island*, 55-56; Miller, William D., *Silversmiths of Little Rest*, 4-8. An Elisha Reynolds was listed as residing in South Kingstown and Exeter in 1774, confirming that the convicted Elisha Reynolds "of Exeter" was not the same Elisha Reynolds of South Kingstown who played such a key role in founding Little Rest. See Bartlett, John (ed.), *Census of the Colony of Rhode Island, 1774* (South Kingstown and Exeter). For the trial of the jail breakers, see King's County Superior Court Records, April 1771 Sess. 291-93 and 313-13 (Nathan Barber of Hopkinton, Timothy Peckham of South Kingstown and John James of Exeter). See also Bartlett, John (ed.), *Records of the Colony of Rhode Island*, v. VII, 22 (reward for jail breakers). For Casey's son, William, fighting as a

Loyalist, see Bunnell, Paul J., *The New Loyalist Index*, Bowie, Maryland: Heritage Books, 1989. William is listed as born in 1760 in South Kingstown and dying in Ontario, Canada. There was still the matter of dealing with the house and land in Little Rest that Casey left behind. In January 1772, the county sheriff sold the property to two South Kingstown men. But William Potter, tavern keeper Thomas Potter's brother, had rented the house from Samuel's brother, Thomas Casey. With villagers Joseph Perkins ("goldsmith"), Benjamin Anthony ("Practitioner of Physick," i.e., doctor), and Abel Cottrel ("taylor"), Potter ejected the new buyers. Potter claimed that prior to Samuel Casey's jailbreak, Casey had sold the land to his brother Thomas Casey. But in a trial held in Little Rest, the jury found that the transfer from Samuel Casey to his brother was fraudulent and that the property belonged to the new buyers. See King's County Superior Court Records, Oct. 1772 Sess. 341-42. Land records indicate that Samuel Casey did transfer his real property to his brother Thomas Casey in 1765. South Kingstown Land Evidence Records, v. 6, 412 (July 16, 1765). Casey also sold land to Nathaniel Gardner in 1768. *Id.*, v. 6, 440 & 442.

Slavery in Colonial Little Rest

For background on slavery in the colonial Narragansett country, see McBurney, Christian M., "The Rise and Decline of the South Kingstown Planters, 1660-1783" (BA Honors Thesis) ch. IV; Fitts, Robert K., *Inventing New England's Slave Paradise, passim*. For references to slaves owned by Hannah, Perkins and Case, see South Kingstown Land Evidence Records, v. 3A, 109-110 (Moore to Perkins); South Kingstown Probate Records, v. 1, 32 (Oct. 14, 1706) (Hannah) and v. 3, 131-32 (Jan. 11, 1739) (Case). For slaves owned by Gardner, William Potter, the Reynolds, Peckham, Thomas Potter and Robert Potter, see Bartlett, John (ed.), *Census of the Colony of Rhode Island, 1774* (South Kingstown). For Reynolds' purchase of Binor, see Elisha Reynolds Papers, Folder 3, Rhode Island Historical Society, Mss 629, SG1. For Peckham's Indian servants, see *id.; Newport Mercury*, July 10, 1775 (advertisement for runaway Indian servant). For the living quarters of slaves, see Fitts, Robert K., *Inventing New England's Slave Paradise*, 142. For town ordinances dealing with slaves, blacks and Indians, see South Kingstown Town Meeting Records, v. 1, 10 (Dec. 1724); 13 (June 1726) & 80-81 (Aug. 30, 1737). For the George Hazard vs. Jonathan Hazard case, see King's County Inferior Court of Common Pleas Records, Aug. 1765 Sess. 10. The decision was affirmed in George Hazard vs. Jonathan Hazard, King's County Superior Court Records, April 1766 Sess. 87. For Elisha Potter Jr.'s quotes, see Updike, Wilkins, *History of the Episcopal Church*, 169-74 (quoting Potter's address to the Rhode Island House of Representatives); Potter, Elisha R., Jr., *An Address Delivered Before the Rhode Island Historical Society, on the Evening of February Nineteenth, 1851*, 13-14. For punishments and terror inflicted on slaves, see Hazard, Thomas R., *Recollections of Olden Times*, 126 (swamp); Fitts, Robert K., *Inventing New England's Slave Paradise*, 108-09 (discussing likelihood that toes were removed as punishment); Goodwin, Daniel (ed.), *A Letterbook and Abstract of Our Services, 1743-1751*, 52 (pothooks); Pearce, Cato, *Brief Memoir of the Life and Religious Experience of Cato Pearce a Man of Color*, 5-

6 (Pearce); Bartlett, Irving H., *From Slave to Citizen,* 15 (Quaker); Sweet, John Wood, *Bodies Politic,* 71 (iron tongs); Bartlett, John R. (ed.), *Records of the Colony of Rhode Island,* v. IV, 27; (dismemberment). For the Quaker anti-slavery movement in South Kingstown, see McBurney, Christian M., "The Rise and Decline of the South Kingstown Planters, 1660-1783" (BA Honors Thesis) 210-12; Crane, Ellen Forman, *A Dependent People,* 81 (Woolman). For the Wamsley case, see Fiske, Jane Fletcher, *Gleanings from Newport Court Files,* case no. 1130; this case is discussed extensively in the Sweet, John Wood, *Bodies Politic,* 228-38. For the 1774 act, see Bartlett, John (ed.), *Records of the Colony of Rhode Island,* v. VII, 251-53. For the North Kingstown incident, see Sweet, John Wood, *Bodies Politic,* 71. For Sarah's story, see Walker v. Blevin, King's County Superior Court, April 1773 Sess. 360-62. For Abigail's story, see Sweet, John Wood, *Bodies Politic,* 247-48; Bartlett, John R. (ed.), *Records of the Colony of Rhode Island,* v. VIII, 576 (ordering that Abigail be delivered to the King's County sheriff) & 618 (reference to act passed in Little Rest restricting sales of slaves out-of-state); John Rice's Petition, Petitions to the General Assembly 1778-79, v. 17, no. 118, Rhode Island State Archives. For the proposal to abolish slavery in 1775, see South Kingstown Meeting Records, v. 1, 388 ((Dec. 27, 1775); see also North Kingstown Town Meeting Records, v. 1, 484 (Dec. 1775).

Little Rest and the Coming American Revolution

For the activities of the town meeting and committee of correspondence in 1774-1775, see South Kingstown Town Meeting Records, v. 1, 373-90; Stutz, Jean, *South Kingstown Town Council Records,* 37-38; *Newport Mercury,* February 21, 1774. For George Rome, see Lovejoy, David S., *Rhode Island Politics and the American Revolution,* 175-76 & 188; Simister, Florence, *The Fire's Center,* 209-10. For William Potter, see Bartlett, John R. (ed.), *Records of the Colony of Rhode Island,* v. VII, 347-48 (Potter letter). For Samuel Fayerweather, see Simister, Florence, *The Fire's Center,* 212 (1775); Stutz, Jean (ed.), *South Kingstown Town Council Records,* 49 (Aug. 23, 1778 meeting). For background on Rhode Island in the American Revolution, see James, Sydney, *Colonial Rhode Island,* ch. 13; Simister, Florence, *The Fire's Center,* ch. I-III. For the Kingston Reds, see Act of the General Assembly Establishing the Kingston Reds, Nov. 11, 1775 (Kingston Free Library, Vertical Files); Bartlett, John R. (ed.), *Records of the Colony of Rhode Island,* v. VII, 383 (approving such Act); Field, Edward, *Revolutionary Defences in Rhode Island,* 113-16 (includes 1776 muster roll); Smith, Joseph Jencks (ed.), *Civil and Military List of Rhode Island, 1647-1800, passim* (officers); Bartlett, John R. (ed.), *Records of the Colony of Rhode Island,* v. VII, 538; v. VIII, 227, 395 & 561 (officers) and v. VIII, 149 (excusing Teft and Sheffield). For Quaker exemptions from military service, see Chamberlain, Mildred, *The Rhode Island 1777 Military Census,* 2 & 97; Stutz, Jean C. (ed.). *South Kingstown, Rhode Island Town Council Records 1771-1795,* 81 (list in clerk's office); Bartlett, John R., *Records of the Colony of Rhode Island,* v. VIII, 204-06 (April 1777 Act). For formation of regiments in 1775 and the service of William Potter, see Smith, Joseph Jencks (ed.), *Civil and Military List of Rhode Island, 1647-1800,* 321-24; Simister, Florence, *The Fire's Center,* 78-79; Bartlett, John R. (ed.), *Records of the Colony of Rhode Island,* v. VII, 322-23; Heitman,

Francis B., *Historical Register of Officers of the Continental Army*, 449. For Thomas Potter's service as an officer of the King's County second regiment, see Bartlett, John R. (ed.), *Records of the Colony of Rhode Island*, v. VIII, 45, 390, 533 & v. IX, 7. For the services of Captain William Potter, see Walker, Anthony, *So Few the Brave*, 101, 117 & 138; Heitman, Francis B., *Historical Register of Officers of the Continental Army*, 449; Field, Edward (ed.), *State of Rhode Island and Providence Plantations*, v. I, 505; Revolutionary War Muster Rolls 1775-1783, Rhode Island (National Archives) (showing several of Captain Potter's muster rolls); Canfield, Rosemary, *Some Rhode Island Descendants of Nathaniel Potter*, 63 ("galling fire" quote from *Providence Journal* obituary). In the *Providence Gazette's* June 7, 1777 edition, Captain William Potter advertised for the return of a deserter from his company "in Col. Angell's Regiment." Taylor, Maureen Alice, *Runaways, Deserters, and Notorious Villains from Rhode Island Newspapers*, 67. For the 1776 raids, see South Kingstown Town Meeting Records, v. 1, 388 (Jan. 4, 1776); v. 2, 10; Simister, Florence, *The Fire's Center*, 74. It was difficult for the author to establish that Captain William Potter was the brother of Colonel Thomas Potter. It does appear that Captain William Potter resided in Little Rest. The town council records indicate that Captain William Potter was included in a list of Little Rest residents appointed to repair streets in Little Rest. Stutz, Jean (ed.), *South Kingstown Town Council Records*, 209 (Sept. 10, 1787 meeting). The 1790 census, which generally went in the order of houses, places a William Potter in the center of Little Rest. Bureau of the Census, *Census of the United States, 1790, Washington County, Rhode Island*, 48. Charles Potter, in his *Genealogies of the Potter Families*, does not make it clear which one of the several William Potters in South Kingstown at the time was the Captain (it was not Judge William Potter who resided up North Road and who later became a disciple of the religious leader Jemima Wilkinson). Charles Potter does report that Ichabod and Margaret Potter had two male children, Thomas, born in 1738, and William, born in 1739. Thomas became the tavern keeper and colonel. *Id.*, Part 4, 21. Evidence indicates that this was the William who resided in Little Rest and became the captain. In a listing of the officers of the 1775 "army of observation," "William Potter (son of Ichabod)" is listed as an ensign. Cowell, Benjamin, *Spirit of '76*, 19. A descendant of the Potter family in the mid-19th century also recollected that Col. Thomas Potter had a brother William who served in the patriot army in the Revolutionary War. See Elizabeth Potter Randolph's recollection written by James B. M. Potter, in the Wells Papers, folio 19, Pettaquamscutt Historical Society.

The British Occupy Newport

For the British invasion and occupation of Newport, and the Battle of Newport, see Dearden, Paul F., *The Rhode Island Campaign of 1778, passim*; Simister, Florence, *The Fire's Center*, ch. V-VI; James, Sydney, *Colonial Rhode Island*, 355-56. For the 1777 military census, see Chamberlain, Mildred, *The Rhode Island 1777 Military Census* (Little Rest is at p. 100; Tower Hill is at p. 97). For the new stone steps, see Bartlett, John (ed.), *Records of the Colony of Rhode Island*, v. VIII, 599. For reimbursements by the General Assembly to Robert Potter and Thomas Potter, see Bartlett, John R. (ed.), *Records of the Colony of Rhode Island*, v.

VIII, 477 (R. Potter), 572 (T. Potter, illegal trade) & 598 (Tories); Petitions to the General Assembly 1780-81, No. 125, Rhode Island State Archives (for raising troops in Col. Green's regiment of Continental soldiers). For Colonel Angell's invitation to dine at Little Rest, see Field, Edward, *Diary of Colonel Israel Angell*, 76 (Oct. 6, 1779). For heavy taxation on South Kingstown during the American Revolution, see notes to "Our Best Blood and Treasure" chapter. For the Rhode Island black regiment, see Buckley, Gail, *American Patriots*, 24-26; Arnold, James, *Narragansett Historical Register*, v. I, 313 (partial muster roll); Bartlett, John R. (ed.), *Records of the Colony of Rhode Island*, v. VIII, 358-60 (General Assembly Act permitting enlistment of slaves) & 361 (protest against the Act); Revolutionary Muster Rolls, 1775-1783, Rhode Island, 1st Regiment (listing Sampson Reynolds and Mingo Reynolds). For a summary of the most recent scholarship regarding the black regiment and other Rhode Island black soldiers in Continental Army units, see Sweet, John Wood, *Bodies Politic*, 197-209. See also Letter from Captain Elijah Lewis to the Speaker of the Assembly, South Kingstown, March 13, 1778, Letters to Rhode Island Governor, v. 12, no. 39, Rhode Island State Archives. For the administration of Sampson Reynolds' estate, see Stutz, Jean (ed.), *South Kingstown Town Council Records*, 309. There may have been other former black slaves who fought in patriot regiments. A Richard Potter enlisted in the Rhode Island black regiment and a Cuff Pekam enlisted in Col. Israel Angell's regiment. See Greene, Robert E., *Black Courage, 1775-1783*, 31 & 103. Richard Potter could have been a former slave of Thomas Potter and Cuff Pekam could have been a former slave of Timothy Peckham's. However, there were several Potters who were slaveholders in South Kingstown and other Peckhams in South County. At least three black slaves from nearby Mooresfield enlisted in the black regiment. Arnold, James, *Narragansett Historical Register*, v. I, 313 (Isaac Rodman, with Daniel Rodman of South Kingstown as former owner; Ceaser Rose and Edward Rose, with John Rose of South Kingstown as former owner). For James Rose, see Elizabeth Potter Randolph's recollection written by James B. M. Potter, Wells Papers, folio 19, Pettaquamscutt Historical Society; Field, Edward, *Revolutionary Defences in Rhode Island*, 113-16 (includes 1776 muster roll of Kingston Reds). For Captain William Potter, see notes to prior chapter; Field, Edward (ed.), *State of Rhode Island and Providence Plantations*, v. I, 505 (Captain William Potter's company in Israel Angell's 2nd Rhode Island Regiment, General James Varnum's Brigade, listed in payroll list of Rhode Island companies in August 1778, the month of the Battle of Newport; Varnum's Brigade fought in Battle of Newport); Walker, Anthony, *So Few the Brave*, 136-38 (same; and retired in April 1779); White, Virgil D. (ed.), *Genealogical Abstracts of Revolutionary War Pension Files*, v. III, 2745 (William Potter; says in 1820 he was 80 years-old and had lived with Samuel R. Potter for many years who supported him; Elisha R. Potter, Sr. submitted a list of William's property in 1820); Hazard, Caroline (ed.), *Nailer Tom's Diary*, 301 (Feb. 8-13, 1808) (Nailer Tom hires Captain William Potter to make him a suit of clothes); 313 (Oct. 24, 1808) (same). See also Schunke, Marjoric, "Potter Family Bible," *Rhode Island Genealogical Register*, 7: 341 (April 1985) (reference to "Wm Potter, Capt in Revolutionary War & Taylor by trade"). For British raids in 1779, see Hazard, Caroline (ed.), *Nailer Tom's Diary*, 6 (Jan. 30,

1779), 8 (May 8 & May 21, 1779; June 6, June 8 & June 12, 1779); Cook, Edward M, Jr. (ed.), "Jeffrey Watson's Diary," *Rhode Island History* 43: 79, 109 (Aug. 1984).

General Washington has a "Little Rest"

     For the French occupation of Newport, see James, Sydney, *Colonial Rhode Island,* 355-56; Haley, John Williams, *Old Stone Bank History of Rhode Island,* v. III, 137-42; Simister, Florence, *The Fire's Center,* ch. VI. For Von Closen's journal, see Acomb, Evelyn M., *The Revolutionary Journal of Baron Ludwig Von Closen, 1780-1783,* 59-63. I thank Nancy Alicia Wayland, the town historian for New Windsor, Connecticut, for bringing Von Closen's journal to my attention and for other assistance on this topic. For Tilghman's expense records, see The Papers of Tench Tilghman, Manuscript Division, Library of Congress (AC 4520, 3). For Elizabeth Potter Randolph's recollection written by James B. M. Potter, see Wells Papers, folio 19, Pettaquamscutt Historical Society. Reverend Wells recalled that "the old barrack in which Washington and his staff had encamped for a night" was demolished. Wells, J. Hagadorn, "Kingston Annals," 29. For more on Washington's visit to Little Rest, see Miller, William Davis, "General Washington at Little Rest," *Rhode Island Historical Society Collections* 47-53 (April 1932); Wells, J. Hagadorn, "Kingston Annals," 27-28; Potter, James B. M., "Recollections of a Paymaster of the Army During the Civil War 1861-1882," 1-2. For Major Lunt, see Helme, Jonathan, "Recollections of South Kingstown," *Providence Journal,* Oct. 31, 1874; Wells, J. Hagadorn, "Kingston Annals." 28-29; White, Virgil D. (ed.), *Genealogical Abstracts of Revolutionary War Pension Files,* v. II, 2145. For Watson and Hazard journal entries, see Hazard, Caroline (ed.), *Nailer Tom's Diary,* 20 (Mar. 6, 1781); Cook, Edward M, Jr. (ed.), "Jeffrey Watson's Diary," *Rhode Island History* 43: 79, 110 (Aug. 1984). For more on Washington's visit to Rhode Island, see Haley, John Williams, *George Washington and Rhode Island;* Haley, John Williams, *Old Stone Bank History of Rhode Island,* v. III, 153-62; Crofut, Florence S. Marcy, *Guide to the History and the Historic Sites of Connecticut,* 56-59 (Connecticut and Rhode Island daily itineraries); Freeman, Douglas, *George Washington,* v. 5, 267-76; Baker, William S., *Itinerary of General Washington,* 208-12; Mitchell, Broadus, *Alexander Hamilton,* 235-39. For the March 6, 1781 town council meeting, see Stutz, Jean C. (ed.), *South Kingstown Town Council Records,* 118. For the stationing of troops outside Newport in 1781, see Acomb, Evelyn M., *The Revolutionary Journal of Baron Ludwig Von Closen, 1780-1783,* 73 & n.29; Field, Edward, *Revolutionary Defences in Rhode Island,* 113-14. The author reviewed the following in attempting to determine the existence of Philip Rose: Arnold, James, *Vital Records of Washington County, Rhode Island;* Heitman, Francis B., *Historical Register of Officers of the Continental Army,* 473-74; White, Virgil D. (ed.), *Genealogical Abstracts of Revolutionary War Pension Files,* v. III; Peterson, Clarence S., *Known Military Dead During the American Revolutionary War, 1775-1783,* Baltimore: Genealogical Publishing Company, 1967; Fitzpatrick, John C. (ed.), *The Writings of George Washington from the Original Manuscript Sources, 1745-1799,* Washington, D.C.: Government Printing Office, 1944, vols. 1-39; Freeman, Douglas, *George Washington,* vols. I-VII. There was a Philip Rose listed in a Rhode Island company of artillery in 1776; where he came from and whether he was killed is not known. See Abernethy, Thomas J., "Crane's Rhode Island Company of Artillery -1775," 29 *Rhode Island History* 46, 51 (Winter 1970).

"Our Best Blood and Treasure"

For Robinson, see Petitions to the General Assembly 1780-81, No. 60, Rhode Island State Archives (petitions in February 1781 from Dr. William Chace and others requesting M. Robinson's release); Payne, Abraham, *Reminiscences of the Rhode Island Bar,* 239-41; Bartlett, John R. (ed.), *Records of the Colony of Rhode Island,* v. IX, 334. For Hazard's journal entry, see Hazard, Caroline (ed.), *Nailer Tom's Diary,* 25 (Oct. 27, 1781). For the change of the name of King's County to Washington County, see Bartlett, John (ed.), *Records of the Colony of Rhode Island,* v. IX, 484. For John Peck Rathbun, see Rider, Hope S., *Valour Fore & Aft, passim;* Atkinson, Amaila Inge, "Captain Rathbun's Last Voyage," *The New England Historical and Genealogical Register, v.* CXV, 164-69; Thomas, Evan, *John Paul Jones,* 56, 61, 74, 80 & 91; *Newport Mercury,* April 2, April 17 & Oct. 19, 1782 (death notices of 17 crew members; death notice of Captain Rathbun; death notice of his wife Mary; Mary predeceased John, dieing on Jan. 17, 1782 at the age of 23). The land record reflecting Rathbun's purchase of the former John Potter tavern describes Rathbun as "late Commander of the ship of War called the Queen of France in the Services of the United States of America." South Kingstown Land Evidence Records, v. 7, 465 (July 10, 1780). For the "our best Blood and treasure" quote, see South Kingstown Town Meeting Records, v. 2, 12 (April 16, 1783). For the court cases approving the seizure of farm animals on South Kingstown shorelines, see Washington County Court of Common Pleas Records, July 1782 Sess. 553; July 1782 Sess. 554-55; Dec. 1783 Sess. 639-43. For South Kingstown's tax burden in colonial times and during the Revolutionary War, see Dyer, Elisha (ed.), *Valuation of the Counties and Towns in the State of Rhode Island from 1860 to 1869,* 32-39. For South Kingstown's tax burden and protests, see Conley, Patrick T., *Democracy in Decline,* 68-71; Polishook, Irwin H., *Rhode Island and the Union,* 44-45; Bartlett, John (ed.), *Records of the Colony of Rhode Island,* v. VIII, 569 (June 1779 protest); v. IX, 167 (allowed to defer payment of grain one month), 169 (S.K. has highest share of tax in 1780), 397 (S.K. has highest share of tax in 1781), 445 (S.K. has highest share of grain requisition) & 606-07; v. X, 34-35 (S.K. town treasurer permitted to delay payment of taxes two months in May 1784); South Kingstown Town Meeting Records, v. 2, 107 (Jan. 6, 1782), 111 (April 1, 1782) & 148 (1784 convention reference); Charlestown Town Meeting Records, March 14, 1782 & April 17, 1782. For $2.05 per capita tax in 1782, see Herndon, Ruth Wallis, "Governing the Affairs of the Town" (Doctoral Thesis) 275-76. For jailing of the South Kingstown town treasurer, see Bartlett, John R. (ed.), *Records of the Colony of Rhode Island,* v. IX, (state authorizes Thomas Potter to sue town treasurer to collect taxes in Oct. 1781), 511 (town treasurer ordered released from jail in Jan. 1782), 593 (town treasurer ordered released from jail in Aug. 1782), 732 (town treasurer ordered released from jail in Oct. 1783); South Kingstown Town Meeting Records, v. 2, 143 (Feb. 16, 1782) (to town treasurer George Babcock for 25 days in jail), 177 (Mar. 29, 1784) (agreement of town to indemnify town treasurer for time in jail), 197 (June 16, 1785), 238 (Aug. 29, 1786), 243 (June 5, 1787), 257 (April 16, 1788, £512 for 1785-86); Beriah Brown Papers, Rhode Island Historical Society (1775 notice for overdue Oct. 1774 taxes and release of warrant against town treasurer). For poor relief for returning soldiers from the Continental Army, see Stutz, Jean C. (ed.), *South Kingstown, Rhode Island Town Council Records 1771-1795*, 172 (Robert Congden, white); 196, 210 (Mingo Rodman, black). The General Assembly had enacted a law ordering town councils to feed and clothe properly former slaves who had joined the Continental battalions and had become unable to support themselves. See Bartlett, John (ed.), *Records of the Colony of Rhode Island*, v. X, 85 (committee formed for this purpose, v. X, 44).

The Indentured Servitude of Alice Franklin

This chapter relies on Herndon, Ruth Wallis, "Governing the Affairs of the Town" (Doctoral Thesis) 183-86; see also generally Creech, Margaret. *Three Centuries of Poor Law Administration, a Study of Legislation in Rhode Island, passim.* See Stutz, Jean C. (ed.), *South Kingstown Town Council Records 1771-1795*, 41 (binding out); 205 (delirious); 215 (Franklin not yet 18); 216 (ordering Gardner to receive Franklin); 217-18 (voting to sue Gardner); 254 (Franklin ordered to support son). For an amendment to "An Act regulating the Proceedings in Cases of Bastardy" (unmarried women giving birth to children), see *Rhode Island Acts & Resolves,* Jan. 1795 Session, v. III, 19-21. For the town council dealing with Alice's mother, Hannah, see South Kingstown Town Council Records, v. 5, 230 (voting to order the overseer of the poor to "keep Hannah Franklin in his service, until she pays him said charge of Lying in Including for her Maintenance of child") (Oct. 4, 1770 meeting). For court cases in which men had bonds executed against them for failure to support an illegitimate child, see King's County Inferior Court of Common Pleas Records, see, e.g., Aug. 1754 Sess. 48; Aug. 1762 Sess. 128-29; Feb. 1768 Sess. 692. For the man committed to jail, see South Kingstown Town Council Records, v. 7, 79 (July 8, 1811). For other instances, see Justices Court Records, Levi Totten, Justice, 1793-98, 81, June 2, 1796 (Robert G. Potter, cordwainer, accused of fathering illegitimate child; ordered to post bond and to appear at next Supreme Court session); *id.* at 105 (Potter found guilty); *id.* at 87, July 18, 1796 (James Sheffield found guilty of fathering an illegitimate child and ordered to pay child support).

Jemima Wilkinson: Prophet of God and Utopian Leader

For Jemima Wilkinson, see McLoughlin, William G., *Rhode Island,* 79-80; Wiseby, Herbert A., *Pioneer Prophetess, passim;* Whyte, J. Bruce, "The Publick Universal Friend," *Rhode Island History* 26: 18-24 (Jan. 1968) & 27: 103-112 (Oct. 1968); Updike, Wilkins, *History of the Episcopal Church in Narragansett,* 233-36; Bowditch, Franklin Dexter, *The Literary Diary of Ezra Stiles,* v. II, 380-81; Potter, Charles, *Genealogies of the Potter Families,* Part 4, 27-31; Hazard, Caroline (ed.), *Nailer Tom's Diary,* 7 (March 2, 1779). For William Potter's dispute with Wilkinson and his attempted return to Little Rest, see all the references in the prior sentence, except for the McLoughlin and Bowditch books. Stephen Card was in the first company in 1788 to migrate to the New York wilderness. He and his brother-in-law John Reynolds sowed the first wheat in western New York near City Hill. They then went back to Rhode Island for their families. New Jerusalem is near present-day Penn Yan in Yates County, New York. See Adamson, Thaire Congdon, "They Left Rhode Island, Part Two, Followers of Jemima Wilkinson to Yates Co., N.Y.," *Rhode Island Genealogical Register,* 103-05 (Oct. 1978). Adamson writes that Card was from Little Rest, but the 1790 census indicates that he lived just west of Little Rest.

The Execution of Thomas Mount

For Caesar Hazard's case, see *Newport Mercury,* Oct. 7, 1771; Bill submitted by Beriah Brown, High Sheriff of King's County, Accounts Allowed by the General Assembly, 1770-1772, Rhode Island State Archives; Rex v. Cezar Hazard, King's County Superior Court Records, Oct. 1771 Sess. 303. The newspaper suggest that the victim died, but not the court records. For Thomas Mount, see Miller, William Davis, "Thomas Mount," *Rhode Island Historical Society Collections* 53-58 (April 1927); Bickford, Christopher, *Crime, Punishment, and the Washington County Jail,* 42-43; Wells, J. Hagadorn, "Kingston Annals," 48 (location of hanging). Cole refers to a "Hanging Lot" where Mount was hung. Cole, J. R., *History of Washington and Kent Counties,* 483. For 1764 hanging in Newport, see Field, Edward (ed.), *State of Rhode Island and Providence Plantations,* v. III, 438. For fees paid to Robert Sands of Little Rest, as deputy sheriff of Washington County, apparently for capturing and guarding Thomas Mount, see *Rhode Island Acts & Resolves,* Feb. 1791 Session, v. I, 20-21 ("for apprehending and committing divers Persons charged with high Crimes and Misdemeanors"); *Rhode Island Acts & Resolves,* May 1791 Session, v. I, 27 (audit of accounts of Sands and another man who helped bring Mount from Newport).

Little Rest in the Census of 1790: Slavery, Freedom and Family

For the 1790 census, see Bureau of the Census, *Census of the United States, 1790,* Washington County, Rhode Island, 48. Another approach to determining who resided in Little Rest (and later Kingston) is to review the South Kingstown Highway Tax Records, 1797-1854. Little Rest is included in Districts 11 and 12. This list includes property owners only and not renters. See also Stutz, Jean C. (ed.), *South Kingstown Town Council Records,* 209 (in 1787, orders to "squadrons" of Little Rest villagers and some outlying residents to maintain and repair the roads in the village; individuals named). For the South Kingstown town meeting's opposition to an emancipation bill, see South Kingstown Town Meeting Records, v. 2, 174 (Feb. 9, 1784). For the gradual emancipation bill, see Melish, Joanne Pope, *Disowning Slavery,* 71-73 and the later chapter, The Town Council Prevents Elisha Gardner from Freeing His Slave. For Cross and Stanton land purchase records, see Tootell, Lucy R. (ed.), *Kingston, Old Houses, Dates and Builders,* 28-29. The 1800 census indicates that West Cross continued to reside in South Kingstown with four other members of his family. Jackson, Ronald V., *Rhode Island 1800 Census*; S-K Publications, *1800 U.S. Census,* Washington County, Rhode Island. For wills of Elisha Reynolds and

Joseph Perkins, see South Kingstown Probate Records, v. 6, 215 (Oct. 28, 1789) (Perkins) & v. 6, 241 (Reynolds) (Nov. 14, 1791). For purchases by the estate of Elisha Reynolds' for slave Tom, see Elisha Potter's Account Book, 33, Pettaquamscutt Historical Society.

The Rise of the Country Party and the Failure of Rhode Island to Ratify the U.S. Constitution in Little Rest in March 1790

For background on Rhode Island and the U.S. Constitution, see Cotner, Robert C., introduction to *Theodore Foster's Minutes of the Convention;* Polishook, Irwin H., *Rhode Island and the Union,* ch. 8-9. For the 1781-82 impost controversy, see McLoughlin, William G., *Rhode Island,* 101; Polishook, Irwin H., *Rhode Island and the Union,* ch. 3. For Jonathan J. Hazard and the rise of the Country Party, see James, Sydney V., *Colonial Rhode Island,* 367-72; Polishook, Irwin H., *Rhode Island and the Union,* ch. 8; Kaminski, John , "Political Sacrifice and Demise – John Collins and Jonathan J. Hazard, 1786-1790," *Rhode Island History* 35: 91, 91-93 (Aug. 1976); Allen, Thomas S., "Landed Versus Paper Property in Rhode Island, 1781-1790," *Rhode Island History* 53: 3, 3-17 (Feb. 1995). For South Kingstown's tax burden problems, see prior chapter, Our Best Blood and Treasure. For the paper money controversy, see McLoughlin, William G., *Rhode Island,* 101-04; Conley, Patrick T., *Democracy in Decline,* 80-106; Polishook, Irwin H., *Rhode Island and the Union,* 118-29. For South Kingstown first opposing the issuance of paper money and then supporting it, see South Kingstown Town Meeting Records, v. 2, 218 (July 20, 1786) (oppose), and 238 (Sept. 26, 1786) & 254 (Mar. 4, 1788) (support). For the Col. Potter quote, see Payne, Abraham, *Reminiscences of the Rhode Island Bar,* 238. For the towns' vote on the U.S. Constitution, see Polishook, Irwin H., *Rhode Island and the Union,* ch. 8; Conley, Patrick T., *Democracy in Decline,* 109-110; Herndon, Ruth Wallis, "Governing the Affairs of the Town" (Doctoral Thesis) 108-14. For South Kingstown's vote on the U.S. Constitution, see South Kingstown Town Meeting Records, v. 2, 252-56 (March 4, 1788). For increasing pressure on Rhode Island, see Conley, Patrick T., *Democracy in Decline,* 107-42. For "one vote for a Convention" quote, see South Kingstown Town Meeting Records, v. 2, 281. For preparations of the Court House, see South Kingstown Town Meeting Records, v. 2, 284 (Feb. 7, 1790). David Douglas, a blacksmith in Little Rest, was described as a "waiter" in Cotner, Robert C. (ed.), *Theodore Foster's Minutes of the Convention,* 1; see also *Rhode Island Acts & Resolves,* Sept. 1790 Session, v. I, 21 (General Assembly paying Douglas "for Attendance as a Waiter upon the Convention which sat in the County of Washington in March last"). For the convention in Little Rest, see Cotner, Robert C. (ed.), *Theodore Foster's Minutes of the Convention, passim;* Conley, Patrick T., *Democracy in Decline,* 124-25; James, Sydney V., *Colonial Rhode Island,* 371-72; *Providence Gazette,* March 6 & 13, 1790. For the later adoption of the U.S. constitution in Newport, see Conley, Patrick T., *Democracy in Decline,* 113-16; Polishook, Irwin H., *Rhode Island and the Union,* 221-30. To compare the rural party in northwest Rhode Island, see Jones, Daniel, *The Economic & Social Transformation of Rural Rhode Island,* 30-35.

A Picture of Little Rest in the Early 1800s

Economic Decline in South County and Golden Age in Little Rest. For causes of the decline of the Narragansett planters, see McBurney, Christian M., "The Rise and Decline of the South Kingstown Planters, 1660-1783" (BA Honors Thesis) ch. VIII; Bidwell, Percy W. & John I. Falconer, *History of Agriculture in the Northern United States, 1620-1860,* 135-37 (West Indies trade); Cotner, Robert C. (ed.), *Theodore Foster's Minutes of the Convention,* 41 & 66-67 (southern planters' wealth). For post-war population decline, see Coleman, Peter J., *The Transformation of Rhode Island,* 220. For migration from rural towns quote, see *What a Ploughman Said,* 30-31. For Elisha Potter's statement that slavery contributed to the laziness of the sons of slave owners, see Potter, Elisha R., Jr., *An Address Delivered Before the Rhode Island Historical Society, on the Evening of February Nineteenth, 1851,* 13-14. A similar comment was made in connection with the eight sons of wealthy Narragansett planter Judge William Potter. "Bred to wealthy and luxurious tastes, the sons, with the exception of Arnold, gave little application to business. Accustomed to the service of slaves, they had no taste for labor. They were well educated, but fast horses and sporting society produced their usual results in this aristocratic family." Potter, Charles, *Genealogies of the Potter Families,* Part 4, 31.

Tavern Life. For the inventory of Charles Barker, see South Kingstown Probate Records, v. 3, 204-07 (Oct. 11, 1819). For Mary Barker's transactions, see Thomas S. Taylor Collection, Baker Library, Harvard Business School, Mss. 77 1807-1863 T238, v. 21 (passbook of Mary Barker, 1824-29). Mary Barker was granted a liquor license to operate the tavern from 1820 to 1827. South Kingstown Town Council Records, v. 7, 171 & 245. For the Joe Reynolds tavern, see Joseph Reynolds Day Book, June 10, 1796-April 30, 1801 (for sale by M&S Rare Books) (the day book indicates that Reynolds was also a blacksmith at this time); Pettaquamscutt Historical Society, *Historic Buildings of South County,* 29; Stedman, Oliver H., *A Stroll Through Memory Lane,* 134-35; Tootell, Lucy (ed.), *Kingston, Old Houses, Dates and Builders,* 39-40 (list of owners); Taylor, Philip K., "Little Rest," *The New England Magazine,* 136 (April 1903) (turkey suppers quote). Joseph Reynolds did not acquire ownership of the tavern until 1813; prior to that time, he must have rented the tavern from its owner, Timothy Peckham. For the Timothy Peckham tavern, see South Kingstown Town Council Records, v. 6, 231 (last license for Robert Potter in July 1796) & 232 (first license for Timothy Peckham in August 1796); MacKenzie, Louise, *Strolling Through Kingston,* 30-31; Helme, Jonathan, "Recollections of South Kingstown," *Providence Journal,* Oct. 31, 1874. For the dates who operated each tavern, see South Kingstown Town Council Records, v. 6-8, *passim.* For example, in 1801, the town council granted following Little Rest tavern keepers liquor licenses: Charles Barker, Joseph Reynolds and Timothy Peckham. *Id.* at v. 6, 5. In 1810, the same persons were granted liquor licenses. *Id.* at v. 7, 68. In 1820, Reynolds and Peckham received liquor licenses, as well as Mary Barker. *Id.* at v.7, 171. These tavern keepers were invariably charged the highest fee by the town council, indicating that they were the most substantial taverns in town. In 1834, the town council granted the following Kingston tavern keepers liquor licenses: John N. Reynolds, Jesse Babcock, and Robinson & Anthony (which took over the Peckham tavern). *Id.* at v. 7, 305. For the town council meeting at Little Rest taverns, see, e.g., South Kingstown Town Council Records, v. 6, 232 (July 1796, Charles Barker); v. 7, 1 (Timothy Peckham, 1800); v. 7, 11, 24 & 18 (1802, Joseph Reynolds); v. 7, 102 (Charles Barker, 1811); v. 7, 202 (Mary Barker, 1822); v. 7, 345 (Jesse Babcock, 1841). The town council, between March 1844 and February 1846, met at Philip Taylor's tavern numerous times in order to correct the town's voting lists, which was necessitated by the adoption of the new state constitution and expansion of eligible voters. *Id.* at v. 7, 357-59, 361, 365 & 371.

A Village of Shopkeepers. For Hazard's journal entries, see Hazard, Caroline (ed.), *Nailer Tom's Diary,* 141 (Sept. 13, 1792) (J. Helme shop); 159 (Feb. 19, 1794) (R. Potter's tavern); 164 (July 27, 1794) (tea at R. Potter's); 235 (Oct. 4, 1800) (hat bound and brushed to make knife to pay for it); (Charles Barker tavern); 284 (Jan. 21, 1807) (tea at E. Potter's); 289 (May 14, 1807) (tea at E. Potter's); 289 (May 20, 1807) (coffee at Dr. Hazard's); 310 (Aug. 11-13, 19 & 22, 1808) (Timothy Peckham and Joe Reynolds taverns); 311 (April 29, 1808 (tea at Joe Reynolds tavern); 325 (June 26 & July 4, 1809) (Wells and Taylor stores); 326 (July 14, 1809) (Wells store; visit E. Potter); 349 (Sept. 15 & 16, 1810) (dined and tea at E. Potter's); 367 (Aug. 12, 1811) (traded beef to E. Potter, Philip Taylor, Joseph Reynolds, John Nichols, and E. Gardner; bought gin from Joseph Reynolds and Philip Taylor); 411 (Sept. 7-9, 1813) (shaved by W. Lunt; bought drugs from Dr. Aldrich; bought gin from J. Reynolds); 414 (Oct. 20, 1813) (gave money to T. Peckham "to pay into Narragansett Bank;" dined at E. Potter's); 445 (April 22-27, 1815) (dined at E. Potter's; lodged at T. Peckham's; bank business with D. Douglas; tea at J. Reynolds by invitation; gin from T. Peckham and J. Reynolds; Wickford bank business with E. Potter; dined at C. Barker's tavern); 464 (April 9, 1816) (hired Capt. William Potter to make clothes; see also May 31 & June 1, 1816, where he finished making the clothes); 465 (May 1, 1816) (bought gingerbread from S. Green); 487 (June 17, 1817) (bought gingerbread from S. Green; Narragansett bank business); 533 (Oct. 29, 1819) (Taylor and Wells stores; Landholders Bank business); 537 (Feb. 29, 1820) (renewed note at Landholders Bank for $280; bought plums from John Clarke's shop; bought glass of gin from J. Reynolds); 669 (April 17-19, 1827) (dined at Dr. Johnson's, P. Taylor's tavern and J. Nichols). For artisans in the village, see also upcoming chapter on the Fayerweathers; Hunt, Arline M., "Industries, Stores, Lawyers, Etc. in Little Rest, Later Kingston," 2-4 (Rose, Greene, Aldrich, Greenman); Wells, J. Hagadorn, "Kingston Annals," 22, 26, 36, 45-46 & 51 (Greene, Eldred, Stanton, Lunt, Cottrell, French & Nichols). In the 1790s, there were also Nicholas Pettis, a hat maker, and Jeremiah N. Sands, a watchmaker and silversmith. South Kingstown Land Evidence Records, v. 9, 30 (transfer of land from James Helme to Nicholas Pettis, "a Hatters (new) shop, Aug. 23, 1793; v. 8-597 (lease to Sands, a "clock and watchmaker," 1793); Washington County Court of Common Pleas Records, Feb. 1802 Sess. 197 & 198 (cases brought by Nicholas Pettis, "hatter"). For the postmasters, see appendix to Gardiner, Thomas, A., "The Early Postal Services of South Kingstown," *The Reporter* (quarterly journal of the Pettaquamscutt Historical Society) (Winter 1988-89). For the doctors, see Helme, Jonathan, "Recollections of South Kingstown," *Providence Journal,* Oct. 31, 1874 (Johnson, Aldrich & Hazard); Wells, J. Hagadorn, "Kingston

Annals," 42 & 65 (Aldrich and Hazard); Cole, J. H., *History of Washington and Kent Counties,* 188-90 (Johnson), 197-98 (Hazard) & 611 (Aldrich); Chappell, Virginia (ed.), "The Diary and Account Book of William Gould, Jr.," *Rhode Island Genealogical Register, v. 3, no. 2: 108* (Oct. 1980) & v. 3, no. 3: 229-33 (Jan. 1981). Day books are held by the University of Rhode Island Library (Special Collections) for Dr. Johnson (1827-1851) and Dr. Hazard (1839-82). For advertisements by dentist J. W. Babcock in Kingston, see *Narragansett Times,* Feb. 21, 1863.

Leisure, Voluntary Associations and Reform Activities. For entertainment in Kingston, see Oatley, Henry Clay, Jr. (ed.), *Daniel Stedman's Journal,* 137, 161, 163 & 255 (all circus, except last one is cattle show); Chappell, Virginia (ed.), "The Diary and Account Book of William Gould, Jr.," *Rhode Island Genealogical Register,* v. 3, no. 3: 231 (Jan. 1981) (circus); *Narragansett Times,* June 24, 1870 (Murray's Circus in Kingston draws 4,000 people); *Narragansett Times,* June 1, 1877 (O'Brien's Circus in Kingston); *South County Journal,* July 10, 1858, 2 (July 4th) & July 24, 1858, 5 (tea); Hunt, Annie M., "Industries, Stores, Lawyers, Etc. in Little Rest," 7 (other social occasions). For the agricultural society, see Hazard, Thomas R., *The Jonny-Cake Papers,* 158-59. For the Kingston Musical Society, see Kingston Musical Society Minutes, Wells Papers, Pettaquamscutt Historical Society. For the establishment of the library, see Titus, David K., "The Kingston Free Library, 1824-1893, A Revised History," 1-7. For the 1848 women's club, see Faella, Betty and Connie Fitzelle, "The Every Tuesday Club" 15 (this club was mentioned in a 1902 meeting; nothing more is known of this club). For French's gardening, see Hazard, Thomas R., *The Jonny-Cake Papers,* 140; South Kingstown Probate Records, v. 4, 152 (April 14, 1826). For the newspapers and journals, see Kingston Post Office Records, Thomas Wells, Postmaster, 1837-40, Wells Papers, Pettaquamscutt Historical Society.

The Rise of the Common Man. For Potter at the Reynolds tavern, see Hazard, Thomas R., *The Jonny-Cake Papers,* 149. For Major Lunt, see *id.* at 130-31; Wells, J. Hagadorn, "Kingston Annals," 28-29; Justices Court Records, 1782-92, George Peckham, Justice, Sept. 9, 1785, 129 & Dec. 18, 1790, 18 (William Lunt, "Peruke Maker" (wigmaker)). For French, Cottrell, Green and Robinson, see Hazard, Thomas R., *The Jonny-Cake Papers,* 112-13, 140-41 & 158-59; Wells, J. Hagadorn, "Kingston Annals," 26, 30 & 46; Helme, Jonathan, "Recollections of South Kingstown," *Providence Journal,* Oct. 31, 1874.

Little Rest's Ties to the Sea. For South Ferry and the ships, see Arnold, James (ed.), *Narragansett Historical Register,* v. II, 66-77; Saunders, Laura S., "A Glimpse of South Kingstown's Maritime Past," *The Reporter* (the quarterly journal of the Pettaquamscutt Historical Society) (Autumn 1986) 3-5; Tootell, Lucy R., "Shipwright Saunders' Shipshape Ships," *The Reporter* (the quarterly journal of the Pettaquamscutt Historical Society) 29 (May 1963); *Rhode Island Advocate,* Sept. 17, 1832, 3 (Taylor announces ship *Kingston* has returned with molasses for sale); South Kingstown Probate Records, v. 5, 261 (Sept. 18, 1835) (James B. M. Potter inherits South Ferry property from Elisha R. Potter, Sr.); Thomas S. Taylor Collection, Baker Library, Harvard Business School, Mss. 77 1807-1863 T238, v. 22 (Daybook,

Wickford, 1830-31); James Brown Mason Potter Papers, Box 1, Folder 5, Rhode Island Historical Society, Mss 629, SG 6 (loose receipts and other papers relating to Potter's expenses of maintaining the sloop *South Kingstown* and the South Ferry).

Little Rest as State, County and Town Seat

For the General Assembly at Little Rest, see Carroll, Charles, *Rhode Island: Three Centuries of Democracy,* v. I, 575 (1844 law changing General Assembly meeting at Kingston once every two years, until 1854). For court of common pleas cases in Little Rest, see Washington County Court of Common Pleas Records, Feb. 1809 Sess. 299 (J. Helme v. C. Barker); Feb. 1818 Sess. 362 (T. Taylor v. Levi Totten); Aug. 1817 Sess. 415 (T. Peckham v. E. Potter); Aug. 1817 Sess. 448 (E. Potter v. T. Peckham); Feb. 1817 Sess. 348-53 (Cuban merchant cases against Providence and Cranston merchants). For the fish dam case, see *id.* Aug. 1803 Sess. 349-51; this case was the subject of several appeals. Washington County Supreme Court Records, Oct. 1804 Sess. 193-95; April 1807 Sess. 343-47; Oct. 1807 Sess. 258-59. For the Peckham v. French case, see Hazard, Thomas R., *The Jonny-Cake Papers*, 142. For the case of Mary Joe, see Washington County Supreme Court Records, Oct. 1805 Sess. 255. Another case involving a Narragansett Indian was Harry Hazard, a Charleston man who was charged with beating his wife to death, but was acquitted at trial. *Id.,* Oct. 1806 Sess. 325. For divorce cases, see *id.,* April 1792 Sess. (two cases); Apr. 1797 Sess. 5; April 1800 Sess. 64, 66, 77, 79 & 80 (5 wives granted divorces, one for husband's adultery; E. Potter the attorney for the wife in two cases); Oct. 1801 Sess. 106 & 108 (two wives granted divorce, one for husband threatening her life). For non-governmental uses of the Court House, see Field, Edward (ed.), *State of Rhode Island and Providence Plantations,* v. I, 320-21 (first convention); *Narragansett Times,* Nov. 4, 1864 (Lincoln meeting); *Narragansett Times,* Oct. 30, 1868 (Grant); Hazard, Caroline (ed.), *Nailer Tom's Diary,* 145 (Dec. 6, 1792) & 469 (July 9, 1816) (Quaker meetings); Letter from William French to Joseph L. Tillinghast, dated Feb. 17, 1840, Misc. Manuscripts Collection, Box 14, Folder 137, University of Rhode Island Library (Special Collections) (speaker from Boston on currency and Whig meeting); broadside, "Law and Order Party of South Kingstown Dissolved by the Ultra Clay Whigs," Misc. Manuscripts Collection, Box 2, Folders 16 & 17, University of Rhode Island Library (Special Collections) (the meeting of the "ultra" Whigs in the Court House in Kingston and the division within the Law and Order Party in 1844); Updike, Wilkins, *History of the Episcopal Church in Narragansett,* 357-58 (Episcopal church in 1857-58 that later moved to Wakefield). For the act to prevent excessive riding near the Court House, see *Rhode Island Acts & Resolves,* Sept. 1790 Session, v. I, 14. For the fence around the Court House, see Wells, J. Hagadorn, "Kingston Annals," 41. For the ordinance prohibiting keeping a "Station House" near the Court House, see South Kingstown Town Council Records, June 1861, 208. For the town meeting at which beer kegs surrounded the court house, see *Narragansett Times,* April 4, 1862. For the ordinance prohibiting sales of liquor on town meeting days, see South Kingstown Town Meeting Records, v. 3, 46 (July 6, 1862). For the criminal system, see Justices Court Records, 1792-1808, South Kingstown Town Hall; Bickford, Christopher, *Crime, Punishment, and the Washington County Jail,* 19-36; Oatley, Henry Clay, Jr. (ed.), *Daniel Stedman's Journal,* 21-22 (Congden). For violently assaulting his wife Elizabeth, Congden was sentenced to pay a fine of $20 and the court costs, and spend 30 days in jail. Washington County Supreme Court Records, April 1827 Sess. 673. The clerk's office for the Washington County court of common pleas and supreme court were located in two small buildings on North Road. See Wells, J. Hagadorn, "Kingston Annals," 16. The town clerk's office was originally in the Landholders Bank building. Hunt, Arline M., "Industries, Stores, Lawyers, Etc. in Little Rest, Later Kingston," 6. For the town clerk's office being built into the Court House, see handwritten notes on important dates in Kingston's history, Elisha R. Potter, Jr. Papers, Series 5, Box 5, Folder 35, Rhode Island Historical Society. For developments in poor relief, see Brennan, Joseph, *Social Conditions in Industrial Rhode Island,* 141-44. For Hazard's journal entries, see Hazard, Caroline (ed.), *Nailer Tom's Diary,* 145 (Dec. 6, 1792) (Quaker monthly meeting at court house); (Gardiner-Brattle arbitration); 203 (Oct. 10-13, 1797) (four days at court); 220 (April 22, 1799) (Nichols-Pettis arbitration); 240 (Mar. 1, 1804) (political caucus on behalf of South Kingstown); 243 (April 24, 1804) (grand jury); 289 (May 20, 1807) (at court for estate administration; coffee at Dr. Hazard's); 296 (Oct. 26-30, 1807) (General Assembly four days; dined with E. Potter's and Dr. Hazard's); 311 (Sept. 12, 1808) (town council meeting; Stanton-Hazard arbitration; dined at T. Peckham's tavern); 327 (Aug. 7 & 8, 1809) (at court for estate administration; Wells store); 360 (April 17, 1811) (town meeting; dined at E. Potter's); 367 (Aug. 12, 1811) (traded beef to E. Potter, Philip Taylor, Joseph Reynolds, John Nichols, and E. Gardner; give evidence in court case; at court for his suit as guardian; bought gin from Joseph Reynolds and Philip Taylor); 385 (June 12, 1812) (town meeting and Joseph Reynolds for gin); 411 (Sept. 7-9, 1813) (served on jury; shaved by W. Lunt; bought drugs from Dr. Aldrich; bought gin from J. Reynolds); 414 (Oct. 20, 1813) (appointed administrator of estate at court); 448 (June 20-21, 1815) (gave evidence in court case involving E. Gardner; Wickford bank business with J. Nichols, including payment of interest); 463 (March 27, 1816) (pay J. Helme to draw deed; settle accounts with J. Helme, E. Gardner; lodged at J. Reynolds tavern); 464 (April 9, 1816) (bought 5 cent stamp from J. Helme); 465 (April 23, 1816) (placed on jury); 469 (Quaker meeting at Court House); 487 (June 14, 1817) (gave bond to get J. Taylor out of jail); 509 (June 11-13, 1818) (gave evidence in court case between J. Nichols and T. Peckham; tea at J. Nichols); 533 (Oct. 29, 1819) ("Gave Evedence for Christopher Robinson before the Ginneral Assembly about the Fisherry"); 557 (April 25, 1821) (gave evidence in court case; bought plums and gin from J. Clarke's store); 587 (Nov. 5 & 11, 1822 (poor man's oath and guardianship for son Tom; cherry run from J. Reynolds); 631 (April 20, 1825) (dined at W. Updike; town meeting); 677 (Oct. 20, 1827) ((gave bond for son Tom to have liberty of the jail bounds); 759 (March 3-5, 1834 (attended "referrance" between Samuel Helme and Wilkins Updike in Kingston; lodged at John N. Reynolds tavern). On August 17, 1797, Nailer Tom wrote in his journal, "went to Little Rest to Arbetrate with Samuel J Potter and James Knowles a dispute between John Gardiner Formolly of Boston Neck and Robert Brattle. We hear the arguments on both sides and agreed to meet tomorrow morning to give Judgment." The next morning, he reported, "I went to Little Rest to Finish the arbetration Between John Gardiner and

Robert Brattle and we Finished it accordingly." On April 22, 1799, Nailer Tom "went to Timothy Peckhams [the tavern in Little Rest] to attent on an arbetration between William Nichols and Nicholas B. Pettice. I was a Refferee." See citations in prior sentence. For government positions, see Smith, Joseph Jencks (ed.), *Civil and Military List of Rhode Island, 1800-1850, passim.* During the War of 1812, Elijah Kenyon reportedly helped to defend against the British raid of Stonington, Connecticut in August 1814. Wells, J. Hagadorn, "Kingston Annals," 7. For Updike, see Woodward, Carl R., *Plantation in Yankeeland,* 165-67. For the attorneys, see *Biographical Cyclopedia,* 309 (Asa Potter); Helme, Jonathan, "Recollections of South Kingstown," *Providence Journal,* Oct. 31, 1874 (Newell, Totten, Aplin, Potter & Updike); Elisha R. Potter, Sr. Papers, Series 3, Box 1, Folder 24, Rhode Island Historical Society (bar association formation). For militia musters in Little Rest, see Wells, J. Hagadorn, "Kingston Annals," 7 & 25 (Captain Kenyon); Oatley, Henry Clay, Jr. (ed.), *Daniel Stedman's Journal,* 138 & 173; Smith, Joseph Jencks (ed.), *Civil and Military List of Rhode Island, 1800-1850, passim*; *Providence Journal,* Sept. 26, 1842; Potter, James Brown Mason, *Oration Delivered at Kingston, R.I., July 4, 1843,* 24. For the incorporation of the Washington Cavalry, see *Rhode Island Acts & Resolves,* June 1792 Session, v. II, 11-13. For John Hagadorn as its first lieutenant, see Appointment by Governor Fenner, dated May 11, 1807, Hagadorn-Wells Papers, Box 1, Folder 7, Rhode Island Historical Society, Mss 629, SG 10.

Elisha Reynolds Potter, Sr.: A Natural Born Great Man

For Potter's early life, see Wells, J. Hagadorn, "Biographical Sketches," 1-5; *Biographical Cyclopedia,* 156; Langer, Kenneth, "Elisha Reynolds Potter, Sr., Politician" (Masters Thesis) 1-5; Cowell, Benjamin, *Spirit of '76 in Rhode Island,* 63-64 & 77 (military service); Hazard, Caroline (ed.), *Nailer Tom's Diary,* 128 (Oct. 18, 1791) (Hazard buys wine from Potter); Elisha Potter Account Book, Pettaquamscutt Historical Society. For Potter's early political career, see *Biographical Encyclopedia of Representative Men of Rhode Island,* 156; Field, Edward (ed.), *State of Rhode Island and Providence Plantations,* v. III, at 249-50 (1796 valuation); *Rhode Island Acts & Resolves,* v. III, 27-29 (1797 taxes, relying on 1796 revaluation) (Providence paid $3,806; Newport $1,870; Smithfield $978; Gloucester $931; South Kingstown $929); Updike, Wilkins, *Memoirs of the Rhode Island Bar,* 127-29 ("Herculean triumph" quote); South Kingstown Town Meeting Records, v. 2, 129 (admitted as freeman). For Potter as U.S. Congressman, see Langer, Kenneth, "Elisha Reynolds Potter, Sr." (Masters Thesis) ch. II. For Potter's character, see Carpenter, Esther B., *South County Studies,* 172 (Helme funeral); Hazard, Thomas R., *The Jonny-Cake Papers,* 131 (red hot Republicans), 149 (natural born great man); Arnold, James (ed.), *Narragansett Historical Register,* v. III, 145 (Helme as Republican elector of Jefferson); Weeden, William, *History of Early Rhode Island,* 306-07 n.37 (court house steps quote); *Biographical Cyclopedia,* 157 (Josiah Quincy quote). For Potter's political influence at the state level, see Field, Edward (ed.), *State of Rhode Island and Providence Plantations,* v. III, 297-328; Langer, Kenneth, "Elisha Reynolds Potter, Sr." (Masters Thesis) ch. III; Grant, Philip A., "Party Chaos Embroils Rhode Island," *Rhode Island History* 26: 113-25 (Oct. 1967) & 27: 24-33

(Jan. 1968); *Reasons Why the Hon. Elisha R. Potter Should Not be a Senator in Congress,* 5 (Potter still alert but not interested in literature); Sweet, Edward F., "The Origins of the Democratic Party in Rhode Island, 1824-1836" (Doctoral Thesis) *passim*; Zuckerman, Michael B. "The Political Economy of Industrial Rhode Island, 1790-1860" (Doctoral Thesis) *passim*; Carroll, Charles, *Rhode Island: Three Centuries of Democracy,* v. I, 564-74; *Rhode Island Advocate,* May 12, 1832 (Potter on manufacturing and farming). For Potter's questionable electioneering tactics, see Conley, Patrick T., *Democracy in Decline,* 242 n.16; Coleman, Peter J., *The Transformation of Rhode Island,* 261-62; *What a Ploughman Said,* 4-5. Potter was accused of offering to help free a man from jail if the man agreed to vote for him, but depositions taken addressing the matter are inconclusive. Elisha R. Potter, Sr. Papers, Series 2, Box 1, Folder 13, Rhode Island Historical Society. For Potter's marriages to Mary Perkins and Mary Mawney, see Cole, J. R., *History of Washington and Kent Counties,* 169-70 (by Mrs. B. F. Robinson); Beers, J. H., *Representative Men and Old Families of Rhode Island,* 53; Langer, Kenneth, "Elisha Reynolds Potter, Sr." (Masters Thesis) 4-6. For Potter's landholdings, see An Account of the Real and Personal Estate of E. R. Potter, August 21, 1816, Elisha R. Potter, Sr. Papers, Series 6, Box 2, Folder 9, Rhode Island Historical Society; South Kingstown Probate Records, v. 6, 215-16 (Oct. 28, 1789) (will of Joseph Perkins); v. 6, 240-42 (Nov. 14, 1791) (will of Elisha Reynolds); v. 5, 261 (Sept. 18, 1835) (will of Elisha Reynolds Potter, Sr.); *Rhode Island Advocate,* Dec. 26, 1831, 3 (Potter properties listed for sale); Deed of land from Elisha Reynolds to Elisha Potter in 1786, Elisha R. Potter, Sr. Papers, Series 4, Box 1, Folder 27, Rhode Island Historical Society; Elisha R. Potter, Sr. Papers, Series 4, Box 4, Folder 27 (note from E. R. Potter, Jr., "June 6, 1786, ER to ERP 10 acres on Knowles place to make him a voter"); Updike, Wilkins, *History of the Episcopal Church in Narragansett,* 235 (E. Potter acquires W. Potter estate); Arnold, James (ed.), *Narragansett Historical Register,* v. II, 107-08 (1810 broadside stating that Potter was "one of the largest landholders in the State"). For Potter's interest in South Ferry and ships, see his will, South Kingstown Probate Records, v. 5, 261 (Sept. 18, 1835) (James B. M. Potter inherits one-half interest in the South Ferry land and ferry boat); discussion of ships in prior chapter, A Picture of Little Rest in the Early 1800s. For Potter's legal quotation, see quotations.com. For Potter's legal case against Gardner, see *Abridgement of the Case of Gardner and Potter vs. Hannah Gardner and Others*; Elisha R. Potter, Sr. Papers, Series 3 Box 1, Folders 1 and 2, Rhode Island Historical Society (including handwritten brief submitted to U.S. Supreme Court). For Potter and Little Rest, see chapters on Kingston Congregational Church, Landholders Bank, Kingston Academy, and A Picture of Little Rest in the early 1800s; South Kingstown Probate Records, v. 6, 215-16 (Oct. 28, 1789) (will of Joseph Perkins). For Potter's death and funeral, see Oatley, Henry Clay, Jr. (ed.), *Daniel Stedman's Journal,* 138; Langer, Kenneth, "Elisha Reynolds Potter, Sr.," (Masters Thesis) 71-72.

The Little Rest Village Club of Practical Jokers

The original version of Charles Comstock's *A History of South Kingstown with a Particular Description of the Hornet's Nest Company, and the Cats Let Out of the Bag* (Newport, 1806) is available at the John Hay Library at Brown University. William Davis Miller reprinted the pamphlet in 1934, with a short forward. In admirable discretion, Miller left out a sentence in which a Little Rest villager is quoted as making an absurdly vile remarks about a man's religious views. For more on Gardner, see Hazard, Thomas R., *The Jonny-Cake Papers*, 112; Wells, J. Hagadorn, "Kingston Annals," 11 ("unpolished intelligence"); Helme, Jonathan, "Recollections of South Kingstown," *Providence Journal*, Oct. 31, 1874 ("large and muscular"). On humor in America in the early Republic generally, see Nickels, Cameron C., *New England Humor*. For establishments that sold alcohol in Little Rest and the temperance movement in Little Rest, see notes on chapters on Little Rest's three taverns, Little Rest in the 1800s (portion on taverns), general stores and the temperance movement in Little Rest. For the "negro election" festival, see chapter on continuing badges of slavery in Little Rest, and for Gardner being prevented by the town council from freeing his slave, see next chapter. For whippings and other punishments inflicted on prisoners, see chapter on Corporal Punishment in Little Rest. For treatment of fathers of illegitimate children, see chapters on the Indentured Servitude of Alice Franklin and Corporal Punishment in Little Rest. For the Massachusetts study on taverns as coffee-houses, see Conroy, David W., *Public Houses*, 161-62. For the inventory of Charles Barker's estate, see South Kingstown Probate Records, v. 3, 204-07 (Oct. 11, 1819). For Nailer Tom drinking tea, see *Nailer Tom's Diary*, Jan 21, 1807, 284 (tea at E. Potter's house); May 14, 1807, 289 (same); Aug. 29, 1808, 311 (tea at Joseph Reynolds tavern), 509 (tea at J. Nichols' boarding house); *see also* May 20, 1807, 289 (coffee at Dr. Hazard's house). Nailer Tom's journal reveals that he drank tea (and coffee) much more frequently than alcohol. For cases brought by Nichols and Comstock, see Justices Court Records, James Helme, Jr. Justice, 1803-1806, 96, 97 & 98, Jan.-Feb. 1805 (Nichols) and 119, April 1, 1805 (Comstock). For Storer and his pig, see Hazard, Thomas R., *The Jonny-Cake Papers*, 114-16. For Gardner's departure from Little Rest, see Helme, Jonathan , "Recollections of South Kingstown," *Providence Journal*, Oct. 31, 1874. The Landholders Bank sued Gardiner to recover $49.29 in 1822. Washington County Court of Common Pleas Records, Aug. 1822 Sess. 72. Elisha Gardner died some time prior to 1825; his wife was permitted to live on his land in Little Rest for the remainder of her life. South Kingstown Probate Records, v. 4, 108-09.

The Town Council Prevents Elisha Gardner from Freeing His Slave.

I extend credit to Professor Joanne Pope Melish for uncovering the Elisha Gardner and Patience case, at page 98, in her excellent *Disowning Slavery: Gradual Emancipation and "Race" in New England, 1780-1860*, which focuses to a considerable extent on southern Rhode Island. See also Elisha R. Gardiner v. South Kingstown Town Council, Washington County Court of Common Pleas, Oct. 1808 Sess. 397; South Kingstown Probate Records, v. 6, 362 (Nov. 22, 1796) (will of Caleb Gardner, with his grandson Elisha Gardner as co-executor); South Kingstown Town Council Records, v. 7, 38 (Aug. 11, 1806) (town council rejecting Gardner's first manumission request), v. 7, 39 (Sept. 8, 1806) (town council rejecting Gardner's second manumission request) & v. 7, 54 (Dec. 12, 1808) (paying attorney John

Hagadorn's fees in manumission case). For Rhode Island's 1784 gradual emancipation legislation, see Bartlett, John (ed.), *Records of the Colony of Rhode Island,* v. X, 7-8; Melish, Joanne Pope, *Disowning Slavery,* 71-73. For the reluctance of the town council to free Patience and other slaves, see *id.* at 97-98. For examples of the town council emancipating slaves under the emancipation legislation, see Stutz, Jean C., *South Kingstown Town Council Records,* 231 (1788); 236 & 239 (1789); 261 (1790); 304 (1793); South Kingstown Town Council Records, v. 5, 287 (1800); v. 6, 14 (1803). In the 1793 meeting, involving Philo Peckham, the first negative vote was registered by a council member. For the town council rejecting Wilkinson Browning's application to manumit his slave Cesar, see *id.*, v. 6, 22 (Aug. 13, 1804) & v. 6, 24 (Sept. 12, 1804). For Elisha Potter manumitting his slave John Potter, see South Kingstown Town Council Records, v. 7, 69 (Aug. 10, 1810). For the wills of Perkins, Reynolds and Peckham, see South Kingstown Probate Records, v. 6, 215 (Oct. 28, 1789) (Perkins); v. 6, 241 (Reynolds) (Nov. 14, 1791); v. 6, 263 (Dec. 7, 1790) (Peckham). For the town council ordering the estate of Josephus Peckham to support Quaim Peckham, "a black man . . . in a suffering state," see South Kingstown Town Council Records, v.7, 106 (Dec. 13, 1813). For the Abolition Society's prosecution of Benjamin Peckham, see Rhode Island Society for the Abolition of the Slave Trade Minutes, 1789-1827, 28-29, Rhode Island Historical Society. An examination of the Federal 1790 census for Rhode Island indicates that there were four heads of households named Benjamin Peckham, one in Newport, one in North Kingstown, and two in South Kingstown. See *Heads of Families at the First Census of the United States Taken in the Year 1790, Rhode Island.* Neither of the Peckhams in Newport nor North Kingstown had slaves or other non-white persons living in their households. By contrast, Benjamin Peckham of South Kingstown, the planter who lived just north of Little Rest on North Road, was reported as owning four slaves. His son, Benjamin Peckham, was reported as having two non-white free persons living in his household. Accordingly, the author believes that the Benjamin Peckham who was prosecuted by the Abolition Society came from South Kingstown, and likely was the elder Peckham who resided near Little Rest (if the individual had been the younger Peckham, one would have expected the Abolition Society to reflect that he was a "jr."). For the cases brought by the free black laborers, see Washington County Court of Common Pleas Records, Aug. 1795 Sess. 195 (Quash and Lydia Peckham vs. Zephamiah Brown); Aug. 1796 Sess. 248 (Prince Vaughn v. John Wescott); Aug. 1797 Sess. 331 (Cudjo Babcock v. Joshua Perry).

Elisha R. Potter and Continuing Badges of Slavery in Little Rest

I extend credit to Robert K. Fitts for rediscovering Cato Pearce's book. See his authoritative study on slavery in colonial Narragansett, *Inventing New England's Slave Paradise, Master/Slave Relations in Eighteenth-Century Narragansett, Rhode Island.* An original copy of Pearce's pamphlet, *A Brief Memoir*, is in the John Hay Library at Brown University. For Stedman's mentions of Cato Pearce and Governor John Potter in his journal, see Oatley, Henry Clay, Jr. (ed.), *Daniel Stedman's Journal,* 31 (Pearce) & 9, 85 (Potter). Pearce must have been put in jail in either 1807 or 1808, as he says the name of the sheriff at the time was Allen. Sheriff Samuel D.

Allen served in the years 1807 and 1808. See Bickford, Christopher, *Crime, Punishment, and the Washington County Jail,* 25. For the "Negro Election" festival in New England generally, see White, Shane, "'It was a Proud Day:' African Americans, Festivals, and Parades in the North, 1741-1834," *Journal of American History* 81: 13-50 (June 1994); Wade, Melvin, "Shining in Borrowed Plummage: Affirmation of Community in the Black Coronation Festivals in New England, 1750-1850," *Western Folklore* 40: 211-31 (July 1981). For the "Negro Election" festival in the Narragansett country, see Updike, Wilkins, *History of the Episcopal Church in Narragansett,* 177-79; Helme, Jonathan, "Recollections of South Kingstown," *Providence Journal,* Oct. 31, 1874. For town meeting ordinances attempting to outlaw the annual "Negro Election," see South Kingstown Town Meeting Records, v. 1, 13 (June 1726) & 80-81 (Aug. 30, 1737). For reports of the last Negro elections, see Oatley, Henry Clay, Jr. (ed.), *Daniel Stedman's Journal,* 26; Hazard, Thomas R., *Recollections of Olden Times,* 121-22. For "Who makes thunder?", see Hazard, Thomas R., *The Jonny-Cake Papers,* 150-51. For a discussion of the exaggerated black speech patterns, see Melish, Joanne, *Disowning Slavery,* 178-82. For black migration, see Snow, Edwin M., *Census of Rhode Island, 1875,* xliii. For mentions of "Governor" John Potter in Nailer Tom Hazard's journal, see Hazard, Caroline (ed.), *Nailer Tom's Diary,* 549-50 (Nov. 1-2, 1820); 560 (April 27, 1821); 583 (Sept. 4-5, 1822); 584 (Sept. 16-17, 1822); 721 (April 20-21, 1830).

George Fayerweather: A Free Man of Color

For information on George I and George II, see Woodward, Carl R., *Plantation in Yankeeland,* 167-70; South Kingstown Probate Records, v. 6, 122 (June 11, 1781) (Samuel Fayerweather's will) & v. 6, 324 (Matthew Robinson's will); Hazard, Caroline (ed.), *Nailer Tom's Diary,* 132 (Jan. 13, 1792) ("Dockter Perry supt here also George Fareweather"), 136 (April 24, 1792) ("then went to mill with a bushel grist that I had of George Faireweather for whitch I gave him a Chest Lock"), 441 (Feb. 14, 1815) (Nailer Tom sold George II a pair of gloves), 465 (April 18, 1816) (Nailer Tom sold George II two "plowshear Moulds"), 466 (May 9, 1816) (Nailer Tom purchased a hoe from George II), 474 (Oct. 16, 1816) (Nailer Tom settled accounts with George II and gave George II's order to George II), 555 (Mar. 24-25, 1821) (Fayerweather made a plow at Nailer Tom's forge and spent the night at Nailer Tom's house, taking breakfast in the morning), 559 (June 6, 1821) (Nailer Tom settled accounts with George II), 712 (Jan. 12, 1830) (Nailer Tom settled accounts with George II); Joseph Reynolds' Day Book, June 10, 1796-April 30, 1801 (for sale by M&S Rare Books) (Reynolds hires George II on Feb. 6, 1800; George II also buys a gill of gin from Reynolds on Feb. 6, 1801); Elisha Potter's Account Book, 45, Pettaquamscutt Historical Society (George II's first purchases in 1804); Kingston Post Office Records, Thomas P. Wells, Postmaster, 1837-40, Wells Papers, Pettaquamscutt Historical Society (newspapers); Oatley, Henry Clay, Jr. (ed.), *Daniel Stedman's Journal,* 196 (George II's death); Wells, J. Hagadorn, "Kingston Annals," 12-13 (location of first blacksmith shop). George II hired Elisha R. Potter, Sr. to keep his horse in Potter's Pastures. For George Fayerweather's Day Book (1809-21), see Fayerweather Family Papers, 1836-1962, MSG #121, University of Rhode Island

Library (Special Collections). For court case, see Washington County Court of Common Pleas Records, Aug. 1824 Sess. 164 & Feb. 1822 Sess. 368 (Levi Totten owes $49.04; Fayerweather wins.) For membership in the Kingston Congregational Church, see Kingston Congregational Church records; Hagadorn-Wells Papers, Box 2, Folder 11, Mss 629 SG 10. For Solomon Fayerweather and the Kingston Congregational Church, see Metz, William D., *History of the Kingston Congregational Church,* 96. For the quote on Solomon's shop, see Taylor, Philip K., "Little Rest," *The New England Magazine,* 138-39. For George Fayerweather III, see Woodward, Carl R., "A Profile in Dedication, Sarah Harris and the Fayerweather Family," *The New England Galaxy* 4-11 (summer 1973). For Elisha Potter's financial assistance to George III, see Elisha Reynolds Potter Papers, letter from George Fayerweather to Elisha Potter, dated Mar. 16, 1836, Mss 629, SG3, Series 1, Correspondence, Box 1, folder 2 & letter from George Fayerweather to Elisha Potter, dated Mar. 27, 1840, Box 1, folder 6, Rhode Island Historical Society; South Kingstown Land Evidence Records, v. 17, 612 (Mar. 30. 1847) (conveying land and blacksmith shop on the old Helme property from George Fayerweather to Elisha R. Potter, Jr., Potter having obtained a mortgage on the property on Nov. 28, 1846). For letters by Sarah Harris Fayerweather and George III, invoices for orders of supplies by the Fayerweather blacksmiths, page from account book of Estate of John H. Teft by Solomon Fayerweather, and the George and Solomon Fayerweather 1868 account book, see Fayerweather Family Papers, 1836-1962, MSG #121, Boxes 1 and 2, University of Rhode Island Library (Special Collections). For work on the jail, see Bickford, Christopher, *Crime, Punishment, and the Washington County Jail,* 14. For a discussion of black employment in 19th century New England, see Melish, Joanne P., *Disowning Slavery,* 135-36. For restrictions on blacks in the 19th century in Rhode Island, see Conley, Patrick T., *Democracy in Decline,* 195 (1822 voting act); Carroll, Charles, *Public Education in Rhode Island,* 157-58 (public school); Bartlett, Irving H., *From Slave to Citizen,* 50-59 (public school) & 63 (juries and public accommodations).

The Kingston Congregational Church

This chapter relies heavily on Metz, William D., *History of the Congregational Church*, ch. 2. For Elisha R. Potter, Sr.'s efforts, see Langer, Kenneth Thomas, "Elisha Reynolds Potter, Sr., Politician" (Masters Thesis) 10-15; South Kingstown Land Evidence Records, v. 13, 296 (Jan. 15, 1821) (Potter sells for $300 the meeting house lot to the Presbyterian Society). For the Kingston Sabbath School, see South Kingstown Sabbath School Society Record Book, Wells Papers, Pettaquamscutt Historical Society. For a discussion of the Rhode Island Sunday School Union, see Schantz, Mark S., *Piety in Providence, Class Dimensions of Religious Experience in Antebellum Rhode Island,* 55-65. For church memberships and pew records, see Kingston Congregational Church Records, Kingston Congregational Church; Hagadorn-Wells Papers, Box 2, Folder 11, Mss 629 SG 10.

The Rise of the Bank and General Store

For Hazard's journal entries, see Hazard, Caroline (ed.), *Nailer Tom's Diary,* 414 ((Oct. 21, 1813) (gave money to T. Peckham "to pay into Narragansett Bank"); 448 (June 21, 1815) (Narragansett Bank business with J. Nichols, including payment of interest); 463 (Mar. 27, 1816) (gave money to J. Nichols to pay interest to Narragansett Bank); 487 (June 17, 1817) (Narragansett Bank business). For banking in Rhode Island in the early 1800s, see Fensternmaker, Joseph Van, *The Development of American Commercial Banking, 1782-1837, passim;* Coleman, Peter J., *The Transformation of Rhode Island,* 183-207; Jones, Daniel , *The Economic & Social Transformation of Rural Rhode Island*, 102-05. For the Landholders Bank, see Hoag & Wade, *History of the State of Rhode Island,* 294-95; *Rhode Island Advocate,* July 20, 1832, 4 (Potter as president); *Providence Gazette,* July 12, 1819 (bank deposits); Landholders' Bank Records, Weekly Reports, Rhode Island Historical Society, Mss 528; Landholders Bank Records, Elisha R. Potter, Sr. Papers, Series 5, Box 2, Folders 1-4, Rhode Island Historical Society (account books from 1839 to 1848; register of dollar bills, 1846-62; weekly reports, 1828-32); South Kingstown Land Evidence Records, v. 13, 87 (Sept. 7, 1818) (John T. Nichols leases rooms to Landholders Bank for $20 annual rent). Of course, the Landholders Bank sued debtors for nonpayment of loans. Washington County Court of Common Pleas Records, Aug. 1819 Sess. 118; Aug. 1822 Sess. 72. The Washington Bank in Westerly and the Narragansett Bank in Wickford started to bring cases against debtors in 1808. *Id.,* Feb. 1808 Sess. 50 (Washington Bank); Aug. 1808 Sess. 234 (Narragansett Bank). In some years, banks brought many cases, indicating that it was a period of economic difficulty. For example, the Washington Bank brought 16 cases in the August 1811 session of the court of common pleas (*id .*at 201-05) and the Narragansett Bank brought 14 cases in the August 1812 session (*id.* at 346-52). For the Kingston Savings Bank, see Hoag & Wade, *History of the State of Rhode Island,* 295; *South County Journal,* July 10, 1858, 4 (officers). For contemporary journal entries related to local banking, see Oatley, Henry Clay, Jr. (ed.), *Daniel Stedman's Journal,* 16, 106, 142 (Wakefield Bank), 206, 212 & 250; Hazard, Caroline (ed.), *Nailer Tom's Diary,* 533 (Oct. 29, 1819); 537 (Feb. 28, 1820) (renewed note for $280); 540 (April 24, 1820). For the United States Bank branch in Providence, see Carroll, Charles, *Rhode Island: Three Centuries of Democracy,* v. II, 795-96.

For barter exchanges in the early 1800s and the rise of the general store generally, see Jones, Daniel, *The Economic & Social Transformation of Rural Rhode Island,* 111-21; Bidwell, Percy W. & John I. Falconer, *History of Agriculture in the Northern United States, 1620-1860,* 132-33 & 247-48. For Immanuel Case's store in Little Rest, see advertisement in the *Newport Mercury,* Aug. 26, 1771. For Joseph Perkins, see chapter above, The Silversmiths of Little Rest. For James Helme, see Helme, Jonathan, "Recollections of South Kingstown," *Providence Journal,* Oct. 31, 1874. For purchase of local products by general stores, see Hazard, Caroline, *Nailer Tom's Diary,* 146 (Dec. 31, 1792) (sale of 500 nails by Nailer Tom to J. Helme). For John Nichols' saddler shop and boarding house, see Cole, J. H., *History of Washington and Kent Counties,* 612-13; *Rhode Island Advocate,* April 27, 1832, p. 3 (advertisement for saddler and harness shop; "Country produce taken in payment").

For Thomas Taylor's account books and ledgers, see Thomas S. Taylor Collection, Baker Library, Harvard Business School, Mss. 77 1807-1863 T238 (Daybooks, 1807-39; ledgers; accounts payable and receivable; miscellaneous accounts of general store); see also *Rhode Island Advocate,* June 15, 1832, 3 (advertisement). For references to the sloop *Kingston,* see notes to chapter, A Picture of Little Rest in the Early 1800s. For Thomas R. Wells' general store, see Wells, J. Hagadorn, "Kingston Annals," 4-5; Helme, Jonathan, "Recollections of South Kingstown," *Providence Journal,* Oct. 31, 1874; *Rhode Island Advocate,* Feb. 9, 1831, 1 (Thomas P. Wells advertising dry goods); Hagadorn-Wells Papers, Folder 9, Rhode Island Historical Society, Mss 629 SG 10 (account of Benjamin Storer's purchases from Thomas R. Wells' store, including brandy, tobacco, tea and sugar). For paragraph on Little Rest as a good market for farm produce, see *Rhode Island Advocate,* Dec. 27, 1831, p. 3 (Elisha R. Potter, Sr. advertised several of his farms for sale, which "are situated within a short distance of the flourishing village of Kingston, where an excellent school is established, and the village affords a good market for all kinds of farming productions"); Wells, J. Hagadorn, "Kingston Annals," 4-5 (Wells general store); Helme, Jonathan , "Recollections of South Kingstown," *Providence Journal,* Oct. 31, 1874 (Helme). For John G. Clarke, Robinson & Anthony, and other storekeepers in Kingston, see *id.*; Beers, J.H., Representative Men…of Rhode Island, 996 (Case Family) & 2133 (Clarke Family). MacKenzie, Louise, *Strolling Through Kingston,* 30-31. For the Palmer store, see *Narragansett Times,* May 16, 1862, 3 (Palmer and Wells opened dry goods and grocery store opposite the Court House). See also Nailer Tom Hazard's journal entries on general stores in chapter above, A Picture of Little Rest in the Early 1800s. The South Kingstown town council sometimes required general stores to be issued retail licenses to sell liquor. Here are some examples. In 1822, Little Rest general storekeeper's John G. Clarke, John P. Case and Thomas Taylor were issued licenses to sell liquor. *Id.* at v. 7, 195 & 199. In 1831, Kingston storekeepers John G. Clarke and Robinson & Anthony were issued licenses to sell liquor. *Id.* at v. 7, 282.

The Kingston Academy and Kingston Female Seminary

For the 1759 school house, see South Kingstown Land Evidence Records, v. 6, 110 (Oct. 20, 1759). For Elisha Potter teaching at the Little Rest school house and the Tower Hill school house, see Elisha R. Potter, Jr. Papers, Series 4, Box 5, Folder 28, Rhode Island Historical Society (notes from E. R. Potter, Sr. and lists of students); Miller, William Davis, "The Samuel Sewall School Land," *Rhode Island Historical Society Collections* 4, 10 (Jan. 1930). Historian Charles Carroll reports that there were four school houses in South Kingstown in 1819 and seven plus the Kingston Academy in 1828. Carroll, Charles, *Rhode Island: Three Centuries of Democracy,* v. I, 415; see also later chapter, Elisha Reynolds Potter, Jr., Wilkins Updike, and the Public School Movement in Rhode Island. For the removal of the Tower Hill school to Kingston and the Kingston Academy, see Trustees of the Academy, *Statement of Facts in Relation to the Funds of the Kingston Academy,* 1836, *passim;* Miller, William Davis, "The Samuel Sewall School Land and the Kingston Academy," *Rhode Island Historical Society Collections* 42-50 (April 1930); *Rhode Island Advocate,* April 20, 1832 & May 18, 1832 (advertisements for Kingston Academy);

Langer, Kenneth, "Elisha Reynolds Potter, Sr., Politician" (Masters Thesis) 10-13; *Catalogue of the Trustees, Instructors and Students of Kingston Academy*; Records of the Pettaquamscutt Academy [Kingston Academy], Misc. Manuscripts Collection, Box 1, Folder 1, University of Rhode Island Library (Special Collections); *October 5, 1833; Catalogue of the Trustees, Instructors and Students of Kingston Academy, for the Term Ending April 20, 1837*; Kingston Academy Minutes Book, 1823-61, Miscellaneous Manuscripts Collection, MSG #20, Box 1, Folder 1, University of Rhode Island Library (Special Collections); *Providence Daily Journal*, Dec. 2, 1829 (report on the Academy); *Rhode Island Republican*, Aug. 22, 1822 (same); South Kingstown Land Evidence Records, v. 12, 204 (purchase of Kingston Academy school house lot by Elisha Potter (16 shares); James Helme (5 shares); Maria Wells (4 shares); John T. Nichols (5 shares), and twelve other villagers (16 shares) (Dec. 23, 1815). For the dispute between E. R. Potter, Jr. and Rev. Brown, see letter from Elisha R. Potter, Jr. to Rev. Oliver Brown, Dec. 10, 1834, Elisha R. Potter, Jr. Papers, Series 1 Box 1, Folder 1, Rhode Island Historical Society. For the Kingston Seminary, see *Catalogue of the Officers and Students of Kingston Classical Seminary, Kingston, R.I. for the Academic Year, 1853-54;* Kingston Academy Minutes Book, 1823-61, Miscellaneous Manuscripts Collection, MSG #20, Box 1, Folder 1, University of Rhode Island Library (Special Collections); *Narragansett Times,* July 21, 1855, 2 & July 28, 1855, 2 (advertisements). For Wells boarding school, see Wells, J. Hagadorn, "Kingston Annals," 11-12. For other private academies in Rhode Island, see Field, Edward, *State of Rhode Island and Providence Plantations,* v. II, 354-76. For Mary Elizabeth Potter, see Mary E. Potter Papers, Box 1, Folders 1-3, Rhode Island Historical Society, Mss 629, SG 7. She attended Mrs. E. Smith's Boarding School for Young Ladies, located at Fifth Avenue in New York City.

Corporal Punishment in Little Rest

This chapter relies heavily on Bickford, Christopher, *Crime, Punishment and the Washington County Jail,* 31-38 & 46-49; see also Brennan, Joseph, *Social Conditions in Industrial Rhode Island,* 144-49. For the sentences of whipping in default of paying fines, see Court Justices Records, 1796-1806, Cyrus French, Justice, Dec. 6, 1796 (Mary and Rebecca Jones defendants; for stealing two plates; ten lashes each on the "Naked Back" if fines not paid); Court Justices Records, 1793-98, Levi Totten, Justice, May 20, 1794, 28-30 (Peter Freeman, a "molatto," for stealing small items including a linen handkerchief; thirty lashes on his "Naked Back" if fines not paid). Mary and Rebecca Jones may have been whipped, as they were not able to pay all of the court costs. The General Assembly ended up paying fees to justices and sheriffs handling the case and witness fees. *Rhode Island Acts and Resolves,* Oct. 1797 Session, v. III, 25. For the whipping sentence for Caleb Church, see *Rhode Island Acts & Resolves,* June 1791 Session, v. I, 22-23. For crimes involving money and property, see Washington County Superior Court Records, Oct. Sess. 148-49 (Short); Oct. 1825 Sess. 581-82 (Hines); April 1823 Sess. 418-20 (Bowen); April 1818 Sess. 69-71 (James); Oct. 1826 Sess. 607 (Church). For violent crimes, see *id.,* April 1814 Sess. 166-69 (five-year old victim); April 1827 Sess. 666-71 (four-month old victim); April 1824 Sess. 469-70 (Casey); April 1815 Sess. 230; Oct. 1825 Sess.

583 ("Life … Greatly Despaired of").   For the background on the debtor laws, see Coleman, Peter, J., *The Transformation of Rhode Island,* 254; Coleman, Peter J., "The Insolvent Debtor in Rhode Island, 1745-1828," *William & Mary Quarterly* 22: 413, 429 (1965) (J. Philips and S. Hazard); Brennan, Joseph, *Social Conditions in Industrial Rhode Island,* 144-45.   For Helme's anecdotes, see Helme, Jonathan, "Recollections of South Kingstown," manuscript at Kingston Free Library & Reading Room. Helme did not cite these anecdotes in the version of his reminiscences that appeared in the *Providence Journal* on October 31, 1874. He wrote that the first instance of corporal punishment was for counterfeiting, but he probably meant forging. Criminals had turned from counterfeiting bills and coins in the 18th century to forging bank notes and promissory notes in the early 1800s. The victim could also have been Palmer Hines of North Kingstown, who in 1825 was convicted of setting fire to a barn filled with nine tons of hay, nine hogs and farming utensils. He was sentenced to pay a fine of $1,000, to be imprisoned in the Little Rest jail for four years, to have his ears cropped, and to be branded with the letter "R." For the 1851 bank theft case, see Washington County Superior Court Records, Feb. 1851 Sess. 630-35 (State v. John Collins; State v. Henry Dasey). For Thomas Potter petitioning the General Assembly for relief under the Act of 1756, see King's County Superior Court, Nov. 1768 Sess. 229. For Samuel Casey's petition of insolvency to the General Assembly, see Petitions to the General Assembly 1770-72, No. 9, Rhode Island State Archives.   For William Lunt's insolvency, see Washington Court Supreme Court Records, April 1813 Sess. 122. For Potter's support of the bills for minor relief of debtors, see *Providence Journal,* Jan. 15-16, 1830 & June 21, 1830. For Potter's opposition to debtor relief, see also Fields, Edward (ed.), *State of Rhode Island and Providence Plantations,* v. I, 314. For Hazard's journal entry, see Hazard, Caroline, *Nailer Tom's Diary,* 587 (Nov. 11, 1822). For Stedman's journal entry, see Oatley, Henry Clay, Jr. (ed.), *Daniel Stedman's Journal,* 112. In October 1793, the General Assembly voted "that the Liberties of the Gaol-Yard in the County of Washington by extended so far Eastward as to allow the Prisoners who have the Liberty thereof to pass into the State-House in the aforesaid County." *Rhode Island Acts & Resolves,* Oct. 1793 Session, v. I, 20. In 1811, a debtor held in the Little Rest jail, James Rose, did "break the wall of the said jail and then removed a piece of plank and made his escape." Washington County Supreme Court Records, April 1811 Sess. 84-85. For Thomas Hazard and his movement to improve the treatment of poor persons, see Brennan, Joseph, *Social Conditions in Industrial Rhode Island,* 142-44. For the use of Butler Asylum, see South Kingstown Town Council Records, v. 8, 132 (Nov. 1, 1855 meeting).

The Village Changes its Name to Kingston

For the resolution changing the name to Kingston, see Wells Papers, Pettaquamscutt Historical Society. See also official federal post office notice confirming change of name to Kingston, dated January 3, 1826, in Wells Papers, Pettaquamscutt Historical Society. For Hazard's discussion of the name of Little Rest, see Hazard, Thomas, R., *The Jonny-Cake Papers,* 111-12. For the suggestion of the name of Kingston, see McBurney, Christian, *Kingston: A Forgotten History,* 12.

Elisha R. Potter, Sr. and his Responsibility for Causing the Dorr Rebellion

This chapter relies heavily on Conley, Patrick T., *Democracy in Decline,* 145-60 (agricultural decline, rural migration and manufacturing growth) (gaping cellar holes quote at 157); 195-213 (first conventions); 217-36 (up to 1829) (Potter quote on serving the Landed Interests at 230 n.28); 236-68 (1834 convention) ("Duke of Kingston" quote at 242). See also Marsis, James L., "Agrarian Politics in Rhode Island, 1800-1860," *Rhode Island History* 34: 13-21 (Feb. 1975). For the Cole quote on the deterioration of the farms of Narragansett planters, see Cole, J. R., *History of Washington and Kent Counties,* 538. For a further discussion on the economic decline in South Kingstown, see A Picture of Little Rest in the Early 1800s. For the foreign born and other population figures, see Snow, Edwin M., *Report of the Census of Rhode Island, 1875,* at xliii & xxxiii. For the pamphlet arguing that manufacturing jobs helped farming families, see *What a Ploughman Said,* 30-31.

Efforts at Manufacturing in Kingston Fail

For the rise in manufacturing in Rhode Island and South County, see Coleman, Peter J., *The Transformation of Rhode Island,* ch. 3, esp. 95 & 134-36; Conley, Patrick T., *Democracy in Decline,* 145-60; Brennan, Joseph, *Social Conditions in Industrial Rhode Island,* 4 & 8-9. For Stedman's journal entries, see Oatley, Henry Clay, Jr. (ed.), *Daniel Stedman's Journal,* 116 & 184 (two factory deaths); 83, 139, 237 & 238 (family members and boarders working at factories); 150, 154 & 167 (Kingston Boot and Shoe factory). For the French's hat business, see Wells, J. Hagadorn, "Kingston Annals," 45-46; Tyler, E. M., "History of Kingston," 8; *Rhode Island Acts & Resolves,* March 1794 Session, v. II, 25 (French buys former jail). For efforts at manufacturing at Biscuit City, see Miller, William Davis, "Biscuit City," *Rhode Island Historical Society Collections* 72-77 (July 1933); Coleman, Peter J., *The Transformation of Rhode Island,* 234 (child labor statistics); Williams, John Haley, *The Old Stone Bank History of Rhode Island,* v. III, 170-72; Stedman, Oliver H., *A Stroll Through Memory Lane,* v. II, 30-32. For Biscuit City land transactions and list of proprietors, see South Kingstown Land Evidence Records, v. 11, 34 (March 16, 1808); v. 11, 136 (May 10, 1809); v. 11, 210 (June 17, 1809). For the Rathbun quote on the mill operations, see *Narragansett Times,* Feb. 2, 1956, letter-to-the-editor; see also Brennan, Joseph, *Social Conditions in Industrial Rhode Island,* 32-35 (discussing the two systems for labor in cotton mills: the Waltham system, which employed chiefly the daughters of farmers and housed them in dwellings built and managed by the company; and the system relying primarily on child labor). For Hazard's journal entries, see Hazard, Caroline (ed.), *Nailer Tom's Diary,* 349 (Sept. 17, 1810 & Sept. 21, 1810); 360 (April 8, 1811); 385 (June 1, 1812); 464 (1816; but this was to have note paid, not to pick up cotton). For the sale of the factory to Rouse Clarke, see South Kingstown Land Evidence Records, v. 13, 89 (Jan. 2, 1819). For Clarke's factory operations, see Wells, J. Hagadorn, *Kingston Annals,* 51-52. For the end of the fish run, see McBurney, Christian, *Kingston: A Forgotten History,* 80. For the water power being limited, see Arnold, James (ed.), *Narragansett Historical Register,* v. I, 147. For a description of the water flume, see *Narragansett Times,*

March 1922, letter-to-the-editor by "G" (copy in vertical files on Biscuit City in the Pettaquamscutt Historical Society); Taylor, Philip K., "Little Rest," *The New England Magazine* (April 1903) 141. For Biscuit City as a picnic area and the ending point after a lover's lane, see *id.* at 140. For the *Rhode Island Advocate*, see Wells, J. Hagadorn, "Kingston Annals," 5-6; *Rhode Island Advocate*, June 15, 1832, 3 (its own insolvency) & Sept. 28, 1832 (auction of its property). For the Kingston Boot and Shoe Company, see Proceedings of the Kingston Boot and Shoe Manufacturing Company, Pettaquamscutt Historical Society; Wells, J. Hagadorn, "Kingston Annals," 6 ("hoping to do much for Kingston"); Oatley, Henry Clay, Jr. (ed.), *Daniel Stedman's Journal*, 150, 154 & 167; South Kingstown Land Evidence Records, v. 16, 382 (sale of current Tavern Hall Club building by E. R. Potter, Jr. to Kingston Boot and Shoe Company, 1838) & v. v. 17, 244 (sale back to E. R. Potter, Jr., 1842). For Daniel Rodman's Mooresfield manufacturing mills, see Rhode Island Historical Preservation Commission, *Historic and Architectural Resources of South Kingstown, Rhode Island*, 22; Hoag & Wade, *History of Rhode Island*, 296. For James B. M. Potter's South Ferry and Usquepaug manufacturing mills, see Tootell, Lucy R. (ed.), *Driftways into the Past (Richmond, Rhode Island)*, 191; Beers, J. H., *Representative Men and Old Families of Rhode Island*, 56-57; Federal Writers' Project, *Rhode Island, A Guide to the Smallest State*, 369; James, B.M. Potter Papers, RIHS. The Usquepaug mill burned down in 1870. *Narragansett Times*, April 15, 1870.

The Railroad Comes to West Kingston

For the Boston and Providence railroad, see Carroll, Charles, *Rhode Island: Three Centuries of Democracy*, v. II, 828-30; Haley, John Williams, *The Old Stone Bank History of Rhode Island*, v. IV, 169-71. For the decision to construct a railroad that would stop at West Kingston and its building, see McCabe, Martha, *The Kingston Train Station, passim;* Haley, John Williams, *The Old Stone Bank History of Rhode Island*, v. IV, 169-74; *Rhode Island Advocate*, July 6, 1832, 2. For the impact of the railroad on Kingston, see Wells, J. Hagadorn, "Kingston Annals," 35; Gardiner, Thomas, A., "The Early Postal Services of South Kingstown," *The Reporter* 1, 2 (quarterly journal of the Pettaquamscutt Historical Society) (Winter 1988-89).

Elisha Reynolds Potter, Jr.: Educator, Historian, Politician and Judge

For short biographies of Potter, see Rider, Sydney S., *Historical Research and Educational Labor Illustrated in the Work of Elisha Reynolds Potter, passim;* Barnard, Henry, "Elisha Reynolds Potter, 1811-1882," *Harvard University Memoirs*, 98-105; Malone, Dumas, *Dictionary of American Biography*, 126-27; Wells, J. Hagadorn, "Biographical Sketches," 14-22; Beers, J. H., *Representative Men and Old Families of Rhode Island*, 53-55; Freeman, Donald McKinley, "South County Reaction to the Dorr Rebellion as Illustrated by Elisha Reynolds Potter" (Master's Thesis) ch. II. For Potter's literary circle, see Rosenfeld, Alvin, "Wilkins Updike to Sarah Helen Whitman: Two Letters," *Rhode Island History* 25: 97, 98-103 (Oct. 1966). On Potter's two runs for governor, see Field, Edward (ed.), *State of Rhode Island and Providence Plantations*, v. I, 369-70. For Potter's financial troubles, see

Letter from Lizzie Robinson to Frank and Lizzie Hagadorn, dated April 16, 1861, Hagadorn-Wells Papers, Box 1, Folder 2, Rhode Island Historical Society, Mss 629 SG 10. For Potter's career as a judge, see Carroll, Charles, *Rhode Island: Three Centuries of Democracy,* v. II, 762-67. For Potter's funeral, see *Providence Daily Journal,* April 11, 1882; and excerpts from other newspapers, vertical files, Kingston Free Library and Reading Room; *Narragansett Times,* April 21, 1882, April 28, 1882. For Mary Elizabeth Potter, see Mary E. Potter Papers, Box 1, Folders 1-3, Rhode Island Historical Society, Mss 629, SG 7. Mary kept a short diary from 1863-65.

Wilkins Updike: Politician, Historian and Lawyer

For short biographies of Wilkins Updike, see Wells, J. Hagadorn, "Biographical Sketches," 14-22; *Biographical Cyclopedia,* 93-94; Letter from Daniel Rodman to the *Narragansett Times,* Feb. 1, 1867; Woodward, Carl R. *Plantation in Yankeeland,* 162-67. See also Updike, Wilkins, "History or the Alleged State Debt of Rhode Island," 1846; Updike, Wilkins, "Hints to the Farmers of Rhode-Island," 1829. For the anti-Updike broadside, see Richmond, John Wilkes, "Facts Relative to the Political and Moral Claims of Wilkins Updike, for the Support of the Whig Electors of the Western District," Providence, 1847. For the two letters by Updike to Sara Helen Whitman, see Rosenfeld, Alvin, "Wilkins Updike to Sarah Helen Whitman: Two Letters," *Rhode Island History* 25: 97-109 (Oct. 1966). Updike, in a letter to Elisha Potter, Jr. in 1845, relates a humorous incident involving Sarah Helen Whitman. See Elisha R. Potter, Jr. Papers, Box 1, Folder 14, Rhode Island Historical Society.

The Roles of Elisha Potter, Jr. and Wilkins Updike in Suppressing the Dorr Rebellion

This chapter relies heavily on Conley, Patrick T., *Democracy in Decline,* 309-79. For other sources on the Dorr War, see McLoughlin, William G., *Rhode Island,* 121-36; Mowry, Arthur May, *The Dorr War, passim*; Hoffman, Charles and Tess Hoffman, *Brotherly Love,* 13-14 & 161 n. 3; Potter, Elisha R., Jr. *Considerations on the Questions of the Adoption of a Constitution and Extension of Suffrage in Rhode Island;* Freeman, Donald McKinley, "South County Reaction to the Dorr Rebellion as Illustrated by Elisha Reynolds Potter" (Master's Thesis) ch. III-IV; Wiecek, William M. "Popular Sovereignty in the Dorr War: Conservative Counterblast," *Rhode Island History* 32: 35-51 (May 1973); Names of Voters on the Constitution in South Kingstown, March 20, 1842, Elisha R. Potter, Jr. Papers, Series 2, Box 4, Folder 1, Rhode Island Historical Society; List of Qualified Voters for the People's Constitution in South Kingstown in 1841, Elisha R. Potter, Jr. Papers, Series 2, Box 4, Folder 8, Rhode Island Historical Society. For the population decline, see Coleman, Peter J., *The Transformation of Rhode Island,* 220; prior chapter, A Picture of Little Rest in the Early 1800s. For the Suffrage Party's call for a town meeting to be held at the Kingston Court House in May 1841 to select delegates to the People's Convention, see DeSimone, Russell J., *The Broadsides of the Dorr Rebellion,* 21-22 (original is at Rhode Island Historical Society). For the Washington Cadets and Washington Grenadiers, see Smith, Joseph Jencks (ed.), *Civil and Military List of*

Rhode Island, 1800-1850, 605-15; Potter, James B. M., *Oration Delivered at Kingston, R.I., July 4, 1843,* 24. For the calling out of the militia, see Oatley, Henry Clay, Jr. (ed.), *Daniel Stedman's Journal,* 204; *The Narragansett Chief,* July 2, 1842 (600 men arrived from Washington County); Arnold, James (ed.), *Narragansett Historical Register,* v. II, 186 (Third Brigade in Providence); Potter, James B. M., "Recollections of a Paymaster of the Army During the Civil War 1861-1882," 3 (Dorr War experience). For the clam bakes and the military review in Kingston, see Freeman's thesis cited above. For voting requirement changes in 1888, see Hoffman, Charles and Tess Hoffman, *Brotherly Love,* 161 n.3. For a discussion of the Know-Nothing movement and the Thomas R. Hazard quote, see Brennan, Joseph, *Social Conditions in Industrial Rhode Island,* 134-39.

The Potter Brothers, Updike and the Aftermath of the Dorr Rebellion

For continued turmoil in state politics, see Freeman, Donald McKinley, "South County Reaction to the Dorr Rebellion as Illustrated by Elisha Reynolds Potter" (Master's Thesis) ch. V; *The Narragansett Chief,* Dec. 24, 1842 (Potter letter regarding continued opposition by Democrats); *The Narragansett Chief,* April 1843 (Potter's election to state senate). For the oration on July 4, 1843, see Potter, James B. M., *Oration Delivered at Kingston, R.I., July 4, 1843.* For the list of "Renegade Democrats," including James and Elisha Potter, and the March 2, 1843 Law and Order Party meeting in Kingston, see *The Narragansett Chief,* Feb. 4, 1843. For James Potter's military experience in the Dorr War, see Potter, James B. M., "Recollections of a Paymaster of the Army During the Civil War 1861-1882," 3. James B. M. Potter rose to become Brigadier General of the Third Brigade. Potter attended Yale in 1836 and 1837, but ended up graduating from Brown. *Id.* For the Massachusetts man killed by the Kentish Guards, see Mowry, Arthur May, *The Dorr War,* 221-2; for the most colorful and detailed description, see summary of *Providence Journal* eyewitness account in Cole, J. H., *History of Washington and Kent Counties,* 143-47. For Potter in Washington, D.C., see Potter, Elisha R., Jr., *Speech of Mr. Potter, of Rhode Island: on the Memorial of the Democratic Members of the Legislature of Rhode Island: Delivered in the House of Representatives, March 7, 9, and 12, 1844;* Freeman, Donald McKinley, "South County Reaction to the Dorr Rebellion as Illustrated by Elisha Reynolds Potter" (Master's Thesis) 100-03. For the meeting of the "ultra" Whigs in the Court House in Kingston and the division within the Law and Order Party, see the broadside, "Law and Order Party of South Kingstown Dissolved by the Ultra Clay Whigs," Misc. Collections, File Box 2, Folders 16 & 17, University of Rhode Island Library (Special Collections). For Potter losing the 1845 election, see Freeman, Donald McKinley, "South County Reaction to the Dorr Rebellion as Illustrated by Elisha Reynolds Potter" (Master's Thesis) 103-07 & Appendix H; Carroll, Charles, *Rhode Island: Three Centuries of Democracy,* v. I, 587 (Rhode Island opposition to the annexation of Texas and the Mexican War); letter from Elisha Potter to his brother Thomas, Thomas M. Potter Papers, Rhode Island Historical Society, Mss 629. For Stedman's journal entries, see Oatley, Henry Clay, Jr. (ed.), *Daniel Stedman's Journal,* 231.

Murder Trials and the Abolition of the Death Penalty

The history of the Gordon murder trial relies heavily on Hoffman Charles and Tess Hoffman, *Brotherly Love,* including at 33 (William Potter background) and at 107 (Updike quote). See also Carroll, Charles, *Rhode Island: Three Centuries of Democracy,* v. II, 754-61 (trial); Beers, J. H., *Representative Men and Families of Rhode Island,* 55-56 (William Potter biography). The history of murder trials in Kingston relies heavily on Bickford, Christopher, *Crime, Punishment, and the Washington County Jail,* 44-45. See also Cole, J. H., *History of Washington and Kent Counties,* 79-80 (Daniel Harry trial); Washington County Supreme Court Records, Oct. 1815 Sess. 293-96 (Billington) & May 1839 Sess. 564-65 (Harry). For John Robinson, see also Oatley, Henry Clay, Jr. (ed.), *Daniel Stedman's Journal,* 11 (Robinson death sentence); Washington County Supreme Court Records, Oct. 1826 Sess. 639-43 (trial record); *Providence Daily Journal,* Nov. 6, 1826 (report of Robinson's age, death sentence and petition to General Assembly). For the abolition of the death penalty in Rhode Island, see Conley, Patrick T., "Death Knell for the Death Penalty: The Gordon Murder Trial and Rhode Island's Abolition of Capital Punishment," *Liberty and Justice,* 276-83; Brennan, Joseph, *Social Conditions in Industrial Rhode Island,* 148-50.

Elisha Reynolds Potter, Jr., Wilkins Updike and the Public School Movement in Rhode Island

For the weakness in Rhode Island public education and segregated schools, see McLoughlin, William G., *Rhode Island,* 138-39; Carroll, Charles, *Rhode Island: Three Centuries of Democracy,* v. I, 537-41; Snow, Edwin, M., *Report Upon the Census of Rhode Island, 1865,* lxxvi-lxxviii. For early history of public schools in Rhode Island and the enactment of Updike's bill, see Carroll, Charles, *Public Education in Rhode Island,* 125-80; Brennan, Joseph, *Social Conditions in Industrial Rhode Island,* 93-101; Flaherty, Thomas Francis, "The History of the Public School Movement in the State of Rhode Island" (Doctoral Thesis) ch. I-II. For the term of Commissioner Potter, see Carroll, Charles, *Public Education in Rhode Island,* 153-75; Potter, Elisha R., *The Rhode Island Educational Magazine,* v. 1, *passim;* Potter, Elisha R., Jr. (ed.), *Reports and Documents Upon Public Schools and Education in the State of Rhode Island,* 9-11 (school prayer); Flaherty, Thomas Francis, "The History of the Public School Movement in the State of Rhode Island" (Doctoral Thesis) ch. IV. For the number of school houses in South Kingstown and other Rhode Island towns in 1821, see newspaper report summarized in Field, Edward (ed.), *State of Rhode Island and Providence Plantations,* v. II, 226-30. For the number of school houses in the town in 1832, see *id.,* v. II, at 335. In handwritten notes on important dates in Kingston's history, Elisha R. Potter, Jr. states that in 1828-29, "Thomas P. Wells first kept the free school for three months." Elisha R. Potter, Jr. Papers, Series 5, Box 5, Folder 35, Rhode Island Historical Society; see also Beers, J. H., *Representative Men and Old Families of Rhode Island Representative Families,* 1034 (short biography of Wells). In the South Kingstown Town Council Records for the July 14, 1834 meeting, v. 7, 305, there is the following entry: "That the Clerk give the Town Treasurer a certificate that all the money that has been received of the State by this Town for public schools has been appropriated for that purpose." Similar resolutions were passed in later years. See *id.* at 320 (July 1836); 325 (July 1837) & 330 (July 1838). For School District No. 3 in Kingston, see Thresher, John C., "Education in Kingston, Part Two -- Kingston Grammar School," *The Reporter* 1-11 (the quarterly journal of the Pettaquamscutt Historical Society) (summer 1998); Potter, Elisha R., *The Rhode Island Educational Magazine,* v. 1, 268-78 (South Kingstown School Report for year ending July 1852); Records of South Kingstown School District No. 3, 1844-1902, Misc. Manuscripts Collection, Box 5, Folder 62, University of Rhode Island Library (Special Collections); South Kingstown Land Evidence Records, v. 18, 83 (lease of Kingston Academy school house to District No. 3 for 20 years).

Kingston in the Temperance Movement

For general store operators, taverns and other sellers of alcohol, see prior chapters, Three Good Taverns, A Picture of Little Rest in the Early 1800s, and The Rise of the Bank and General Store, and notes thereto. For Reverend Wells' count of six rum establishments and the rum-making concern, see Wells, J. Hagadorn, "Kingston Annals," 29 (rum-making concern) & 69 ("six rum concerns, these last all in full blast at one and the same time"). For the "best of liquors" quote, see Helme, Jonathan, "Recollections of South Kingstown," *Providence Journal,* Oct. 31, 1874. Helme counted five stores that sold alcohol; he did not recall that his grandfather, James Helme, sold alcohol, but town council records in the last quarter of the 18th century indicate that he did. However, in the 1790s and early 1800s, Nailer Tom Hazard, in his journal, mentions shopping at Helme's store on many occasions, but he never reported purchasing any alcohol from Helme (as he did from other Little Rest storekeepers and tavern keepers). For South County quote, see Coleman, Peter J., *The Transformation of Rhode Island,* 249. For Elisha Gardner buying rum, see Philip K. Taylor Journal, 13 (in author's possession). For the Case store and Clarke store quotes, see Wells, J. Hagadorn, "Kingston Annals," 12 & 29. Wells did not name Clarke as the proprietor, but this can be determined by consulting land evidence records showing Clarke as owning the buildings that Wells described. In 1797, the town council dealt with Samuel Curtis, a "Gentleman" and former town council member for many years. Because Curtis "for a considerable time past has been squandering his estate by giving himself up to the practice of a daily enebriation," there was a risk he would become a town charge, so a guardian was appointed for him. South Kingstown Town Council Records, v. 6, 253 (Dec. 15, 1797). For the temperance movement in the 19th century, see Tyrell, Ian R., *Sobering Up: From Temperance to Prohibition in Antebellum America, 1800-1860.* For the temperance movement in Rhode Island generally, see Jones, Daniel, *The Economic & Social Transformation of Rural Rhode Island,* 156-160; Gilkeson, John S., Jr., *Middle-Class Providence, 1820-1940,* 23-35; Brennan, Joseph, *Social Conditions in Industrial Rhode Island,* 80-87. For the South Kingstown Temperance Society, see South Kingstown Temperance Society Records, Wells Papers, South Kingstown Temperance Folder, Pettaquamscutt Historical Society; Wells, Thomas R., *An*

Address, Delivered at Kingston, R.I., July 5, 1830, Before the South Kingstown Temperance Society; *Rhode Island Advocate,* June 15, 1832, 3 (announcing annual meeting at Kingston Congregational Church on July 4th). For Stedman's journal entries on temperance, see Oatley, Henry Clay, Jr. (ed.), *Daniel Stedman's Journal,* 106, 119, 123, 176, 188, 196, 200, 201, 213, 223, 227 & 302. For Kingston Congregational Church and John Hawkins, see Metz, William D., *History of the Kingston Congregational Church,* 69-70. For the church's temperance resolution, see *id.*; draft resolutions in Hagadorn-Wells Papers, Box 2, Folder 11, Mss 629 SG 10. For the struggle to eliminate sales of alcohol by Kingston taverns, see Oatley, Henry Clay, Jr. (ed.), *Daniel Stedman's Journal,* 200 & 201; for the fining of rum sellers, see *id.* at 212-213. See also South Kingstown Town Council Records, v. 7, 349 (June 10, 1842) (granting liquor licenses for taverns to W. Hazard and Taylor); v. 7, 351 (July 11, 1842) (rejecting W. Hazard's request for liquor license and instructing town treasurer to prosecute all liquor license violations); v. 7, 355 (Dr. Thomas Hazard and Thomas P. Wells of Wakefield permitted to sell liquor for medicinal purposes only); v. 7, 36 (town council meets at Philip Taylor's tavern); v. 7, 374 (June 25, 1846) (license to keep a tavern without privilege of selling liquor granted to Taylor); v. 7, 375 (Oct. 12, 1846) (same, John Perry). For the alcohol-free dinner served by Taylor at the July 4, 1843 celebration, see Potter, James B. M., *Oration Delivered at Kingston, R.I., July 4, 1843,* 24. For temperance legislation enacted by the General Assembly, see Carroll, Charles, *Rhode Island: Three Centuries of Democracy,* v. II, 648-49; Brennan, Joseph, *Social Conditions in Industrial Rhode Island,* 85-86. For Elisha Potter, Jr.'s leading the repeal movement in 1863, see Hoffman, Charles and Tess Hoffman, *Brotherly Love,* 168 n.35; for the 1863 legislation, see *Narragansett Times,* March 27, 1863, 2.. For the two reminiscences that report no alcohol in the village, see Helme, Jonathan, "Recollections of South Kingstown," *Providence Journal,* Oct. 31, 1874 (express statement to that effect); Wells, J. Hagadorn, "Kingston Annals" (reporting no sellers of alcohol currently around 1897). In 1868, for example, a letter writer complained that while the town council did not grant liquor licenses, it also did not enforce the law against the use of alcohol in the town. *Narragansett Times,* Aug. 7, 1868. For temperance activities in the late 19th century in Kingston and Rhode Island College, see Eschenbacher, Herman F., *The University of Rhode Island,* 97 (college graduation speech); *Narragansett Times,* June 16, 1871 (Christian temperance meeting).

The Kingston Anti-Slavery Society and Other Antislavery Activities

For the antislavery movement in Rhode Island generally, see Broekhoven, Deborah Bingham Van, *The Devotion of These Women,* 1-53, 142-43 & 158-60; Gilkeson, John S., Jr., *Middle-Class Providence, 1820-1940,* 36-53; Brennan, Joseph, *Social Conditions in Industrial Rhode Island,* 138-40. For South Kingstown's participation in the antislavery convention, see *Proceedings of the Rhode Island Anti-Slavery Convention,* 4-16 & 84-85. For Asa Potter, see *Biographical Cyclopedia,* 309. For John G. Clarke, see Helme, Jonathan, "Recollections of South Kingstown," *Providence Journal,* Oct. 31, 1874; Wells, J. Hagadorn, "Kingston Annals," 42, 70; Tootell, Lucy R. (ed.), "Kingston, Old Houses, Dates and Builders," 12-13 & 51 (land purchases and sales). For the Rhode Island Anti-Slavery Society meeting in Kingston, with agent William L. Chaplin, see *The Liberator,* June 30, 1837; Myers, John L., "Antislavery Agents in Rhode Island, 1835-1837," *Rhode Island History* 30: 31 (Winter 1971). For the Kingston Anti-Slavery Society, see Kingston Anti-Slavery Society Minutes, University of Rhode Island Library (Special Collections); Broekhoven, Deborah Bingham Van, *The Devotion of These Women,* 88-90 and accompanying notes, 183, 203. Deborah Bingham Van Broekhoven deserves the credit for bringing the minutes to the attention of the public, with the assistance of librarians from the Kingston Free Library and Reading Room, where the minutes were stored for many years. For the letter from Thomas R. Wells, representing the Kingston Anti-Slavery Society, to Elisha R. Potter, Jr., see Elisha R. Potter, Jr. Papers, Series 1, Box 1, Folder 2, Rhode Island Historical Society. For the draft January 22, 1836 statement in opposition to abolitionist's activities in the state in Elisha R. Potter, Jr.'s handwriting, see Elisha R. Potter, Jr. Papers, Series 7, Box 6, Folder 4, Rhode Island Historical Society. For antislavery literature subscribed to by Kingston residents, see Kingston Post Office Records, Thomas Wells, Postmaster, 1837-40, Wells Papers, Pettaquamscutt Historical Society. For the Congregationalist schism, see Meyer, Henry, *All on Fire: William Lloyd Garrison and the Abolition of Slavery,* 226-27 & 233-37; Broekhoven, Deborah Bingham Van, *The Devotion of These Women,* 63-64. For the Kingston Congregational Church and the Reverend Grosvenor, see Metz, William D., *History of the Kingston Congregational Church,* 73 & 75-76. For the church's antislavery resolution, see *id.;* Hagadorn-Wells Papers, Box 2, Folder 11, Mss 629 SG 10. For Stedman's journal entries, see Oatley, Henry Clay, Jr. (ed.), *Daniel Stedman's Journal,* 188-89 & 222. For William Wells Brown, see *Narragansett Times,* Mar. 15, 1856, 2. For lukewarm support for antislavery activities in South Kingstown, see prior chapter on manufacturing (Rodman and James B. M. Potter sold garments to clothe black slaves); Oatley, Henry Clay, Jr. (ed.), *Daniel Stedman's Journal,* 167 (Hazard brothers selling Negro cloth); Stachiw, Myron O., "'For the Sake of Commerce': Slavery, Antislavery, and Northern Industry," *The Meaning of Slavery in the North,* 33-43 (Hazard family's trade with the South); Russell, Howard S. *A Long, Deep Furrow, Three Centuries of Farming in New England,* 340 (potato trade with South). For the Hazards' commercial relations with the South and Rowland G. Hazard, see Stachiw, Myron O., "'For the Sake of Commerce': Slavery, Antislavery, and Northern Industry," *The Meaning of Slavery in the North,* 33-43. For records of Thomas Wells' accounts printing tags for Samuel Rodman and James B. M. Potter, see Account Book of T. Wells, Wells Papers, 17, 20-21 & 27, Pettaquamscutt Historical Society. For Biscuit City as a possible refuge on the underground railroad, see *South County Yearbook* 31 (12th ed. 1959); Philip K. Taylor Journal, 27 (in author's possession). For blacks residing in Biscuit City, see Wells, J. Hagadorn, "Kingston Annals," 51 -53.

The Restoration of Black Voting Rights in Rhode Island

For the disenfranchisement of blacks, see Melish, Joanne Pope, *Disowning Slavery,* 164, 185 & 189. For the challenges and discrimination Rhode Island blacks faced in the post-abolition period, see *id.*; Sweet, John Wood, *Bodies Politic,*

Negotiating Race in the American North, 1730-1830, passim. For the struggle for the re-enfranchisement of black voters from 1840 to 1843, see Lemons, Stanley J. & Michael A. McKenna, "Re-enfranchisement of Rhode Island Negroes," *Rhode Island History* 30: 5-13 (Winter 1971); Conley, Patrick T., *Democracy in Decline, 345 & 372; Field, Edward (ed.), *State of Rhode Island and Providence Plantations,* v. I, 345; Broekhoven, Deborah Bingham Van, *The Devotion of These Women,* 42. For French's letter, see the *Providence Journal,* March 19, 1842. For the Frederick Douglass quote and his comment on the Stonington railroad, see Douglass, Frederick, *Life and Times of Frederick Douglass,* 205 & 207. For Fayerweather men as voters, see List of Freeholders of South Kingstown, 1856, South Kingstown Town Hall.

Elisha R. Potter, Jr. and Wilkins Updike: Rationalizing the Slaveholding of Their Forefathers with Pre-Civil War Opposition to the South

The idea for this chapter and its contents relies heavily on Fitts, Robert K., *Inventing New England's Slave Paradise, Master/Slave Relations in Eighteenth-Century Narragansett, Rhode Island,* 21-32. See also Updike, Wilkins, *History of the Episcopal Church in Narragansett,* 168-88 (including Potter's 1841 speech quoted); Potter, Elisha R., Jr., *An Address Delivered Before the Rhode Island Historical Society, on the Evening of February Nineteenth, 1851,* 10-14; Potter, Elisha R., Jr., *Speech of Hon. Elisha R. Potter of South Kingstown, March 14, 1863, Upon the Present National Difficulties,* 29-35. The 1847 Updike broadside is held by the Library of Congress, Rare Books and Manuscripts Division. For the letter from Elisha Potter to his brother Thomas, see Thomas M. Potter Papers, Rhode Island Historical Society, Mss 629, SG 7. For the letter from Elisha Potter to his brother James, see James Brown Mason Potter Papers, Box 1, Folder 3, letter dated Jan. 5, 1845, Rhode Island Historical Society, Mss 629, SG 6. For the case record involving Patience, see earlier chapter on Town Council preventing Elisha Gardner from freeing his slave.

Sarah Harris Fayerweather: Heroine and Abolitionist

For Sarah Harris Fayerweather's early life and Prudence Crandall's school, see Kozlowski, Kazimiera and David A. Porter, "...To Get A Little More Learning", Prudence Crandall's Female Boarding School," *Cultural Resource Management* 20, 3: 40-43 (1997); Meyer, Henry, *All on Fire: William Lloyd Garrison and the Abolition of Slavery,* 145-47; Woodward, Carl R., "A Profile in Dedication, Sarah Harris and the Fayerweather Family," *The New England Galaxy* (summer 1973) 5-7. For Sarah Harris Fayerweather in Kingston, the letter from Crandall's daughter, Sarah's letter to Crandall, Sarah Fayerweather's death, and naming the residence hall in her name, see Woodward, Carl R., "A Profile in Dedication, Sarah Harris and the Fayerweather Family," *The New England Galaxy* (summer 1973) 7-14. For Garrison and Crandall letters to Sarah Fayerweather, the *Liberator* receipt, see Fayerweather Family Papers, 1836-1962, MSG #121, University of Rhode Island Library (Special Collections) with copies in Carl R. Woodward Papers, Boxes 64-65. For the wedding cake, see Meyer, Henry, *All on Fire: William Lloyd Garrison and the Abolition of*

Slavery, 600. It has been reported that Sarah hosted Frederick Douglass at her home in Kingston, but I have found no support for that in local newspapers or letters, or in books on Douglass. It was likely the case that Sarah, who traveled to New York and Boston to attend antislavery meetings, was acquainted with Douglass, as she was with many of the abolitionist leaders.

Kingston During the Civil War

For Isaac P. Rodman and the formation of the new regiment, see Bartlett, John (ed.), *Memoirs of Rhode Island Officers in the Civil War,* 357-62; Stedman, Oliver H., *A Stroll Through Memory Lane,* v. I, 184-89. For the town meeting on payment for enlistment, see South Kingstown Town Meeting Records, v. 2, 229-30 (May 4, 1861) (Elisha R. Potter, Jr. moderator). For the farewell hosted by the Wells, see Stedman, Oliver H., *A Stroll Through Memory Lane,* v. I, 184-89; *Narragansett Times,* June 7, 1862, 2. For Rodman's Civil War experiences, see Bartlett, John (ed.), *Memoirs of Rhode Island Officers in the Civil War,* 357-62; Cole, J. R., *History of Washington and Kent Counties,* 529-30. For his return to South Kingstown, see *id.*; Stedman, Oliver H., *A Stroll Through Memory Lane,* v. I, 184-89; Letter from Elizabeth Robinson, dated July 9, 1862, Hagadorn-Wells Papers, Box 2, Folder 1, Rhode Island Historical Society, Mss 629, SG 10 (recovering Rodman in Kingston). For the Pettaquamscutt Light Infantry, see *Narragansett Times,* May 9, 1862, 2, July 7, 1862, 1, & Sept. 25, 1863, 2. For the 8th Regiment, see *Narragansett Times,* June 26, 1863. For the fates of the men in the 7th Regiment, see Hopkins, William, *The Seventh Regiment of Rhode Island Volunteers.* For John Hull's letters, see Barrett, Shirley L., *Voices from the Civil War,* 17-47. For Union soldiers in regiments, I relied heavily on Leo Dery who recently completed an unpublished listing of all Civil War soldiers from South and North Kingstown and a summary of the service of each regiment, which is on file at the Pettaquamscutt Historical Society. For Samuel Potter, see *id*; *Narragansett Times,* Aug. 28, 1863, p. 3, c. 1. For Amos Wells, see Hagadorn-Wells Papers, Box 2, Folder 6, Amos Wells Correspondence, Rhode Island Historical Society, Mss 629 SG 10. For the Case sons, see Beers, J. H., *Representative Men . . . of Rhode Island,* 996. For Carroll H. Potter, see *Narragansett Times,* July 11, 1862, p. 2, c. 2 & Nov. 14, 1862, p. 2, c. 3; *Biographical Cyclopedia,* 309; military pension records for Carroll H. Potter and James B. M. Potter (National Archives). For Potter's Senate speech, see Potter, Elisha R., Jr., *Speech of Hon. Elisha R. Potter, of South Kingstown, upon the Resolution in Support of the Union,* 2-11; *Naragansett Times,* Aug. 31, 1861, p.1. For Potter's efforts to extend the vote to Irish-American soldiers, see Conley, Patrick T., *An Album of Rhode Island History, 1636-1986,* 107. For the town meeting against extending the vote to native born citizens, see South Kingstown Town Meeting Records, v. 3, 38-39 (June 7, 1862; Wilkins Updike, moderator). For reference to the attack on Updike, see *Narragansett Times,* Sept. 19, 1862, 2. For Potter's resolution on freed slaves from the South voting in Rhode Island, see the *Narragansett Times,* Feb. 13, 1863, 2. For John White, former slave from Virginia, see Balch, Lewis, "Old Folks in Little Rest," 1; Old Fernwood Cemetery gravestone ("Born a Slave in Virginia Died in Rhode Island July 15, 1895" inscribed on his gravestone). For federal taxes, see *Narragansett Times,* Sept. 25, 1863. For Potter's 1863 resolution, see Potter, Elisha R., Jr., *Speech of Hon. Elisha R. Potter of South Kingstown, March 14, 1863,* 20-23 & 29-35. For the McClellan meeting, see *Narragansett Times,* Oct. 28, 1864, p. 2, c. 2. For the Lincoln meeting and Presidential election vote in Kingston, see *Narragansett Times,* Nov. 4, 1864, p. 2, c. 2; letter from Elizabeth (Wells) Hagadorn to Frank Hagadorn, dated Nov. 11, 1864, Hagadorn-Wells Papers, Box 2, Folder 2, Rhode Island Historical Society, Mss 629, SG 10 (election day). For Dr. Thomas M. Potter, see Miller, William Davis, "An Early Rhode Island Collector," 1-2; Beers, J. H., *Representative Men and Families of Rhode Island,* 55; Thomas M. Potter Papers, Rhode Island Historical Society. For James B. M. Potter, see chapters above, on Elisha Potter; Efforts at Manufacturing in Kingston Fail; and The Potter Brothers, Updike and the Aftermath of the Dorr Rebellion; see also *Narragansett Times,* Feb. 15, 1861 (involuntary assignment of mills); letter from Elizabeth (Wells) Hagadorn to Amos Wells, dated July 29, 1861, Hagadorn-Wells Papers, Box 2, Folder 6, Rhode Island Historical Society, Mss 629 SG 10 (opposition to war); Potter, James B. M., "Recollections of a Paymaster of the Army During the Civil War 1861-1882," *passim* (appointment as paymaster and service in Union army). For James B. M. Potter's letter regarding President Lincoln's assassination, see letter of James B. M. Potter to J. G. Nicolay and John Hay, dated Jan. 7, 1890, John Hay Correspondence, 1854-1914, "Platt" to "Ray," John Hay Library, Brown University.

Post-War Public School Developments

For the integration of public schools in Rhode Island, see Bartlett, Irving H., *From Slave to Citizen,* 50-59; Grossman, Lawrence, "George T. Downing and Desegregation of Rhode Island Public Schools, 1855-1866," *Rhode Island History* 36: 99 (Nov. 1977); Carroll, Charles, *Public Education in Rhode Island,* 157-58. For the Sunday School attendance in 1833, see South Kingstown Sabbath School Society Record Book, Wells Papers, 59-60, Pettaquamscutt Historical Society. For the proposal to fund a high school in Peace Dale, see Quinn, Catherine Harvey, "Rowland Hazard of Peace Dale, Rhode Island" (Master's Thesis) 90-92; Field, Edward, *State of Rhode Island and Providence Plantations,* v. II, 335; *Narragansett Times,* March 24, 1876; Letter-to-the-Editor, *Narragansett Times,* Sept. 10, 1875. For Kingston's public school, see Thresher, John C., "Education in Kingston, Part Two -- Kingston Grammar School," *The Reporter* (the quarterly journal of the Pettaquamscutt Historical Society) 1-11 (summer, 1998) (including the 1884 photograph); Records of School District No. 3, South Kingstown, University of Rhode Island Library (Special Collections); *Narragansett Times,* Nov. 21, 1879, p. 2, c. 1 (Kingston school opens in residential house in village). For the literacy figures, see Snow, Edward M., *Report Upon the Census of Rhode Island, 1865,* lxxvi to lxviii.

The Opening of the Narragansett Pier Railroad

For the idea, funding and construction of the Narragansett Pier Railroad, see Henwood, James N. J., *A Short Haul to the Bay,* 5-12; Stedman, Oliver H., *A Stroll Through Memory Lane,* v. I, 142-46; McCabe, Martha, *The Kingston Train Station, passim.* For the dispute regarding its route, see letters published in Hazard, Rowland (ed.), *Notable Correspondence Between Judge Elisha R. Potter and R. G. Hazard, Esq.,* 1-16; Stedman, Oliver H., *A Stroll Through Memory Lane,* v. I, 142-46;

Narragansett Times, Mar. 8, 1876 (Kingston shut out); *Providence Journal,* June 28, 1876 (Kingston meeting on alternative railroad line to South Ferry). For the railroad's impact on Kingston, see Wells, J. Hagadorn, "Kingston Annals," 12 (marble shop) and 35 (tavern and railroad quote); Wells, Herbert G., "A Restful Corner of Rhode Island," 1 (Taylor tavern); Balch, Lewis, "A Sketch of Old Kingston," 2 (marble shop). For the departure of Rowland Hazard from the Kingston Congregational Church, see Metz, William D., *History of the Kingston Congregational Church,* 81; Hagadorn-Wells Papers, Box 2, Folder 11, Rhode Island Historical Society, Mss 629 SG 10 (withdrawal notice and acceptance).

The Removal of the Town Hall and Court House from Kingston

For the last session of the General Assembly in Kingston, see Stedman, Oliver H., *A Stroll Through Memory Lane,* v. I, 8; *Historic Buildings of South County,* 36; Rhode Island Historical Preservation Commission, *Historic and Architectural Resources of South Kingstown, Rhode Island,* 51. For the renovations to the Court House building, see *id.; Narragansett Times,* Oct. 29, 1875 (weather vane); Wells, J. Hagadorn, "Kingston Annals," 41 (fence and strays); *Narragansett Times,* August 13, 1875 ($3,000 for Mansard roof and tower; in prior year $1,000 was spent repairing rotten sills and posts); July 22, 1876 (stairs in tower). For the renovations to the County Jail, see Bickford, Christopher, *Crime, Punishment and the Washington County Jail,* 12-15. The source of the granite for the jail is not known for certain, but there is reference in Eldred's records of stone coming from a place called "the ledge." This may have been the same "ledge" near the current athletic fields at the University of Rhode Island that was used to supply granite for the first college buildings in the late 1880s and 1890s. For the Hoag and Wade quote, see Hoag & Wade, *History of the State of Rhode Island,* 296. For the 1875 post office count, see Metz, William D., *History of the Kingston Congregational Church,* 63. For the removal of the town hall from Kingston, see Stedman, Oliver H., *A Stroll Through Memory Lane,* v. I, 106-11 & 135; South Kingstown Town Council Records, v. 6, 195 (Jan. 11, 1878) (last meeting of the Town Council at the Court House) & 197-98 (Jan. 28, 1878) (first Town Council meeting at new Town Hall; order to remove records to new Town Hall). For the Westerly dispute and the removal of the county court from Kingston, see *Narragansett Times,* March 9, 1877, p.2, c. 5; April 20, 1877 (Judge Potter denies motion to transfer 56 cases to Westerly); April 20, 1877; Feb. 27, 1891, Mar. 6, 1891, Mar. 13, 1891, Aug. 4, 1893, May 1, 1896; Rhode Island Historical Preservation Commission, *Historic and Architectural Resources of South Kingstown, Rhode Island,* 51. For the prisoner escapes, see *Narragansett Times,* Aug. 2, 1878; June 7, 1879. For the tramps, see *Narragansett Times,* Sept. 17, 1875; April 14, 1876.

The Kingston Free Library: Its Proud Founding and a Bitter Feud

For the founding of the library and its early years, and its expansion in the 1870s, see Titus, David K., "The Kingston Free Library, 1824-1893, A Revised History," *passim; Catalogue of the Library at Kingston, R.I.* (1855); Hoag & Wade, *History of the State of Rhode Island,* 296; *Narragansett Times,* May 6, 1873 (library dedication). On Reverend Wells and the feud, see Metz, William D., *History of the Kingston Congregational Church,* ch. 4; Titus, David K., "The Kingston Free Library, 1824-1893, A Revised History," 12-19; *Representative Men of Rhode Island,* 1036-37; *Narragansett Times,* Mar. 30, 1877 (reopening as a free library). For the incorporation of the Kingston Free Library and Reading Room, see Titus, David K., "The Kingston Free Library, 1824-1893, A Revised History," 22-24. For the use of the old Court House to hold the library, see Pettaquamscutt Historical Society, *Historic Buildings of South County,* 36; Stedman, Oliver H., *A Stroll Through Memory Lane,* v. II, 8. For a colorful description of an afternoon in the reading room, see Balch, Lewis, "In Kingston Library," 1-3.

Bucolic Kingston: A Future "as Bright as Pewter"

　　For the Stedman quote, see Stedman, Oliver H., *A Stroll Through Memory Lane,* v. I, 135. For the decline of farming in New England, see notes to next chapter. For the Aldrich quote, see Thresher, John C., "More Information about the Eldred Family," *The Reporter* 5 (quarterly journal of the Pettaquamscutt Historical Society) (Summer 1998). On Madame Lucca, see Federal Writers' Project, *Rhode Island, A Guide to the Smallest State,* 372; Stedman, Oliver, *A Stroll Through Memory Lane,* v. I, 137. In the *Narragansett Times,* Oct. 27, 1855, 2, editor Thomas P. Wells wrote, "Since the arrival of the railroad, Kingston has become quite a resort for families that desire to spend a few weeks in the country during the dog days." For the lover's lane, see Taylor, Philip Kittredge, "Little Rest," *New England Magazine* (April 1903) 140; Wells, J. Hagadorn, "Kingston Annals," 46. For the Wells letter quote, see Metz, William D., *History of the Kingston Congregational Church,* 102-03. For the county sheriff's refusal to permit a band to hold a concert in the Court House, see *Narragansett Times,* Mar. 18, 1871. For the Kingston Fair and agricultural society, see Stedman, Oliver H., *A Stroll Through Memory Lane,* v. I, 229-33; Cole, J. H., *History of Washington and Kent Counties,* 91-92; Federal Writers' Project, *Rhode Island, A Guide to the Smallest State,* 370. For William Potter, see Helme, Jonathan , "Recollections of South Kingstown," *Providence Journal,* Oct. 31, 1874; Beers, J. H., *Representative Men and Families of Rhode Island,* 55-56. For Dr. Thomas Potter, see Miller, William Davis, "An Early Rhode Island Collector." For the careers of Thomas Wells and his sons, see Beers, J. H., *Representative Men of Rhode Island,* 1033-36; Cole, J. H., *History of Washington and Kent Counties,* 96 & 584. For the black community arising in Biscuit City, see Wells, J. Hagadorn, "Kingston Annals," 51-53; Recollections of Biscuit City, no author or date, Wells Papers, Pettaquamscutt Historical Society. For Henry Thomas, see Balch, Lewis, "in Kingston Library," 3. For John White, see Balch, Lewis, "Old Folks in Little Rest," 1; Old Fernwood Cemetery gravestone for John White (("Born a Slave in Virginia Died in Rhode Island July 15, 1895" inscribed on his gravestone). For Jane Hull, see Balch, Lewis, "M.M. Journeys Back to Little Rest," 3. For other black families living in or near Kingston, see Wells, J. Hagadorn, "Kingston Annals," 23, 29 & 67. For the equal rights laws in the 1880s, see Bartlett, Irving H., *From Slave to Citizen,* 63. For the Matunuck race riot, see Whaley, Carder, "The Hills of Matunuck," (1941, unpublished manuscript in local libraries). The *Narragansett Times* does not mention this incident. For the founding of the Kingston Lyceum, see *Narragansett Times,* Dec.

8, 1865; see also Jan. 19, 1866. For the Kingston Improvement Association, see its Constitution as Adopted April 14, 1884, Wells Papers, Pettaquamscutt Historical Society; various entries in Helme, Nathaniel, *Diaries of Nathaniel Helme*. For the old elm trees, see Federal Writers' Project, *Rhode Island, A Guide to the Smallest State,* 370 (main street lined with elm trees; some are 150 to 200 years old; 1937). For modern changes to Kingston, see Stedman, Oliver H., *A Stroll Through Memory Lane,* v. I, 135 & v. II, 77-80; Helme, Nathaniel, *Diaries of Nathaniel Helme,* July 26, 1888 & Oct. 30, 1889; *Narragansett Times,* Dec. 22, 1893, p. 2, c. 1 & Dec. 10, 1893, p. 7, c. 2. For John Perry as inventor, see *Narragansett Times,* Nov. 14, 1863 (meat cutters) & July 26, 1867, 2 (mower).

Bernon Helme and the Founding of the University of Rhode Island: An Idea to Save Kingston and Farming in Rhode Island

On Bernon Helme, see Wells, J. Hagadorn, "Kingston Annals," 37 (storekeeper); Leslie, James W., "The Key to URI's Beginnings," *Horizons,* URI Alumni Association (Feb. 1988); Helme, Nathaniel, *Diaries of Nathaniel Helme, passim.* For the decline of farming in Rhode Island, see Russell, Howard S., *A Long, Deep Furrow, Three Centuries of Farming in New England,* ch. 40; Snow, Edwin S., *Report Upon the Census of Rhode Island, 1865,* lxxxvi, xc, xcvi, 97 (1865 figures); Perry, Amos, *Rhode Island State Census, 1885,* 264-65, 506-17 & 596-99 (1885 figures); Carroll, Charles, *Rhode Island: Three Centuries of Democracy,* v. II, 892 (loss to the West of market for livestock due to refrigeration, as well as poultry, eggs, butter and cheese); Bidwell, Percy I. & John I. Falconer, *History of Agriculture in the Northern United States, 1620-1860,* 373-78 (potatoes); 396-98 (cattle and western railroads) & 421-26 (New England dairy farming). For the Rhode Island demographer quotes, see Snow, Edwin S., *Report Upon the Census of Rhode Island, 1865,* 40-41. For how Helme came up with his idea, see Wells, J. Hagadorn, "Kingston Annals," 44-45. On the founding of Rhode Island College, the chapter relies heavily on Eschenbacher, Herman F., *The University of Rhode Island,* ch. 1-6 and the *Narragansett Times,* Aug. 30, 1878; Feb. 3, 1888; Feb. 10, 1888; Mar. 23, 1888; April 4, 1888; May 25, 1888; June 1, 1888; Feb. 19, 1889; Feb. 22, 1889; Mar. 1, 1889; Feb. 2, 1894; April 27, 1894; May 18, 1894; see also Leslie, James W., "The Key to URI's Beginnings," *Horizons;* Metz, William D., *History of the Kingston Congregational Church,* 127-34; Carroll, Charles, *Rhode Island: Three Centuries of Democracy,* v. II, 974-1000; South Kingstown Town Council Records, v. 10, 113-14 (Feb. 20, 1888 meeting; vote on contributing funds to establish a college in the town). For the list of books for the 1895 term, see *Rhode Island School Report, 1895, passim.* For the founding of the Every Tuesday Club, see Faella, Betty and Connie Fitzelle, "The Every Tuesday Club," 1-9. For the founding of the Tavern Hall Club, see Stedman, Oliver, *A Stroll Through Memory Lane,* v. I, 136-38. For Helme's support of the South County Art Association, see Pettaquamscutt Historical Society, *Historical Buildings in South County,* 33. For Mary LeMoine Potter's support of the Kingston Improvement Association and the Kingston Free Library, see newspaper and other excerpts in the Vertical Files, Kingston Free Library, on Mary LeMoine Potter. A "new literary and social club" was established in Kingston in 1894 "embracing the faculty of the College and prominent people of the village," but it did not survive. *Narragansett Times,* Nov. 23, 1894.

Index

Newport merchants, 8-11, 14, 20, 22, 29, 31, 36, 40, 53, 69, 85, 87-88, 158-59
Newport Mercury, 37, 40, 46, 50, 52
Newport, 2, 4, 8-9, 11-12, 15, 20-22, 28-29, 31, 34-37, 40-41, 44, 46, 48, 52-54, 57-61, British occupy Newport, 61-66, General Washington visits, 68-69, 73, 77-80, Thomas Mount, 85-91, 94, 101-4, 118, 128-29, 150, 158, 160, 165, 176, 187, 194, 211, 232, 235, 278, 285, 294-96
Newport, Battle of, 58-60
Nichols, Benjamin, 205
Nichols, Bill, 100, 188
Nichols, John (father and son), xiv, 14, 81, 83, 97, 120, 131-32, 139, 156-58, 162-63, 182, 185, 205, 297
Nichols, William, 100, 237
Nicolay, John, 261
Niles, Javin, 135
North (Civil War era), 133, 190, 207, 214, 232, 243, 245-47, 253, 255, 257, 259-60
North Carolina, 49-50, 87-88, 254
North Ferry, 75
North Kingstown, town of, 6, 8, 21, 33, 44, 49, 53, 72, 77, 90, 141, 156, 167, 196, 221, 225, 258-59, 326
North Road, 1, 5-6, 9, 11, 18, 23-24, 31, 34, 45, 52, 56, 64, 73, 83, 116, 119, 135-36, 145-46, 160-61, 163, 165-66, 225, 233, 265, 277, 286, 323, 327, 342
North Scituate, town of, 165
Northrop, George, 167
Norton, Massachusetts, 165
Norwich, Connecticut, 61-62
Noyes, Robert F., 162

O

Old, Fernwood Cemetery, 5, 116, 148, 153, 252, 358, 361
Opera, 44
Orphans, 24, 69-70
Oxen, 5, 44, 68, 117, 131, 288

P

Paine, Thomas, 84
Palmer, Benjamin, xvi, 161, 226, 279
Pawcatuck River, 103
Pawtucket Bridge, 209
Peace Dale Congregational Church, 267, 270
Peace Dale, vii, 94, 100-1, 119, 172, 180-182, 185-86, 188, 219, 222, 253, 258, 260, 264-68, 270, 272, 277, 282-84
Pearce, Cato, viii, ix, 48, 141-46, 164, 166, 192
Pease and Niles *Gazetteer*, 101
Peckham, Anna, 291
Peckham, Benjamin, 11, 45, 52, 56-57, 83, 135, 145, 196, 320
Peckham, George, 81

Peckham, Jeremiah, Jr., 286-87
Peckham, Josephus, 45, 83, 136
Peckham, Nathaniel, xiii, 225, 285
Peckham, Philo, 135-36
Peckham, Quash, 146
Peckham, Quom, 135
Peckham, Timothy, xiv, xv, 17, 45, 81-83, 88, 96, 103, 156, 335, 338-39
Peckham, William, 181, 212-13
Pennsylvania, 133, 260
People's Constitution, 201, 210-11, 233, 241
Perkins, Abraham, 6, 44, 315
Perkins, Joseph, xiii, 14, 17, 32, 35-36, 55, 88, 109, 135, 158, 161, 294-96, 325
Perkins, Mary (Gardner), 36, 109, 117, 121, 142, 146
Perkins, Nathaniel, xiii, 17, 55
Perry, John G., xiii, 105, 161, 281
Pettaquamscutt Historical Society, x, xiv, 193, 294
Pettaquamscutt Light Infantry, 258-59
Pettaquamscutt Purchasers, 2, 4-5, 8
Pettaquamscutt, settlement, 3
Pettis, Nicholas, xv
Philadelphia, 39, 52, 100, 102, 126, 148, 160, 237, 281
Phillips, John, 170
Phillips, Wendell, 237, 249
Plainfield Academy, 108, 162, 196
Poe, Edgar Allen, 200
Point Judith, 56, 60, 102, 116, 187
Pollack, William Wilson, xiv, 26, 32, 79, 81, 83
Poor, treatment of, viii, 23-24, 32, 45, illegitimate children, 69-71, 105-6, 137, improvement, 171, 227, 271, see also "Binding Out" and Town farm
Portsmouth, town of, 6, 20, 57, 176, 286
Post Office, xiv, 64, 97, 99, 148, 159-61, 172, 188, 270, 282
Post Road, 100
Potter Family Cemetery, 195
Potter Hall, 191
Potter Homestead, 2, 116-17, 141-43, 190, 193-95, 277-79, 315, 364
Potter Homestead, 2, 141-43, 190, 193-95, 277, 279
Potter Lane, 35
Potter Woods, 140
Potter, Aaron, 140
Potter, Alice, 73
Potter, Asa, Jr., xiii, 100, 104, 161, 165, 185, 233, 236, 239, 278-79
Potter, Asa, Sr., 64, 153, 159, 196, 273
Potter, Cesaer, 73, 135
Potter, Carroll H., 258
Potter, Elisa, 159

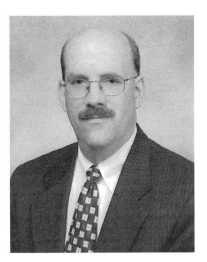

Christian M. McBurney was raised in Kingston, Rhode Island in the Potter Homestead. He graduated from South Kingstown High School in 1977 and Brown University in 1981. In high school he wrote *Kingston: A Forgotten History* (1975) and at Brown he wrote an undergraduate history thesis paper on colonial South Kingstown planter society. After graduating from New York University School of Law in 1985, he embarked on a career as an attorney. Currently, he is a partner with the law firm of Nixon Peabody LLP in its Washington, D.C. office. He lives with his wife, Margaret, and three children, Ryan, Kyle and Victoria, in Kensington, Maryland.